Teacher Companion

MyMaths

for Key Stage 3

2A

Powered by  MyMaths.co.uk

OXFORD
UNIVERSITY PRESS

OXFORD
UNIVERSITY PRESS

Great Clarendon Street, Oxford, OX2 6DP, United Kingdom

Oxford University Press is a department of the University of Oxford.
It furthers the University's objective of excellence in research, scholarship,
and education by publishing worldwide. Oxford is a registered trade mark of
Oxford University Press in the UK and in certain other countries.

British Library Cataloguing in Publication Data
Data available

978-0-19-830459-3

10 9 8 7 6 5 4 3 2 1

Paper used in the production of this book is a natural, recyclable product made
from wood grown in sustainable forests. The manufacturing process conforms
to the environmental regulations of the country of origin.

Printed in Great Britain by Bell and Bain Ltd., Glasgow

Acknowledgements

The editors would like to thank Mike Heylings, Katie Wood and Ian Bettison
for their excellent work on this book.

Contents

This Teacher Companion is part of the MyMaths for Key Stage 3 series which has been specially written for the new National Curriculum for Key Stage 3 Mathematics in England. It accompanies Student Book **2A** and is designed to help you have the greatest impact on the learning experience of lower ability students towards the end of their Key Stage 3 studies.

The author team collectively brings a wealth of classroom experience to the Teacher Companion making it easy for you to plan and deliver lessons with confidence.

The structure of this book closely follows the content of the student book so that it is easy to find the information and resources you need. These include for each

Lesson: objectives; a list of resources – including MyMaths 4-digit codes; a starter, teaching notes, plenary and alternative approach; simplification and extension ideas; an exercise commentary and full answers; the key ideas and checkpoint questions to test them; and a summary of the key literacy issues.

Chapter: National Curriculum objectives; any assumed prior knowledge; notes supporting the Student Book introduction and starter problem; the associated MyMaths and InvisiPen resources – including those offering extra support to weaker students; questions to test understanding; and how the material is developed and used.

The accompanying CD-ROM makes all the lesson plans available as Word files, so that you can customise them to suit your students' needs. Also on the CD are full sets of answers for Homework Book **2A** and Workbook **2**.

The integrated solution

This teacher guide is part of a set of resources designed to support you and your students with a fully integrated package of resources.

MyMaths
Direct links to the ever popular site's lessons and auto-marked homeworks.

Online Student Book
Digital versions of the student books for home and classroom use.

Online Testbank
A complete suite of assessment tests: Good to Go, formative (including feedback), auto-marked and print based.

InvisiPen solutions
Student friendly videos explaining just what is needed to solve a sample problem.

Homework Book
Handy, pocket-sized books, tailored to the content of each student book lesson.

Workbook
Accessible, write-in books designed to support weaker students making the transition from KS2 to KS3.

Student Book
The three books in a phase are organised to cover topics in the same order but at three ability levels.

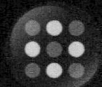

Learning outcomes

N1 Understand and use place value for decimals, measures and integers of any size (L4)

N2 Order positive and negative integers, decimals and fractions; use the number line as a model for ordering of the real numbers; use the symbols $=, \neq, <, >, \leq, \geq$ (L5)

N3 Use the concepts and vocabulary of prime numbers, factors (or divisors), multiples, common factors, common multiples, highest common factor, lowest common multiple, prime factorisation, including using product notation and the unique factorisation property (L5)

N7 Use integer powers and associated real roots (square, cube and higher), recognise powers of 2, 3, 4, 5 and distinguish between exact representations of roots and their decimal approximations (L5)

N13 Round numbers and measures to an appropriate degree of accuracy (for example, to a number of decimal places or significant figures) (L5)

Introduction

The chapter starts by revising ordering negative integers. The main focus is working with multiples, factors and prime numbers. Ordering decimal numbers and rounding are also covered. Finally square numbers are discussed together with square roots.

The introduction discusses sending sensitive information, such as credit card details, over the internet where there is a risk that it can be intercepted. The first step is to convert any message into a number, say using ASCII codes. The number is then encrypted to turn it into apparent gibberish that can only be decrypted using a secret key. The difficulty is in giving someone enough information to be able to encrypt a message without making it obvious how to also decrypt the message.

One solution called public key encryption is RSA, named after Rivest, Shamir and Adleman. This involves sending, via the internet, two numbers, e and N, to allow a message to be encrypted. The trick is that the decryption requires N to be factored into two primes. N is typically 100 digits long and factorising such large numbers is ferociously difficult making the encryption practically unbreakable if you don't already know the two primes.

The technical details involve modulo arithmetic and Fermat's little theorem. A discussion is available here http://www.claymath.org/publications/posters/primes-go-forever

Prior knowledge

Students should already know how to...

- Use place value with integers and decimals
- Interpret negative numbers
- Do basic integer arithmetic

Starter problem

The starter problem is a classic puzzle where 100 prisoners are locked into their cells and then doors are opened or closed in sequence depending on whether the door number is a multiple of the respective prison guard's number. For example, after the first guard visits the cells, all of the doors are opened, but then the second guard locks all the even numbered doors. The third guard changes the status of all the doors that are multiples of three. The even multiples of three are opened again, while the odd multiples of three are opened again. This continues until all 100 guards have completed their rounds.

The solution to the puzzle is that the open doors at the end are the square numbers. This is since square numbers have an odd number of factors, while all other numbers have an even number of factors.

This kind of exercise could be simulated with a class (obviously with a smaller number of 'prisoners') standing or sitting in turn. The students with square numbers should all be standing at the end, while all other students should end up sitting down.

Resources

⊞ MyMaths

Rounding decimals	1004	Factors and primes	1032	LCM	1034
Square and cubes	1053	Negative numbers 2	1068	Negative numbers 1	1069
Ordering decimals	1072	Decimal place value	1076		

Online assessment

Chapter test	2A–1
Formative test	2A–1
Summative test	2A–1

InvisiPen solutions

Place value	111	Rounding	112
Negative numbers	113	Multiples and factors	171
HCF and LCM	172	Primes and prime factors	173
Powers and roots	181		

Topic scheme

Teaching time = 8 lessons/3 weeks

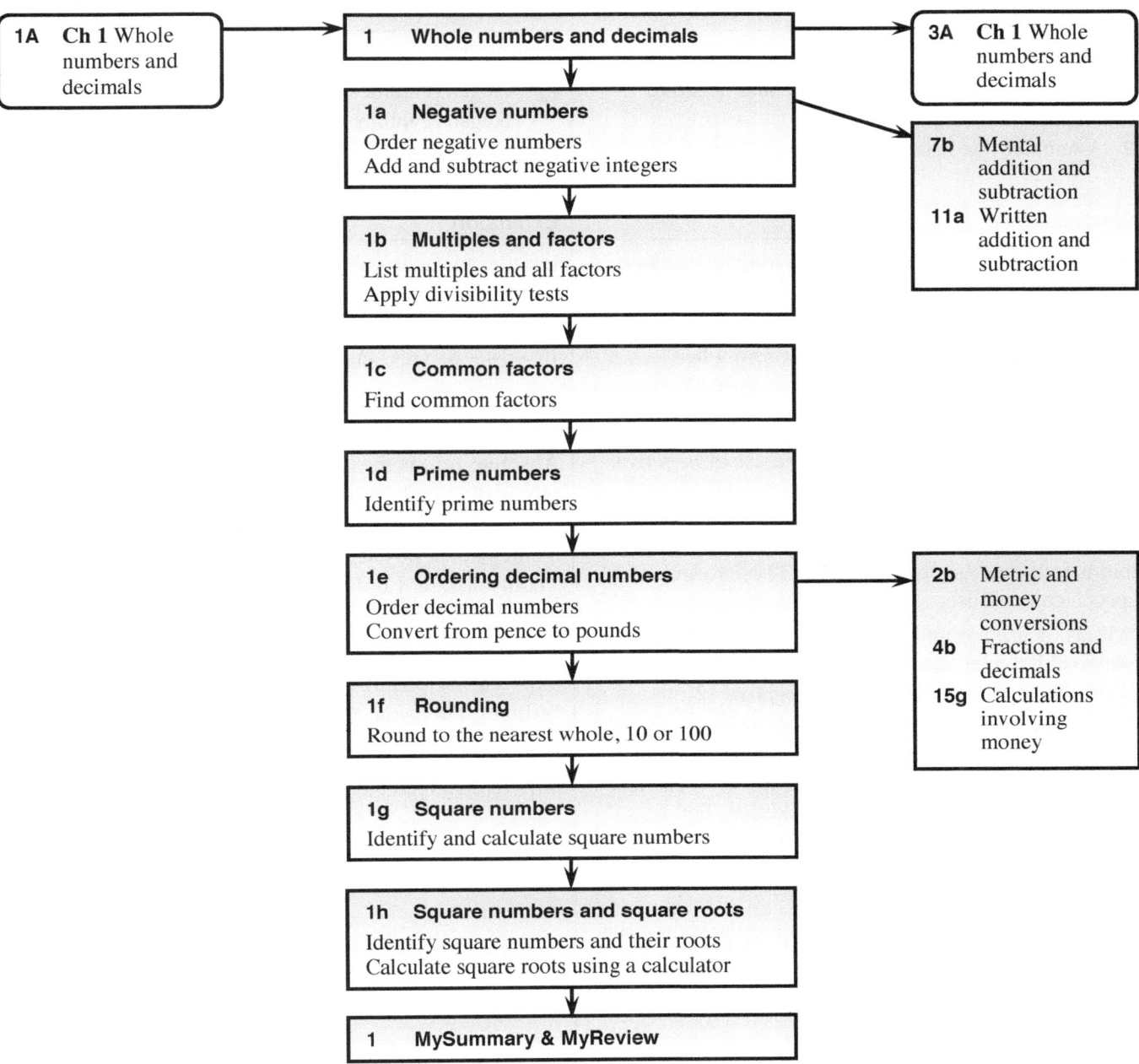

1A Ch 1 Whole numbers and decimals

1 Whole numbers and decimals

3A Ch 1 Whole numbers and decimals

1a Negative numbers
Order negative numbers
Add and subtract negative integers

7b Mental addition and subtraction
11a Written addition and subtraction

1b Multiples and factors
List multiples and all factors
Apply divisibility tests

1c Common factors
Find common factors

1d Prime numbers
Identify prime numbers

1e Ordering decimal numbers
Order decimal numbers
Convert from pence to pounds

2b Metric and money conversions
4b Fractions and decimals
15g Calculations involving money

1f Rounding
Round to the nearest whole, 10 or 100

1g Square numbers
Identify and calculate square numbers

1h Square numbers and square roots
Identify square numbers and their roots
Calculate square roots using a calculator

1 MySummary & MyReview

Differentiation

Student book 2A 2 – 23	Student book 2B 2 – 23	Student book 2C 2 – 21
Negative numbers	Integers and decimals	Factors, multiples and primes
Multiples and factors	Multiplying and dividing integers	Prime factor decomposition
Common factors	Multiples and factors	LCM and HCF
Prime numbers	Prime numbers	Square roots and cubes
Ordering decimal numbers	LCH and HCF	Indices
Rounding	Squares and cubes	Rounding and estimation
Square numbers	Square roots	Trial-and-improvement 1
Square numbers and square roots	Cube roots	

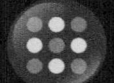

1a Negative numbers

Objectives

- Understand negative numbers as positions on a number line   (L4)
- Order, add and subtract integers on a number line and in context   (L5)

Key ideas	Resources
1 Positive numbers are above zero and negative numbers are below zero 2 A number line is used to add and subtract numbers	Negative numbers 1 (1069) Negative numbers 2 (1068) Horizontal and vertical display number line, individual number lines, mini whiteboards

Simplification	Extension
Provide weaker students with an individual number line as in the book (–10 to 10). They should decide the *start number* and the *direction of motion* for each calculation. Students often miss out zero when counting between negative and positive numbers.	Invite students to calculate with larger numbers (include non-multiples of 10) and where use of a number line is not appropriate; for example, 17 – 14 – 5 (-2) and -42 + 32 + 18 (8)

Literacy	Links
There is general inconsistency in the use of *negative, minus, subtract* and *take away*. The number -12 is spoken as 'negative 12' and 'minus 12'. The operation 6 – 4 is a subtraction which is often spoken as 'six minus four' and 'six take away 4'. These forms of speech can confuse. 'Minus' is used as an adjective and as a verb and so is best avoided in either spoken form. The number -12 should always be spoken as 'negative 12'. The operation 'subtraction' can be performed by 'taking away'. For example, 20 – 3 found by counting back 3 from 20 is 'taking away'. However, it can also be performed by complementary addition. For example, 20 – 18 found by counting on 2 from 18 is an addition. So, in this exercise, simply use the word 'subtract' in speech. By convention the MyMaths books use the short - sign for 'negative 3' and the long – sign for the operation 'subtract'. This distinction is not easy to maintain when writing by hand.	Absolute zero is the temperature at which (in classical physics) all molecules and atoms stop moving. The idea was established by the pre-eminent Victorian mathematical physicist and engineer William Thomson, later Lord Kelvin, in the 19th century. A unit of temperature, the kelvin, is named in his honour. There is more information about Lord Kelvin at http://en.wikipedia.org/wiki/William_Thomson,_1st_Baron_Kelvin And about absolute zero at http://en.wikipedia.org/wiki/Absolute_zero

Alternative approach

Start with negative numbers in contexts, for example, with heights above and below sea level or ground level and then with temperatures on a thermometer. Number lines are thus vertical rather than horizontal. The notion of negative numbers being 'below' zero or 'less than' zero is thus acquired naturally. Ask questions such as 'A builder is 5 m above the ground when he goes into a trench 2 m below ground level. How many metres has he dropped?' (7 m) and 'It's 5 °C now but it was -3 °C early this morning. How many degrees has it gone up?' (8 °C). Refer to the vertical number line to find the answers.

Once confident with these contexts, then progress to the abstract horizontal number line.

Checkpoint

1 Which is bigger, -5 or 2, and how much bigger?   (2; it is 7 bigger than -5)

2 Consider the calculation -3 + 5
   a Where do you start on the number line?   (-3)
   b Which direction will you go and how far?   (To the right 5 *or* up 5)
   c Where do you get to?   (2; Saying 3 suggests they did not count 0 as a step)

Starter – Guess my number

Choose a number between -10 and 10 and then invite students to guess the number.

After each guess, say whether the next guess should be higher or lower (with a vertical number line) or larger or smaller (with a horizontal number line).

This game can be extended by using numbers with one decimal place.

Teaching notes

Taking two positive numbers, say 2 and 7, discuss the relative size of these numbers and their respective positions on the number line. Extend the discussion to negative numbers, say 2 and -4, highlighting that the bigger number (2) is further to the right than the smaller number (-4). Some students will say that -4 is bigger than 2.

Give students a starting number, say 11, and ask a student to add 4. Go around the class, giving an addition or subtraction to each student.

Repeat with the starting number 5 and the first student subtracts 6. Discuss and demonstrate with a number line that extends below zero, and continue with more additions and subtractions. (Avoid subtracting a negative number. This is not dealt with here.)

Introduce the keywords **positive** and **negative** and ensure students understand that on a number line positive numbers are to the right of zero and negative numbers are to the left of zero.

Highlight that with any calculation there is a *starting number* and a *directional jump* – an addition moves to the right along the number line; a subtraction moves to the left.

Plenary

Test students understanding by asking them questions with and without a context.
 For example:
What temperature is 5 degrees warmer than -1 °C? (4 °C)
What is the answer if you start at -1 and subtract 3? (-4)
Find -4 + 6 (2)
Use mini whiteboards, if available, and discuss answers as necessary.

Exercise commentary

Have a vertical and a horizontal number line on display for students to refer to.

Question 1 – Encourage students to start by positioning the numbers on a number line, even if only mentally by looking at a number line. Check for students who argue -8 is bigger than -5 because 8 is bigger than 5.

Question 2 – Emphasise 'Where do you start?' and 'In which direction do you go?'

Questions 3 and **4** – The vertical number line on the classroom wall is used as a surrogate thermometer. In this context larger corresponds to *hotter* and smaller corresponds to *colder*.

Question 5 – Answers come by direct calculation from the diagram. A number line is not likely to be needed for most students.

Answers

1	a	-8,-5, 3, 5	b	-4, -3, 2, 10	c	-6, -3, 7, 9
	d	-9, -4, 0, 2	e	-10, -5, -3, -1	f	-9, -8, 0, 8
2	a	-2	b	2	c	-3	d	-2
	e	4	f	-7	g	-4	h	-9

3 a 13°C
   b Aberdeen, Birmingham, Edinburgh, Newcastle, London, Belfast, Cardiff

4 a

Between	Temperature
8am and 9am	goes down 2 °C
9am and 10am	goes up 6 °C
10am and 11am	goes up 5 °C
11am and 12pm	goes up 2 °C
12pm and 1pm	goes up 3 °C
1pm and 2pm	goes up 2 °C
2pm and 3pm	goes down 6 °C
3pm and 4pm	goes down 4 °C
4pm and 5pm	goes down 2 °C

   b Between 9am and 10am

5 a 40 m   b 33 m   c 15 m   d 8

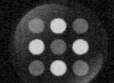

Objectives

- Recall multiplication facts and quickly derive associated division facts (L4)
- Recognise and use multiples and factors (L4)
- Use simple tests of divisibility (L4)

Key ideas	Resources	
1 Factors and multiples are found in the 'times tables'	Factors and primes	(1032)
2 A number has many multiples but has few factors	LCM	(1034)
	Multiplication square	
	Dictionaries	

Simplification

Many students confuse the definitions of factors and multiples. It is worth spending time giving concrete examples to refer to; for example, 6 is a **factor** of 18, 18 is a **multiple** of 6. This diagram can help:

$$6 \xrightarrow[\text{of} \;\; \xleftarrow{\text{a multiple}} \;\; \text{is}]{\text{is} \;\; \xrightarrow{\text{a factor}} \;\; \text{of}} 18$$

The work relies heavily on multiplication and division facts, and weaker students may need a multiplication ('times table') square.

Extension

6 is a *perfect number*; that is, the sum of its factors (except itself) is equal to 6. Challenge students to find other perfect numbers. (There are not many small ones, as they get big very quickly, but 28 is another one!)

Literacy

There are an infinite number of *multiples* of a number, with the smaller multiples being found in the 'times tables'.

Factors of a number occur in pairs which multiply to give the number; such as $3 \times 4 = 12$. So, 3 and 4 are both factors of 12.

Links

Provide dictionaries for the class to use. The word *divisibility* has 5 i's, the word *indivisibilities* has 7. Ask the class to find other words with at least 4 i's. Some examples include *infinitesimal* (4), *impossibilities* (5), *invisibility* (5) and *indistinguishability* (6). The dictionary will probably not include *supercalifragilisticexpialidocious* (7)!

Alternative approach

You can think of finding factors and finding multiples as the 'opposite' of each other. The fact that $5 \times 7 = 42$ tells us (a) that 5 and 7 are both factors of 42, and (b) that 42 is a multiple of 5 and also a multiple of 7.

Use the 'times tables' to write down multiples. For example, 3, 6, 9, 12, 15, … are all multiples of 3.

Use the 10×10 multiplication grid to find (pairs of) factors. For example, 1×6, 2×3, 3×2 and 6×1 are all on the grid, so 1, 2, 3 and 6 are all factors of 6.

On a 100 square, shade all the multiples of 2 and repeat for the multiples of 3, 4, 5, 9, 10 and discuss the patterns.

On axes labelled from 0 to 30, plot points $(1, 24)$, $(24, 1)$, $(2, 12)$, $(12, 2)$, … for the factor pairs of 24 and discuss the pattern. Join with a smooth curve and discuss where you can find $\sqrt{24}$.

Checkpoint

1 Which of these numbers are divisible by 2, 3, 4?

    11, 15, 16, 22, 24, 25, 30, 33, 34   (2: 16, 22, 24, 30, 34; 3: 15, 24, 30, 33; 4: 16, 24)

2 Is 125 divisible by 5? Explain how you know.   (Yes, because 125 ends in 5)

Starter – Differences

Write down the following numbers on the board:

359   275   311   247   409   294.

Ask students which two numbers give

the biggest difference	(409, 247)
the smallest difference	(294, 311)
a difference of 19	(275, 294)
a difference in the 5 times table	(359, 409)
a difference in the 7 times table	(247, 275).

Teaching notes

Ask students to say all that they know about a number, say 50. For example, it is even; it is not a prime. Use their statements to highlight key terms and re-word as necessary; so,

'It is in the 10 times table' becomes 'It is a **multiple** of 10' and

'It divides into 200 exactly becomes 'It is a **factor** of 200'.

Invite students to define multiple and factor. Ensure students understand that a **factor** of a number divides into it **exactly** and a **multiple** of a number is in its times table. Refer to a multiplication grid to highlight that all multiples of, say 7, are in its **row**.

Ask for 'a multiple of 8', 'a factor of 50', and so on for students to gain confidence.

Ask students to list **all** the factors of 24 by finding it in the multiplication square and elicit the reciprocal relationship between factor and multiple – each number is a **factor** of 24, so 24 is a **multiple** of each number. Highlight that each factor is one of a pair, for example, 3 and 8. Ensure students understand that 24 is a factor of itself and 1 is a factor of every number.

Plenary

Invite students to find all the factors of 12 and write them in pairs. Repeat for 35 and 42. Notice that each number has an even number of factors. Challenge students to find numbers with an odd number of factors and discover that they are the square numbers.

Exercise commentary

Question 1 – This requires sequences of multiples. Students can find them in the 'times tables'.

Question 2 – 'Halving and halving again' immediately discards all odd numbers.

Question 4 – Students can use their 'times tables' in reverse; finding divisions from multiplications.

Question 5 – In identifying all the factors of a given number, many students will forget $1 \times n$ as a factor pair of n. Encourage them to start at this point; 1 is a factor of every number.

Question 6 – This question requires students to differentiate between the multiples and factors.

Answers

1 a 15, 21, 24   b 44, 55, 66
   c 30, 42, 54   d 32, 48, 56
2 84, 16, 56, 40, 156
3 a Yes   b No   c No   d Yes
   e Yes   f No
4 a 2   b 5   c 4   d 3
   e 3   f 5   g 9   h 2
   i 7   j 3   k 14   l 1
5 a 2, 3   b 2, 5   c 2, 4, 6
   d 1, 3, 5, 15   e 1, 2, 4, 5, 10, 20
   f 1, 2, 3, 4, 6, 8, 12, 24
   g 1, 2, 3, 5, 6, 10, 15, 30
   h 1, 2, 3, 4, 6, 9, 12, 18, 36
6 a 13   b 18   c 9   d 7

Objectives

• Recognise and use factors and common factors	(L4)

Key ideas	Resources	
1 Pairs of factors of a number can be found from that number's 'times table' 2 Two numbers can have the same factors. They are called 'common factors'	Factors and primes Multiplication square	(1032)

Simplification	Extension
Weaker students have a multiplication grid to identify factors of numbers up to 10 (or 12).	Students find the highest common factor of two (or three) numbers and also find the lowest common multiple. Challenge students to find two numbers where the LCM is *not* just the product of the two numbers, such as 4 and 6 with a product of 24 and an LCM of 12.

Literacy	Links
Alliteration is useful when remembering the meaning of a multiple and a factor: **M**ultiples are **M**any, but **F**actors are **F**ew. To help remember HCF and LCM, the *highest* common factor is a *low* number, whereas the *lowest* common multiple is a *high* number, when compared with the two numbers under consideration.	Ask the class how many ways there are to make £1 using coins of the same denomination. All 26 000 million circulating coins in the UK are factors or multiples of £1. All the coins have a portrait of the reigning monarch on the front, but a variety of designs on the reverse. There is more information about British coinage at http://www.royalmint.gov.uk/ Corporate/BritishCoinage/british_coinage.aspx and pictures showing the designs for all coin denominations since 1971 at http://www.ukcoinpics.co.uk/dec/index.html

Alternative approach

Students have met Venn diagrams in student book **1A**. Factors of two numbers can be entered in a Venn diagram and the common factors found from it. The HCF is then easy to choose.

For example, a Venn diagram of two circles can be used for the factors of 12 and 20. The common factors, 1, 2 and 4, are entered in the intersection (the overlap) and the other factors are entered outside the intersection. Of the common factors, the highest common factor is 4.

A similar Venn diagram can represent multiples of two numbers. The sizes of the sets are infinite as there are an infinite number of multiples, so only list the multiples up to a certain limit.

For example, for the multiples of 2 and 3 up to 20, the intersection of the Venn diagram contains the multiples 6, 12 and 18, with the other multiples outside the intersection. The LCM is then easy to choose as 6.

Checkpoint

1	a	Name one factor of 12.	(1, 2, 3, 4, 6 or 12)
	b	How do you known that 4 is a factor of 12?	(Because 4 divides into 12 exactly)
	c	What are the other factors of 12?	
2	a	What are all the factors of 20?	(1, 2, 4, 5, 10, 20)
	b	Why is 6 not a factor of 20?	(Because 6 does *not* divide into 20 exactly)
3		What are the common factors of 12 and 20?	(2 and 10)

Starter – Tables bingo

Ask students to draw a 3 × 3 grid and enter numbers from the 4, 5 and 6 times tables. Give questions; for example, what is the product 6 × 3? The winner is the first student to cross out all numbers.

This game can be differentiated by the choice of tables.

Teaching notes

Invite students to list all the factors of 32, recalling from the previous lesson that **factor** of a number is a number that divides into it **exactly**. Encourage students to think in terms of factor pairs and recall that 1 is always a factor of any number.

Repeat for factors of 24. Discuss which factors are common to both 32 and 24.

Introduce students to the term **Highest Common Factor (HCF)** and, looking at the common factors identified, find the HCF of 32 and 24.   (8)

Repeat the exercise for 12 and 16.   (4)

Plenary

Ask questions such as 'List the factors of 16', 'What numbers less than 10 have factors of 1, 2 and 3?' and 'List the factors of 8 and 12 and circle the common factors'. Students respond on mini whiteboards and discuss results.

Exercise commentary

Questions 1 and **2** – Many students are likely to forget $1 \times n$ as a factor pair. Encourage them to start at this point with $1 \times n$ and to be systematic.

Questions 3–5 – Write out the full list for each number before identifying the common factors. Be systematic in approach.

Question 6 – Amaze students with some factor magic!

Answers

1 a 1, 2, 3, 6   b 1, 2, 4, 8   c 1, 2, 5, 10
   d 1, 2, 3, 4, 6, 12   e 1, 3, 5, 15   f 1, 2, 4, 8, 16
   g 1, 2, 3, 6, 9, 18   h 1, 19
2 a 1, 2, 3, 4, 6, 8, 12, 24   b 1, 2, 4, 7, 14, 28
   c 1, 2, 3, 5, 6, 10, 15, 30
3 a 1, 2, 3, 4, 6, 9, 12, 18, 36   b 8, 24, 72
4 a 1, 2, 4   b 1, 3   c 1, 3, 9
   d 1, 2, 3, 6   e 1, 2, 4   f 1, 3
5 a 1, 5   b 1, 2, 4   c 1, 2, 4
6 Student dependent
7 10

Objectives

- Recognise and use primes (less than 100) (L4)

Key ideas	Resources
1 A prime number has no factors except for 1 and the number itself **2** 1 is not a prime number	Factors and primes (1032) A 10 by 10 number square A multiplication square Small squares Computer spreadsheet

Simplification	Extension
Provide students with a multiplication square to help correctly identify factor pairs.	Use the internet to find (a) a list of all prime numbers below 1000, and (b) the highest prime number that has been discovered.

Literacy	Links
The word *prime* comes from Latin and means 'first in importance'. 'Prime-time television' is the most popular time for watching TV. A 'prime cut of meat' is the best cut. Prime numbers are important because all non-prime numbers can be made from primes. For example, 14 is not a prime number and is made from the two primes 2×7. The number 12 is not prime and is made from $2 \times 2 \times 3$.	Some varieties of the insect cicada have long life cycles of a prime number of years, usually thirteen but sometimes seventeen. They live for years underground as grubs and then emerge from their burrows for a few weeks to breed and then die. The population is synchronised so that huge numbers of insects become adults and emerge together. It is believed that this helps them to escape from natural population control by predators and parasites. The males make a distinctive drumming or singing noise. There is more information about periodical cicadas at magicicada.org/magicicada.php and at biology.clc.uc.edu/steincarter/cicadas.htm

Alternative approach

Use a spreadsheet to find prime numbers.

In column A, let cell A1 = 1 and cell A2 = A1 + 1. Drag down to, say, 32 to generate the numbers 1 to 32.

In column B, let B1 = 32 and drag down so that 32 appears in each cell from 1 to 32.

In column C, let cell C1 = B1/A1 and drag down as far as 32. Inspect this column to see if the divisions create any integer answers other than 1 and 32. Yes, there are several integer answers, so 32 is not a prime number. (The integer answers, by the way, are the factors of 32.)

Change cell B1 to 31. As the formulae are already set up, the answers to the divisions appear immediately. Integer answers only exist for 1 and 31, so 31 is a prime number. Repeat for other values of cell B1.

Checkpoint

1 a Is 5 a prime number? (Yes)
  b Why is it prime? (Because only 1 and 5 will divide into it a whole number of times.)
  c So is 6 prime and, if not, why not? (No, 6 isn't prime, because 2 and 3 divide into it exactly.)
  a Is 7 a prime? (7 is a prime number, as it has no factors except 1 and 7.)
2 List the first five prime numbers. (2, 3, 5, 7, 11)

Starter – Quick fire

Recap basic number work so far in this chapter and more especially from student book **1A**. Include questions on fractions, decimals and percentages and questions using mental and written computation. Ask rapid response questions. Students reply by writing on their mini whiteboards. Discuss questions when their answers indicate a need.

Teaching notes

Students list the factors of 12 by thinking of them in pairs. They do the same with 13 and 7. They note that both 13 and 7 have only two factors. Do the students know any more numbers with only two factors?

Introduce the 'sieve of Eratosthenes' as described in the students' book to the whole class, with students crossing out (in pencil) each set of multiples.

Plenary

Show students a random scatter of identical squares. They use 2 squares, and then 3 squares, to sketch a rectangle on their mini whiteboards. With 4 squares, ask them to sketch as many rectangles as they can and to classify a square as a rectangle. (They draw 1 × 4 and 2 × 2). Repeat with 5, 6, 7 8, 9 squares.

Ask students which numbers only give one possible rectangle (2, 3, 5, 7, …) and what name is given to these numbers. (Primes)

Exercise commentary

Questions 1–3 – These questions all require students to identify prime numbers. Watch for students who do not list all the factors and so falsely declare a number prime.

Question 5 – Students need to be systematic. Can they devise an efficient method? A possible method is to subtract each prime number in turn to see if it gives a prime number as an answer.

Answers

1	d	1 and 5	Prime
	e	1, 2, 3, 6	Non-prime
	f	1 and 7	Prime
	g	1, 2, 4, 8	Non-prime
	h	1, 3, 9	Non-prime
	i	1, 2, 5, 10	Non-prime
	j	1, 11	Prime
	k	1, 2, 3, 4, 6, 1 2	Non-prime
	l	1 and 13	Prime
	m	1, 2, 7, 14	Non-prime
	n	1, 3, 5, 15	Non-prime
	o	1, 2, 4, 8, 16	Non-prime
	p	1 and 17	Prime
	q	1, 2, 3, 6, 9, 18	Non-prime
	r	1 and 19	Prime
	s	1, 2, 4, 5, 10, 20	Non-prime

2	a	7	b	17	c	23	d	31
3	a	11	b	23	c	37		
	d	3 (41, 43 and 47)						
	e	2 (53, 59)						
4	a	D	b	B				
5	a	7, 5	b	31, 5	c	47, 5	d	97, 3

Objectives

• Understand and use decimal notation and place value	(L3)
• Compare and order decimals in the context of money	(L4)

Key ideas	Resources
1 The place of a digit in a decimal determines its value 2 Decimal place values are tenths, hundredths and thousandths	Ordering decimals (1072) Decimal place values (1076) 10 × 10 squares Overlapping place value cards Number line with 100 divisions

Simplification	Extension
Questions 1 to 4 focus on decimals within the context of money and most students will have an intuitive approach. In question 5 onwards with abstract decimals, students can still think in terms of monetary value. Watch for students who write 3p as £0.3 (Question 1a i, 3a, 4e).	Encourage students outside the context of money to write decimals such as 0.30 as 0.3 by asking 'Do you need to say there are no hundredths?' Extend students to addition and subtraction of decimal values.

Literacy	Links
There are linguistic points to note when using money as an introduction to decimal notation. The number 'nought point three' has no meaning with money, neither spoken nor written; £1.20 is spoken as 'one pound twenty', but 1.2 is spoken as 'one point two'. The third decimal place has no physical meaning in money. Care has to be taken later when the transfer is made to other measures, such as length, mass and capacity.	Gold was discovered along the Klondike River in the Yukon in north-west Canada in 1896. Word quickly spread and thousands of prospectors stampeded to the area to find their fortunes. The journey was difficult and there was not enough transportation to handle the huge numbers of people. Many of the prospectors turned back and, of those who did reach the Klondike, only a small number found any gold. There is more about the Klondike Gold Rush at http://library.thinkquest.org/5181/ and a game to simulate the journey to the Klondike at http://www.virtualmuseum.ca/Exhibitions/Klondike/English/main.html

Alternative approach

The diagrammatic representation of a decimal in the students' book (using a 100 square as the unit 1) is not set in the context of money and so the general language of decimals can be used. A full column is worth one tenth, a small square is worth one hundredth, and tiny squares (too small to be drawn in the students' book) are worth thousandths. An exercise based on a several of these diagrams can lead to each diagram being written, for example, as:

$$\text{4 tenths, 5 hundredths and 5 thousandths} = \frac{4}{10} + \frac{5}{100} + \frac{5}{1000} = 0.4 + 0.05 + 0.005 = 0.4\,5\,5 = 0.455$$

U t h th

Overlapping place value cards is another visual representation that can be used.

Checkpoint

1 a What is £0.30 in pence?   b What is £0.03 in pence?   (30p, 3p)

2 Which is the larger – nought point three or nought point three three?   (Nought point three three)

3 Is there any difference between 0.6 and 0.60?   (There is no difference in these two values)

Starter – Quick fire

Continue the recap of basic number work begun in the last lesson's Starter activity. Include questions on fractions, decimals and percentages and questions using mental and written computation. Ask rapid response questions. Students reply by writing on their mini whiteboards. Discuss questions when their answers indicate a need.

Teaching notes

Show the whole class a number line from 0 to 1 with 100 divisions. Invite students to label any point on the line with the appropriate decimal or fraction. Elicit that each division is $\frac{1}{100}$ and that this is written as the decimal 0.01 (recalling place value: 'no units, no tenths, and 1 hundredth'). Link to money and highlight each penny is $\frac{1}{100}$ of a pound. Invite students to include monetary values on the number line; for example, 10p, 1p, 50p. Challenge students to mark various monetary amounts, such as £0.17, £0.78, 29p. Take a particular interest in £0.20 and £0.02.

Discuss which is larger: 26p, £0.27 or 34p.

Plenary

Students say which of two sums is the bigger, such as 25p and £0.20, and which of two numbers is the bigger such as 0.3 and 0.03. Students add two sums together such as 30p and £0.15 and add two numbers together such as three-hundredths and 0.2. All answers are written on mini whiteboards and discussed.

Exercise commentary

Questions 1 and **2** – Watch for the answers such as 3p written as £0.3 or £0.30 instead of £0.03.

Question 4 – Extends to consider the relative size of decimals within the context of money.

Question 5 – Shading a grid to represent each answer is strongly recommended. It will show the students' understanding more clearly.

Question 6 – A new context of mass is introduced here. Insist on the change in spoken language; for example 0.13 g is *not* 'nought point thirteen grams'.

In part **d**, some students may find it easier to add 0.13 and 0.09 together, and then add on 1.01, etc., rather than all six amounts together.

Answers

1 i a £0.03   b 3p
   ii a £0.09   b 9p
   iii a £0.13   b 13p
   iv a £0.20   b 20p
   v   a £0.34   b 34p
   vi a £0.01   b 1p

2 a £0.30   b £0.90   c £0.70   d £0.50
   e £0.10   f £0.33   g £0.45   h £0.17
   i £0.02   j £1.00

3 a £0.09, (£0.10)   b (£0.30), £0.04

   c £0.01, (£0.10)   d (£0.35), 29p

   e (3p) £0.02

4 a 0.38 (0.41)   b 0.05 (0.10)

   c 0.07 (0.70)   d 0.08 (0.80)

   e 0.27 (0.50)   f 0.06 (0.40)

5 a 0.07, 0.10, 0.15, 0.21
   b 1.09, 1.35, 1.51, 1.80
6 a Wed and Sat
   b 0.09 g
   c 0.09 g, 0.13 g, 0.31 g, 0.93 g, 1.01 g, 1.12 g
   d 3.59 g
7 Juice, Milk, Butter, Bread, Crisps

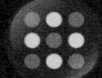

1f Rounding

Objectives

- Round positive whole numbers to nearest 10, 100, 1000 and decimals to nearest whole number (L4)
- Read and interpret scales, and round readings from scales (L5)

Key ideas

1 Rounding gives a 'ball-park' figure when the headline is more important than the detail
2 Always round up from the midpoint

Resources

Rounding decimals (1004)
Number lines for various ranges.

Simplification

Students often become confused about the degree they are rounding to when, for example, rounding a number to the nearest 10 instead of the nearest 100.

They should first consider the two tens (or hundreds) that the number lies between. Use a number line and write the two values, one on either side.

In addition, place value headings (H T U t h) emphasise the value of the digits in each number and help students to identify the *decider* digit.

Extension

Challenge students to consider upper and lower bounds. If a number has been rounded to 50 to the nearest 10, what could that number be? What is the highest possible value is could be before it becomes 60? What is the lowest value before it becomes 40?

Literacy

'Rounding' is used generally in the sense of 'making something complete or whole' like a rounded personality and a rounded education. So, in mathematics, 'rounding' can be thought of as removing the unwanted smaller 'bits' of a number to give a more rounded size.

Links

In parliamentary elections in Germany in 1992, a rounding error caused the wrong results to be announced. Under German law, a party cannot have any seats in parliament unless it has 5.0% or more of the vote. The Green Party appeared to have exactly 5.0%, until it was discovered that the computer which had printed out the results had only used one place after the decimal point, and it had rounded the vote up to 5.0%. The Green Party only had 4.97% of the vote and the results had to be changed.

Alternative approach

The following approach does not replace the use of a number line to straddle the required number between two boundary numbers. But it gives the number line more force. For example, when finding the number 1357 to the nearest hundred, the number line will indicate 1300 and 1400 as the two boundary numbers.

Write the number with its column headings and place a card over the parts that are to be rounded (the 'unwanted bits'). For example, when rounding 1357 to the nearest 100, write Th H T U above 1357 and cover the T and U columns with the card – we are only interested in hundreds and bigger; we are not interested in tenths and smaller (so cover them up). Under the card will only be zeros, but the part removed (the unwanted 57) is more than halfway to 400 and so it makes the 3 hundred into a 4 hundred.

Checkpoint

1 a What is the number 1357 rounded to the nearest 100? (1400)
  b What is it rounded to the nearest 10? (1360)

2 a What is the number 24.6 rounded to the nearest whole number? (25)
  b What is it rounded to the nearest 10? (20)

3 a What is the decimal 0.62 rounded to the nearest tenth? (0.6)
  b How big does it have to become before it is 0.7 rounded to the nearest tenth? (0.65)

Starter – Quick fire

Continue the recap of basic number work begun in the last lesson's Starter. The overall aim is to have students able to answer speedily and accurately basic questions on, for example, the equivalence between fractions, decimals and percentages, and questions using mental and written computation. Ask rapid response questions. Students reply by writing on their mini whiteboards. Discuss questions when their answers indicate a need.

Teaching notes

Invite students to tell you how long it takes to get to school. Discuss whether this is an exact measurement or an approximation. Write answers, discuss rounding them to the nearest 5 minutes, and write the rounded values alongside.

Write the number 12 on the board and ask 'What two multiples of 10 does 12 lie between?'

Draw a number line from 10 to 20. Discuss which 'ten' (multiple of 10) 12 is closer to. Label the line from 10 to 15 with 'closer to 10' and from 15 to 20 with 'closer to 20'. Discuss other numbers in the range 10 to 20 and rounding them 'to the nearest 10'.

Discuss how to round 473 to the nearest ten.

- First consider which two tens it lies between; use a number line to illustrate this.
- Using the next place value digit (the U column in this case) to decide whether to round up or down.
- If this digit is below 5, the number rounds down. If it equals 5 or is above 5, it rounds up.

Discuss the idea of 'exactly halfway' being rounded up.

Move on to consider rounding a decimal number to the nearest whole number. Again, consider first which two whole numbers it lies between.

Plenary

Give students several numbers, both integers and decimals, to round to different degrees of accuracy. Students respond on mini whiteboards and, from their responses, judge whether to discuss any particular question.

Exercise commentary

Questions 1 and **2** – Sketches of number lines are needed with the two boundary values straddling the given number, or decide in question **1** which tens the number lies between and which one it is closer to, similarly hundreds in question **2**.

Question 4 – Round all to the nearest 10 first. Encourage students to write down the number before rounding to nearest 100.

Question 5 – If the number in the tenths column is 5 or more, the number rounds up.

Question 6 – If the number in the hundredths column is 5 or more, the tenths column rounds up.

Question 7 – This is a jump as the students need to understand than only the hundreds column affects the rounding. They can ignore the tens and units. Cover up the T and U. Look at the hundreds column then decide whether to round up or not.

Question 8 – Students might find the answer rather 'fussy'. But emphasise that there has to be evidence that the rounding 'to one decimal place' has actually taken place.

Answers

1	a	10	b	30	c	60	d	0
	e	100	f	130	g	150	h	220
	i	400	j	110				
2	a	600	b	600	c	0	d	400
	e	400	f	400	g	0	h	100
	i	1000	j	1400				
3	a	5	b	6	c	10		
	d	15	e	22	f	21		
4	a	i	70	ii	100		
	b	i	130	ii	100		
	c	i	360	ii	400		
5	a	4	b	20	c	32	d	51
	e	1	f	30	g	100	h	0
	i	101	j	122	k	130	l	131
6	a	3.6	b	0.1	c	9.8	d	2.5

7
Blackpool	9000
Bristol City	16 000
Hull City	18 000
Ipswich	21 000
Leicester	23 000
Southampton	20 000
Stoke	16 000
Watford	17 000

8 Kaye

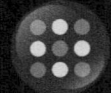

Objectives

- Recognise the squares of numbers to at least 12×12 (L4)

Key ideas	Resources
1 A square number is found by multiplying a number by itself 2 The notation for a square number is x^2	Squares and cubes (1053) Multiplication square Calculator Computer spreadsheet

Simplification	Extension
Some students may need a multiplication square of 'times tables'. Students often confuse ^{2} with multiplying by 2. Students should be encouraged to link back to the multiplication grid and visualise the diagonal pattern of square numbers.	Students calculate $x^2 - y^2$ where x and y are consecutive integers. For example, they calculate $32^2 - 31^2$. They look for a pattern in their answer and use it to predict other values of $x^2 - y^2$. (The pattern is that all answers are $x + y$)

Literacy	Links
The notation 5^2 is spoken in two different ways. It is spoken as '*five squared*' or as '*five to the power 2*'. The first of these is the more popular, but the second is the only way used for higher powers (other than the power 3). The number 2 is called an *index* or *power*. The plural of index is indices.	Tiananmen Square in Beijing in China is the largest city square in the world. It measures 880 m by 500 m and has room for a million people to gather. It has been the site of many rallies and demonstrations, including the student protests in 1989. 'Tiananmen' means 'Gate of Heavenly Peace' and the square is named after the Tiananmen Gate to the north of the square. There is a panoramic view of Tiananmen Square at http://www.thebeijingguide.com/tiananmen_square/index.html

Alternative approach

Use a spreadsheet to generate square numbers.

Let cell A1 = 1, cell A2 = A1 + 1, cells B1 = A1 * A1. Drag these formulae down, say, 25 rows. Column B displays the square numbers.

Use the tool bar (Insert Chart and Line) to draw a line graph of both columns. See how the square numbers rise far faster than the numbers themselves.

If you need the square of a large number, is it quicker to use this spreadsheet or to use a calculator? (Most likely quicker on a calculator.)

Does every calculator have a 'square' key on it? (The cheapest calculators may not have.)

Checkpoint

1 What are the first five square numbers? $(1, 4, 9, 16, 25)$

2 Which one of the following numbers is a square number?   62, 63, 64 (64)

Starter – Quick fire

Continue the recap of basic number work begun in the last lesson's Starter. Include questions on fractions, decimals and percentages and questions using mental and written computation. Ask rapid response questions. Students reply by writing on their mini whiteboards. Discuss questions when students' answers indicate the need.

Teaching notes

Draw squares with these sizes 1×1, 2×2, and 3×3. Invite volunteers to draw the next square in the sequence (until you have 6×6). Students allocate a number to each diagram (1, 4, 9, etc.).

Explain that these numbers 1, 4, 9, … are **square numbers**. Explain the name 'square' by linking the numbers with areas of squares.

Introduce index notation. The fourth square number is 4 squared $= 4^2 = 4 \times 4 = 16$

Demonstrate the pattern of square numbers in a 10×10 multiplication square as a diagonal of numbers.

Plenary

Practise students' mental number skills by asking straightforward calculations, such as, finding the value of $2^2 + 3^2$, $4^2 - 2^2$, 3×5^2. Students respond on mini whiteboards and answers are discussed when necessary.

Exercise commentary

Question 1 – It may be necessary to draw the 4th and 5th square shapes.

Question 3 – The 'tiles' are the nine cells of the rectangles. All can be paired.

Question 4 – Encourage writing down the middle step, e.g. $4^2 + 3 = 16 + 3 = 19$. Watch out for $4 + 3$ which is then squared.

Question 5 – Counting the row and the column in each diagram shows that they are indeed squares.

Question 6 – The next step is $1^2 + 4^2 + 5^2$

Answers

1 a 16   **b** 25

2

Number	Calculation	Power	Value
1	1×1	1^2	1
2	2×2	2^2	4
3	3×3	3^2	9
4	4×4	4^4	16
5	5×5	5^2	25
6	6×6	6^2	36
7	7×7	7^2	49
8	8×8	8^2	64
9	9×9	9^2	81
10	10×10	10^2	100
11	11×11	11^2	121
12	12×12	12^2	144

3 $5^2 = 25$, $9^2 = 81$, $3^2 = 9$, $7^2 = 49$, $6^2 = 36$, $12^2 = 144$

4 a 19   **b** 5   **c** 16   **d** 1
   e 36   **f** 40   **g** 42   **h** 80
   i 66   **j** 19

5 a 36   **b** 64   **c** 121

6   Student dependent

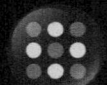

Objectives

- Recognise the squares of numbers to at least 12×12 and the corresponding square roots (L5)
- Use the square root key on a calculator (L5)

Key ideas	Resources
1 Squaring and square-rooting are inverse operations 2 For example, if $12^2 = 144$, then $\sqrt{144} = 12$	⊞ Squares and cubes (1053) OHT of (picture pattern of) square numbers Unit cubes Cards numbered 1-9 Mini whiteboards

Simplification	Extension
Some students will become confused between the square number and the square root. Ensure they have a clear example to refer to: $4 \times 4 = 16$ (16 is a square number) and the square root of 16 is 4. This diagram might help:	Extend students to cubed numbers. Provide them with unit cubes and challenge them to find how many cubes would be required in a $1 \times 1 \times 1$ cube, $2 \times 2 \times 2$ cube, $3 \times 3 \times 3$ cube, ... and use the notation $1^3, 2^3, 3^3, \ldots$

$$4 \xrightarrow{\text{squared}} \text{is } 16$$
$$4 \text{ is} \xleftarrow{\text{square-rooted}}$$

Literacy	Links
The use of square roots in Europe goes back about 500 years. But the Ancient Babylonians wrote about $\sqrt{2}$ on clay tablets nearly four thousand years ago. The Ancient Egyptians about the same time showed how to find square roots. There are writings from India about 2700 years old and from China about 2200 years old which also tell how to find them. When using the symbol $\sqrt{\ }$, we write $\sqrt{2}$. But, if the number is long, we write it with a line across the top, like $\sqrt{2.375}$ or by using brackets, like $\sqrt{(2.375)}$. The line on the top acts like a bracket.	Show sheets of A3, A4 and A5 paper and other ISO sizes. Ask the class to measure the paper. The length is $\sqrt{2}$ times the width for each size. Fold a sheet of A4 in half and compare with a sheet of A5 – it is the same size. ISO paper sizes are designed so that A0 has an area of one square meter but with a length : width ratio of $\sqrt{2} : 1$. A sheet of A0 cut in half makes two sheets of size A1, each with a length : width ratio of $\sqrt{2} : 1$. Similarly, a sheet of A1 produces two A2 sheets, and an A2 sheet produces two A3 sheets. There is a chart showing ISO paper sizes at http://en.wikipedia.org/wiki/Image:A_size_illustration.svg

Alternative approach

Use a graphical method to find square roots.

Write the factor pairs of 36 as coordinates of points: $(1, 36), (2, 18), (3, 12), \ldots (18, 2), (36, 1)$. Draw axes labelled from 0 to 40, plot the points and draw a smooth curve through them. Ask students to find a point where the coordinates are the same. They find $(6, 6)$. Draw the square $(0, 0), (6, 0), (6, 6), (0, 6)$ and ask for its area, which is $6 \times 6 = 36$. Say that 6 squared gives us 36 and introduced the square root of 36. Write $6^2 = 36$ and introduce the symbol $\sqrt{\ }$ by writing $\sqrt{36} = 6$. Say that finding the square root is the opposite of finding the square.

Repeat for factor pairs of 64. Eventually, write $8^2 = 64$ and $\sqrt{64} = 8$.

Repeat for the factor pairs of 12. Finding the coordinates that are the same gives a non-integer answer. Read the graph as accurately as possible. A more accurate answer can be found on a calculator. Use the $\sqrt{\ }$ key and find it. Write out the whole display. Write $3.46^2 = 12$ and $\sqrt{12} = 3.46$ (to 2 decimal places).

Checkpoint

1 Match the following numbers in pairs. Which number is the odd one out?

8^2 $\sqrt{16}$ 49 4 7^2 10 $\sqrt{25}$ 9 64 $\sqrt{100}$ 5 (9)

Starter – Stamps

A package costs 40 pence to post.

Ask students how many ways 40 pence can be made using 5p and 7p stamps. (There are 2 ways: 8 × 5p and 1 × 5p + 5 × 7p.)

Challenge students to find the largest postage amount that cannot be made using 5p and 7p stamps. (23p)

Teaching notes

Show a picture pattern of the square number sequence. Discuss how the number of tiles grows and challenge students to describe the position-to-term rule (that is, for example, the 3rd diagram has 3 rows of 3 tiles, so the position-to-term rule gives $3 \longrightarrow 3 \times 3 = 9$). Link the area of a square to its side and elicit:

a square number = the number × the number.

List the square numbers up to the 12th square number. Students should memorise them.

Introduce the notation and key language: for example,

5^2 *is spoken as '5 squared' and* $5^2 = 5 \times 5 = 25$

Remind students that 5^2 means '5 squared' and not '5 doubled'.

Provide students with calculators and ask them to evaluate 1.5^2, 72^2, etc. Extend to discuss how to find the input given various outputs (for example, what is the number that gives the squares 64, 100, etc.).

Highlight this as the inverse and introduce students to the keyword *square root* and its symbol $\sqrt{}$. Introduce the calculator button and sequence of keys to evaluate a square root.

Introduce students to Pauline and Rob's number game in the students' book. Show students the cards for the number 65; they use the calculator to find $\sqrt{65}$ and write it on mini whiteboards. Discuss why they should expect a number slightly bigger than 8. They check their answer by finding the square of it to get back to 65.

Repeat to gain confidence. Show students a two-digit number; they use a calculator to evaluate its square root.

Plenary

Show students the numbers, say, 25, 4, 9, 81, 5, 8, 11, 12, 7, 64, 3. Invite them to connect pairs of numbers using squares and square roots. For example, for the pair 8 and 64, they write $8^2 = 64$ and also $\sqrt{64} = 8$ on their mini whiteboards. Discuss their results. Repeat for other pairs.

Exercise commentary

Questions 2–5 – These questions refer back to the previous page where Pauline and Rob are playing with number cards and a calculator.

Question 4 – Have students write the full calculator display in each case, before any rounding takes place. Note the '1 dp' means 'one decimal place'.

Question 5 – Remind students of a two-stage number machine (function diagram) and using it in reverse.

Question 6 – The jagged edges indicate that this is only part of the floor. So the student cannot simply count the tiles that fit into the diagram that is drawn here.

Question 7 – Refer back to Eratosthenes sieve in **1d**, to have a list of the prime numbers up to 35 to work with is helpful.

Answers

1	a	2		b	$4 \times 4 = 16$	c	36
	d	$3 \times 3 = 9$		e	$5 \times 5 = 25$	f	100
2	a	4	b 36	c	64	d	25
	e	0	f 1	g	81	h	49
	i	100					
3	a	5	b 4	c	7	d	10
	e	6	f 8	g	1	h	0
	i	9					
4	a	400	b 30	c	13	d	6.25
	e	1.4	f 0.3	g	3.2	h	5.8
	i	1.69					
5	a	9	b 36				

6 Yes, $\sqrt{1600} = 40$

7 $4 = 2 + 2$, $9 = 7 + 2$, $16 = 13 + 3$, $25 = 23 + 2$, $36 = 31 + 5$

Key outcomes		Quick check	
Order, add and subtract negative numbers.	L5	Which is the smallest, -5 or 2?	(-5)
		Which is the smallest, -3 or -4?	(-4)
		4 + - 7	(-3)
		-3 – 5	(-8)
Recognise and use multiples and factors.	L4	Is 5 a factor of 8?	(No)
		Is 4 a factor of 8?	(Yes)
		Which number is a factor of all numbers?	(1)
		Is 28 a multiple of 7?	(Yes)
		Is 34 a multiple of 7?	(No)
Use divisibility tests.	L4	Is 123 divisible by 3?	(Yes)
		Is 125 divisible by 5?	(Yes)
		Is 121 divisible by 2?	(No)
Recognise prime numbers.	L5	From the folllowing four numbers two are prime and two are not. Which ones are prime? 1 2 7 9	(2 ,7)
Find squares and square roots.	L5	What is 5 squared?	(25)
		What is the square root of 36?	(6)
Order decimals.	L4	Which is the smallest, 0.9 or 0.89?	(0.89)
		Which is the smallest 1.01 or 1.11?	(1.01)
Round whole numbers and decimals.	L4	Round 439 to the nearest ten.	(440)
		Round 5.6 to the nearest whole number.	(6)
		Round 4.45 to one decimal place.	(4.5)

MyMaths extra support

Lesson/online homework			Description
Rounding to 10, 100	1003	L3	Rounding numbers to the nearest 10, 100 and 1000
Ordering whole numbers	1217	L3	Ordering whole numbers up to 1000
Place value hundreds thousands	1352	L4	Ordering whole numbers, decimals and negatives
Solving problems by rounding	1373	L3	Estimating amounts up to 100; rounding numbers to the nearest 10 and 100

MyReview

Check out

You should now be able to ...

Test it ➡
Questions

✓ Order, add and subtract negative numbers.	⑤ 1
✓ Recognise and used multiples and factors.	④ 2 – 5
✓ Use divisibility tests.	④ 6
✓ Recognise prime numbers.	⑦ 7
✓ Find squares and square roots.	⑤ 8 – 10
✓ Order decimals.	④ 11
✓ Round whole numbers and decimals.	④ 12

Language	Meaning	Example
Integer	A whole number without a decimal part	7 and 342 are integers
Multiple	A number which is part of another number's times table	12 and 18 are both multiples of 6
Factor	A number which exactly divides into another number	4 and 6 are both factors of 12
Square number	A number which is found by multiplying an integer by itself twice	$9 = 3^2$ is the square of 3 and $25 = 5^2$ is the square of 5
Square root	The opposite of a square number	$3 = \sqrt{9}$ is the square root of 9 and $5 = \sqrt{25}$ is the square root of 25
Decimal	A number which has digits after the decimal point	3.25 and 4.13 are decimal numbers
Rounding	You can round up or down to a particular accuracy	Rounding 16 to the nearest 10 is 20

1 Put these numbers in order from smallest to largest.
  a 4   -2   0   -3
  b -6   6   -5   -4

2 Which of the following numbers are factors of 8?
  1   2   3   4
  6   8   16   20

3 Which of the following numbers are multiples of 8?
  1   2   3   4
  6   8   16   20

4 Find all the factors of
  a 20
  b 32.

5 Find the common factors of
  a 10 and 15
  b 24 and 30.

6 Use divisibility tests to answer these questions and explain your answer.
  a Is 2 a factor of 458?
  b Is 134 divisible by 5?
  c Is 540 a multiple of 10?
  d Is 3 a factor of 457?

7 Which of these numbers are prime? Explain your answers.
  a 1   b 2   c 4
  d 7   e 9   f 13

8 Which of the these numbers are square numbers?
  a 1   b 2   c 3
  d 4   e 6   f 9

9 Write down the value of these square roots.
  a $\sqrt{81}$
  b $\sqrt{16}$

10 Work out these calculations.
  a 5^2
  b $14 - 3^2$

11 Put these numbers in order from smallest to largest.
  0.49, 0.52, 1.02, 0.6, 0.07

12 Round 192.5 to the nearest
  a whole number
  b 10
  c 100.

What next?

Score		
0 – 5		Your knowledge of this topic is still developing. To improve look at Formative test: 2A-1; MyMaths: 1004, 1032, 1034, 1053, 1068, 1069, 1072 and 1076
6 – 9		You are gaining a secure knowledge of this topic. To improve look at InvisiPen: 111, 112, 113, 171, 172, 173 and 181
10 – 12		You have mastered this topic. Well done, you are ready to progress!

Question commentary

Question 1 – Students can use a number line to help.

Question 2 – Remind students that a factor of 8 is a number that divides into 8 an exact number of times.

Question 3 – Remind students that multiples of 8 are numbers that 8 divides into.

Question 4 – Factors include 1 and the number itself.

Question 5 – Write out all the factors of each number first.

Question 6 – Remind students that the test for divisibility by 3 is that the sum of the digits of the number is divisible by 3.

Question 7 – 1 is not a prime number.

Question 8 – 1 is a square number.

Question 9 – What number multiplies by itself to give 81?

Question 10 – In part **b** encourage $14 - 3^2 = 14 - 9$

Question 11 – Read numbers from left to right. It is easier to order from largest to smallest and swap them round.

Question 12 – In part **c** do we write 200 or 200.5? The former as it is rounding.

Answers

1 a -3, -2, 0, 4   b   -6, -5, -4, 6

2 1, 2, 4, 8

3 8, 16

4 a 1, 2, 4, 5, 10, 20   b 1, 2, 4, 8, 16, 32

5 a 1, 5   b 1, 2, 3, 6

6 a yes   b no
    c yes   d no

7 a no   b yes
    c no   d yes
    e no   f yes

8 a yes   b no
    c no   d yes
    e no   f yes

9 a 9   b 4

10 a 25   b 5

11 0.07, 0.49, 0.52, 0.6, 1.02

12 a 193   b 190
     c 200

1 MyPractice

1 Use the number lines to answer these.

a 4 − 11 =   [number line −8 to 4]

b 6 − 13 =   [number line −6 to 6]

c -4 + 12 = [number line −4 to 9]

d -6 + 11 = [number line −6 to 7]   c -2 − 4 =

2 Answer these problems involving negative numbers.

a 5 − 14 =   b -8 + 11 =   c -2 − 4 =

d -7 + 15 =   e -6 − 9 =

3 Find all the factors of each of these numbers.

a 8   b 9   c 16   d 18

4 Find *five* multiples for each of the following numbers:

a 3   b 11   c 7   d 9

5 a Write four numbers of which 2 is a factor.

b Write four numbers of which 5 is a factor.

6 What is the number ☐ in each of these?

a ☐ is a factor of all of these numbers … | 10, 15, 20, 25, 30 | … and all these numbers are multiples of ☐

b ☐ is a factor of all of these numbers … | 9, 12, 15, 18, 21 | … and all these numbers are multiples of ☐

c ☐ is a factor of all of these numbers … | 21, 28, 35, 42, 49 | … and all these numbers are multiples of ☐

7 Which of these numbers are prime?

a 85   b 91   c 87   d 69   e 59   f 79

8 Answer these problems involving square numbers.

a $3^2 + 12 =$ b $5^2 − 12 =$ c $6^2 + 4 =$ d $4^2 − 10 =$

e $4^2 − 2^2 =$ f $4^2 + 2^2 =$ g $5^2 − 3^2 =$ h $5^2 + 3^2 =$

9 Write these amounts as decimals of one pound (£).

a 40p   b 60p   c 10p   d 20p   e 80p

f 31p   g 52p   h 22p   i 1p   j 5p

10 Copy and circle the larger amount in each pair.

a £0.29, £0.40   b £0.10, £0.04   c £1.01, £0.90

d £1.35, 129p   e 7p, £0.08

11 Copy and circle the larger decimal number in each pair.

a 0.26, 0.3   b 0.6, 0.58   c 0.09, 1.01

d 0.20, 0.02   e 0.15, 0.09   f 1, 0.09

12 Round each number to the nearest 10. Choose the correct answer.

a **12**   b **3**   c **27**   d **15**   e **106**   f **145**

10 or 20   0 or 10   20 or 30   10 or 20   100 or 110   140 or 150

13 Round each number to the nearest 100. Choose the correct answer.

a **94**   b **139**   c **604**   d **45**   e **461**   f **351**

0 or 100   100 or 200   600 or 700   0 or 100   400 or 500   300 or 400

14 Use a calculator to evaluate these amounts.
If your answers are not whole numbers, round them to 1dp.

a 30^2 b $\sqrt{400}$ c $\sqrt{225}$ d 2.5^2

e $\sqrt{6}$ f 0.25^2 g $\sqrt{169}$ h $\sqrt{55}$

i 1.41^2 j 4.5^2 k $\sqrt{196}$ l $\sqrt{625}$

15 Use these three signs to order the pairs of numbers ($<$, $>$, $=$)

a 2^2 3   b $\sqrt{16}$ 2^2 c 5 $\sqrt{22}$ d 5^2 $\sqrt{196}$

e 3^2 8   f 18 $\sqrt{81}$ g $\sqrt{100}$ 10   h $\sqrt{625}$ 6^2

16 a What do you know about the terms in this sequence?

1, 4, 9, 16, 25, 36, …………

b What is the next term in the sequence?

17 A square room has an area of 121 m².

a What is the length of each side?

b What is the perimeter of the room?

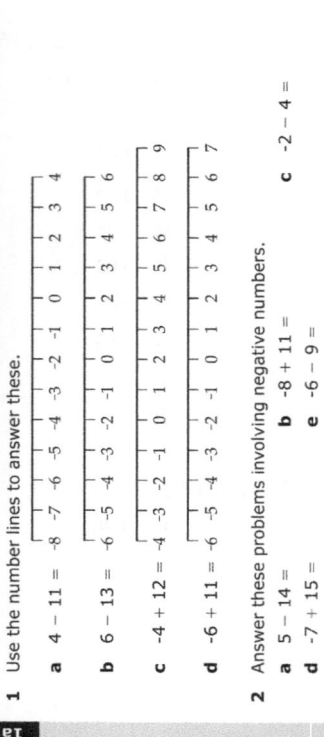

m   m   Area = 121 m²

Question commentary

Questions 1 and **2** – Encourage use of number line. May have to extend line unless able to picture the answer.

Question 3 – Encourage a systematic way by writing in pairs, e.g. 1 and 8, then 1, 2, 4, 8.

Question 4 – For example, numbers that 3 divides into, or 3 times table.

Question 5 – Another way of asking for multiples.

Question 6 – Again, shows the relationship between factors and multiples.

Question 7 – Try dividing by primes. 3 divides into 87 and 69. 5 divides into 85. 7 divides into 91. Once you have passed the square root of the number, you need look no further.

Question 8 – Encourage writing out steps.

Questions 9 and **10** – 40p = £0.40, not £0.4 or £0.40p.

Question 11 – Emphasis larger is being asked for.

Questions 12 and **13** – In 13, it is the tens column that matters, not the units.

Question 14 – Write down full calculator display.

In part **i** 1.9881 rounds to 2.0

Question 15 – These symbols have not been used in this chapter yet. Students should evaluate numbers first then decide on symbol. '<' reads 'is less than' and '>' reads 'is greater than' or the pointed end points at the smaller number.

Question 16 – Students may recognise these as square numbers and/or may see that the pattern goes up in odd numbers.

Question 17 – Part **a** requires the square root. Remind students how to find the area of a square.

Answers

1. **a** -7   **b** -7   **c** 8   **d** 5
2. **a** -9   **b** 3   **c** -6
    d 8   **e** -15
3. **a** 1, 2, 4, 8   **b** 1, 3, 9
    c 1, 2, 4, 8, 16   **d** 1, 2, 3, 6, 9, 18
4. Various answers possible as *any* 5 multiples are asked for. Most will give first 5 multiples, i.e.
    a 3, 6, 9, 12, 15   **b** 11, 22, 33, 44, 55
    c 7, 14, 21, 28, 35   **d** 9, 18, 27, 36, 45
5. **a** 4, 6, 8, 10   **b** 10, 15, 20, 25
    (Various answers possible)
6. **a** 5   **b** 3   **c** 7
7. **a** No   **b** No   **c** No
    d No   **e** Yes   **f** Yes
8. **a** 21   **b** 13   **c** 40   **d** 6
    e 12   **f** 20   **g** 16   **h** 34
9. **a** £0.40   **b** £0.60   **c** £0.10   **d** £0.20
    e £0.80   **f** £0.31   **g** £0.52   **h** £0.22
    i £0.01   **j** £0.05
10.
    a £0.29 (£0.40)   **b** (£0.10), £0.04
    c (£1.01), £0.90   **d** (£1.35), 129p
    e 7p, (£0.08)
11. **a** 0.26 (0.3)   **b** (0.6) 0.58
    c 0.09 (1.01)   **d** (0.20) 0.02
    e (0.15) 0.09   **f** (1) 0.09
12. **a** 10   **b** 0   **c** 30
    d 20   **e** 110   **f** 150
13. **a** 100   **b** 100   **c** 600
    d 0   **e** 500   **f** 400
14. **a** 900   **b** 20   **c** 15
    d 6.25 (6.3 to 1 dp)   **e** 2.4
    f 0.1   **g** 13   **h** 7.4
    i 2.0   **j** 20.3   **k** 14   **l** 25
15. **a** >   **b** =   **c** >   **d** >
    e >   **f** >   **g** =   **h** <
16. **a** They are all square numbers
    b 49
17. **a** 11 m
    b 44 m

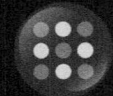

Learning outcomes

R1 Change freely between related standard units (for example time, length, area, volume/capacity, mass) (L4/5)

G1 Derive and apply formulae to calculate and solve problems involving: perimeter and area of triangles, parallelograms, trapezia, volume of cuboids (including cubes) and other prisms (including cylinders) (L5)

G2 Calculate and solve problems involving: perimeters of 2D shapes (including circles), areas of circles and composite shapes (L5)

Introduction

The chapter starts by reviewing which metric units to use to measure everyday lengths, weights and capacities. It then covers how to convert between metric units, between metric and imperial units and how to read scales. After reviewing how to calculate perimeters and areas of rectangles and simple shapes the main focus becomes using the formula for the area of a rectangle. Composite shapes made from rectangles are covered in the final section.

The introduction discusses the origin of geometry. The word itself is Greek for *measuring the earth* and the Greek historian Herodotus claimed it developed in Egypt from the need to re-measure fields after the annual river Nile floods. As a practical subject for surveying and building, geometry is certainly very old. An early Egyptian geometry textbook the Rhind (Ahmes) papyrus is about 4000 years old. Formal geometry, involving proofs and deriving results from first principles, developed later around 500 BC with the ancient Greeks and is associated with the name Euclid.

Students could be asked for examples of real-life areas and how they could be broken down into definite mathematical shapes. For example the floor of a classroom might be broken down into different sized rectangles.

Prior knowledge

Students should already know how to...

- Multiply and divide by 10, 100 and 1000
- Do basic arithmetic
- Classify units of measurement as length, weight, time or capacity
- Understand perimeter and area by counting edges and squares

Starter problem

The starter problem requires students to draw shapes onto a square dotty grid that have an area of exactly one unit. The example gives an isosceles triangle and students should quickly identify the square option. Less obvious options will include the right-angled triangle and parallelogram. Other, less 'regular' shapes are possible and students should be expected to explain how they know the area is exactly equal to one square.

The starter then invites the students to investigate different areas. Two squares and three squares are clearly obvious options to choose but more able students might try and find shapes equal to one and a half squares, or two and a half squares. The grid could even be extended to provide alternative options such as four or five squares, depending on the time available and the ability of the students.

Resources

MyMaths

Metric conversion	1061	Area of rectangles	1084	Converting measures	1091
Units of length	1101	Units of capacity	1104	Units of mass	1105
Perimeter	1110	Imperial measures	1191	Measures	1232

Online assessment

Chapter test	2A–2
Formative test	2A–2
Summative test	2A–2

InvisiPen solutions

Perimeter	312
Area of shapes made from rectangles	313
Measuring lines and reading scales	331
Metric measures	332
Metric and imperial measures	333

Topic scheme

Teaching time = 7 lessons/3 weeks

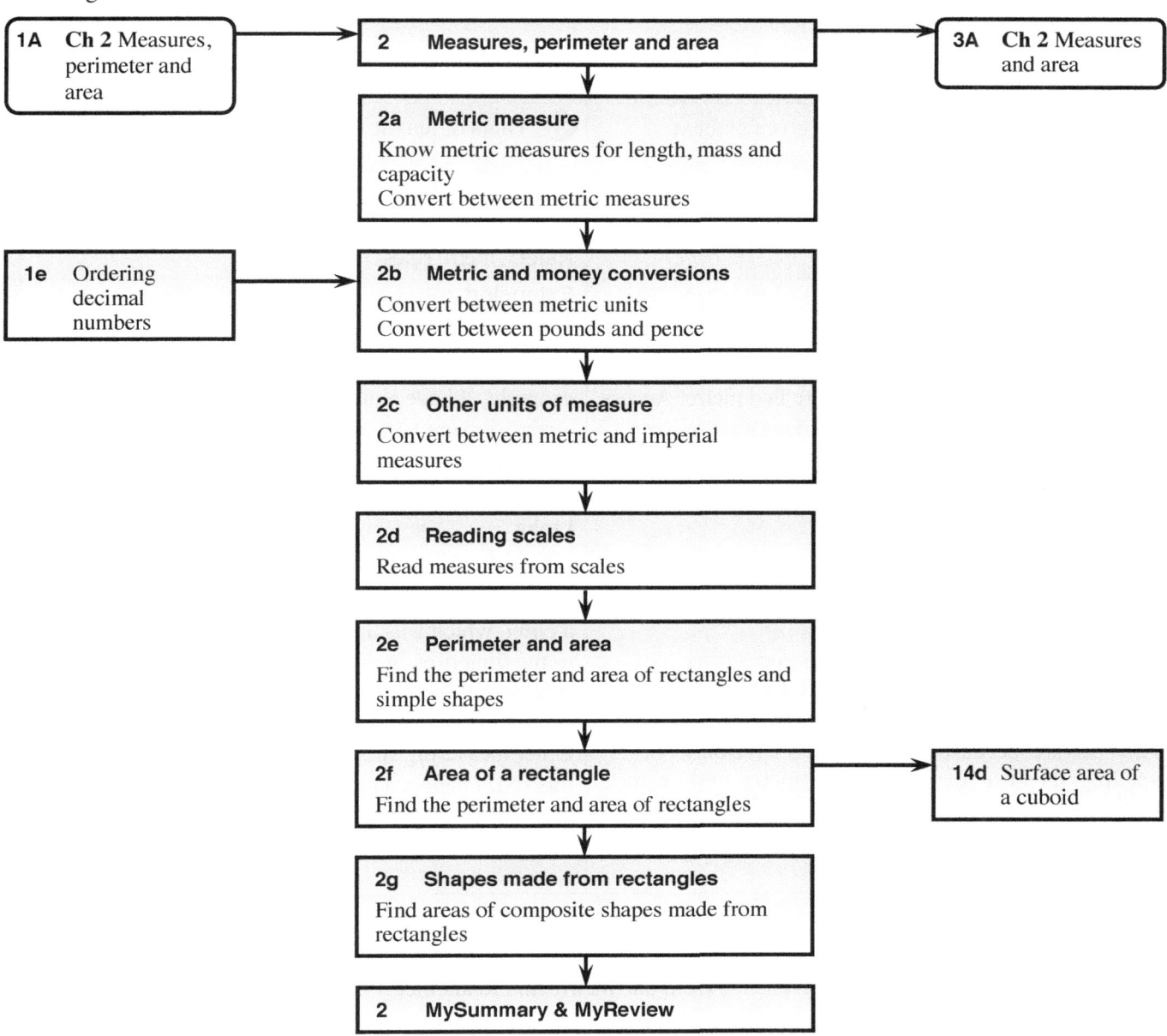

1A **Ch 2** Measures, perimeter and area

2 **Measures, perimeter and area**

3A **Ch 2** Measures and area

2a **Metric measure**
Know metric measures for length, mass and capacity
Convert between metric measures

1e Ordering decimal numbers

2b **Metric and money conversions**
Convert between metric units
Convert between pounds and pence

2c **Other units of measure**
Convert between metric and imperial measures

2d **Reading scales**
Read measures from scales

2e **Perimeter and area**
Find the perimeter and area of rectangles and simple shapes

2f **Area of a rectangle**
Find the perimeter and area of rectangles

14d Surface area of a cuboid

2g **Shapes made from rectangles**
Find areas of composite shapes made from rectangles

2 **MySummary & MyReview**

Differentiation

Student book 2A 24 – 43	**Student book 2B** 24 – 39	**Student book 2C** 22 – 39
Metric measure	Metric measure	Metric measure
Metric and money conversions	Imperial measure	Imperial measure
Other units of measure	Perimeter and area of a rectangle	Area of a rectangle and a triangle
Reading scales	Area of a triangle	Area of a parallelogram and a trapezium
Perimeter and area	Area of a parallelogram and a trapezium	Circumference of a circle
Area of a rectangle		Area of a circle
Shapes made from rectangles		

Objectives

- Choose and use units of measurement to measure, estimate, calculate and solve problems in everyday contexts   (L4)
- Convert one metric unit to another metric unit   (L5)

Key ideas	Resources	
1 Know appropriate units for the given context 2 The conversions in the metric system are based on 10, 100 and 1000	Units of length	(1101)
	Units of capacity	(1104)
	Units of mass	(1105)
	Squared grid paper	
	Rulers, metre rules, tape measures	

Simplification	Extension
Some students will lack a general knowledge of the relative size of metric units – for example, they may not know how many centimetres are in a metre. Access to rulers and metre rules will provide reference for some units of length.	Students invent questions similar to **5, 6** and **7** where they convert units of length, mass and volume. For example, 'I have a distance of 3 km to walk. I have already covered 46 000 cm. How many more metres do I have to go?' Challenge them to create similar questions for one another.

Literacy	Links
The word *metre* comes from a Greek word meaning 'measure'. The prefixes 'milli', 'centi' are from Latin and 'kilo' from Greek. Beware – a 'meter' is a machine for measuring quantities of something, such as a gas-meter. Get the spelling of 'metre' and 'meter' right! Also beware, because the Americans have only one spelling: they use 'meter' for both 'metre' and 'meter'; so they write 'centimeter' which is incorrect in Britain. And they spell *litre* as 'liter' which is a spelling never used in Britain.	Measurement of length was originally based on the human body. The ancient Egyptians used a unit called a *cubit*, which was the length of an arm from the elbow to the fingertips. As everybody's arm was a different length, the Egyptians developed the standard Royal cubit and preserved this length as a black granite rod. Other measuring sticks were made the same length as this rod. There is a picture of a cubit rod at http://www.globalegyptianmuseum.org/detail.aspx?id=4424

Alternative approach

Use place values on squared grid paper with headings labelled Th (for 1000), H, T, U, t, h, th (for $\frac{1}{1000}$).

Discuss how the grid can be used to change from one metric unit to another. For example, enter 1250 ml in the appropriate columns and then change to litres by writing 1.25 litres in the next row.

Measure the heights of students in cm and use the grid to write heights in mm and metres.

For example, 184 cm becomes 1840 mm and 1.84 m, written on three rows under the headings.

Checkpoint

1 What are the two units used for capacity or volume?   (millilitres and litres)

2 Would you measure the length of a football pitch in centimetres, metres or kilometres?   (metres)

3 What is 5 kilograms in grams?   (5000 grams)

Starter – Quick fire

Continue the recap of basic number work begun in previous Quick fire Starters. Include questions on fractions, decimals and percentages and questions using mental and written computation. Ask rapid response questions. Students reply by writing on their mini whiteboards. Discuss questions when their answers indicate a need.

Teaching notes

Draw a table with three columns labelled 'Length', 'Weight' and 'Volume/Capacity'. Invite students to write any unit used to measure one of these. (Give two different coloured pens for metric and imperial units, without saying why.) Seek correct spellings. Include abbreviations of units. Give one example of what this unit might be used; for example, mm to measure the length of an ant.

Ask why two colours have been used. Introduce the words *metric* and *imperial*. Say that this lesson is about the metric system. (Imperial units come later.)

Invite students to order the remaining measures from smallest to largest. Discuss how many of each smaller unit is in a larger unit and highlight the focus around powers of 10. Explain that these are all **metric** measures.

Challenge students with oral questions: How many cm in 2 m, 3 m, and 47 m? Encourage intuitive understanding of simple conversions to help with more challenging questions.

Plenary

Invite students to consider other units of measurement which don't fall into the three categories from the introductory activity; such as the units of time, area, temperature.

Students use mini whiteboards to give conversions of lengths, weights and volume given the teacher.

Exercise commentary

A class list of units for length, mass and volume/capacity would make for easy reference. The previous page in the students' book is also a reference.

Explore the units used for time and temperature.

Questions 1 and **2** – Encourage students to use the abbreviations for the units although the abbreviation for litre can be an l, we often write out the word in full.

Questions 4–7 – These questions require students to solve word problems. Question **4** involves the subtraction of decimals; the other questions use integers if the larger units are converted to smaller units.

Question 8 – Requires students to convert from a smaller to a larger unit. Ask if they expect whether there will be more or fewer cm than mm.

Answers

1	**a** litre	**b** kg		**c** m		**d** tonne	
	e cm	**f** g		**g** ml		**h** km	
2	**a** km, litres, minutes			**b** years, kg, cm			
	c grams, ml, °C						
3	**a** 10	**b** 1000		**c** 1		**d** 100	
	e 1						
4	**a** 5.6 kg	**b** 4.4 kg					
5	350 g						
6	800 m						
7	1 litre						
8	16 cm × 46 cm × 27 cm						
9	grams						

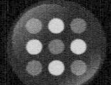

2b Metric and money conversions

Objectives

- Know metric units for length, weight, capacity and volume   (L4)
- Convert from one metric unit of length, weight and capacity/volume to another.   (L4)

Key ideas	Resources
1 Converting from one metric unit to another involves multiplying or dividing by 10, 100 or 1000	Metric conversion (1061) Converting measures (1091) Model coins and notes Rulers graded in millimetres and centimetres Metre rules Various objects to measure

Simplification	Extension
Students often struggle with the decimal structure of currency and hence model coins and notes could be used for counting money. Having physical objects to measure is also a good way of helping students understand the relative sizes of things. Bottles, jugs, small masses and metre rules are all good ways of stimulating discussion and interest among the students.	Invite students to complete statements using metric units: I walk approximately _____ to school. My height is approximately _____. I weigh approximately _____. In pairs, discuss which metric units have been used and whether the answers are reasonable. Re-write each sentence using alternative metric units.

Literacy	Links
It is usual that units are written as initials in lower case letters. For example, *kilogram* is *kg*. But to abbreviate *litre* with an l is to confuse it with the number 1. So, Australia, Canada and USA use a capital letter L and Japan and South Korea use a scripted letter *ℓ*. Europe uses the lower case l for millilitres (ml) but writes the word 'litre' in full for whole litres, such as *3 litres*. There is no international agreement. Also, be aware that the USA spells *litre* as 'liter'.	Measurement of length was originally based on the human body. The ancient Egyptians used a unit called a cubit, which was the length of an arm from the elbow to the fingertips. As everybody's arm was a different length, the Egyptians developed the standard Royal cubit and preserved this length as a black granite rod. The metre as we know it now was standardised in a very similar way by French scientists and the standard 'metre stick' and 'kilogram' are still in use today.

Alternative approach

Many rulers are marked with one edge in millimetres and the other edge in centimetres. So, when measuring a line, you can convert from mm to cm by simply using the other edge.

This idea of a line being labelled differently can be used for any conversion. For example, to change from kilograms to grams, draw a line 10 cm long and marked every 1 cm. Label the marks on one side of the line from 0 to 1000 g in steps of 100 g. Label the other side of the line from 0 to 1 kg in steps of 0.1 kg. Each point on the line gives a weight in both units.

Checkpoint

1 a Convert £ 5.50 into pence.   (550p)

   b Convert 6.4 kilometres into metres.   (6400 cm)

   c Convert 14.3 litres into millilitres.   (14 300 ml)

2 a Convert 205 pence into pounds.   (£2.05)

   b Convert 315 centimetres into metres.   (3.15 m)

   c Convert 450 grams into kilograms.   (0.45 kg)

Starter – Metric pairs

Write the following measurements on the board:

2 km	20 cm	2000 ml	2000 kg	200 cm
2 litres	2000 g	2 kg	2 tonnes	200 mm
2 m	2000 m			

Ask students to find the equivalent pairs. They can write on their mini whiteboards, starting with 2 km.

This activity can be extended by asking students to make their own equivalent pairs.

Teaching notes

There are two main elements to this lesson. Firstly, the lesson deals with the conversion of money to and from pounds and pence. This should not take a huge amount of time but if students struggle you could have some 'money' on hand to help them.

The second aspect is metric conversion. The three main types may need to be discussed separately although the language of 'milli' and 'centi' are used throughout. Check students understand that the numerical value gets smaller as we convert *up* to unit scale, i.e. 2 metres is a smaller numerical value than 20 centimetres.

Plenary

Students convert between metric units for length, mass, capacity and volume. They write their answers on mini whiteboards and discuss their answers where appropriate.

Exercise commentary

Have the column headings Th H T U t h th readily to hand.

Questions 1–4 – These questions offer straightforward conversions.

Question 5 – Convert kilograms into grams first.

Question 6 – This involves multiplying or dividing by 1000.

Question 7 – You multiply to convert to a smaller unit and divide to convert to a larger unit.

Answers

1	**a**	£4.99	**b**	£3.03	**c**	£9.70	**d**	£0.53
	e	£6.01	**f**	£5.00	**g**	£2.15	**h**	£0.09
2	**a**	645p	**b**	900p	**c**	367p	**d**	406p
	e	200p	**f**	301p	**g**	770p	**h**	75p
	i	40p	**j**	110p	**k**	10p	**l**	1p
3	**a**	3.2 m	**b**	4.5 m	**c**	1.5 m	**d**	2.65 m
	e	8 m	**f**	0.8 m	**g**	1.5 m	**h**	0.5 m
	i	0.3 m						
4	**a**	1	**b**	1000	**c**	10	**d**	1
	e	1000	**f**	1000	**g**	50	**h**	5
	i	500	**j**	100				
5	**a**	25	**b**	6				
6	**a**	3.2 litres	**b**	8300 ml	**c**	9.3 kg		
	d	2030 g	**e**	3.025 km	**f**	9235 m		
7	**a**	200 000; 2	**b**	1.8; 1800 000	**c**	38 000; 38		
	d	6 150 000; 6150	**e**	485 000	**f**	0.126		

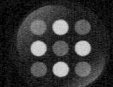

Objectives

- Know approximate metric equivalents of imperial measure in common use   (L5)
- Convert between metric and imperial measures   (L5)

Key ideas	Resources
1 Conversions between metric and imperial measures are approximate **2** Conversions involve a multiplication or division by a scale factor	Converting measures (1091) Imperial measures (1191) A 1pint glass, a 1litre bottle A 1 lb (pound) weight, a 1kg weight A 1 metre rule, a tape measure in cm

Simplification	Extension
Draw up a comprehensive list of common conversion factors, such as 1 mile ≈ 1.5 km, 1 km ≈ $\frac{5}{8}$ miles. Students refer to it, as when answering questions **5** and **6**.	Invite students to complete statements using imperial units: I walk approximately _____ to school. My height is approximately _____. I weigh approximately _____. In pairs, discuss which imperial units have been used and whether the answers are reasonable. Re-write each sentence using alternative imperial units.

Literacy	Links
The word *pound* is used for money and imperial weight. The word has travelled around much of western Europe over the years, originally coming from a Latin word meaning 'weight'. A pound weight of silver gave its meaning to a pound as a unit of money. The symbols £ and lb are both from the Latin word 'libra' meaning 'pound'. The symbol £ is a very curvy letter L.	The United States has its own system of weights and measures which is largely similar to the imperial system. Yards, feet, inches and pounds are all in everyday use in the USA. However, the US pint and US gallon are both smaller than the imperial pint and gallon. There is more information about the differences between the two systems at http://home.clara.net/brianp/usa.html and at http://en.wikipedia.org/wiki/Imperial_units

Alternative approach

For conversion between metric and imperial units, draw a line with imperial units marked off on one side and metric units on the other. As a simple example, use a ruler with cm on one edge and inches on the other edge. Draw a line 10 inch long, marking each inch. Then, use the cm scale on the other edge to mark the other side of the line each centimetre. Similar lines can be drawn for pints/litres and pounds/kilograms.

Some scales are already marked in two ways. Bathroom scales often measure in stones/pounds and in kg.

Checkpoint

1 If 1 mile is 1.5 km, how many kilometres is 6 miles equivalent to?   (9 km)
2 If 1 pint is 0.5 of a litre, how many litres is 8 pints equivalent to?   (4 litres)

Starter – Quick fire

Continue the recap of basic number work begun in previous Quick fire Starters. Include questions on fractions, decimals and percentages and questions using mental and written computation. Ask rapid response questions. Students reply by writing on their mini whiteboards. Discuss questions when their answers indicate a need.

Teaching notes

Write both imperial and metric units grouped together in terms of measures of length, weight and volume/capacity. Circle a metric unit in red and an imperial in blue, and ask students to give others to circle red or blue.

Define the two groups as **imperial** and **metric.** Note that the metric system is now in general use in Britain, but that some people still use imperial measures. This is an opportunity to discuss the European Union's use of metric measures. There are only three countries that have not adopted the metric system as their official system of measurement: Burma, Liberia and the USA.

Show students various imperial and metric measures side by side (for example, a pint bottle of milk and a litre bottle) to discuss equivalences. Refer to the students' book to formalise these approximate equivalences. Challenge students to convert from metric to imperial and vice versa, using a list of approximate equivalents. Set questions in context. For example, 'When I buy 3 pints of milk, how many litres is this?'

Plenary

Speak a sentence but do not finish it; for example, 'Mr Smith drove to Derby the other day. He travelled 70 _____'. Students finish the sentence by writing an appropriate metric unit and an appropriate imperial unit.

Give a measure, such as 5 pints, and ask for an approximate equivalent in litres. Repeat with other conversions.

Students write their answers on mini whiteboards and discuss their responses when necessary.

Exercise commentary

Questions 1–4 – These questions involve no conversions between metric and imperial.

Questions 5 and **6** – Require students to convert from imperial to metric. Students need the conversions from the box on page 30.

Question 7 – This question is straightforward.

Answers

1.   a 30   b 180   c 5500
     d 250
2.   a 245 ml   b 590 g
3.   a mile   b litre
4.   a -12°C   b $5\frac{1}{2}$ hr
5.   a 2.5 litres   b 90 cm or 0.9 m   c 3 kg
     d 9 km   e 100 m   f 16.5 km
6.   a 400 yards $\approx$ 400 m
     b Nescliff 7.5 km
         Chirk 21 km
7.   5 min

Objectives

- Read and interpret scales on a range of measuring instruments   (L5)

Key ideas	Resources
1 Scales give readings between the labelled numerical values on the scale 2 It is necessary to find how much each division is worth on a scale	⚫ Measures (1232) A clock face with independent hands Various scales marked in different ways A counting stick

Simplification	Extension
Some students may benefit from a photocopy of the scales in these exercises, so that they can label each division shown.	Working in pairs, students each draw a scale accurately (with as many equal intervals as required) for their partner to read. They place pointers on their scales and exchange them with their partner. Their partner reads the pointers.

Literacy	Links
There are digital and analogue scales. Only analogue scales are used in this exercise. Scales can be read in two ways. When the needle or dial points exactly at a mark on the scale, then read that value. When the needle or dial points between two marks on the scale, then *either* go to the nearest mark and read that, *or* make an estimate of the position of the needle or dial.	Until the 18th century, measuring scales were marked by hand. This made them expensive as they could only be made one at a time and it meant that they were not very accurate. In 1773, Jesse Ramsden invented a machine that could divide circular scales accurately and consistently. There is more information about Ramsden's dividing engine at http://www.surveyhistory.org/ the_dividing_engine1.htm

Alternative approach

Practise counting in different steps using a counting stick, forwards and backwards, starting at various starting points. Then, do the same without the counting stick but, instead, by pointing at an unnumbered graduated scale.

For example, using a counting stick, start at 40 and count up to 60 and back in 1s, then in 2s, and then in 5s.

Without a counting stick but pointing at an unnumbered graduated scale, start at 120 and count forwards and backwards in 1s and then 2s to 140, in 5s and then 10s to 200, and in 20s to 300.

Now show various numbered graduated scales and ask students to say what they need to count in to get from one numbered value to the next. Do they count in 1s, 2s, 5s, 10s, 20s, 25s? They make their choice and count out loud to confirm that they have made the correct choice.

Finally, place pointers on the scales and ask what values the pointers are giving. The pointers can be indicating a value at a mark or a value between marks (in which case an estimation is required).

Checkpoint

1 Draw a scale from 10 to 20 kilograms, marking every two kilograms in between. Indicate on your scale where 18 kg is.

2 Draw a scale from 100 to 200 kilograms, marking every 100 grams in between. Indicate on your scale where 140 g is.

Starter – Up, up and away

The London Eye has a height of 135 m and a weight of 2100 t. The Beijing Great Wheel in China has a height of 208 m and a weight of 2800 t.

Ask students for the heights in cm and also mm and for the weights in kg and also in grams.

How much bigger is the Beijing wheel than the London wheel? (In this case, 'bigger' can mean 'taller' or 'heavier'. It is 73 m taller and 700 t heavier.)

Teaching notes

Show a clock face showing 12:15. Ask for the angle between the hands. (90° - almost) Invite students to give other times that show an angle of 90°. Ask students how many degrees are shown in the time 12:05 and discuss how this is derived. Note that, if 90° is represented by 3 divisions on the clock face, then 30° is only 1 division. So how many minutes does the minute hand go through when it turns through an angle of 30°, 60°, 120°, …?

For divisions other than on a clock face, discuss how to calculate the value of each smaller division within each larger interval. Ensure students understand to divide the interval value by the number of divisions to calculate the value of each smaller interval.

Students give examples of where scales are seen in everyday life (such as on weighing scales, speedometers, thermometers, petrol gauges, etc.).

Plenary

Show students pointers drawn on various scales. For each, ask how much each division on the scale is worth and what reading does the pointer give. Students write on their mini whiteboards and discuss their results.

Exercise commentary

Questions 1 and **2** – All but the last two scales are graduated in tenths.

Question 3 – The scale for **3a** is straightforward. The scales for **3b, 3c** need careful counting to realise they are graduated in 5s and 20s.

Question 4 – Students may not know how to give the answer. 1300 ml or point to it on the scale.

Question 5 – This question has the scale reading clockwise and anticlockwise.

Answers

1	**a**	4.3 kg	**b**	5.9 kg	**c**	0.8 kg		
2	**a**	1.2 cm	**b**	1.9 cm	**c**	2.6 cm	**d**	71.9 cm
	e	73.2 cm	**f**	75.2 cm	**g**	115 °C	**h**	170 g
3	**a**	27.5			**b**	34		
	c	370						
4	1400 ml							
5	**a**	34 g	**b**	66 g	**c**	18 g	**d**	118 g

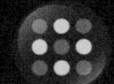

2e Perimeter and area

Objectives

- Know and use the formula for the area of a rectangle   (L4)
- Find the perimeter and area of a triangle   (L4)

Key ideas	Resources
1 Find the area and perimeter of a rectangle	Area of rectangles (1084)
2 Find the perimeter of triangles	Perimeter (1110)
3 Find the area of other shapes by informal methods	Square grid paper

Simplification	Extension
Using an accurate scale diagram on grid paper and counting squares can be used to give confidence in the numerical approach to finding perimeters and areas.	Challenge students with a problem like such as: A rectangle has a perimeter of 28 cm, what different areas might this rectangle have? You are told that the area of this rectangle is 30 cm². What could the dimensions be?

Literacy	Links
The language of 'perimeter' and 'area' are likely to be familiar to students but check they can define both terms. Emphasise the importance of including correct units when recording values for perimeter and/or area	An area of 10 000 m² is called a hectare and is a common unit used to measure an area of land. Measure or estimate the size of the classroom. What fraction is this of a hectare? Estimate how many hectares the school field or other local open space covers.

Alternative approach

Students may be familiar with the formula for the area of a rectangle and if this is the case, the counting squares approach could be glossed over. Students could be given more general rectangles and asked to work out the areas directly although the informal method for working out the perimeter may still be necessary. The non-rectangle shapes will still require a counting squares approach but this could be used as a lead-in to more formal work on the areas of these shapes.

Checkpoint

1 What is the perimeter of a square of side length 10 cm?   (40 cm)
2 What is the area of a rectangle that measures 5 cm by 6 cm?   (30 cm²)

Starter – Estimation

Draw lines on the board.

Ask students to estimate the length of the lines in cm.

Use a scoring system for the estimations, for example, within 10% score 3 points, within 20% score 1 point.

Teaching notes

It is important for students to be aware of the units used and convert where necessary.

The emphasis in the lesson is on counting squares but it is useful at this point to introduce the formula for the area of a rectangle. Checking that the area counted agrees with that calculated by the formula should give the students confidence that either method will work.

Questions 1c and 4 have shapes other than rectangles so ensure students have a clear understanding of the counting squares method for area and the general approach required for perimeter.

Plenary

Ask students to work in pairs on a problem like: A rectangular towel is folded in half and the dimensions are now 20 × 30 cm. What is the area of the towel and what could the dimensions of the towel be?

(1200 cm^3; 20 cm by 60 cm or 40 cm by 30 cm)

Exercise commentary

Question 1 – Straightforward questions on perimeter.

Questions 2 and **3** – Encourage students to find answers by multiplying dimensions.

Question 4 – Students may find answers by completing a rectangle around the triangle and halving it, or by adding the parts of squares together – good for pair work.

Answers

1	a	18 cm	b	38 cm	c	41 cm		
2	a	6	b	15	c	12	d	50
	e	30	f	70				
3	a	25			b	40		
4	a	4	b	6	c	8	d	8
5	2 cm and 3 cm							

Objectives

- Know and use the formula for the area of a rectangle (L5)

Key ideas	Resources
1 Find the area of a rectangle 2 Formula for finding the area of a rectangle	⊞ Area of rectangles (1084) Multiplication square

Simplification	Extension
In question **1** weaker student should be encouraged to verify their use of the formula by counting the squares in each rectangle. In question **2**, direct students to use the dimensions to consider the number of rows and the number of squares in each row. Multiplication squares will help students who have weak multiplication recall.	Carpet costs £6 per metre square. Challenge students to approximately calculate how much it will cost to carpet every classroom in the school.

Literacy	Links
The word *area* comes from a Latin word meaning 'level ground'. The level ground need not be rectangular. It is important that students do not associate 'area' with only rectangles and the formula 'length × width'. Some students may try to use this formula for all shapes. It is worthwhile drawing irregular areas or L-shaped areas that can be broken into rectangles (see the next exercise) where the formula cannot be used or can only be used in part.	Where possible, a new carpet is laid in a room in a single piece. The size of the piece of carpet has to be as long and as wide as the longest and widest dimensions of the room. Carpet is produced in standard widths, usually 3.7 m and 4.6 m, but it is priced per square metre. So a strip of carpet 1 m wide cut from a roll 3.7 m wide will be charged as 3.7 m^2. There is a guide to measuring a room for new carpet at http://m6carpets.co.uk/info_03.html and at http://www.simplifydiy.com/floors/carpet/measuring-carpet (EP)

Alternative approach

To find the area of an irregular shape, such as a map of France, cover it with a transparent grid of centimetre squares. Find the area by (a) counting the individual squares and using the rule 'more than half in, count it; more than half out, don't'; or (b) patching the map with as many rectangular patches as can be fitted into it. Method (a) is seen as inefficient. Method (b) is quicker, as the formula *length × width* can be used for each rectangle. The fiddly bits between the rectangles and the edge of the map have to be counted separately.

Each student's patchwork of rectangles will be different. Collect the different results and compare them. Do they all seem to be reasonably in agreement? What do the students decide as a reasonable answer for the area?

Checkpoint

1 A rectangle is 10 cm long and 3 cm wide.
   a How many cm^2 can be fitted into one row?   (10)
   b How many rows are there?   (3)
   c Therefore what is the area of the rectangle?   (30cm²)

2 A carpet is 5 metres long and 4 metres wide.
   a What is its area?   (20 m²)
   b A rectangle has an area of 30 cm². If it is 5 cm wide, what is its length?
      Show how you worked out your answer.   (6 cm; 30 ÷ 5 = 6)

Starter – Estimation

Draw lines on the board. Ask students to estimate the length of the lines in cm. Ask how much this would be in mm.

Then recap work of previous chapter and this chapter so far. Ask rapid response questions. Students reply by writing on their mini whiteboards. Discuss questions when their answers indicate a need.

Teaching notes

Draw a 5 cm × 3 cm rectangle with grid lines showing the cm intervals. Students find how many cm squares are in the rectangle. Explain that 15 cm^2 is the **area** of the rectangle as area is as a measure of the space inside the shape.

Draw a 6 cm × 4 cm rectangle. Ask for its area. Discuss whether it is necessary to **count** the squares. Pint out that in each row there are 6 squares and there are 4 rows, so
$6 + 6 + 6 + 6 = 4 \times 6 = 24$ cm^2.

Draw a 7 cm × 3 cm rectangle without any division lines. Discuss how many rows there are and how many cm squares in each row. Students offer the calculation
$7 + 7 + 7 = 3 \times 7 = 21$ cm^2.

Label a rectangle 60 cm × 10 cm and discuss how many rows (indicating **width**) and how many squares in each row (indicating the **length**) there are. Progress to the formula:

- area of a rectangle = length × width.

Students measure the length and width of the classroom using a metre rule and calculate the area of the floor in m^2. This figure could be used to buy carpet for the classroom. Point out that m^2 is a larger unit than cm^2 for use with larger areas such as rooms, car parks, road surfaces, etc.

Plenary

Ask students how to find the number of cm^2 in 1 m^2. Draw 1m^2 as a 1 m × 1 m square and begin to draw inside it a few 1cm^2. Ask for a quicker method. Students find how many rows and how many 1cm^2 in each row, from which they find their answer. Write as a conclusion that $1m^2 = 100 \times 100 = 10\,000$ cm^2.

Exercise commentary

Question 2 – There are no grid lines, so the formula is needed. Weaker students could place a transparent grid over the rectangle or draw their own grid and then count squares. Ask how many squares in a row and how many rows.

Question 4 – There is scope for misunderstanding as area and perimeter are often confused. It may be best to draw the rectangles on centimetre-squared paper to find the perimeters.

Question 5 – The tiles are counted directly from the diagram. Students should count rows and columns.

Question 6 – Those needing support could be asked, for part **a**, 'How many in a row do you need if 5 rows give a total of 25 cm^2?'

Answers

1	a	24 cm^2	b	20 cm^2	c	40 cm^2	
2	a	12 cm^2	b	18 cm^2	c	16 cm^2	
	d	28 cm^2	e	30 cm^2	f	32 cm^2	
3	a	40 cm^2	b	48 cm^2	c	77 cm^2	
	d	45 cm^2	e	48 cm^2	f	42 cm^2	
4	a	P = 28 cm			b	P = 28 cm	
	c	P = 36 cm			d	P = 28 cm	
	e	P = 32 cm			f	P = 26 cm	
5	A	20	B	18	C	30	
	D	36	E	12	F	35	
6	a	5 cm	b	4 cm	c	8 cm	
	d	10 cm					

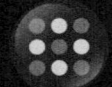

Objectives	
• Know and use the formula for the area of a rectangle	(L5)

Key ideas	Resources	
1 Find the area of a rectangle using the formula 2 Find the area of a compound shapes made from rectangles	Area of rectangles Multiplication square	(1084)

Simplification	Extension
Encourage students to first calculate the lengths of every side on the shape before beginning to calculate the area. Ensure students draw a sketch of each shape and separate it into its rectangular components before considering area.	Challenge students to make up a question/shape of their own with just enough information for someone else to derive all dimensions required to calculate the area.

Literacy	Links
Understanding that 'length' and 'width' are arbitrary but that 'length' is usually the *longer* side should be explained to the students.	Areas of countries are measured in square kilometres. https://www.cia.gov/library/publications/the-world-factbook/fields/2147.html lists all the countries of the world by area. Which is the largest country? (Russia, 17 075 200 km^2) Which is the smallest? (Holy See or Vatican City 0.44 km^2).What is the area of the United Kingdom? (244 820 km^2) You could give students the area of a particular country, say the UK, and ask them to estimate the area of other given countries – the closest estimates win!

Alternative approach
Instead of splitting the shape up into separate rectangles, the students could be encouraged to think about the compound shapes in question **2** for example as being a larger single rectangle with bits cut out of it. This then links nicely into questions **3** and **4** where this approach is easier than splitting up.

Checkpoint
1 A piece of paper measuring 10 cm by 7 cm has a rectangle cut out of it measuring 4 cm by 5 cm. What is the area of paper left?   (70 – 20 = 50 cm^2)
2 A square measuring 4 cm by 4 cm is joined to a rectangle which is 4 cm by 7 cm. They are joined down the 4 cm side. What is the perimeter of the shape that is formed?   (2 × 11 + 2 × 4 = 30 cm)

Starter – Area bingo

Ask students to draw a 3×3 grid and enter numbers from the 4, 6 and 7 times tables.

Give questions, for example, 'What is the area of a rectangle that has a length of 7 cm and a width of 5 cm?' The winner is the first student to cross out all numbers.

Teaching notes

Ask students to close their eyes and listen to the description of a shape:

I am a rectangle 7 cm long and 4 cm wide. On top of me there is a rectangle 2 cm long and 5 cm wide – pushed over to the left so I look like an L shape.

Invite students to draw the shape in their books. Highlight that rectangles can be placed together to create more complex shapes.

Draw an L, a C and an H on the board and invite students to come and split them into rectangles.

Discuss how to use this fact to calculate the area of shapes made from rectangles and add dimensions to one of the shapes to initiate working out.

Recall formula for area of a rectangle and demonstrate naming each composite part A and B or 1) and 2) to clarify working out.

Plenary

Draw a square within a rectangle with the outside section shaded:

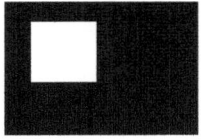

Discuss how to calculate the shaded area.

Exercise commentary

Question 1 – Students can count the squares in each shape and should certainly be encouraged to check their work by doing this to add conviction to the process.

Question 2 – Focuses on splitting a shape into its rectangular components before calculating area. This question progresses to shapes where critical dimensions must first be calculated.

Question 3 – Students may find area of gravel by dividing into two rectangles or by taking away the area of the lawn form the area of the garden.

Question 4 – In this question, students should be encouraged to subtract area of windows from area of wall.

Question 5 – Possibly in pairs, draw out shape using scale of 1 cm to 1 m.

a Divide into three triangles (there are several ways to do this) and write in lengths of sides of rectangles before calculating area.

b Write in all the lengths of the sides before adding them together

Answers

1 **a** 21 cm² **b** 27 cm² **c** 34 cm² **d** 29 cm²
2 **a** 46 cm² **c** 60 cm²
3 **a** 15 m² **b** 35 m²
4 24 m²
5 **a** 33 m² **b** 30 m

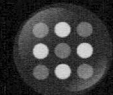

Key outcomes	Quick check
Use, read and write standard metric units. L4	Name the three metric measurements for length. (mm, cm and km) How many millilitres are there in a litre? (1000) Convert 4500 grams to kilograms. (4.5 kg)
Convert between metric and imperial units. L5	If 1 pint is roughly equivalent to 0.5 litres, how many litres are roughly equivalent to 4 pints? (2 litres) If 1 foot is roughly the same as 30 cm, how many feet are there in 90 cm? (3 feet)
Read measurements from scales. L5	Draw the scale from 100 g to 200 g, dividing the scale into five divisions. Mark where 160 g is on your scale.
Find the perimeter and area of a rectangle. L5	A rectangle measures 2 cm by 8 cm. What is its area? (16 cm^2) What is its perimeter? (20 cm)
Calculate the area of shapes made from rectangles. L5	One rectangle measures 5 cm by 6 cm. Another measures 5 cm by 8 cm. They are joined together along their 5 cm sides. What are the lengths of the sides of the rectangle that has been formed? (5 cm by 14 cm) What is the perimeter of this rectangle? (38 cm)

⊞ MyMaths extra support

Lesson/online homework			Description
Measuring lengths	1146	L3	Testing measuring skills with an interactive ruler; converting between cm and mm
2D and 3D shapes	1229	L2	Names and properties of 2D and 3D shapes
Describing shapes	1390	L1	Names of simple 2D and 3D shapes, counting sides and corners

MyReview

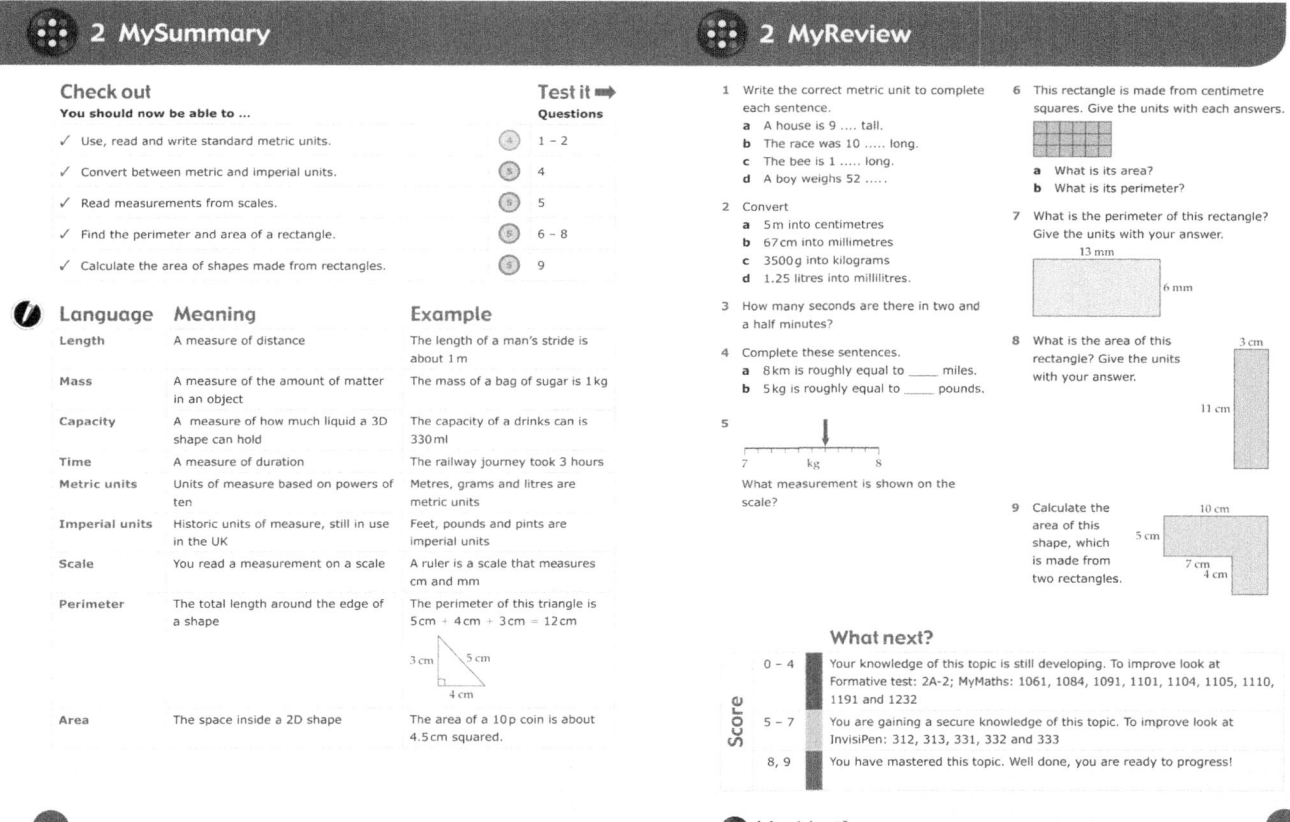

Check out

You should now be able to ...

✓ Use, read and write standard metric units.

✓ Convert between metric and imperial units.

✓ Read measurements from scales.

✓ Find the perimeter and area of a rectangle.

✓ Calculate the area of shapes made from rectangles.

Test it ➡

Questions

4️⃣ 1 - 2

5️⃣ 4

9️⃣ 5

6️⃣ 6 - 8

9️⃣ 9

Language	Meaning	Example
Length	A measure of distance	The length of a man's stride is about 1 m
Mass	A measure of the amount of matter in an object	The mass of a bag of sugar is 1 kg
Capacity	A measure of how much liquid a 3D shape can hold	The capacity of a drinks can is 330 ml
Time	A measure of duration	The railway journey took 3 hours
Metric units	Units of measure based on powers of ten	Metres, grams and litres are metric units
Imperial units	Historic units of measure, still in use in the UK	Feet, pounds and pints are imperial units
Scale	You read a measurement on a scale	A ruler is a scale that measures cm and mm
Perimeter	The total length around the edge of a shape	The perimeter of this triangle is 5 cm + 4 cm + 3 cm = 12 cm
Area	The space inside a 2D shape	The area of a 10p coin is about 4.5 cm squared.

40 **Geometry and measures** Measures, perimeter and area

MyReview

1 Write the correct metric unit to complete each sentence.
  a A house is 9 .... tall.
  b The race was 10 ..... long.
  c The bee is 1 ..... long.
  d A boy weighs 52 .....

2 Convert
  a 5 m into centimetres
  b 67 cm into millimetres
  c 3500 g into kilograms
  d 1.25 litres into millilitres.

3 How many seconds are there in two and a half minutes?

4 Complete these sentences.
  a 8 km is roughly equal to _____ miles.
  b 5 kg is roughly equal to _____ pounds.

5

What measurement is shown on the scale?

6 This rectangle is made from centimetre squares. Give the units with each answers.
  a What is its area?
  b What is its perimeter?

7 What is the perimeter of this rectangle? Give the units with your answer.
  13 mm
  6 mm

8 What is the area of this rectangle? Give the units with your answer.
  3 cm
  11 cm

9 Calculate the area of this shape, which is made from two rectangles.
  10 cm
  5 cm
  7 cm
  4 cm

What next?

Score	
0 – 4	Your knowledge of this topic is still developing. To improve look at Formative test: 2A-2; MyMaths: 1061, 1084, 1091, 1101, 1104, 1105, 1110, 1191 and 1232
5 – 7	You are gaining a secure knowledge of this topic. To improve look at InvisiPen: 312, 313, 331, 332 and 333
8, 9	You have mastered this topic. Well done, you are ready to progress!

⠿ **MyMaths**.co.uk

41

Question commentary

Questions 1 and **2** – May need a quick review of metric units and their connections.

Question 3 – Should be straightforward.

Questions 4 and **5** – 1.5 miles is roughly equivalent to one kilometer. 8 ÷ 1.5 is approximately 5. Students will find this quite tricky.

Question 6–9 – Check that students remember the calculations for area and perimeter. They can be mixed up.

Question 10 – This can be divided in two ways. Students could be encouraged to check that they get the same answer both ways.

Answers

1 a m   b km
   c cm   d kg

2 a 500 cm   b 670 mm
   c 3.5 kg   d 1250 ml

3 150 s

4 a 5   b 11

5 7.6 kg

6 a 18 cm^2 b 18 cm

7 38 mm

8 33 cm^2

9 62 cm^2

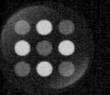

2 MyPractice

2 MyPractice

2a

1 Copy and complete these statements.

a There are ____ mm in a cm.
b There are ____ g in a kg.
c 1000 ml are equal to ____ litre.
d There are ____ cm in 1 m.
e 1000 m are equal to ____ km.

2b

2 Choose the correct unit of measure to complete these sentences.

distance	capacity	time	weight	temperature

a Degrees Celsius is a measure of ____.
b Grams are a measure of ____.
c Kilometres are a measure of ____.
d Hours are a measure of ____.
e Litres are a measure of ____.

2c

3 What reading is shown on each dial? Include the unit of measure in your answer.

a   b
c   d

2d

4 Calculate the perimeter of each shape.

a 1.8 m
b 5.6 cm
c 13.5 mm, 6.7 mm

2e

5 Using the formula $l \times w = A$, calculate the area of these shapes. Give your answers in cm².

a 3 cm, 5 cm
b 4 cm, 10 cm
c 7 cm, 5 cm

6 The table shows the length and width, in centimetres, of some rectangles. Calculate the area of each rectangle. Give your answers in cm².

Length (cm)	Width (cm)	Area (cm²)
4	8	
7	5	
6	7	
11	5	
3	15	
20	4	
9	6	

2f

7 The yellow rectangular shapes are made from shapes A, B, C and D. What is the area of each yellow shape in square units?

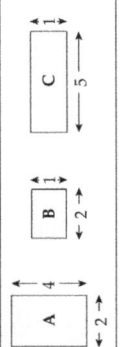

a   b
c   d

Question commentary

Question 1 – Students need metric conversions.

Question 2 – May need reminding that Celsius is a measure of temperature.

Question 3a – Students may find this difficult. Encourage them to work out the value of each division, and then add on to 210.

Question 4 – Students may need to be told that the little lines drawn on the sides show which sides are equal.

Questions 5 and **6** – Students should be multiplying sides together to find area.

Question 7d – Ask students which letter corresponds to the area that is not named.

Answers

1. **a** 10   **b** 1000   **c** 1
   d 100   **e** 1
2. **a** temperature   **b** mass   **c** distance
   d time   **e** capacity
3. **a** -4 °C   **b** 96 kg   **c** 0.6 km   **d** 160 ml
4. **a** 5.4 m   **b** 22.4 cm   **c** 40.4 mm
5. **a** 15 cm^2 **b** 40 cm^2 **c** 35 cm^2
6. Areas are 32 cm^2, 35 cm^2, 42 cm^2, 55 cm^2, 45 cm^2, 80 cm^2, 54 cm^2.
7. **a** 14   **b** 13   **c** 11   **d** 32

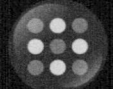

3 Expressions and formulae

Learning outcomes

A1 Use and interpret algebraic notation, including:
- ab in place of $a \times b$
- a^2 in place of $a \times a$, a^3 in place of $a \times a \times a$; a^2b in place of $a \times a \times b$
- a/b in place of $a \div b$
- $3y$ in place of $y + y + y$ and $3 \times y$
- coefficients written as fractions rather than as decimals
- brackets (L5)

A2 Substitute numerical values into formulae and expressions, including scientific formulae (L5)

A3 Understand and use the concepts and vocabulary of expressions, equations, inequalities, terms and factor (L5)

A4 Simplify and manipulate algebraic expressions to maintain equivalence by:
- collecting like terms
- multiplying a single term over a bracket (L5)

A6 Model situations or procedures by translating them into algebraic expressions or formulae and by using graphs (L5)

Introduction	Prior knowledge
The chapter starts by revising algebraic notation and doing simple substitutions. Collecting like terms, expanding a single bracket and slightly harder simplifications are covered followed by evaluating and creating simple formulae.	Students should already know how to… • Use basic algebraic notation • Carry out arithmetic operations in the correct order • Extract information from a written description • Calculate perimeters of simple shapes

The introduction discusses the Voyager 1 space probe. Its primary goal was to investigate Jupiter and Saturn and their moons before heading into the outer solar system and beyond. It has been sending back information for over 36 years and is currently almost 20 billion kilometres away – the furthest any manmade object has ever been. It takes a signal over 19 hours to reach us at that distance. Should 'anyone' encounter the space probe they will find a gold record which contains, amongst other things, whale song, greetings in 50 languages and a recording of Chuck Berry's *Johnny B Goode*. Voyager 1 has a sister probe Voyager 2, actually launched 16 days earlier, which also visited Neptune and Uranus before heading into outer space.

Algebra is the language mathematicians use to write down general statements that can apply to one or more numbers. An equation for an unknown is a familiar example. Likewise, formulae tell you what one thing equals given the value of another arbitrary quantity. For example, the total cost as a function of the number of items sold. Learning how to write and manipulate algebraic expressions allows you to solve more complex problems – like successfully sending a satellite into outer space.

Starter problem

This is a problem which gives you the opportunity to demonstrate the use of algebra.

Students could be encouraged to use algebra to describe the particular staircase you are building, for example, S(10) = the tenth staircase.

You can use this shorthand to describe the number of blocks for a particular staircase for example S(10) = 55

Students should see that S(10) = 1 + 2 + 3 + 4 + 5 + 6 + 7 + 8 + 9 + 10 but the question is how do you work this out quickly… using algebra!

(You could tell the story of Carl Gauss adding up all the numbers from 1 to 100 by spotting that the addition = 50 × 101.)

Students could use the geometry of two identical staircases joined to make a rectangle and finally algebra to express it more succinctly as $n(n + 1)/2$ where n is the number of steps.

Emphasise that the algebra describes every possible staircase made to this pattern no matter what the size.

Students could investigate a tower built to some repeating pattern of their own choosing.

Resources

MyMaths

Rules and formulae	1158	Simplifying 2	1178	Simplifying 1	1179
Substitution 1	1187	Single brackets	1247		

Online assessment

Chapter test	2A–3
Formative test	2A–3
Summative test	2A–3

InvisiPen solutions

Using symbols	211	Collecting like terms	212
Multiplying and dividing terms			213
Expanding brackets	214	Formulae	251
Creating a formula	252	Substitution	254

Topic scheme

Teaching time = 7 lessons/3 weeks

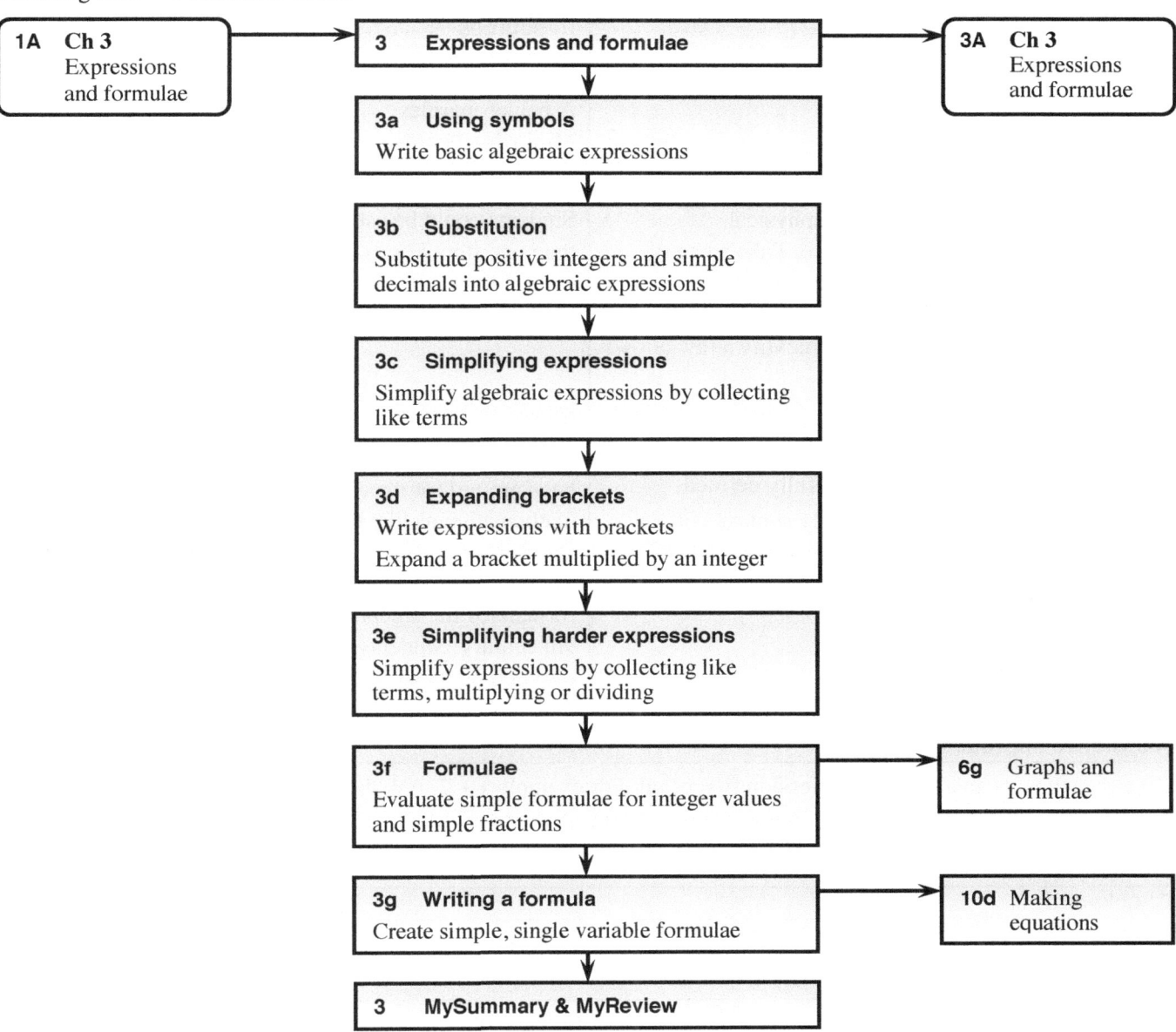

1A Ch 3
Expressions
and formulae

3   Expressions and formulae

3A Ch 3
Expressions
and formulae

3a   Using symbols
Write basic algebraic expressions

3b   Substitution
Substitute positive integers and simple
decimals into algebraic expressions

3c   Simplifying expressions
Simplify algebraic expressions by collecting
like terms

3d   Expanding brackets
Write expressions with brackets
Expand a bracket multiplied by an integer

3e   Simplifying harder expressions
Simplify expressions by collecting like
terms, multiplying or dividing

3f   Formulae
Evaluate simple formulae for integer values
and simple fractions

**6g   Graphs and
formulae**

3g   Writing a formula
Create simple, single variable formulae

**10d Making
equations**

3   MySummary & MyReview

Differentiation

Student book 2A	44 – 63

Using symbols
Substitution
Simplifying expressions
Expanding brackets
Simplifying harder expressions
Formulae
Writing a formula

Student book 2B	40 – 57

Simplifying and substituting
Indices
Like terms
Expanding brackets
Substitution into formulae
Writing a formula

Student book 2C	40 –63

Indices in algebra
Index laws
Collecting like terms including
    powers
Expanding brackets
Factorising expressions
Formulae 1
Rearranging formulae
Writing expressions
Algebraic fractions

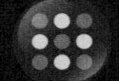

3a Using symbols

Objectives	
• Model situations or procedures by translating them into algebraic expressions	(L5)

Key ideas	Resources	
1 Form simple algebraic expressions	Rules and Formulae	(1158)
	A bag of marbles	
	Mini whiteboards	

Simplification	Extension
Some students may benefit from a physical demonstration of the principles here. Take a bag of marbles, for example, and say there are *x* marbles in the bag. Having a few spare marbles will enable the demonstration of '+' to the bag, removing a few allows '−' to be demonstrated.	Students could be asked to form expressions with more than one step. For example, double the original amount and subtract 3 from it.

Literacy	Links
The words 'expression' and 'unknown' may be new to the students so they should be carefully defined. Question **5** highlights one of the key syntaxes of algebra and could be explored further using other multiplication examples.	The use of a letter to stand for an unknown number has been around for many hundreds of years. Ancient mathematicians like Diophantus used an algebraic structure of sorts to pose and solve problems and it was Muḥammad ibn Musa al-Khwarizmı who first formalised the algebraic notation we use today in the 9th century. Students could be asked to do some research on these or other famous mathematical pioneers.

Alternative approach
Give the students an algebraic expression first of all. For example $x + 2$. Ask them to think up a scenario that this could be used to represent (I have *x* pounds and someone gives me £2 more). This can be repeated with different expressions before students attempt to find their own expressions from the contexts given in the exercise.

Checkpoint		
1	If Joe is *x* years old now, how old will he be in 6 years' time?	$(x + 6)$
2	If Meg has £*y* and spends £15, how much does she have now?	$(y - 15)$

Starter – Number Chain

Give the students a starting number, say 2, then give them a quick-fire chain of operations to do, in sequence. What is the final number?

An example might be $\times 2, + 1, \times 3, - 4, \times 2, + 3$ (25)

Teaching notes

This is a very basic introduction to the language of algebra and it can be worked through as slowly as required to ensure students get a complete understanding of the principles of using an unknown. Give lots of whole-class examples, use mini whiteboards for students to jot answers down on, plan and explore the scenarios given.

Plenary

Give students two or three more examples, read out rather than written, and get them to write the expressions on mini whiteboards. Finish with a simple two-step expression such as that in question **5**.

Exercise commentary

Questions 1–3 – These are very similar to the introductory questions on page 46. If students are struggling to choose letters, they may get used to x, y and n.

Question 4 – **4d** is a little trickier. The unknown could stand for the total cost of the loaves or the cost of one loaf of bread (assuming they all cost the same).

Answers

1 a Different answers possible, e.g. There are x grains of sand in the picture.

   b $x - 10$

2 a Different answers possible, e.g. There are x people in this crowd.

   b $x + 5$

3 b $y + 2$ c $12 + x$ d $30 - n$

4 a $a - 5$ b $50 - b$ c $160 + c$ d $10 - 3d$

5   Both mean the same thing.

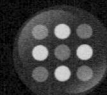

Objectives

- Substitute positive integers into expressions and formulae (L5)

Key ideas	Resources
1 Expressions involve letters (variables) and numbers 2 Expressions have values when numbers are substituted for letters	Substitution 1 (1187) Large dice Computer spreadsheet

Simplification	Extension
The layout helps understanding. The student copies any expression or formula and, below it, writes the same expression or formula with the numerical value replacing the algebraic variable. For example, in question **2a**, the student writes $5 \times d = 5 \times 10$ and then proceeds to find the answer. Remind students that, for example, $4b$ means $4 \times b$	Students meet more complicated formulae in various contexts, such as finding the speed of a car from its initial speed and acceleration using $v = u + a \times t$ where three substitutions are needed to find v.

Literacy	Links
As from above, the layout is an aide to success. For example, the cost of taxi fare is given by $3m + 2$ where m is the number of miles travelled. Find the cost of a journey of 6 miles. Cost $= 3m + 2$ and remember that $3m$ means $3 \times m$ $ = 3 \times 6 + 2$ $ = 18 + 2$ $ = 20$ So the cost is £20.	A substitution cipher conceals a message by replacing or scrambling its letters. Each letter is substituted for another in the alphabet according to a pre-agreed rule. For example A might be substituted for E which is 5 letters further into the alphabet, so B for F, C for G and so on. There is more information about substitution ciphers at http://www.codasaurus.com/Cipher-1.htm and at http://en.wikipedia.org/wiki/Substitution_cipher

Alternative approach

Substitution takes on particular meaning when it is set in a context. An expression can be represented as a 'function machine' with an input and output.

Referring to the taxi fare above, various values of m can be substituted, a table of values created, a graph plotted and predictions made. For example, the layout of working above is repeated several times and answers tabulated to give:

m miles	1	2	3	4	…
Cost, £C	5	8	11	14	…

Axes are drawn and labelled, the points $(1, 5), (2, 8), (3, 11), (4, 14), …$ are plotted and a graph drawn.
Questions can be asked about the cost of journeys of 5 miles or 2.5 miles.

A further development is to use a computer spreadsheet.
Label cells A1 and B1 as m and C. Create a formula (using the expression for the fare) where cell B2 $=3*A2 + 1$
Drag down both A2 and B2 together and see the table appear.
Use the tool bar to draw the graph.

Checkpoint

1 What is the value of $10x$ when $x = 4$? (40)
2 What is the value of $y \div 3$ when $y = 15$? (5)
3 What is the value of $10 \div n$ or $\frac{10}{n}$ when $n = 2$? (5)

Starter – Quick fire

Continue the recap of basic number work begun in previous Quick fire Starters. Include questions on fractions, decimals and percentages and questions using mental and written computation. Ask rapid response questions. Students reply by writing on their mini whiteboards. Discuss questions when their answers indicate a need.

Teaching notes

Write a number of expressions on the board
$d + 3$, $d - 2$, $3d$, $3d + 1$, $\frac{d}{2}$ and d^2.

Roll a dice to generate the number for d. Students must **evaluate** the expressions by substituting the score for d. The student who correctly evaluates an expression gets to roll the dice. Recall 'hidden multiplications' (where $3d$ means $3 \times d$) and algebraic division as well as the use of powers.

Highlight key term 'substitution' and link it to a football match where one player **replaces** another.

Refer to the examples in the student book and especially 'Park and Ride'. Demonstrate how to substitute a given value for n. Remind students to give answers with units when the problem is set in a context; for 'Park and Ride', the units are £.

Plenary

Discuss where substitution, as in the 'Park and Ride' formula, is found in 'real-life' contexts; such as, cooking times for meat (20 min per kilogram + 30 minutes) and telephone tariffs (£25 line rental plus 6p per minute).
Give formulae, make substitutions and have students respond on mini whiteboards. Monitor answers and discuss as appropriate.

Exercise commentary

Questions 1–5 – All offer straightforward substitutions, though there are a few points to watch for:

Question **1** does not define n, but it is defined on the previous page.

Question **2** parts **g**, **h**, **i**, **j** involve fractions and decimals for the first time.

Question **3** has fractional values for $n \div 4$ and, for the first time, has $2n + 2$ without mentioning that $2n$ involves a multiplication. Check that students know that multiplication is first, then addition.

Question **5** Check students divide the right way round.

Answers

1	a	£4.50	b	£8.50	c	£11.50		
	d	£13.50	e	£25.50	f	£37.50		
2	a	50 cm	b	15 cm	c	5 m	d	30 cm
	e	45 cm	f	100 cm	g	12.5 cm	h	7.5 cm
	i	1 cm	j	3 cm				

3
a   4 plates, 0 apples, 1 carton, 6 rolls
b   7 plates, 1 apple, 2 cartons, 12 rolls
c   12 plates, 6 apples, 3 cartons, 22 rolls
a   27 plates, 21 apples, 7 cartons, 52 rolls

4	a	18	b	30	c	100	d	250
	e	40	f	36	g	70	h	120
	i	72						
5	a	3	b	1	c	10	d	5
	e	4	f	1	g	8	h	2
	i	20						
6	a	100	b	2000	c	24	d	20

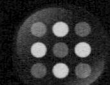

Objectives	
• Simplify linear algebraic expressions by collecting 'like terms'	(L5)

Key ideas	Resources
1 'Like terms' can be simplified 2 Terms which are not 'like' cannot be added or subtracted	Simplifying 1 (1179) Bags of beads and cubes Boxes of cards showing 'like terms'

Simplification	Extension
Students highlight 'like terms' (with the associated operation) in the same colour and read the 'like terms' out loud to emphasise the operations. Watch for expressions where the first term is negative, as in question **2g,** and refer students to a negative number on a number line.	Students give as many expressions as they can find in a given time that would simplify to $4x - 9y$; for example, $2x + 2x - 8y - y$.

Literacy	Links
In algebra, 'like terms' are terms that have the same variable raised to the same power. So, $3x$ and $5x$ are 'like terms', but $3x$ and $5x^2$ are not 'like terms'. 'Like terms' can be added and subtracted, so $3x + 5x = 8x$ and $3x - 5x = -2x$ (using a number line), but $3x + 5x^2$ cannot be simplified. Note that: $1 \times x$ is not written as $1x$, but as just x, and $0 \times x$ is not written as $0x$, but as just 0.	'Like terms' can be thought of as terms having something in common. In English, a word used to describe a group of something is called a 'collective noun'. The words shown here in italics are collective nouns; a *range* of mountains, a *herd* of elephants, a *school* of fish. Some more unusual examples are a *parliament* of owls and a *kindle* of kittens. Ask students if they know any other collective nouns. There is a comprehensive list at http://users.tinyonline.co.uk/gswithenbank/collnoun.htm and terms for animals at http://www.askoxford.com/asktheexperts/collective/?view=uk

Alternative approach
Create a set of cards with 'like terms' containing x in one colour and those containing y in another colour. Each 'like term' contains a + or – sign. For example, red cards can be $+3x$, $-2x$, $+x$, $-4x$, ... and blue cards can be $+4y$, $-3y$, $+2y$, $-y$, ... They are all placed in the same box.   Students work in pairs and select in turn 2 or 3 cards each from the box. They line them up in any order. They write them as an expression and then agree how to simplify the expression. They are reminded that they can use a number line to help the simplification.

Checkpoint
1 Simplify these expressions

a	$4x + 5x$	$(9x)$
b	$7y - 6y$	(y)
c	$7n + 6n - 2n$	$(11n)$
d	$4x + 6y - 2x - y$	$(2x + 5y)$

Starter – Quick fire

Continue the recap of basic number work begun in previous Quick fire Starters. Include questions on fractions, decimals and percentages and questions using mental and written computation. Ask rapid response questions. Students reply by writing on their mini whiteboards. Discuss questions when their answers indicate a need.

Teaching notes

Show students a bag containing a large number of beads. State that there are too many to count, so the number will be represented by the letter n. Produce another two similar bags with similar contents. The total contents of all three bags is written as $n + n + n$ which is 'three lots of n' and written more simply as $3 \times n$ or even more simply as $3n$ (recalling the algebraic convention of the 'hidden' multiplication sign).

Introduce another bag holding a different large number of cubes, so a different letter must be used for this number, say, c. Produce a second similar bag and have students offer $2c$ as the total contents of both bags.

Discuss what to write to express the contents of all five bags; namely, $3n + 2c$. Discuss whether we can combine the $3n$ and the $2c$ into one symbol. Agree that only 'like terms' can be **simplified** in an expression.

Link simplification to an everyday **collection**. For example, instead of saying 'I had a cup of tea and a cup of tea and a cup of coffee and a cup of coffee', you would say 'I had two cups of tea and two cups of coffee'. Discuss how to write an expression for the volume of liquid drunk and agree on $2t + 2c$, where t and c are the volumes of one tea cup and one (smaller) coffee cup.

Plenary

Write an expression of 'like terms' in x. Students simplify the expression onto their mini whiteboard. Repeat for an expression having 'like terms' in both x and y. Repeat where students have to use a number line to simplify negative terms. Discuss students' responses as necessary.

Exercise commentary

Question 1 – Refers back to the previous page in the students' book.

Questions 2 and **3** – Question **2** simplifies terms in **one** variable (for the first time in this lesson). Question **3** involves **two** variables, as in question **1**. Emphasise that the operation, + or −, only refers to the term it is immediately in front of

Question 4 – This is similar to question **1**. The student creates the expression from the context.

Answers

1. **a** $2b + c; 3b + 4c; b + 3c$
   b $6b + 8c$
2. **a** $4x$ **b** $11a$ **c** $14m$ **d** $20q$
   e $6u$ **f** $2y$ **g** $12p$ **h** 0
3. **a** $5x + 2y$ **b** $2v$ **c** $12b + 11c$ **d** $6h - 4k$
   e $6j + 4k$ **f** $12m - 6n$ **g** $5x$ **h** $8z + 2w$
4. **a** $3m$ **b** $5n$ **c** $m + n$
   d $2n + 6m$ **e** $7n$ **f** $3m + 2n$
5. Various answers possible – discuss with students

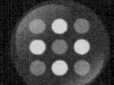

Objectives

- Understand why and how brackets are used (L5)
- Multiply a single term over a bracket (L5)

Key ideas	Resources
1 Brackets are used when expressions are multiplied 2 The term outside the bracket multiples all the terms inside the bracket	Single brackets (1247) Two identical bags with cards inside Selection of books and magazines

Simplification	Extension
Use only positive values and terms in the first instance. When negatives are first used, use them as in Questions such as **3d** and **4d**, rather than **3e** and **4c**.	Students simplify more complex expressions; for example, $4(n + 2) + 3(n - 1)$ by expanding and then collecting 'like terms'.

Literacy	Links
The earliest use of brackets to group terms was suggested by a German mathematician in 1608. Brackets are now used in many different ways in mathematics. In this lesson, they are used to group terms that are multiplied. In earlier lessons, they have been used for coordinates of points (x, y).	Provide a selection of books and magazines. Students find examples of brackets and list the different kinds. Round brackets (also known as *parentheses*) are often used for explanations or to add to the information already given. They can also be used for translations and abbreviations. What is the purpose of the brackets in the examples found? Different types of brackets can be found at http://en.wikipedia.org/wiki/Bracket

Alternative approach

$\left(x + 4\right)$ $\left(x + 4\right)$

$\left(x + 4\right)$ $\left(x + 4\right)$

Imagine a bag with an x and a 4 in it. Draw the bag and its contents. Imagine another identical bag. Draw it with its contents. How can these two bags be represented using the keys of the keyboard? One idea is to only draw the essential part of the bag that is closest to the contents. This gives us curved lines that look like the brackets on a keyboard. So we can type each of them as $(x + 4)$. Since there are two bags and we have two lots of contents, we can type both bags as $2 \times (x + 4)$.

Now, if we empty both bags into one pile, what do we have? There are two xs and two 4s all added together. We have $2 \times (x + 4) = 2x + 8$. This process of removing the brackets is called 'expanding brackets'.

Everything inside the bracket (or bag) has to be multiplied by the number outside the bracket. For example, $3 \times (z + 5) = 3z + 15$ and $4 \times (y - 2) = 4y - 8$.

Checkpoint

1 Expand these brackets

   a $2(x + 5)$ $(2x + 10)$

   b $5(a - b)$ $(5a - 5b)$

   c $6(3a + 2b)$ $(18a + 12b)$

Starter – ABC

Each letter of the alphabet represents a number:

$a = 1, b = 2, c = 3, d = 4, e = 5$, etc.

Challenge students to decode the following message:

$f + g, \ d - c, \ 10b, \ 2d, \ i + j, \ c^2, \ 3f + 1, \ 2c, \ 3g, \ 7b$

[maths is fun]

Students can create their own coded message.

Teaching notes

Draw a straight line on the board, length labelled $x + 3$, divided into an x part and a 3 part. Draw this line four times to make a square. The students give the total length (that is, the perimeter of the square) orally as: '4 lots of x plus 3' or '4 lots of x and 4 lots of 3' or '$4x$ and 12'.

Demonstrate the use of brackets written as $4 \times (x + 3)$ to distinguish it from (4 lots of x) + 3 more. Emphasise $4 \times (x + 3)$ is equivalent to $4x + 12$. Introduce the word 'expanded' by saying 'The bracket has been expanded'.

Return to numerical values. Say that if x had the value 5, then $4 \times (x + 3)$ can be written as $4 \times (5 + 3)$. There are two ways of working to find its value:

(a) By expanding the bracket to give
$4 \times 5 + 4 \times 3 = 20 + 12 = 32$

(b) By writing $4 \times (5 + 3) = 4 \times 8 = 32$

The first method practises expanding brackets, but the second method is quicker.

Plenary

Write expressions such as $2 \times (a + 3)$ for students to expand on their mini whiteboards.

Write expressions such as $3 \times (4 + 1)$ for students to write their values on their mini whiteboards.

As a final question, draw a rectangle with lengths of $x + 1$ and $y + 5$. Students write an expression for its perimeter. Discuss alternative valid expressions and agree the simplest expression.

Exercise commentary

Questions 1 and 2 – These questions are an abstraction of the MP3 player's perimeter dealt with on the previous page of the students' book. Because of the pairs of opposite and equal sides, the perimeter for question **1a** can be written as:

$2 \times (5 + 7)$ cm   or $2(5 + 7)$ cm.

Question 3 – Expanding the brackets as the first step is not the most efficient way of calculating the values. Nevertheless, the more efficient way, such as for question **3a**, of writing $5 \times (3 + 4) = 5 \times 7 = 35$ can be used as a check.

Question 5 – The order of the multiplication does not matter.

Question 6 – Using brackets is rather a contrived request, as there is a far easier way of writing the perimeters. Even so, for **6a**, use the line symmetry of the arrow to see $2 \times (a + b + c)$ and the rotational symmetry of the cross to see $4 \times (x + 2 + 2)$.

Answers

1   a $2(5 + 7)$ cm   b $2(9 + 12)$ cm
    c $2(14 + 10)$ cm   d $2(4 + 9)$ cm

2   a $2(10 + x)$ cm   b $2(a + 8)$ cm
    c $2(d + f)$ cm   d $2(x + y)$ cm

3   a   35   b   18   c   24   d   35
    e   18   f   24   g   36   h   40
    i   200   j   10   k   8   l   36

4   $3(a + 5) = 3a + 15, 6(a + 1) = 6a + 6$
    $2(2a + 1) = 4a + 2, 2(a + 2) = 2a + 2$
    $2(a + 4) = 2a + 8, 3(a + 2) = 3a + 6$

5   a $5a + 5$ b $3x + 15$ c $4y - 32$
    d $6q - 12$ e $8m + 16$ f $4v + 20$
    g $2x - 2y$ h $3a + 3b$ i $20x + 20y$
    j $9m - 9n$ k $10p + 10r$ l $25h - 25t$

6   a $2(a + b + c)$ cm   b $4(x + 4)$ cm
    c $4(x + y + 5)$ cm

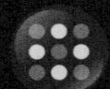
Objectives

- Simplify linear expressions by collecting like terms   (L5)

Key ideas	Resources
1 Expressions can be simplified by using any of the four basic operations 2 The 'rules' that apply to numbers also apply to letters	Simplifying 2 (1178) Templates and three packs of coloured cards

Simplification	Extension
Simplifying divisions is likely to cause some students difficulty. Point out that the divisions of question **5** are partly numerical and partly algebraic, and it is the numerical parts that can be simplified by doing a division.	Students find the dimensions of as many rectangles as possible with area 24*ab*. For example, 6*a* by 4*b* and 24*a* by *b*.

Literacy	Links
Simplifying expressions is a common activity in mathematics. It is the equivalent of rearranging words in sentences to make better sense of what you want to say. Earlier lessons have looked at simplifying 'like terms' when they are added and subtracted. When multiplying, take the letters and the numbers separately. For example, $6x \times 4y$ means $6 \times x \times 4 \times y$ and the multiplication is in any order. So $6 \times 4 = 24$ and $x \times y = xy$, to give a final answer $24 \times xy = 24xy$. Similarly when dividing. For example, with $\frac{8x}{4}$, think of the number part only where $\frac{8}{4} = 2$, giving the final answer $2x$.	People who collect and study postage stamps are called philatelists. Some philatelists collect stamps from a particular country while others collect stamps showing a particular theme such as trains, birds or insects. All postage stamps from across the world give the country of issue, except those from UK which instead carry an image of the head of the ruling monarch. There are collections of stamps showing insects at http://www.bugsonstamps.com/country_master.htm and of birds at http://www.bird-stamps.org/

Alternative approach

☐☐ × ■☐ = ...

$\dfrac{■ \times ☐}{☐} = $ ....

Select coloured cards and place on either template. Simplify the expression.
Create four red cards with the numbers 8, 12, 16 and 24 on them.
Create four yellow cards with the number 2, 4, 6, and 8 on them.
Create four blue cards with the letters *w, x, y* and *z* on them.
Create different expressions.

☐ = Yellow   ■ = Blue   ■ = Red

Checkpoint

1 Simplify these expressions

a $5a + 4b - 2a - 2b$ $(3a + 2b)$

b $a + 2b + a - 2b$ $(2a)$

c $5m \times 6$ $(30m)$

d $2a \times 4b$ $(8ab)$

e $6a \div 3$ $(2a)$

f $10a \div 5b$ $(2\frac{a}{b})$

Starter – Power bingo

Ask students to draw a 4×2 grid and enter eight square numbers (up to 144). Give possible numbers; for example, 'What is six squared?'

The winner is the first student to cross out all their numbers.

The activity can be extended by including cube numbers.

Teaching notes

Invite students to match equivalent expressions:

$12ab$	$\frac{a}{b}$
$8p + 9p$	$2b \times 6a$
$a \times 4$	$4a$
$a \div b$	$9p - 8p$
p	$17p$

- Letters are used to represent unknown numbers and letters follow the same 'rules' as numbers.

- Numbers and letters are multiplied separately and in any order.

- Terms are written with numbers first, followed by letters in alphabetical order.

- Remember the 'hidden' multiplication sign when using algebra.

- 'Like terms' can be collected together by addition and subtraction.

- $1 \times x$ and $1x$ is written as just x.

- Use the link between division and fractions.

Emphasise that, with algebra, you don't always seek to get a numerical answer: sometimes you just want to simplify expressions.

Plenary

Students simplify expressions such as those in questions **2**, **4** and **5**, giving their answers on mini whiteboards. When necessary, discuss responses with the whole class. This plenary and subsequent starter activities provide an efficient way of skilling students in this aspect of algebra and nipping misunderstandings 'in the bud'.

Exercise commentary

Question 1 – This question is harder than question **2**, as it involves understanding perimeter and being able to write it algebraically.

Questions 2 and **3** – Question **2** revises work from earlier lessons and question **3** is a continuity of question **1**.

Questions 4 and **5** – These questions will be more successful if there has been plenty of groundwork and practice done in an earlier whole-class session.

Question 6 – This is best attempted by students who have met this idea of building numbers and expressions using a brick wall. It is harder than question **7**.

Answers

1. **a** $x + 5y + 5$ **b** $5z + t + 8$ **c** $2a + 3b + c$
2. **a** $6c + 4d$ **b** $7t + 10s$ **c** $5r + 7s$
   d $9x + 5y$ **e** $6f + g$ **f** $x + 5y$
   g $j - 6i$ **h** $8q$ **i** $t + 20s$
3. $4x + 2y$ cm
4. **a** $20m$ **b** $6n$ **c** $10b$ **d** $21n$
   e $4mn$ **f** $10tv$ **g** $8rs$ **h** $50xy$
   i $30ce$ **j** $36pr$ **k** $30bf$ **l** $100uv$
5. **a** a **b** $2a$ **c** $5n$ **d** $5t$
   e $5a$ **f** $5p$ **g** $5k$ **h** $8r$
   i $\frac{2r}{s}$ **j** $\frac{2d}{e}$ **k** $\frac{3m}{n}$ **l** $\frac{3j}{k}$
6. $2(a + b) + 1$
   $\qquad\qquad 2b \qquad\qquad 3c + 1$
7. $30ab$ cm^2

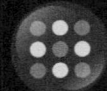

Objectives

- Substitute positive integers into simple formulae (L5)
- Use simple formulae in various contexts (L5)

Key ideas	Resources
1 Formulae can be used in many contexts, both in subjects like science and in real-life situations 2 When substituting numbers into formulae, the order of the operations matters	Rules and formulae (1158) Squared grid paper Computer spreadsheet Calculators

Simplification	Extension
Students use calculators with large numbers and decimal multiplications.	Students use formulae which include powers, for example, $E = mc^2$. Students research this formula to ascertain what each letter represents.

Literacy

Mathematics is written in a very precise and succinct language. The way it is written follows clear rules.

For example, the mobile phone contract which says that the cost in £ is calculated at 5 pence per minute plus a standing charge of £6 per month, is reduced to:

Monthly cost = 5 pence per minute + £6 per month

This reduces to:

Monthly cost, C = 5 pence × time, t (min) + £6

This reduces to:

$C = 5 \times t + 600$, where C is in pence and t in minutes

This reduces to:

$C = 5t + 600$

Links

The formula $V = IR$ is called Ohm's Law and was discovered by the German physicist George Ohm who published the results of his work in 1827. At first, other German scientists did not accept his work and it was only after the Royal Society in London awarded Ohm a medal in 1841 that he became a professor at the university in Munich. There is more information about Georg Ohm at
http://en.wikipedia.org/wiki/Georg_Ohm

Alternative approach

A natural extension is to create a table of values, draw graphs and make conclusions.

For example, for the two mobile phone contracts with formulae $C = 10t$ and $C = 5t + 600$, tables of values from $t = 0$ to $t = 200$ are appropriate with values of t in steps of 20 or 50. The two graphs intersect at the point (120, 1200). Interpret this as both contracts charging the same (1200 pence = £12) for 120 minutes a month. Discuss the circumstance in which one contract is better than the other.

A computer spreadsheet could be used to create the tables of values and to draw two graphs on the same axes.

A different context for two similar formulae would be the cost of hiring a taxi for different lengths of journey.

Checkpoint

1 For the formula $C = 5t + 600$:

  a i Suppose that $t = 10$, what is the value of $5t$? (Show how you work that out.)   (50; 5 × 10)

    ii So what is the value of C and how did you work that out?   (650; 50 + 600)

  b i So, if $t = 10$, then $C = 650$. If the formula represents the cost of a mobile phone contract, what does that tell you?   (It costs 650 pence for 10 minutes of phone calls)

    ii Is that a good contract to have? If not, why not?   (No, too expensive)

Starter – Quick fire

Continue the recap of basic number work begun in previous Quick fire Starters. Include questions on fractions, decimals and percentages and questions using mental and written computation. Also include questions on the algebra of this chapter. Ask rapid response questions. Students reply by writing on their mini whiteboards. Discuss questions when their answers indicate a need.

Teaching notes

Discuss with the class where they might have seen formulae before: science lessons (using distance/speed/time), mobile phone contracts, conversion between units of currency and between temperature scales.

Write two mobile phone 'contracts' on the board:

- Cost = 10p per minute
- Cost = £6 monthly fee + 5p per minute

Demonstrate the use of symbols and the need to convert to the same units.

Students calculate the monthly cost for each contract based upon different times: 30 minutes, 1 hour, 80 minutes of calling, etc. Show the working and point out that students are 'substituting' values into each formula. Discuss how the formulae can be written using symbols (that is, letters rather than words to get $C = 10 \times t$ and $C = 5 \times t + 600$, or $C = 10t$ and $C = 5t + 600$).

Discuss the merits of each contract and encourage students to consider what kind of customer might be interested in each one.

Plenary

Provide a list of formulae; explain the context that each formula relates to. Students substitute values into each formula and write their answers on mini whiteboards. Discuss answers when necessary.

Exercise commentary

Question 1 – Question **1** has a one-step formula.

Questions 2 and **3** – These questions have two-step formulae.

Question 4 – This offers several multi-step formulae.

Answers

1	a	30p	b	£2	c	£2.50	d	80p
	e	£1.20	f	£1.70	g	£2.30	h	£3.20
	i	£4.50	j	£6	k	£8	l	£10
2	a	£6	b	£6.25	c	£6.50		
	d	£5.75	e	£7.50	f	£7.25		
	g	£8	h	£8.10	i	£8.20		
	i	£8.60						
3	a	22	b	37	c	57		
	d	32	e	12	f	9.5		
	g	207						
4	a	12	b	31	c	7	d	10
	e	4	f	8	g	3	h	9
5	Students' answers							

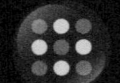

Objectives

- Derive an algebraic formula from a scenario described in words
- Substitute positive integers into formulae   (L5)

Key ideas	Resources
1 A formula is a symbolic way of describing a relationship given in words 2 The value of a variable can be found by substitution into a formula	Rules and formulae (1158) Computer spreadsheet

Simplification	Extension
Students, in pairs, discuss how to write an algebraic relationship in words and, if possible, contextualise it. Then, write a word sentence to describe the algebraic relationship.	Show students various 'match-stick' sequences and challenge them to write a formula connecting the pattern with the number of lines used.

Literacy	Links
The comments from the previous lesson apply here also. The written word can be condensed into a succinct algebraic formula. For example, the mobile phone contract which says that the cost in £ is calculated at 5 pence per minute plus a standing charge of £6 per month, is reduced to: Monthly cost = 5 pence per minute + £6 per month and then to $C = 5t + 600$ where C is in pence and t in minutes.	There are over 600 species of spider in Britain, all of which are harmless to humans. House spiders can measure up to 18 mm in length but the male is slightly smaller than the female. After mating, the male usually dies and is then eaten by the female. There are pictures of different spiders found in Britain at http://www.uksafari.com/spiders.htm

Alternative approach

A computer spreadsheet can be used to illustrate substitution into a formula.

For example, for the above mobile phone where $C = 5t + 600$ with C in pence and t in minutes, place labels 't (min)' into cell A1 and 'C (pence)' into cell B1.

For cell B2, create the formula B2 = 5*A2 + 600. Enter any time (in minutes) into cell A2 and get the monthly cost in pence in cell B2.

If the cost is needed in pounds, then place the label 'C (£)' in cell C1 and, in cell C2, create the formula C2 = B2/100. Enter any time (in minutes) into cell A2 and get the cost in pence and in pounds. Format the cells in column C to display numbers as currency with two decimal places (e.g. £8.50 instead of 8.5).

Enter different times (in minutes) in column A. If cells B2 and C2 are dragged down, the formulae are copied to each new row, and costs are automatically calculated.

Checkpoint

1 Meg is 6 years older than Joe. Use m to stand for Meg's age and j to stand for Joe's age.
   Write a formula to connect their ages. $(m = j + 6$ or $j = m - 6)$

2 Isabella does some gardening for pocket money. She is paid £5 per hour and £7 bonus per week.
   Use h to stand for the number of hours and w to stand for the wage per week.
   a Write a formula $w = $ _____ $(w = 5h + 7)$
   b If she works 4 hours, how much does she earn that week? $(w = 5 \times 4 + 7 = 27)$

Starter – Priceless!

If A costs 1p, B costs 2p, C costs 3p, etc., how much is your name worth?

Are you more expensive than the person beside you?

Which of your school subjects is worth the most?

How much does your favourite hobby cost?

Teaching notes

Discuss how many eyes 4, 10, 15, … people have. Students justify their answer in each case. Students generalise: 'The number of eyes is always two times the number of people'.

Students write this statement more mathematically by using symbols (that is, letters) to represent the unknown values. Mention the use of the algebraic convention of 'hidden' multiplication. So, for example, $e = 2 \times p$ becomes $e = 2p$.

Repeat with different scenarios; how many fingers will people have; how many legs will cats have? Include non-multiplicative relationships such as: 'If John is three years older than Ahmed, how old is John when Ahmed is …?'

For each example encourage students to:
- articulate their calculations
- generalise using words
- progress to an algebraic formula.

Revise substituting values into a formula to check that it works.

Plenary

Students consider two-step formulae. Discuss the formulae to describe the cost of a taxi journey (such as $C = 2m + 3$), the number of rungs on a ladder (such as $n = 2L + 1$), the total cost of buying several identical items with a delivery charge ($C = 6n + 10$).

Substitute values into various formulae. Students use mini whiteboards and discuss answers.

Exercise commentary

Question 1 – Students create formulae using addition.

Question 2 – This is a two-step formula $l = 5w + 2$

Question 3 – takes students through the stages of creating and then using a formula. They could record their results in a mapping diagram.

Question 4 – Assume that the connection between the width and the height is by adding or subtracting an amount.

Answers

1 a $k = c + 7$ b 20
2 a $h = 5w + 2$ b 22
3 a i 40   ii 80   iii 200
   b Total number of drawing pins = 20n
   c 140
4 a $w = h + 4, w = h - 4, w = h + 2$
   b i 24 cm   ii 40 cm
     iii 8 cm   iv $x + 4$ cm
   c Because the width never equals the height

Key outcomes		Quick check
Use symbols to make simple expressions.	L5	Amy receives twice as much pocket money as Beth. If Amy has £a and Beth has £b, write a formula $a = $ _____ ($a = 2b$)
Substitute values into simple expressions.	L5	Calculate the value of the expression $2a + b$ when $a = 4$ and $b = 5$ $(2 \times 4 + 5 = 8 + 5 = 13)$
Simplify expressions by collecting like terms.	L5	Simplify $3x + 5x - 2x$ $(6x)$ Simplify $3a + 5b - 2a + 5b$ $(a + 10b)$
Expand brackets.	L5	Expand the brackets $4(a + b)$ $(4a + 4b)$ $3(4 - b)$ $(12 - 3b)$
Substitute values into formulae.	L5	Find a when $b = 6$ $a = 10 - b$ $(a = 4)$ $a = \dfrac{b + 6}{4}$ $(a = 12 \div 4 = 3)$
Recognise and write formulae.	L5	Dan earns £6 an hour on his newspaper round and an £8 bonus per week. If h is the number of hours he works in a week and w is the wage per week, write this as a formula $w = $ _____ $(w = 6h + 8)$
Multiply and divide algebraic terms.	L5	Simplify $5a \times 6b$ $(30ab)$ $\dfrac{12a}{6b}$ $\left(2\dfrac{a}{b}\right)$

MyMaths extra support

Lesson/online homework			Description
Order of operations	1167	L5	Carrying out arithmetic in the correct order, dealing with brackets

MyReview

Check out
You should now be able to ...   **Test it ➡**
     Questions

✓ Use symbols to make simple expressions.	⑤ 1
✓ Substitute values into simple expressions.	⑤ 2
✓ Simplify expressions by collecting like terms.	⑤ 3
✓ Expand brackets.	⑤ 4
✓ Substitute values into formulae.	⑤ 5, 6
✓ Recognise and write formulae.	⑤ 7, 8
✓ Multiply and divide algebraic terms.	⑤ 9

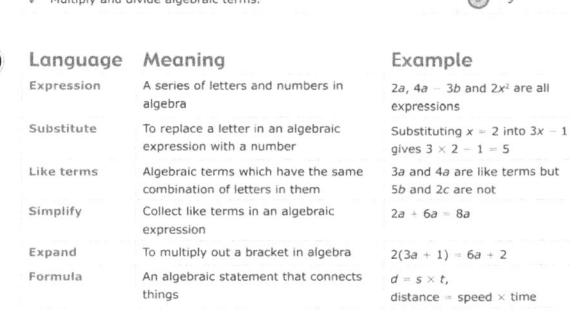

Language	Meaning	Example
Expression	A series of letters and numbers in algebra	$2a$, $4a - 3b$ and $2x^2$ are all expressions
Substitute	To replace a letter in an algebraic expression with a number	Substituting $x = 2$ into $3x - 1$ gives $3 \times 2 - 1 = 5$
Like terms	Algebraic terms which have the same combination of letters in them	$3a$ and $4a$ are like terms but $5b$ and $2c$ are not
Simplify	Collect like terms in an algebraic expression	$2a + 6a = 8a$
Expand	To multiply out a bracket in algebra	$2(3a + 1) = 6a + 2$
Formula	An algebraic statement that connects things	$d = s \times t$, distance = speed × time

1. Jack has $£x$ and Jill has $£y$. How much do they have altogether?

2. Calculate the value of these expressions when $a = 3$ and $b = 8$.
   a $6 \times a$ b $a + b$
   c $4b$ d $b \div 2$
   e $10 - a$ f $\frac{16}{b}$

3. Simplify these expressions.
   a $2y + 3y + y$
   b $12z - 7z$
   c $7a + 2a + 3b - b$
   d $9w - v + 5v - 6w$

4. Expand the brackets.
   a $9 \times (a + b)$
   b $3 \times (3 - c)$

5. Calculate the value of A by substituting the values $b = 3$, $c = 10$ into these formulae.
   a $A = 15 + c$
   b $A = 20 - b$
   c $A = \frac{c + 6}{2}$
   d $A = \frac{b \times c}{6}$

6. Tables (T) are arranged in such a way that the number of chairs required is given by C where $C = 4 \times T - 2$.
   Calculate the number of chairs needed when there are 3 tables.

7. Write an expression for the perimeter of the rectangle.

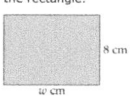

8 cm
w cm

8. There are 30 sweets in a packet. How many sweets are there in
   a 4 packets
   b n packets?

9. Simplify these expressions.
   a $12p \times 3$
   b $5r \times 6t$
   c $14n \div 7$
   d $\frac{25d}{5}$

What next?

Score	
0 – 4	Your knowledge of this topic is still developing. To improve look at Formative test: 2A-3; MyMaths: 1158, 1178, 1179, 1187 and 1247
5 – 7	You are gaining a secure knowledge of this topic. To improve look at InvisiPen: 211, 212, 213, 214, 251, 252 and 254
8, 9	You have mastered this topic. Well done, you are ready to progress!

Question commentary

Students should recognise that $6 \times a$ is usually written as $6a$.

Question 1 – Straightforward.

Question 2 – Substituting given values into simple expressions.

Question 3 – Simplifying expressions by collecting like terms.

Question 4 – Expanding brackets.

Questions 5 and **6** – Substituting given values into formulae. In parts **5c** and **5d**, students may need guidance as to the order of operations.

Question 7 – With brackets the formula is $2(w + 8)$, without it is $2w + 16$

Question 8 – Part **b** is the general case.

Question 9 – Straightforward simplification of expressions involving multiplication and division.

Answers

1. $x + y$

2. a 18   b 11
   c 32   d 4
   e 7   f 2

3. a $6y$ b $5z$
   c $9a + 2b$ d $3w + 4v$

4. a $9a + 9b$ b $9 - 3c$

5. a 25   b 17
   c 8   d 5

6. 10

7. $16 + 2w$

8. a 120   b $30n$

9. a $36p$ b $30rt$
   c $2n$ d $5d$

3a

1 Write an expression for the number of songs on these MP3 players if there are x songs on each.

3b

2 Calculate the value of $30 - y$ if y is

  a 10   **b** 1   **c** 30

3c

3 Simplify these expressions by adding or subtracting the terms.

  a $x + x + x$ **b** $4a + a + 3a$ **c** $4q + 5q + q$

  d $8u - 2u + 9u$ **e** $9h - 3h - 2h$ **f** $45d - 15d - 30d$

4 Add or subtract like terms to simplify these expressions.

  a $5x + 8x + 5y - 3y$ **b** $10g + 6h + 2g - 3h$ **c** $15t - 5t + 6s + 4s$

  d $20b - 8c + 10c - 10b$ **e** $39p + 20q - 13q + 15q$ **f** $23e - 6g + 8g + 4g + 7e$

3d

5 Expand these expressions by removing the brackets.

  a $2 \times (5 + 4)$ **b** $3 \times (6 + 2)$ **c** $6 \times (6 + 6)$

  d $8 \times (12 - 10)$ **e** $4 \times (12 - 4)$ **f** $10 \times (12 - 7)$

6 Expand these expressions by removing the brackets.

  a $6 \times (e + 5)$ **b** $4 \times (x + 5)$ **c** $10 \times (x + 8)$

  d $7 \times (v - 5)$ **e** $9 \times (g + 1)$ **f** $3 \times (12 + h)$

3e

7 Use the 'Pay As You Go' formula, $\text{Cost} = 6 \times t$, to calculate the cost of these calls, where t is time in minutes. Write your answers in pounds whenever you can.

  a 5 minutes   **b** 8 minutes

  c 9 minutes   **d** 1 minute

  e 20 minutes   **f** 50 minutes

8 The distance you travel depends on how long you travel and the speed at which you move.

The formula is: $d = t \times s$ (distance = time × speed)

Use the formula to calculate the distances travelled on these journeys.

  a $t = 4$ hours and $s = 5$mph   **b** $t = 6$ hours and $s = 4$mph

  c $s = 2.5$km/h and $t = 4$ hours   **d** $s = 30$mph and $t = 4$ hours

  e $t = 15$ seconds and $s = 5$m/s   **f** $s = 80$mph and $t = 1.5$ hours

3e

9 Calculate the value of y by substituting different values of x into these formulae.

  a $y = x - 3$ if $x = 14$ **b** $y = x + 29$ if $x = 15$ **c** $y = 21 - x$ if $x = 12$

  d $y = \dfrac{x}{3}$ if $x = 45$ **e** $y = \dfrac{x - 3}{5}$ if $x = 28$ **f** $y = \dfrac{7 \times x}{2}$ if $x = 6$

3f

10 James is 4 years older than Lizzie.

  a Complete the table to show the link between their ages.

James's age	Lizzie's age
5	
12	
15	
20	
32	

  b Write a formula to connect James's and Lizzie's ages. Use j to stand for James's age and l to stand for Lizzie's age.

  Start: $j = \ldots\ldots$

11 There are 30 crisps in a packet.

  a How many crisps are there in

    i 2 packets   **ii** 5 packets   **iii** 10 packets?

  b Write a formula for the number of crisps in any number of packets. Use n for the number of packets of crisps.

  Start: Total number of crisps, $c = \ldots\ldots$

  c Use your formula to calculate the number of crisps in 6 packets. Show your working.

3g

12 a Jason delivers 150 newspapers in 3 hours. How many papers will he deliver in 1 hour?

  b Explain how you calculated your answer. What did you do?

  c Keith delivered x newspapers in 2 hours. How many papers will he deliver in 1 hour?

13 Simplify these expressions. Be careful as there are unlike terms in some of the questions.

  a $6a + 2a + 2d$ **b** $7x + 4y + 3x + 2y$ **c** $9h + h + 5j + 2j - 2h$

  d $10x + 5x + 7y + 8y$ **e** $5t + 2s + 3s - 5t$ **f** $3m + 9n + 8m + 2i$

  g $3a \times 3$ **h** $5 \times 2e$ **i** $6 \times 5t$

  j $5a \times b$ **k** $4q \times 3r$ **l** $20r \times 5s$

14 Simplify these expressions by dividing the numerator by the denominator.

Remember that $a \div b$ is written as $\dfrac{a}{b}$.

  a $2a \div 2$ **b** $4a \div 2$ **c** $10n \div 2$ **d** $25t \div 5$

  e $16v \div 4$ **f** $24y \div 2$ **g** $60b \div 20$ **h** $45e \div 5$

  i $\dfrac{8a}{2}$ **j** $\dfrac{20p}{10}$ **k** $\dfrac{18t}{2}$ **l** $\dfrac{26z}{2}$

MyMaths.co.uk

Question commentary

Questions 1–7 – Straightforward

Question 8 – Most question parts are in hours and give answers in miles, but part **c** has the answer in kilometres. Part **e** also just requires multiplying together but it involves seconds and the answer is in metres.

Questions 9–14 – Straightforward practice of working with formulae and expressions.

Answers

1 $3x$

2 a 20 **b** 29 **c** 0

3 a $3x$ **b** $8a$ **c** $10q$
  d $15u$ **e** $4h$ **f** 0

4 a $13x + 2y$ **b** $12g + 3h$ **c** $10t + 10s$
  d $10b + 2c$ **e** $39p + 22q$ **f** $30e + 6g$

5 a 18 **b** 24 **c** 72
  d 16 **e** 32 **f** 50

6 a $6e + 30$ **b** $4x + 20$ **c** $10x + 80$
  d $7v - 35$ **e** $9g + 9$ **f** $36 + 3h$

7 a 30p **b** 48p **c** 54p **d** 6p
  e £1.20 **f** £3.00

8 a 20 miles **b** 24 miles **c** 10 km
  d 120 miles **e** 75 metres **f** 120 miles

9 a 11 **b** 44 **c** 9
  d 15 **e** 5 **f** 21

10 a James's age   Lizzie's age
       5 $\longrightarrow$ 1
       12 $\longrightarrow$ 8
       15 $\longrightarrow$ 11
       20 $\longrightarrow$ 16
       32 $\longrightarrow$ 28

   b $j = l + 4$

11 a **i** 60 crisps **ii** 150 crisps **iii** 300 crisps
   b $c = 30n$ **c** 180

12 a 50 **b** 150 divided by 3 **c** $\frac{x}{2}$

13 a $8a + 2d$ **b** $10x + 6y$ **c** $8h + 7j$
   d $15x + 15y$ **e** $5s$ **f** $11m + 9n + 2i$
   g $9a$ **h** $10e$ **i** $30t$
   j $5ab$ **k** $12qr$ **l** $100rs$

14 a a **b** $2a$ **c** $5n$
   d $5t$ **e** $4v$ **f** $12y$
   g $3b$ **h** $9e$ **i** $4a$
   j $2p$ **k** $9t$ **l** $13z$

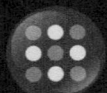

Related lessons		Resources	
Mental multiplication and division problems	7e	Best buys and value for money	(1243)
Written multiplication	11b	Multiply double digits	(1025)
Written division	11c		

Simplification

Most of the calculations required here are straightforward but some students might focus on two or three of the different items rather than considering the whole range. The numbers in tasks **2** and **3** could be simplified to aid the use of mental strategies.

Extension

All of the information given is about 'typical' costs and savings. Students could be asked to consider a *range* of savings and/or costs which will affect the time over which the savings/repayment costs are made. They could also investigate further the effects of the location of things like solar panels and wind generators in terms of their effectiveness at generating the required amounts of electricity.

Links

Most energy companies now offer government subsidised deals on things like new home insulation and solar panels. Private contractors also have access to these deals and students could look up the various offers on the internet and in both local and national newspapers. Can they find a range of suppliers that could provide all of the various installations free of charge?

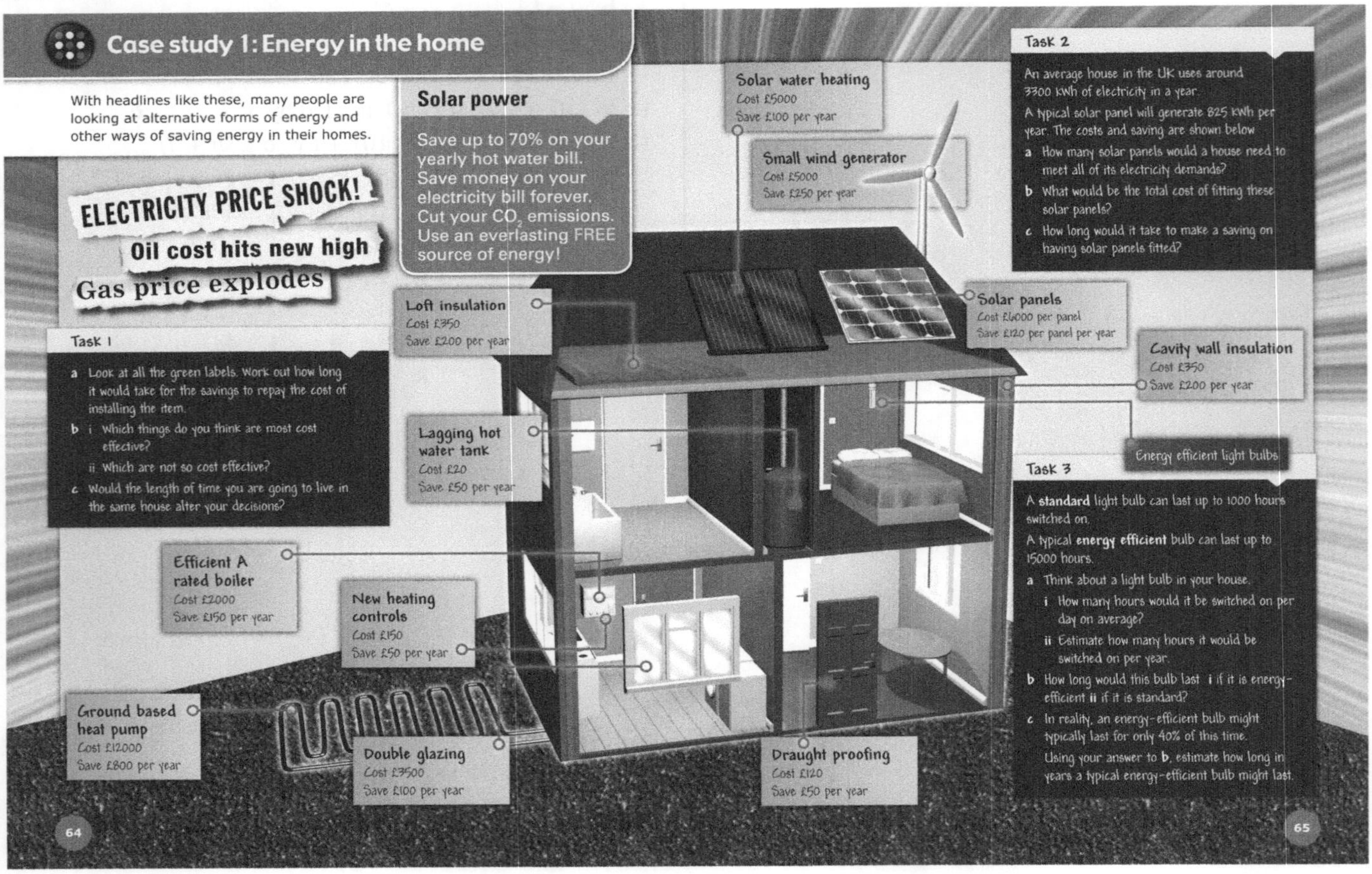

Case study 1: Energy in the home

With headlines like these, many people are looking at alternative forms of energy and other ways of saving energy in their homes.

ELECTRICITY PRICE SHOCK!

Oil cost hits new high

Gas price explodes

Solar power

Save up to 70% on your yearly hot water bill. Save money on your electricity bill forever. Cut your CO_2 emissions. Use an everlasting FREE source of energy!

Task 1

a Look at all the green labels. Work out how long it would take for the savings to repay the cost of installing the item.
b i Which things do you think are most cost effective?
ii Which are not so cost effective?
c Would the length of time you are going to live in the same house alter your decisions?

Solar water heating
Cost £5000
Save £100 per year

Small wind generator
Cost £5000
Save £250 per year

Loft insulation
Cost £350
Save £200 per year

Solar panels
Cost £6000 per panel
Save £120 per panel per year

Cavity wall insulation
Cost £350
Save £200 per year

Lagging hot water tank
Cost £20
Save £50 per year

Energy efficient light bulbs

Efficient A rated boiler
Cost £2000
Save £150 per year

New heating controls
Cost £150
Save £50 per year

Ground based heat pump
Cost £12000
Save £800 per year

Double glazing
Cost £3500
Save £100 per year

Draught proofing
Cost £120
Save £50 per year

Task 2

An average house in the UK uses around 3300 kWh of electricity in a year.
A typical solar panel will generate 825 kWh per year. The costs and saving are shown below
a How many solar panels would a house need to meet all of its electricity demands?
b What would be the total cost of fitting these solar panels?
c How long would it take to make a saving on having solar panels fitted?

Task 3

A **standard** light bulb can last up to 1000 hours switched on.
A typical **energy efficient** bulb can last up to 15000 hours.
a Think about a light bulb in your house.
  i How many hours would it be switched on per day on average?
  ii Estimate how many hours it would be switched on per year.
b How long would this bulb last i if it is energy-efficient ii if it is standard?
c In reality, an energy-efficient bulb might typically last for only 40% of this time.
Using your answer to b, estimate how long in years a typical energy-efficient bulb might last.

Teaching notes

With energy prices rising and environmental concerns about the climate, there is much interest in reducing energy use around the house and obtaining energy in a cheaper or cleaner way.

This case study looks at a number of things that can be done to a house to make it more energy efficient. It looks at them in terms of how much they could reduce the cost of energy used over a year at current costs and considers their cost effectiveness by working out how long it would take for the savings to pay back the cost of purchase and installation of the items.

Look at the case study and explain that the house shows ways of either saving energy or of providing the energy in a different way. Ask the students some general questions such as: which items would save energy and which are alternative sources of energy? Do you have any of these things in your house? Why do you think that there is so much interest in saving energy these days? Establish that rising energy costs and concerns for the environment can both drive people to think about the way they use energy.

Task 1

Look at the information about loft insulation. What do you notice about the information that is given? Roughly how long would it take for the savings in costs to repay the cost of installing the insulation? Discuss how figures for items such as this are often given as ranges, as the actual figure will vary from house to house depending on its size, type and construction. Do you think that is a reasonable time in which to recoup the cost? What will happen for every year after that? Now look at the information for the A rated boiler and ask similar questions. The payback time is considerably longer. Discuss whether this is cost effective by asking questions such as if you have a perfectly good working boiler at the moment, do you think that it would be worth paying to have it changed for a new one? If you needed to change your current boiler, would it be worth having an A rated boiler as the replacement?

Task 2

Work through the section about the solar panels. When discussing answers, ensure that students comment on the fact that the payback time might shorten due to the electricity costs of supplied electricity increasing over time thereby increasing the annual savings.

Task 3

Look at the information about the energy efficient light bulbs. The students are guided through the working for both types of bulb using a series of estimates. Is there another way to save money when considering lighting the home? (Turn off the lights!)

Answers

1 a Loft insulation: 1.75 years; Lagging hot water tank: 0.4 years; Boiler: 13.3 years; Controls: 3 years; Heat pump: 15 years; Double glazing: 35 years: Draught proofing: 2.4 years; Cavity wall insulation: 1.75 years; Solar panels: 50 years; Wind generator: 20 years; Solar heating: 50 years.

   b i Lagging hot water tank, loft insulation, cavity wall insulation.

      ii Double glazing, efficient boiler, heat pump.

   c More likely to buy expensive items like solar panels if you intend to stay longer. May not see the benefit, could increase the value of house.

2 a 4 panels

   b £24 000

   c 50 years

3 a i 4–5 hours/day ii 1500 hours/year

   b i 10 years ii 8 months

   c 4 years

Students' estimates may vary.

Learning outcomes

N2 Order positive and negative integers, decimals and fractions; use the number line as a model for ordering of the real numbers; use the symbols =, ≠, <, >, ≤, ≥ (L5)

N4 Use the 4 operations, including formal written methods, applied to integers, decimals, proper and improper fractions, and mixed numbers, all both positive and negative (L4)

N9 Work interchangeably with terminating decimals and their corresponding fractions (such as 3.5 and 7/2 or 0.375 and 3/8 (L5)

N10 Define percentage as 'number of parts per hundred', interpret percentages and percentage changes as a fraction or a decimal, interpret these multiplicatively, express 1 quantity as a percentage of another, compare 2 quantities using percentages, and work with percentages greater than 100% (L5)

Introduction

The chapter starts by looking at equivalent fractions, ordering fractions, converting simple fractions to decimals and ordering decimals. Adding and subtracting fractions are covered, then calculating fractions and percentages of an amount. Converting between fractions, decimals and percentages are covered in the final section.

The introduction discusses places where fractions are used in everyday life. For example one penny is one-hundredth of a pound and in telling the time one might say a quarter (of an hour) to four O'clock or half (an hour) past one O'clock. Up until 1984 halfpenny coins were legal tender and in pre-decimal currency a farthing – quarter penny – was used until 1960. Earlier coins included a half-farthing and a quarter-farthing.

It may be interesting to review the fractions that arise due to our units of time and money. A day is a seventh of a week, and hour a twenty-fourth of a day, a minute a sixtieth of an hour and a second a sixtieth of a minute. A shilling is a twentieth of a pound and a penny a fifth of a shilling. In pre-decimal currency a pound contained twenty shillings and a shilling contained 12 pence, so 240 pence in a pound.

The students should be able to think of lots of real-life examples of where you use fractions.

NCTEM have produced a booklet on fractions which you might find useful.

https://www.ncetm.org.uk/public/files/257666/fractions_booklet.pdf

Prior knowledge

Students should already know how to...

- Interpret place value notation for decimals
- Carry basic arithmetic including division

Starter problem

The starter problem has statements relating to 'facts' about fractions and percentages. Students are invited to see whether they are true or not. A basic approach would be to test for simple examples and try and find a counter-example, or use a mathematically sound deductive argument.

The first statement is clearly false since one half is equivalent to 14/28 and 15/28 is greater than this.

The second statement is true since the fraction in question is not 'top heavy'.

The first part of statement three is true but what follows is clearly false. 5% is smaller than 10% but 1/5 is bigger than 1/10.

Statement four implies that 1/3 is bigger than ½ which is clearly false.

Statement five is true since 0.2 × 30 = 0.3 × 20. We can convert between the two calculations by moving the digits in one sum and showing it is equivalent to the other: 0.2 × 30 = 2 × 3 = 20 × 0.3 (= 0.3 × 20)

Resources

🌐 MyMaths

Fractions, decimals and percentages		1015	Fractions to decimals	1016
Adding fractions	1017	Fractions of amounts	1018	
Fractions, decimals and percentages introduction		1029	Percentages of amounts 1	1030
Percentages of amounts 2	1031	Finding fractions	1062	Simple equivalent fractions	1371

Online assessment		**InvisiPen solutions**			
Chapter test	2A–4	Equivalent fractions	141	Fractions of amounts	142
Formative test	2A–4	Adding and subtracting fractions			145
Summative test	2A–4	Percentage of an amount	151	Fractions and decimals	161
		Percentages, fractions and decimals			162

Topic scheme

Teaching time = 7 lessons/3 weeks

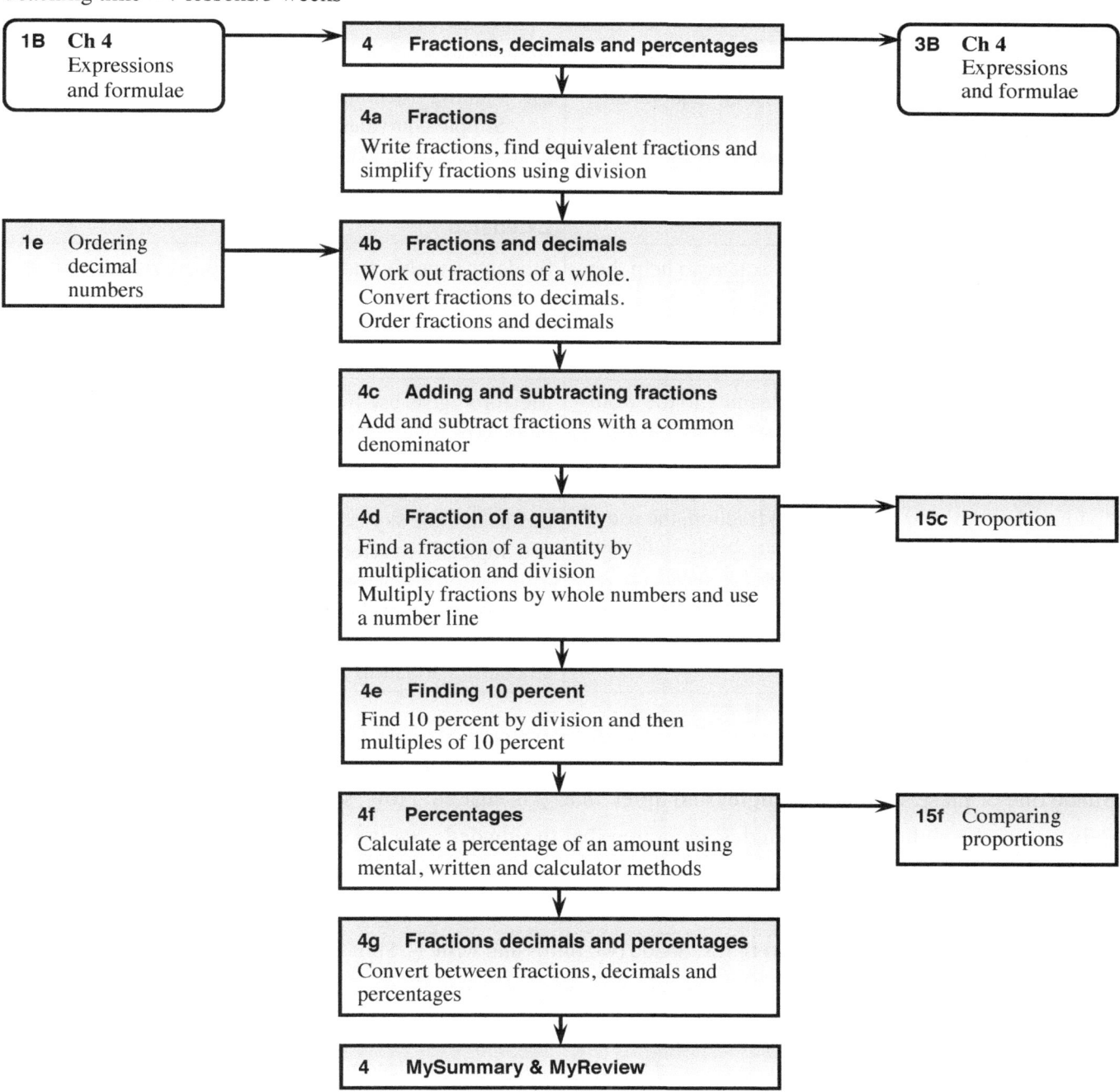

1B   Ch 4
Expressions and formulae

4   Fractions, decimals and percentages

3B   Ch 4
Expressions and formulae

4a   Fractions
Write fractions, find equivalent fractions and simplify fractions using division

1e   Ordering decimal numbers

4b   Fractions and decimals
Work out fractions of a whole.
Convert fractions to decimals.
Order fractions and decimals

4c   Adding and subtracting fractions
Add and subtract fractions with a common denominator

4d   Fraction of a quantity
Find a fraction of a quantity by multiplication and division
Multiply fractions by whole numbers and use a number line

15c   Proportion

4e   Finding 10 percent
Find 10 percent by division and then multiples of 10 percent

4f   Percentages
Calculate a percentage of an amount using mental, written and calculator methods

15f   Comparing proportions

4g   Fractions decimals and percentages
Convert between fractions, decimals and percentages

4   MySummary & MyReview

Differentiation

Student book 2A 66 –85	Student book 2B 60 – 77	Student book 2C 66 –83
Fractions	Ordering decimals	Fractions and decimals
Fractions and decimals	Fractions and decimals	Adding and subtracting fractions
Adding and subtracting fractions	Adding and subtracting fractions	Multiplying and dividing fractions
Fraction of a quantity	Fraction of a quantity	Percentage change
Finding 10 percent	Percentages of amounts	Percentage problems
Percentages	Fractions, decimals and	Fractions, decimals and
Fractions, decimals and	percentages	percentages
percentages		

Objectives

- Express a smaller whole number as a fraction of a larger one (L4)
- Simplify fractions by cancelling all common factors and identifying equivalent fractions (L5)

Key ideas	Resources
1 Fractions of the same value are called 'equivalent fractions' 2 Multiplication or division are used to find equivalent fractions	Finding fractions (1062) Simple equivalent fractions (1371) Multiplication square Rectangles divided into various fractions.

Simplification	Extension
Students may need a multiplication square to help them calculate equivalent fractions and identify common factors of two numbers.	Students simplify fractions where the divisor by which to divide is not given such as $\frac{15x}{10}$.

Literacy	Links
The word 'equivalent' is close in meaning to the word 'equal'. We can say that, if two fractions are equal, then they are equivalent fractions. When finding equivalent fractions by multiplying or dividing the 'top' and 'bottom' of a fraction, the use of two curved arrows (as in the students' book), labelled by the operation (such as × 2) is a useful visual support. As the labelled arrows are eventually internalised, write them in pencil and write the equivalent fractions in pen.	Meteorologists use fractions to estimate the amount of cloud covering the sky. The entire sky is divided into eighths and meteorologists estimate how many eighths or *oktas* of the sky are covered in cloud. Zero oktas means that the sky is clear, 8 oktas means that the sky is completely covered by cloud. There is more information about the symbols used to show cloud cover on weather charts at http://www.metoffice.gov.uk/education/secondary/students/charts.html

Alternative approach

Pose the situation where you are making a patio in your garden and you can choose between two sizes of paving stones. Show a large rectangle to represent the patio and divide it into four equal rectangles. Shade one of these smaller rectangles and agree that $\frac{1}{4}$ is shaded. Now, split each of the four rectangles in two to make eight equal rectangles and agree that the shaded area is $\frac{2}{8}$. The total number of rectangles has doubled from four to eight and the number of shaded rectangles has doubled from one to two. But the shaded area is the same. So $\frac{1}{4} = \frac{2}{8}$ and these are equivalent fractions.

Repeat with a rectangle divided into thirds. Shade two thirds and write $\frac{2}{3}$. Split each of the thirds into two equal pieces to make sixths. The same shaded part is now $\frac{4}{6}$. So, $\frac{2}{3} = \frac{4}{6}$; doubling 3 means that the 2 has to double too.

Repeat with $\frac{1}{2} = \frac{3}{6}$; trebling the 2 means that the 1 has to treble also.

By making the paving stones smaller, you need more of them. So, if the denominator increases, so does the numerator. Ask what the missing number is if $\frac{3}{4} = \frac{?}{12}$.

Checkpoint

1 Lily has £60 and spends £40.
 a What fraction did she spend? b What is this fraction in its simplest form? (40/60, 2/3)
2 What fraction is 75 cm of 1 m? There are 100 cm in a metre. Simplify your answer. (75/100 = ¾)

Starter – Quick fire

Continue the recap of basic number work begun in previous Quick fire Starters. Also include recent work in algebra. Ask rapid response questions. Students reply by writing on their mini whiteboards. Discuss questions when their answers indicate a need.

Teaching notes

Ask students 'Would you rather have $\frac{1}{2}$ of a pizza or $\frac{3}{6}$ of a pizza?' Draw 2 circles on the board and demonstrate the equivalence of these two fractions. Ensure students recognise that the **denominator** indicates **total** number of equal parts and that the **numerator** indicates the number of parts shaded (or, in this case, eaten).

Invite students to give other fractions equivalent to $\frac{1}{2}$. Repeat for the fraction $\frac{1}{4}$.

Continue with other fractions and emphasise that you need to multiply numerator and denominator by the same number.

Explain that fractions can be **simplified** using a similar method by *dividing* numerator and denominator. Students consider 'Can I find a number that divides both the numerator and denominator? Is there a common factor?' or 'In what times-table are both the numerator and the denominator?'

Plenary

Discuss which is bigger, $\frac{5}{8}$ or $\frac{4}{8}$. Ask why this question is straightforward.(Both fractions are in the 'same family'; the eighths.)

Invite students to compare $\frac{4}{5}$ and $\frac{3}{4}$. Elicit that when the denominators are different, you cannot compare directly. Discuss how to change them so that the denominators are the same.

Show two fractions and ask if they are equivalent or not. Students respond on mini whiteboards.

Exercise commentary

Question 3 – This requires two points not yet practised. (a) The fraction cannot be written until the units are compatible. (b) If the question wants the equivalent fraction in its lowest terms, then questions **6** and **7** practise the method.

Questions 5–7 – These questions all deal with finding equivalent fractions.

Question 8 – In part **c**, only one of the fractions listed is equivalent to four-fifths.

Answers

1	a	$\frac{7}{10}$	b	$\frac{3}{5}$	c	$\frac{1}{9}$	d	$\frac{5}{6}$
2	a	$\frac{7}{8}$	b	$\frac{5}{8}$	c	$\frac{3}{8}$	d	$\frac{1}{8}$
3	a	$\frac{1}{5}$	b	$\frac{2}{5}$	c	$\frac{13}{20}$		
	d	$\frac{6}{25}$						
4	a	$\frac{3}{8}$	b	$\frac{2}{3}$				
5	a	$\frac{4}{6}$	b	$\frac{12}{15}$	c	$\frac{15}{25}$	d	$\frac{9}{12}$
6	a	$\frac{3}{4}$	b	$\frac{1}{3}$	c	$\frac{1}{4}$	d	$\frac{1}{2}$
7	a	$\frac{2}{5}$	b	$\frac{2}{3}$	c	$\frac{4}{5}$		
	d	$\frac{3}{10}$	e	$\frac{5}{7}$	f	$\frac{5}{7}$		
8	a	40 ml	b	$\frac{4}{5}$	c iii	$\frac{40}{50}$	d	yes

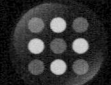

Objectives

- Use diagrams to compare two or more simple fractions   (L4)
- Order fractions by writing them with a common denominator or by converting them to decimals   (L5)

Key ideas	Resources
1 Decimals can be written as fractions in tenths and hundredths 2 Both decimals and fractions can be compared and written using the =, < and > signs	Fractions to decimals (1016) Several 10 × 10 square grid Number lines labelled from 0 to 1

Simplification	Extension
Provide students with 10 × 10 square grids so that they draw fractions on the grid to compare them.	Students draw a 3 × 5 grid and make up three 'true' and one 'false' statement as in question **6** of Exercise **4b**. For example, ' $\frac{2}{3}$ is bigger than $\frac{9}{15}$ ' (False). Students then swap their statements and identify the false one.

Literacy	Links
Part of being 'mathematically literate' or 'numerate' is to be confident in knowing and using equivalences of fractions and decimals. Avoid using money to illustrate decimals, as its use of decimals in speech and writing does not follow the general conventions. Time spent generating confidence in knowing that, for example, $\frac{3}{10}$ and $\frac{30}{100}$ are equivalent fractions and equal to 0.3 and 0.30 is time well spent in preparation for percentages.	Provide some sheet music for the class to use. The inequality signs are similar to the musical symbols *crescendo* (becoming louder) and *decrescendo* or *diminuendo* (becoming softer). Ask the class to find examples of these symbols on the music.

Alternative approach

Another visual aid offers an alternative approach and uses a number line from 0 to 1. One side of the line is labelled in tenths from 0.1 to 0.9 and then sub-divided into hundredths. The other side of the line is labelled in tenths from $\frac{1}{10}$ to $\frac{9}{10}$.

Place a pointer at various positions and express the reading as a decimal and as a fraction, both orally and in writing. Start with decimals such as 0.3 before moving to 0.31.

Checkpoint

1 Which is the larger of each pair?

   a 3/5 or 7/10   (7/10)

   b 9/10 or 95/100   (95/100)

   c 0.5 or 48/100   (0.5)

Starter – Quick fire

Continue the recap of basic number work begun in previous Quick fire Starters. Also include recent work in algebra and last lesson's work on fractions. Ask rapid response questions. Students reply by writing on their mini whiteboards. Discuss questions when their answers indicate a need.

Teaching notes

Show a 10 × 10 grid and invite students to shade $\frac{1}{2}$, $\frac{1}{4}$, $\frac{1}{10}$, $\frac{1}{100}$. Link one hundredth denoted by $\frac{1}{100}$ to the place value headings (H T U t h) and the decimal 0.01. Repeat for one-tenth as $\frac{1}{10}$ and 0.1 with shading on the grid. Repeat for multiples of 0.1 and 0.01 on the grid. The aim is for fluency in knowing the equivalences of, say, $\frac{3}{10}$ as both 0.3 and $\frac{30}{100}$; and also of $\frac{39}{100}$ as 0.39.

Plenary

Write, say, 0.7 and ask for an equivalent fraction in hundredths and an equivalent fraction in tenths. Students use mini whiteboards to respond. Repeat for equivalences of such as 0.19, $\frac{7}{10}$, $\frac{51}{100}$ and $\frac{9}{100}$. Particularly watch for responses to $\frac{9}{100}$ and discuss the response 0.9.

Exercise commentary

Questions 1–3 – These questions link the diagram with basic fraction and decimal equivalents.

Question 4 – Students to choose whether to change to tenths or hundredths. Also have to use the less than and greater than signs.

Question 5 – Part **e** is tricky linguistically.

Question 6 – Students need to read question carefully as once again it is tricky linguistically.

Answers

1 **a** $\frac{3}{100}$ **b** $\frac{10}{100} = \frac{1}{10}$ **c** $\frac{20}{100} = \frac{1}{5}$

d $\frac{27}{100}$ **e** $\frac{13}{100}$ **f** $\frac{27}{100}$

2 **a** 0.03 **b** 0.1 **c** 0.2
d 0.27 **e** 0.13 **f** 0.27

3 **a** $\frac{1}{10}$ **b** $\frac{2}{10}$ **c** $\frac{41}{100}$

d $\frac{3}{10}$ **e** $\frac{7}{10}$ **f** $\frac{100}{100}$

4 **a** $0.1 = \frac{1}{10}$ **b** $\frac{1}{10} < 0.9$ **c** $0.21 > \frac{19}{100}$

d $\frac{1}{100} < 0.1$ **e** $0.07 < \frac{70}{100}$ **f** $\frac{10}{100} = 0.10$

g $\frac{47}{100} < 0.50$ **h** $\frac{25}{100} > 0.03$ **i** $0.8 < \frac{90}{100}$

5 **a** True **b** False **c** True
d True **e** False

6 No

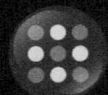

Objectives	
• Add and subtract fractions which have the same denominator	(L4)

Key ideas	Resources
1 Fractions with the same denominator can be added and subtracted on sight	Adding subtracting fractions (1017) Circles and/or rectangles marked with grids Fraction wall

Simplification	Extension
Initially, work with converting one whole into fractions of various sizes. Diagrams of a circle or rectangle split into halves, thirds, … will help them convert wholes into various fractions.	Students use PowerPoint to create an animation of $\frac{1}{5} + \frac{2}{5} = \frac{3}{5}$. Students work with additions that give a mixed number as an answer, such as $\frac{8}{10} + \frac{3}{10}$.

Literacy	Links
The precision of the teacher's spoken language is important in the teaching of fractions. Use the language of 'families' as describe in 'Alternative approach' to determine whether two fractions can be added or subtracted immediately.	Show the class an imperial foot-long ruler. Foot-long rulers are marked in inches and fractions of inches. What does each division on the ruler represent? ($\frac{1}{8}$, $\frac{1}{16}$ or $\frac{1}{32}$ inch, depending on the ruler) How are different-sized divisions distinguished? (By different lengths of the marked lines.) A printable ruler can be found at http://www.vendian.org/mncharity/dir3/paper_rulers/UnstableURL/ruler_foot_a4.pdf

Alternative approach

The language of 'families' is useful in describing the addition and subtraction of fractions. Fractions can only be added and subtracted when they are in the same 'family'; that is, when they have the same denominator. The 'quarters' and 'fifths' are two examples of families.

So $\frac{1}{5} + \frac{2}{5}$ can be added immediately to give $\frac{3}{5}$, with the answer being in the same 'family of fifths'. Fractions not in the same family, such as $\frac{2}{5}$ and $\frac{3}{10}$, cannot be added immediately and are not considered in this lesson.

Checkpoint	
1 Add 5/8 and 2/8	(7/8)
2 Add 2/8 and 3/8 and 4/8	(9/8 or 1 1/8)
3 Subtract 2/5 from 4/5	(2/5)
4 Subtract 2/9 from 1 whole	(7/9)

Starter – Quick fire

Continue the recap of basic number work begun in previous Quick fire Starters. Also include recent work with algebra and fractions. Ask rapid response questions. Students reply by writing on their mini whiteboards. Discuss questions when their answers indicate a need.

Teaching notes

Imagine sharing a pizza between three friends. One friend gets $\frac{5}{8}$ of the pizza; the second friend gets $\frac{3}{8}$ of the pizza. How many eighths does the third friend get? He gets none. Why? Students say that all the pieces have gone because there are only 8 eighths in a whole pizza.

Reinforce that the denominator tells you the **size** of the parts. Draw a circle split into eight equal parts. Have students give the name of the parts (eighths) and demonstrate that the total of 3 parts and 5 parts equals the whole. So, $\frac{5}{8} + \frac{3}{8} = \frac{8}{8} = 1$.

Discuss how many thirds are needed for one whole; and how many quarters; and how many fifths, etc.

Work through several examples of addition and subtraction of fractions with equal denominators.

Plenary

Write various additions and subtractions such as $\frac{5}{8} + \frac{2}{8}$ and $\frac{5}{8} - \frac{2}{8}$. Students write answers on their mini whiteboards. Also write such as $\frac{5}{8} + \frac{?}{8} = 1$ where students find the missing fraction. Discuss answers as necessary.

Exercise commentary

Questions 2–4 – These questions deal with addition and subtraction of fractions, extending to subtraction from a whole in questions **3d** and **3f**. (One whole can be 9/9.)

In part **4e** the answer can be 14/9 or 1 5/9.

Question 5 – This question extends to a real-life context again. Students need to know how many twentieths in a whole cake and in half a cake.

Answers

1	a $\frac{1}{5}$	b $\frac{1}{5}$	c $\frac{2}{5}$		
	d $\frac{4}{5}$	e $\frac{2}{5}$	f $\frac{4}{5}$		
2	a $\frac{5}{8}$	b $\frac{3}{8}$	c $\frac{6}{8}$		
	d 1	e $\frac{7}{8}$	f $\frac{7}{8}$		
3	a $\frac{5}{9}$	b $\frac{4}{9}$	c $\frac{1}{3}$		
	d $\frac{4}{9}$	e $\frac{1}{9}$	f $\frac{2}{9}$		
4	a $\frac{3}{5}$	b $\frac{2}{7}$	c $\frac{4}{9}$	d $\frac{9}{10}$
	e $\frac{14}{9}$	f 1		
5	a $\frac{1}{20}$	b Unal	c $\frac{1}{10}$	d Unal

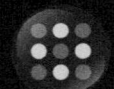

Objectives	
• Calculate simple fractions of quantities and measurements to give integer answers	(L4)
• Multiply a fraction by an integer	(L5)

Key ideas	Resources	
1 A unitary fraction of a quantity is found by dividing by the denominator	Fractions of amounts	(1018)
	Sheets of card with circles on them	
2 A multiple fraction of a quantity is found by multiplying the unitary fraction	Counters	

Simplification	Extension
Deal with fractions that are halves, thirds, quarters or fifths only. Use the method offered in the 'Alternative approach' below.	Word problems similar to question **7** make an appropriate extension. Extend calculations to include mixed numbers.

Literacy	Links

The layout of students' work step-by-step will help their understanding.
For example,
$\frac{3}{4}$ of 28 = $\frac{3}{4} \times 28$ = $3 \times \frac{1}{4} \times 28 = 3 \times 7 = 21$
Another way is to use the short division notation (which will be useful in question **7**) for $\frac{3}{4}$ of 248.
 	
  6 2   then   6 2   to give an answer of 186.
4) 2 4 8   × 3
                  1 8 6
	The Ancient Egyptians represented all their fractions as Egyptian fractions. An Egyptian fraction is the sum of a number of unit fractions, where all the unit fractions are different. All positive rational numbers can be represented by Egyptian fractions. More information about Egyptian fractions, including a calculator to convert a fraction to an Egyptian fraction can be found at http://www.mcs.surrey.ac.uk/Personal/R.Knott/Fractions/egyptian.html

Alternative approach

Have sheets of card with 2, 3, 4 or 5 circles drawn on them. Provide a pile of counters for students.

A student has 12 counters and uses the 2-circle card to divide them into two equal piles, giving a half of 12.

Using the 3-circle card, a student creates three equal piles and finds a third or two thirds of 12.

The 4-circle card creates quarters to find one, two or three quarters of 12 – and also a discussion about two quarters being the same as a half.

The 5-circle card is used with 15 counters to find fifths of 15. Repeat with other numbers of counters.

To reinforce the physical separation of counters with a calculation, check the answers using a calculator. Emphasise that pressing the ÷ key finds just one third, quarter or fifth (the unitary fraction) and that pressing the × finds the multiple fraction.

Checkpoint

1 Calculate

    a ¼ of 20   (5)

    b ¾ of 20   (15)

    c 20 × ¾   (15)

    d 5 × ¾   (15/4)

Starter – Fraction sort

Write the following fractions on the board.

$\frac{1}{4}, \frac{3}{15}, \frac{1}{3}, \frac{4}{6}, \frac{1}{5}, \frac{6}{8}, \frac{6}{10}, \frac{2}{3}, \frac{2}{8}, \frac{3}{4}, \frac{9}{27}, \frac{3}{5}$

Students, in pairs, sort the fractions into three sets of equivalent fractions. Discuss the results with the whole class.

Teaching notes

Start by linking fraction of a quantity to dividing an original amount into equal sized parts. That is, divide by 2 for a half, divide by 3 for thirds, divide by 99 for ninety-ninths and, in general, divide by the denominator for any fraction. Practise by finding $\frac{1}{2}$, $\frac{1}{3}$, ... of a quantity such as 24 kg.

Pose the question about finding $\frac{2}{5}, \frac{3}{5}$, ... of a quantity. Students suggest the rule of 'divide by the denominator and multiply by the numerator'.

The word 'of' is equivalent to 'multiply'. So, finding $\frac{2}{5}$ of 30 is the same as $\frac{2}{5} \times 30$. The same method applies: find one fifth by dividing by 5 and the two-fifths by multiplying by 2. (12)

Plenary

Ask students to find various fractions of quantities mentally. $\frac{1}{8}$ of 32, $\frac{3}{8}$ of 32, $\frac{5}{6}$ of 30. They answer on mini whiteboards and discuss their answers.

Exercise commentary

Question 2 – This requires students to calculate the fraction of a quantity with a unit numerator. The division calculations are fairly straightforward.

Question 3 – The denominators and quantities exactly match those in the parts in question **1**. Only the numerator has changed. So, students can use their answers to question **1** and then multiply them.

Questions 4 and **7** – These questions require students to write the logical steps to calculate simple fractions of a quantity. In question **6**, the order of the multiplication changes. In question **7**, the calculations use larger numbers.

Question 7 – This requires students to know the equivalence of the word 'of' and multiplication. In this question, all the parts are more easily done by dividing by the denominator first and then multiplying by the numerator.

Questions 6–9 – Students should write the intermediate stages of the calculation and not just an answer.

Answers

1 a $\frac{1}{2}$ b $\frac{1}{3}$
   c $\frac{5}{12}$ d $\frac{1}{2}$
2 a £10   b 6 kg
   c 4 apples   d 4 students
   e 7 shops   f £20
   g 9 marks   h 9 m
   i £9   j 25 cm
3 a £20   b 42 kg
   c 20 apples   d 20 students
   e 21 shops   f £140
   g 27 marks   h 36 m
   i £45   j 75 cm
4 a £32   b 21 sheep
   c 60 seconds   d 10p
   e 24 pencils   f $76
   g £13.50   h 60 MB
5 a $\frac{5}{4}=1\frac{1}{4}$ b $\frac{3}{5}$ c $\frac{6}{5}=1\frac{1}{5}$ d $\frac{10}{7}$
6 a 9   b 6   c 4   d 50
   e 4   f 15   g 9   h 15
7 a £35   b 100 m   c $210   d 42 cats
   e 90 kg   f £4000   g 100 km h 90 MB
8 a £24   b £60.80

Objectives

* Define percentage as 'number of parts per hundred', interpret percentages as a fraction or a decimal, interpret these multiplicatively   (L3)

Key ideas	Resources
1 Find 10% of quantities **2** Find multiples of 10%	 Percentages of amounts 1 (1030) Mini whiteboards

Simplification	Extension
Concentrate on finding 10% through division of the base number by 10 before moving on to multiples of 10%.	Students can work through examples where they have to find 1% by dividing by 100. This can be further developed by getting them to find simple divisions for 20%, 5% or 2%. Multiples of these can then also be worked through (e.g. 6%, 40%).

Literacy	Links
Ensure students are confident with the definition of 'percent' (per hundred).	Ask students to think of situations in real-life where they might encounter simple percentages, particularly multiples of 10% (or 5%). Examples might include in shops where items are often seen on sale with '20% off', or in the media where newspaper reports often say things like 'the level of unemployment has risen by 10%'. They could find good examples using the internet, for example, or be asked to do some research as part of a homework task.

Alternative approach

There isn't really an alternative approach to finding 10% quickly but students could be given a matching exercise to replace the questions in the exercise. Two sets of cards, one set containing amounts and the other 10% of the amounts could be used. This could be extended by giving additional sets containing 20%, 30%, etc. or by mixing it up together.

Checkpoint

1	Find 10% of 40	(4)
2	Find 20% of 40	(8)
3	Find 70% of 40	(28)
4	Find 30% of £50	(£15)

Starter – Quick-fire division

Ask students to perform quick-fire divisions by 10. They can record their answers on mini whiteboards.

Example questions:

$300 \div 10$ (30)

$250 \div 10$ (25)

$700 \div 10$ (70)

$30 \div 10$ (3)

$25 \div 10$ (2.5)

Teaching notes

Finding 10% of a number is quite straightforward for most students, so concentrate on working out multiples of 10% by following the examples in the student book and the questions in the exercise.

Plenary

A final quick-fire quiz: Use questions similar to those in the exercise but emphasise speed of working. Mini whiteboards can be used for quick checking of solutions and speed of response.

Exercise commentary

Questions 1–4 – A set of straightforward questions

Question 5 – In part **5a** students can change 15 tonnes to 15 000 kg or work with tonnes which will involve the decimal 1.5×7

Question 6 – This can be done by finding the percentage of what is left $(10 + 20 + 30)\% = 60\%$ so find 40% of £152.

Most students may choose to find 10% of £152, 20% of £152 and 30% of £152, etc.

Answers

1	a	£3	b	9 kg	c	1 cm	d	4l	
	e	$5	f	7 km	g	10 miles	h	13 kg	
2	a	8 cm	b	40 cm	c	16 cm	d	56 cm	
	e	32 cm							
3	a	12 cm	b	60 cm	c	24 cm	d	84 cm	
	e	48 cm							
4	b	120 g	c	200 g	d	280 g	e	240 g
	f	160 g	g	360 g	h	80 g	i	320 g
5	a	10.5 t	b	10 000					
6	£76								

4f Percentages

Objectives

- Understand percentage as the 'number of parts per 100' (L4)
- Calculate simple percentages of quantities (L5)

Key ideas	Resources
1 1% can be found by dividing a quantity by 100 **2** Any other percentage of a quantity can be found by multiplying the value of 1%	Percentages of amounts 1 (1030) Percentages of amounts 2 (1031) Calculators Newspapers and magazines

Simplification	Extension
From question **2** onwards, students can build up their answers based on 1%. For example, if one block (that is, 1%) = 4 kg, then two blocks gives 2% = 2 × 4 kg = 8 kg and three blocks gives 3% = 3 × 4 kg = 12 kg, and so on for other percentages.	Encourage students to use mental methods throughout this lesson. Extend students to consider percentage increases. A jumper costs £30. Its price increases by 15%. What is its new cost?

Literacy	Links
The word *percentage* means 'by a hundred' and the very word reinforces the equivalence between, say, 7%, $\frac{7}{100}$ and even 0.07. This is a good opportunity to refresh these equivalences. Throughout this lesson, use the spoken word to reinforce any percentage, such a 40% as forty hundredths.	Provide newspapers or magazines for the class to use. Students find any article or advertisement where a decimal, percentage or fraction is used. Which format is used most frequently? What value percentage is used most frequently? Are there any examples where the percentage is not a multiple of 5 or 10?

Alternative approach

When using a calculator, the words themselves say which keys to press.
For example, to calculate 15% of 400,

the words: fifteen per cent of four hundred is
the keys: 1 5 ÷ 1 0 0 × 4 0 0 =

to give the answer 60.

Checkpoint

1 a Find 1% of 500 (5)
  b Find 10% of 500 (50)
  c Find 21% of 500 using your answers to the previous two questions. (2 × 50 + 5 = 105)
  d Use your calculator to find 21% of 500 by working out 21 ÷ 100 × 500 (105)

Starter – Crazy clocks

A clock chimes every six minutes. A second clock chimes every five minutes. At a certain instant, the clocks chime together.

How many minutes before the clocks chime together again? (30 min)

If the second clock now chimes every seven minutes, how long before they chime together again? (42 min)

This problem can be extended by asking how many times the clocks will chime together in 24 hours.

Teaching notes

Discuss how to find $\frac{3}{4}$ of 60: find one quarter and then multiply by 3 to find three-quarters. Derive calculator sequence as $60 \div 4 \times 3$. Repeat with different fractions to gain confidence.

Write the words *century, cent, centenary, centimetre* and students suggest the common link of 100. Discuss the word *percent* and its meaning of 'out of 100'.

Explain that a percentage is just a fraction with 100 as the denominator. So, 27% is just $\frac{27}{100}$.

Discuss how to find 27% of 200. Think of 27% as $\frac{27}{100}$. Use the above sequence of keys to find one hundredth and then multiply by 27. Derive the calculation sequence as $200 \div 100 \times 27$. Repeat with different percentages to gain confidence.

As an introduction to question **1**, have a 10×10 grid on which students shade 14%; that is, 14 squares out of the 100 squares. Imagine the brick wall weighing 200 kg and discuss how to calculate 14% of 300 kg.

Plenary

Students use mini whiteboards to answer mixed questions:

What percent is the same as $\frac{1}{2}$ or $\frac{1}{4}$?
What is 5% of £800?
What is the calculator sequence to find 23% of 450?
Discuss answers where appropriate.

Exercise commentary

Question 2 – Each block is 1% of the patio. The students find percentages of 400 kg.

Question 3 – Answers for parts **c** to **f** can be found from parts **a** and **b**.

Questions 4–6 – Students can use written methods of calculation or a calculator.

Answers

1	a	10	b	7	c	21	d	17
	e	55	f	99	g	1	h	100
2	a	4 kg	b	8 kg	c	16 kg	d	40 kg
	e	80 kg	f	200 kg	g	100 kg	h	400 kg
3	a	3 kg	b	30 kg	c	60 kg		
	d	15 kg	e	120 kg	f	45 kg		

4   $30 \div 100 \times 250 = 75$ Jake is correct.

5   a   £20
     b   i   £13.60   ii   £4.40
        iii   £9.60   iv   £0.48

6   a   375 ml   b   1125 ml

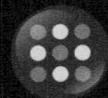

Objectives	
• Understand percentage as the 'number of parts per 100'	(L4)
• Calculate simple percentages of quantities	(L5)

Key ideas	Resources	
1 Convert fractions, decimals and percentages	Frac dec perc 2	(1015)
	Frac dec perc 1	(1029)
2 Order and compare fractions, decimals and percentages	Calculators	
	Newspapers and magazines	

Simplification	Extension
Provide copies of the 10×10 grid for students to shade for each question. This will be useful in particular for question **3** where students must give the simplified fraction equivalent to a given percentage.	Challenge more able students with complex questions: Which is greater: $\frac{3}{5}$ of 800 or 0.72 of 700?

Literacy	Links
Understanding the language of 'percent' is important. Emphasise to the students that it means 'per hundred' and that when converting fractions and decimals to percentages, we are always looking at hundredths.	Bring in some newspapers or magazines for the class to use. Ask students to find any article or advertisement where a decimal, percentage or fraction is used. Which format is used most frequently? What value percentage is used most frequently? Are there any examples where the percentage is not a multiple of 5 or 10?

Alternative approach

The exercise focuses on converting decimals and fractions to percentages but an alternative approach might be to start with percentages (per hundred) and ask students to write these as first decimals (to 2 decimal places) and then convert the decimals into fractions by writing them over 100 and simplifying. This gives a reference point for converting back to percentages when the fractions have to be 'unsimplified'.

Checkpoint

1 Write $\frac{1}{2}$ as a percentage and as a decimal fraction. $\qquad$ (50%, 0.5)

2 What is 75% of 200? $\qquad$ (150)

3 Write in order of size, smallest first. 60%, $\frac{4}{10}$, 0.7 $\qquad$ ($\frac{4}{10}$, 60%, 0.7)

Starter – Crazy clocks

Ask students to find the odd ones out in the following lists and explain why.

$0.1, \frac{1}{10}, 1\%, \frac{4}{40}$

$5\%, \frac{5}{100}, 0.05, \frac{1}{5}$

$\frac{3}{4}, 75\%, \frac{6}{8}, 7.5$

20% of 50, $\frac{1}{3}$ of 30, 10% of 25, $\frac{1}{4}$ of 40.

Teaching notes

Show a 10×10 grid.

Highlight each cell is $\frac{1}{100}$ of the whole and refer to the place value table to link to 0.01.

Invite students to shade 50%, $\frac{1}{4}$, 0.03, etc.

At each example ask students to give equivalent percentages, decimals and fractions – simplifying and demonstrating the equivalent fraction with 100 as denominator where appropriate.

Plenary

Extend students by linking to previous lesson. Discuss how to calculate 0.17 of 200.

Highlight 0.17 as equivalent to $\frac{17}{100}$ and recall calculator sequence $200 \div 100 \times 17$.

Students use mini whiteboard to answer mixed questions: 5% of 300, 13% of 200, etc.

Exercise commentary

Question 1 – Each can be written as a fraction over 100. Students can cancel too if required.

Question 2 – It can be explained that if the number is a fraction with 100 in the denominator, the numerator is a percentage. Alternatively a hundredth is equivalent to 1%

Question 3 – Again, read off the numerator when the denominator is 100. Change **d, e, f** to equivalent fractions with the denominator 100.

Question 4 – If this is not intuitive, change all numbers to percentages.

Questions 5–7– Students can change all numbers to percentages.

Question 8 – Students need to add 70% , 3/100 and 0.27 together. Again, possibly as percentages.

Question 9 – Students may need reassurance that the answer is expected in pounds.

Answers

1 a $\frac{4}{100}$ b $\frac{1}{100}$ c $\frac{7}{100}$ d $\frac{6}{100}$

   e $\frac{10}{100}$ f $\frac{60}{100}$ g $\frac{90}{100}$ h $\frac{67}{100}$

   i $\frac{43}{100}$ j $\frac{99}{100}$

2 a 4%   b 1%   c 7%   d 6%
   e 10%   f 60%   g 90%   h 67%
   i 43%   j 99%

3 a 20%   b 75%   c 90%
   d 30%   e 50%   f 10%

4 $\frac{23}{100} = 0.23, \frac{3}{4} = 75\%, \frac{1}{5} = 20\%, \frac{4}{5} = 0.8$

   $\frac{3}{5} = 0.6, 8\% = 0.08$

5 a $49\% < \frac{1}{2}$ b $\frac{1}{4} > 21\%$ c $0.8 < 90\%$

6 Rosa

7 a Science   b History

8 Check
   $70\% + 3\% + 27\% = 100\%$
   $0.7 + 0.03 + 0.27 = 1.00$
   $\frac{70}{100} + \frac{3}{100} + \frac{27}{100} = 1$ Meg is correct

9 £4

Key outcomes		Quick check
Simplify equivalent fractions.	L5	Simplify 6/9 and 15/25 (2/3 and 3/5)
Use decimal conversions to order fractions.	L5	Write in order of size, smallest first 0.31 3/10 32/100 (3/10, 0.31, 32/100 or 0.3, 0.31, 0.32)
Add and subtract fractions.	L4	Add together 1/4 + 2/4 (¾) Subtract 6/7 – 2/7 (4/7)
Find a fraction of a quantity.	L4	Find 1/4 of 24 (6) Find ¾ of 24 (18)
Calculate percentages of amounts.	L5	Find 20% of 300 (60) Find 5% of 300 (15) Find 15% of 300 (45)
Convert fractions and decimals into percentages.	L5	Write the following as percentages 23/100 (23%) 3/10 (30%) ¾ (75%) 0.3 (30%) 0.45 (45%)

MyMaths extra support

Lesson/online homework			Description
Improper and mixed fractions	1019	L4	Learning about improper and mixed fractions
Simple fractions	1220	L3	Looking at fractions such as halves, thirds, quarters and fifths
More fractions	1370	L3	Using simple equivalent fractions

MyReview

Check out
You should now be able to ...

Test it ➡
Questions

✓ Simplify equivalent fractions.	(5)	1
✓ Use decimal conversions to order fractions.	(5)	2
✓ Add and subtract fractions.	(4)	3
✓ Find a fraction of a quantity.	(4)	4, 5
✓ Calculate percentages of amounts.	(5)	6 – 8
✓ Convert between fractions, decimals and percentages.	(5)	9, 10

Language	Meaning	Example
Fraction	A way of describing a part of a whole. A fraction is written as the *ratio* of the numerator and the denominator	$\frac{3}{4}$ is a fraction with numerator 3 and denominator 4
Equivalent fractions	Fractions which have the same value	$\frac{1}{3}, \frac{2}{6}, \frac{3}{9}$ and $\frac{10}{30}$ are all equivalent fractions
Decimal	A number which has digits after the decimal point, representing tenths, hundredths, thousandths, etc	$1.27 = 1 + \frac{2}{10} + \frac{7}{100}$ is a decimal
Percentage	A fraction out of 100	85% means $\frac{85}{100}$

---

1 Simplify these fractions.
 a $\frac{12}{14}$ b $\frac{6}{9}$
 c $\frac{15}{20}$ d $\frac{8}{16}$

2 Which of these pairs of numbers is larger?
 a $\frac{12}{100}$ or $\frac{2}{10}$
 b $\frac{3}{10}$ or 0.4
 c $\frac{9}{100}$ or 0.6

3 Add or subtract these fractions.
 a $\frac{1}{5} + \frac{2}{5}$ b $\frac{5}{7} - \frac{2}{7}$

4 Calculate these fractions of amounts.
 a $\frac{1}{5}$ of £25
 b $\frac{1}{6}$ of 24 students
 c $\frac{3}{10}$ of 200 m
 d $\frac{5}{8}$ of 40 p

5 Work out these calculations.
 a $6 \times \frac{1}{5}$
 b $\frac{1}{4} \times 9$
 c $21 \times \frac{6}{7}$
 d $\frac{5}{6} \times 36$

6 Calculate 10% of
 a 60 kg
 b 120 cm.

7 Find these percentages of amounts.
 a 30% of 80
 b 20% of 60
 c 50% of 150
 d 70% of 90

8 Find these percentages of amounts.
 a 1% of 500
 b 5% of 60
 c 15% of 120
 d 99% of 600

9 Write these decimals as fractions.
 a 0.8
 b 0.06
 c 0.45

10 Write these fractions as decimals without using a calculator.
 a $\frac{3}{10}$ b $\frac{42}{100}$
 c $\frac{9}{100}$ d $\frac{1}{4}$

What next?

Score		
	0 – 5	Your knowledge of this topic is still developing. To improve look at Formative test: 2A-4; MyMaths: 1015, 1016, 1017, 1018, 1029, 1030, 1031, 1062 and 1371
	6 – 8	You are gaining a secure knowledge of this topic. To improve look at InvisiPen: 141, 142, 145, 151, 161 and 162
	9, 10	You have mastered this topic. Well done, you are ready to progress!

 MyMaths.co.uk

Question commentary

Question 1 – Make sure the fractions are in their simplest form.

Question 2 – Possibly change both to decimals for ease of comparison.

Questions 3–5 – Straightforward questions involving fractions

Questions 6–8 – Straightforward questions involving percentages

Question 9 – Converting decimals to fractions

Question 10 – Part **d** is the only part where denominator is not 10 or 100: ¼ = 25/100 = 25%

Answers

1 a $\frac{6}{7}$ b $\frac{2}{3}$
   c $\frac{3}{4}$ d $\frac{1}{2}$

2 a $\frac{2}{10}$ b 0.4
   c 0.6

3 a $\frac{3}{5}$ b $\frac{3}{7}$

4 a £5   b 4 students
   c 60 m   d 25p

5 a $1\frac{1}{5}$ b $2\frac{1}{4}$
   c 18   d 30

6 a 6 kg   b 12 cm

7 a 24   b 12
   c 75   d 63

8 a 5   b 3
   c 18   d 594

9 a $\frac{8}{10}$ b $\frac{6}{100}$
   c $\frac{45}{100}$

10 a 0.3   b 0.42
   c 0.09   d 0.25

4 MyPractice

1 Make new equivalent fractions by multiplying the numerators and denominators by the numbers in brackets.

a $\frac{4}{5}(\times 4)$ b $\frac{5}{7}(\times 2)$ c $\frac{9}{10}(\times 10)$ d $\frac{4}{9}(\times 3)$ e $\frac{3}{8}(\times 3)$

2 Jake has made some equivalent fractions by multiplying.
What numbers has he used to multiply for each pair?

a $\frac{3}{8} = \frac{6}{16}$ b $\frac{4}{5} = \frac{20}{25}$ c $\frac{3}{4} = \frac{18}{24}$ d $\frac{6}{7} = \frac{18}{21}$ e $\frac{5}{6} = \frac{25}{30}$

3 Use $<$, $>$ or $=$ to order these pairs of numbers.

a 0.1 $\frac{1}{10}$ b $\frac{13}{100}$ 0.9   c 0.2 $\frac{25}{100}$

d $\frac{13}{100}$ 0.19   e 0.07 $\frac{70}{100}$ f $\frac{10}{100}$ 0.10

g $\frac{47}{100}$ 0.50   h $\frac{2}{8}$ 0.03   i 0.8 $\frac{77}{100}$

4 Use the drawing to add these fractions.

a $\frac{1}{8}$ and $\frac{2}{8}$ b $\frac{2}{8} + \frac{2}{8}$

c $\frac{2}{8} + \frac{3}{8} + \frac{1}{8}$ d $\frac{5}{8} + \frac{1}{8}$

e $\frac{5}{8} + \frac{3}{8}$ f $\frac{5}{8} + \frac{8}{8} + \frac{1}{8}$

5 Use the drawing to subtract these fractions.

a Subtract $\frac{1}{6}$ from $\frac{5}{6}$ b Take $\frac{2}{6}$ from $\frac{3}{6}$

c Subtract $\frac{3}{6}$ from $\frac{5}{6}$ d Take $\frac{5}{6}$ from 1 whole

e $\frac{4}{6} - \frac{1}{6}$ f $1 - \frac{5}{6}$

6 a What fraction of these shapes are rectangles?

b What fraction of these shapes are triangles?

c What fraction of these shapes are coloured blue?

7 Niki invites 19 friends to a 'Home-alone' party and they all turn up.

a How many people are there at the party?

b If there are 13 girls what fraction are boys?

8 Calculate

a $\frac{2}{3}$ of 120m   b $\frac{3}{10}$ of 50p   c $\frac{3}{5}$ of 40cm

d $\frac{4}{7}$ of $35   e $\frac{6}{11}$ of 77 litres   f $\frac{8}{9}$ of 108km

g $\frac{7}{12}$ of 72g   h $\frac{9}{13}$ of 78kg   i $\frac{14}{15}$ of 105°C

j $\frac{8}{17}$ of 85 miles   k $\frac{13}{20}$ of £580   l $\frac{2}{25}$ of 900g

9 Calculate

a $16 \times \frac{7}{8}$ b $\frac{3}{8} \times 32$ c $42 \times \frac{3}{7}$ d $\frac{4}{11} \times 99$

e $18 \times \frac{2}{3}$ f $48 \times \frac{7}{12}$ g $\frac{3}{13} \times 65$ h $120 \times \frac{11}{5}$

10 Find 10% of these amounts.

a 20   b 240   c 410ml   d 362cm

11 Calculate these percentages.

a 50% of £90   b 50% of 260m   c 10% of 120cm

d 10% of £350   e 1% of £300   f 20% of 60 minutes

12 Convert these amounts to tenths and complete the sentences.

a 10 hundredths are the same as .... tenths.

b 40 hundredths are the same as .... tenths.

c 200 hundredths are the same as .... tenths.

d 100 hundredths are the same as .... tenths.

13 Express these fractions as percentages.

a $\frac{27}{100} = $ %

b $\frac{80}{100} = $ %

c $\frac{100}{100} = $ %

Question commentary

Questions 1 and **2** – Straightforward questions involving equivalent fractions

Question 3 – Convert fraction into decimal and then order pairs of numbers. **3h** 2/8 = ¼ = 25/100 = 0.25

Questions 4–7 – Straightforward questions involving fractions

Questions 8 and **9** – Students can check answers with a calculator.

Questions 10 and **11** – Straightforward questions involving percentages

Question 12 – Convert hundredths to tenths. Straightforward but students have to read fractions in words.

Question 13 – In part **c** students may need to be reminded that $\frac{100}{100} = 1 = 100\%$

Answers

1 a $\frac{16}{20}$ b $\frac{10}{14}$ c $\frac{90}{100}$

   d $\frac{12}{27}$ e $\frac{9}{24}$

2 a 2 b 5 c 6
   d 3 e 5

3 a $0.1 = \frac{1}{10}$ b $\frac{13}{100} < 0.9$ c $0.2 < \frac{25}{100}$

   d $\frac{13}{100} < 0.19$ e $0.07 < \frac{70}{100}$ f $\frac{10}{100} = 0.10$

   g $\frac{47}{100} < 0.50$ h $\frac{2}{8} > 0.03$ i $0.8 > \frac{77}{100}$

4 a $\frac{3}{8}$ b $\frac{4}{8} = \frac{1}{2}$ c $\frac{6}{8}$

   d $\frac{6}{8}$ e $\frac{8}{8} = 1$ f $\frac{8}{8} = 1$

5 a $\frac{4}{6}$ b $\frac{1}{6}$ c $\frac{2}{6}$

   d $\frac{1}{6}$ e $\frac{3}{6}$ f $\frac{1}{6}$

6 a $\frac{4}{9}$ b $\frac{3}{9} = \frac{1}{3}$ c $\frac{3}{9} = \frac{1}{3}$

7 a 20 b $\frac{7}{20}$

8 a 80 m b 15p c 24 cm d $20
   e 42 litres f 96 km g 42 g h 54 kg
   i 98 °C j 40 miles k £377 l 72 g
9 a 14 b 12 c 18 d 36
   e 12 f 28 g 15 h 264
10 a 2 b 24 c 41 ml d 36.2 cm
11 a £45 b 130 m c 12 cm
   d £35 e £3 f 12 minutes
12 a one b four c twenty d ten
13 a 27% b 80% c 100%

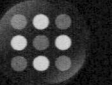
These questions will test you on your knowledge of the topics in chapters 1 to 4.
They give you practice in the types of questions that you may eventually be given in your GCSE exams. There are 70 marks in total.

1 The temperature over a 12 hour period was measured every hour from 9 p.m.
The temperature recorded was

2°C, 2°C, 1°C, 0°C, -2°C, -4°C, -6°C, -5°C, -3°C, -1°C, 0°C, 1°C

  a What was the coldest temperature recorded that evening?   (1 mark)

  b What was the difference in temperature between the coldest and warmest?   (1 mark)

  c Place these temperatures in order from lowest to highest.   (2 marks)

2 Using the numbers 2, 3, 5, and 10, use divisibility tests to find two numbers
in the list that are not divisible.

162, 485, 901, 394, 270, 659, 802   (2 marks)

3 **a** Write down all the factors of 28.   (2 marks)

  b What are the common factors of 12, 20 and 28?   (2 marks)

4 Here is a list of numbers less than 100

1, 9, 17, 22, 36, 41, 42, 51, 64, 67, 71, 81, 93, 97

  a Which numbers in the list are prime numbers?   (2 marks)

  b Which numbers in the list are square numbers?   (2 marks)

  c Write these square numbers as a power.   (2 marks)

5 Round these numbers to the accuracy indicated.

  a 479 (nearest 10)   (1 mark)   **b** 961 (nearest 100)   (1 mark)

  c 1455 (nearest 100)   (1 mark)   **d** 2765 (nearest 1000)   (1 mark)

6 **a** Use your calculator to find the value of these.
Round any values to 2dp if necessary.

  i $\sqrt{69}$ (1 mark)   **ii** $\sqrt{35}$

  iii $\sqrt{2}$ (1 mark)   **iv** $\sqrt{3}$

  b Place the decimal values in order largest to smallest.   (1 mark)

7 Convert these quantities to the units indicated.

  a 0.42kg (to grams)   (1 mark)   **b** 3.1m (to cm)   (1 mark)

  c 1200ml (to litres)   (1 mark)   **d** 72km (to miles)   (1 mark)

  e 4 pounds (to kg)   (1 mark)   **f** 4 litres (to pints)   (1 mark)

8 Use your calculator to work out these times.

  a The number of seconds in one day.   (1 mark)

  b The number of hours in one year (assume 365 days).   (1 mark)

  c The number of minutes in 60 days.   (1 mark)

9 What are the readings given by these scales?   (3 marks)

  a   **b**   **c**

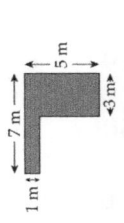

10 Here is a plan for a garden patio.

  a Calculate the perimeter of the patio.   (1 mark)

  b Calculate the area of the patio.   (2 marks)

11 Using values of $a = 3$ and $b = 4$ find the values of these expressions.

  a $4a$ (1 mark)   **b** $3ab$ (1 mark)

12 Add or subtract like terms to simplify these expressions.

  a $3p + 2q - p + 7q$ (1 mark)   **b** $9x + 4y - 7x - 4y$ (1 mark)

13 This formula is used by engineers to determine power:

$$P = F \times v$$

Substitute the values for F and v into the formula to calculate the power P.

  a $F = 40000$ and $v = 15$ (1 mark)   **b** $F = 10000$ and $v = 20$ (1 mark)

14 Simplify these expressions.

  a $7 \times 3x$ (1 mark)   **b** $9u \times 6v$ (1 mark)

  c $24h \div 8$ (1 mark)   **d** $45k \div 9m$ (1 mark)

15 **a** Simplify these fractions as much as possible.

  i $\dfrac{16}{20}$ (1 mark)   **ii** $\dfrac{10}{30}$ (1 mark)

  b Write these simplified fractions as decimals.   (2 marks)

  c Add these two fractions together and leave your answer in its simplest form.   (2 marks)

  d Subtract the smallest from the largest of these two fractions and leave your
answer in its simplest form.   (2 marks)

16 Calculate

  a $\frac{3}{5}$ of £95   (1 mark)   **b** $\frac{5}{8}$ of 416km   (1 mark)

  c 30% of 900ml   (1 mark)   **d** 75% of 180kg   (1 mark)

  e 0.6 of £1000   (1 mark)   **f** 0.1 of 30 litres   (1 mark)

17 Write these values in the form needed.

  a $\frac{7}{20}$ as a decimal   (1 mark)   **b** 0.6 as a fraction   (1 mark)

  c $\frac{1}{10}$ as a percentage   (1 mark)   **d** 9% as a fraction   (1 mark)

  e 78% as a decimal   (1 mark)   **f** 0.08 as a fraction   (1 mark)

Mark scheme

Questions 1 – 4 marks

a   1   -6°C

b   1   8°C

c   2   -6, -5, -4, -3, -2, -1, 0, 0, 1, 1, 2, 2

Questions 2 – 2 marks

2   901, 659

Questions 3 – 4 marks

a   2   1, 2, 4, 7, 14, 28; -1 each error/omission

b   2   1, 2, 4; -1 each error or omission

Questions 4 – 6 marks

a   2   17, 41, 67, 71, 97

b   2   1, 9, 36, 64, 81

c   2 $1^2, 3^2, 6^2, 8^2, 9^2$

-1 mark each error/omission

Questions 5 – 4 marks

| **a** | 1 | 480 | **b** | 1 | 1000 |
| **c** | 1 | 1500 | **d** | 1 | 3000 |

Questions 6 – 5 marks

| **a i** | 1 | 8.31 | **ii** | 1 | 5.92 |
| **iii** | 1 | 1.41 | **iv** | 1 | 1.73 |

b   1   8.31, 5.92, 1.73, 1.41 ; correct order only

Questions 7 – 6 marks

a	1	420 grams	**b**	1	310 cm
c	1	1.2 litres	**d**	1	45 miles
e	1	2 kg	**f**	1	8 pints

Questions 8 – 3 marks

a   1   86 400 seconds

b   1   8760 hours

c   1   86 400 minutes

Questions 9 – 3 marks

a   1   66 kph

b   1   40 ml

c   1   100 ml

Questions 10 – 3 marks

a   1   24 m

b   2   19 m^2

Questions 11 – 2 marks

a   1   12

b   1   36

Questions 12 – 2 marks

a   1 $2p + 9q$

b   1 $2x$

Questions 13 – 2 marks

a   1   600 000

b   1   200 000

Questions 14 – 4 marks

a   1 $21x$; accept only these answers

b   1 $54uv$

c   1 $3h$

d   1 $5\frac{k}{m}$

Questions 15 – 7 marks

| **a i** | 1 | $\frac{4}{5}$ | **ii** | $\frac{1}{3}$ |

b   2   0.80, 0.33

c   2 $\frac{17}{15}$ or $1\frac{2}{15}$

d   2 $\frac{7}{15}$

Questions 16 – 6 marks

a	1	£57	**b**	1	260 km
c	1	300 ml	**d**	1	135 kg
e	1	£600	**f**	1	3 litres

Questions 17 – 6 marks

a	1	0.35	**b**	1	$\frac{3}{5}$ or $\frac{6}{10}$
c	1	10%	**d**	1	$\frac{9}{100}$
e	1	0.78	**f**	1	$\frac{2}{25}$ or $\frac{8}{100}$

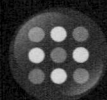

5 Angles and 2D shapes

Learning outcomes

G5 Describe, sketch and draw using conventional terms and notations: points, lines, parallel lines, perpendicular lines, right angles, regular polygons, and other polygons that are reflectively and rotationally symmetric (L5)

G7 Derive and illustrate properties of triangles, quadrilaterals, circles, and other plane figures (for example, equal lengths and angles) using appropriate language and technologies (L5)

G10 Apply the properties of angles at a point, angles at a point on a straight line, vertically opposite angles (L5)

G12 Derive and use the sum of angles in a triangle and use it to deduce the angle sum in any polygon, and to derive properties of regular polygons (L5)

Introduction

The chapter starts by a review of angles in a straight line and angles at a point. Vertically opposite angles are covered before moving on to the properties of triangles and angles in a triangle. The principles of parallel lines, identifying and marking them and then the properties of quadrilaterals are covered in the final two sections.

The introduction discusses the use of basic geometrical shapes, principally triangles, in the creation of 3D images for computer games. This process, which significantly simplifies the creation of 3D graphics, is used in many other areas as well such as architecture and 3D product design (e.g. in the design of cars).

Vector graphics, as opposed to 'bitmap' graphics, defines the points, lines and planes using simple mathematical equations rather than single point definitions and it significantly reduces the amount of computer power and storage requirements and can therefore be a lot more efficient, saving time and computational complexity for the designers.

This website gives a brief description of some of the differences between vector and bitmap graphics: http://www.animationpost.co.uk/tech-notes/bitmaps-vs-vectors.htm

Prior knowledge

Students should already know how to...

- Do simple arithmetic using whole numbers
- Find missing angles in a variety of contexts, at a basic level
- Name and describe some of the basic properties of triangles and quadrilaterals

Starter problem

The starter problem is an investigation into quadrilaterals on a 9-pin geoboard. Students are invited to investigate how many different triangles they can find. Encourage them to think about triangles that look different, even when rotated and/or reflected.

As an extension, students could be asked to find examples of other polygons on the geoboard, for example different quadrilaterals or pentagons. The discussion could develop into finding polygons that are concave as well as the more commonly identifiable convex versions. The geoboard could also be extended to 16-pin or even 25-pin if time and ability allows.

Resources

MyMaths

Angle reasoning	1080	Angle sums	1082	Lines and quadrilaterals	1102
Properties of triangles	1130	Positioning and turning	1231		

Online assessment

Chapter test	2A–5
Formative test	2A–5
Summative test	2A–5

InvisiPen solutions

Measuring and classifying angles	341
Types of triangles and angles	343
Properties of quadrilaterals and angles	344
Opposite angles	345

Topic scheme

Teaching time = 6 lessons/2 weeks

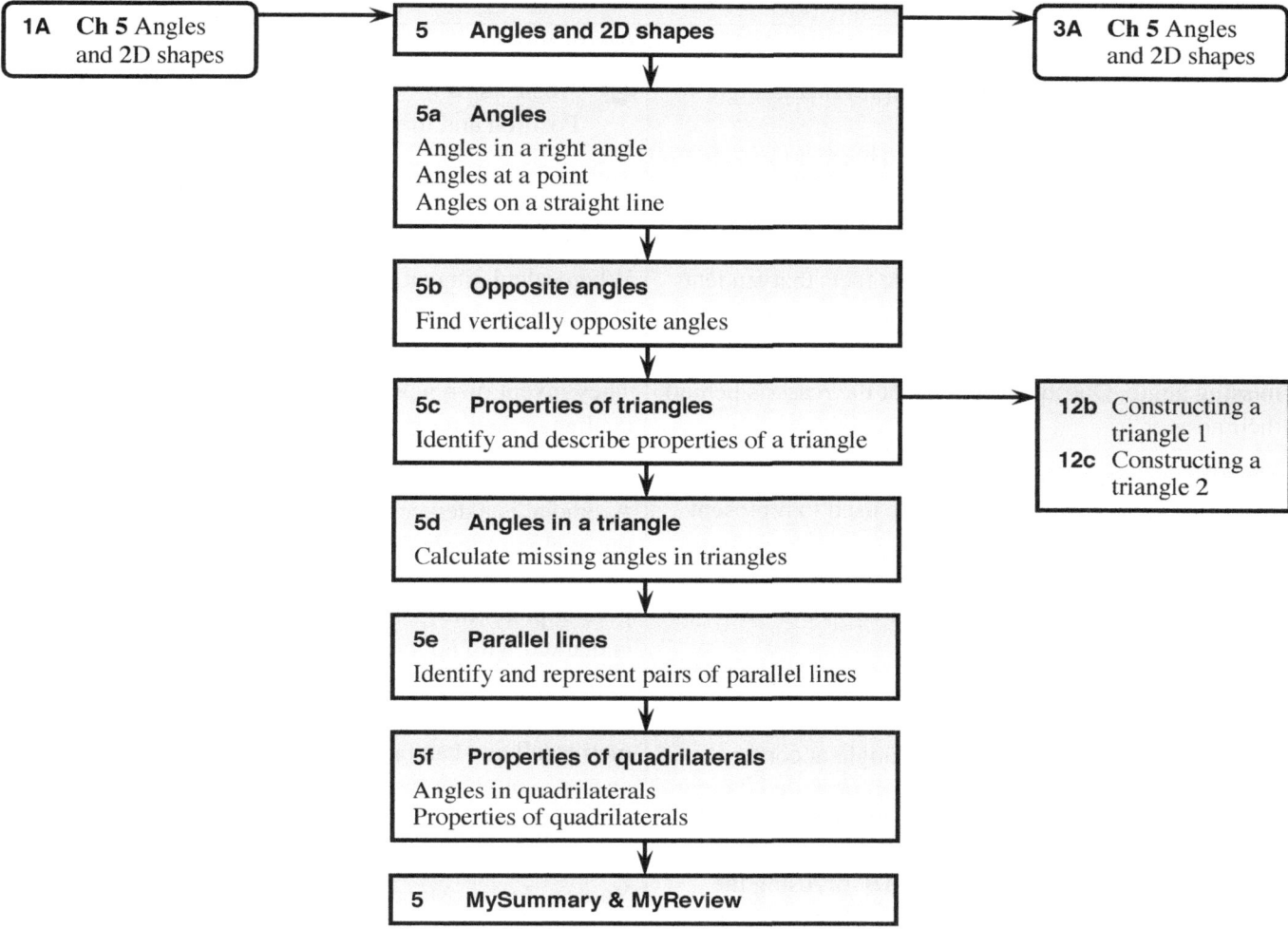

| 1A   Ch 5 Angles and 2D shapes |

| 5   Angles and 2D shapes |

| 3A   Ch 5 Angles and 2D shapes |

5a   Angles
Angles in a right angle
Angles at a point
Angles on a straight line

5b   Opposite angles
Find vertically opposite angles

5c   Properties of triangles
Identify and describe properties of a triangle

12b Constructing a triangle 1
12c Constructing a triangle 2

5d   Angles in a triangle
Calculate missing angles in triangles

5e   Parallel lines
Identify and represent pairs of parallel lines

5f   Properties of quadrilaterals
Angles in quadrilaterals
Properties of quadrilaterals

5   MySummary & MyReview

Differentiation

Student book 2A   88 – 105

Angles
Opposite angles
Properties of triangles
Angles in a triangle
Parallel lines
Properties of quadrilaterals

Student book 2B   80 – 97

Angles
Properties of a triangle
Angles in parallel lines
Properties of a quadrilateral
Properties of a polygon
Congruent shapes

Student book 2C   86 – 99

Angles and parallel lines
Properties of a triangle and a quadrilateral
Properties of a polygon
Congruent shapes

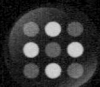

Objectives	
• Use correctly the vocabulary, notation and labelling conventions for lines, angles and shapes	(L5)
• Know various facts about angles at points, on lines and in triangles	(L5)

Key ideas	Resources	
1 Angles on a straight line and angles in a triangle add up to 180°	Angle sums	(1082)
2 Angles meeting at a point to make a full turn add up to 360°	Position and turning	(1231)

Simplification	Extension
Make a list of all the different angle facts that students have met and should know. In question **2**, students may intuitively know the missing angle. Question them about the reasons behind their answer.	When calculating angles in shapes, students should always state the angle fact they are using and show their calculation. They invent own new shapes and diagrams and challenge their neighbour to calculate missing angles.

Literacy	Links
There are various notations that are used to represent angles. The simplest notation is a lower case letter (in either the Roman or Greek alphabet) written within the angle, as in question **3** of Exercise **5a**. Other ways use the uppercase letters which label the corners of a shape. For example, triangle *ABC* has an angle at corner *A* which can be written as $\angle A$ or as $\hat{A}$, provided there is no ambiguity. If, however, the triangle is part of a greater diagram with several angles at point *A*, then the angle is written as $\angle BAC$ or $\angle CAB$ or, using the circumflex symbol, as $B\hat{A}C$ or $C\hat{A}B$. This last method is used in question **4** of Exercise **5a**.	A sundial is a device that measures time according to the angle of the shadow cast by the sun. As the sun moves across the sky, the shadow cast by a vertical pole or plate (the gnomon) moves across a dial which is marked with hours like a clock. The largest sundial in the world is the Samrat Yantra (The Supreme Instrument) at Jantar Mantar in Jaipur in India. It is 27 metres tall and can be used to tell the time to an accuracy of about two seconds. There are pictures of the Samrat Yantra at http://commons.wikimedia.org/wiki/Image:Samrat_Yantra,_Jantar_Mantar,_Delhi,_early_19th_century.jpg and at http://en.wikipedia.org/wiki/Jantar_Mantar_(Jaipur)

Alternative approach
Calculating angles in this exercise gives a good context for practising the students' algebraic skills. Although students will often calculate angles mentally, they can write simple equations to set out their reasoning. For example, if the three angles *x*, 125° and 165° meet at a point and make a full turn, then:

$$x + 125° + 165° = 360°$$
$$x + 290° \ = 360°$$
$$x = 360° - 290°$$
$$x = 70°$$

Checkpoint		
1 When solving a problem, such as finding angle *x* on a straight line formed from angles *x* and 130°:		
	a Which angle fact are you going to use?	(Angles on a straight line add up to 180°)
	b What does the angle fact tell you about this particular angle?	(*x* and 130° add to make 180°)
	c So what calculation do you have to do to find the angle?	(Add onto 130° to make 180°)
	d What is the size of the angle you want?	(130 + 50 = 180, so *x* = 50°)

Starter – Angle estimation

Draw a mixture of acute, obtuse and reflex angles on the board. Students name each angle and estimate its size in degrees. They then measure the angles using a protractor.

Teaching notes

Brainstorm students' existing knowledge of angles. Encourage them to note down important points such as:

A full turn is 360°
A half turn is 180°
A quarter turn or right angle is 90°

Draw a rectangle ABCD with diagonals crossing at E. Ask students which line is the longest. Explain that there needs to be a way of describing a line precisely. Describe the convention of labelling the line by its end points. Ask questions about the rectangle that require students to use the convention.

Now point to an angle and ask students for suggestions on how to describe it. Note that there are three angles at point B so just to say 'angle B' is not clear. Explain the convention of using three letters to describe a 'journey' from start to finish that 'includes' the angle. Using a highlighter, demonstrate the journey from B to E to D that defines the angle BED. Practise by asking questions such as, which angles are acute, obtuse and right.

Students recall existing knowledge and calculate angles in the rectangle. For example, if $C\hat{A}E$ is 60°, what is $E\hat{A}B$? They give reasons for their answers.

Plenary

Show various diagrams of angles. Students calculate missing angles, writing answers on mini whiteboards. Discuss responses as necessary.

Exercise commentary

Question 2 – Students may need explanation of notation.

Questions 2 and **3** – Students discover that the angles in a triangle add up to 180°.

Answers

1	a	30°	b	130°	c	260°
	d	45°	e	45°	f	110°
	g	53°	h	120°	i	120°
2	a	50°	b	70°	c	60°
	d	40°	e	50°	f	90°
	g	Add to 180°			
3	a	$a = 90°, b = 40°, c = 50°$			
	b	Make 180°			
4	190°				

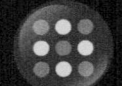

Objectives		
• Recognise vertically opposite angles		(L5)
• Know the sum of angles at a point and on a straight line		(L5)

Key ideas	Resources	
1 Vertically opposite angles are equal	Angle sums	(1082)
2 When two straight lines cross, pairs of adjacent angles make straight angles of 180°	Board protractor	
	Two metre rules	
	Card	
	Dynamic geometry software	

Simplification	Extension
Give students vertically opposite angles drawn accurately, say 60° and 120°. Students use protractors to measure all four angles and note where the equal angles are.	Students should always state the angle fact they are using and show their calculation.
Mention that, in Exercise **6b**, the angles are sketches and not necessarily drawn accurately. So they do not use protractors and have to calculate angles instead.	Students design their own geometrical problem, similar to that in question **5** of the exercise for their partner to work out. They use PowerPoint to animate the logical progression of the solution.
Students consider whether the angles are acute or obtuse to help decide which ones are equal.	

Literacy	Links
Spatial literacy is the ability to use the properties of space to communicate, reason, and solve problems. Some students need help in 'seeing' the relevant part of a diagram.	Scissors consist of two crossed blades, pivoted in the middle. Cross-bladed scissors were invented by the Romans but the first cast steel scissors were produced in England in 1761 by Robert Hinchcliffe. There are pictures of vintage scissors at http://www.collectorsweekly.com/sewing/scissors
For example, in question **4a** of Exercise **5b**, covering up angles s and t so the student sees only r and 60° may help the student calculate angle r.	

Alternative approach

A dynamic approach provides an alternative way to the static introduction.

For vertically opposite angles, have two metre rules rotating about a common central point. Watch opposite pairs of angles opening up or closing. Mark vertically opposite angles with the same colour and, as the two rules open further, mark the angles in a different colour. Notice that there are two pairs of vertically opposite angles. As one pair of angles is increasing in size, the other pair is decreasing.

Draw pairs of vertically opposite angles. Mark one angle and cut card to fit the angle. Show that the card also fits exactly on the opposite angle, making an X shape.

Use dynamic geometry software to demonstrate vertically opposite angles.

Checkpoint

1 For vertically opposite angles labelled a, b as one pair, and labelled c, 60° for the other pair:
  a i Which angle is opposite the 60° angle? **ii** How big is angle c? $(c, 60°)$
  b Which angle makes a straight line with the 60°? (Either a or b)
  c What is the size of the the angle (a or b) that makes the straight line with c? (120°)

Starter – Straight-line pairs

Write the following list of angles on the board:

75° 156° 116° 15° 105° 104° 35° 64° 145° 49° 89° 151° 131° 55° 24° 76° 29° 165° 125° 91°.

Challenge students to match up the pairs that add up to 180° in the shortest possible time.

The task can be extended by using pairs that add up to 360°.

Teaching notes

Draw two intersecting lines (preferably using different colours). Measure one angle using a board protractor and encourage students to **calculate** the remaining angles, pointing out the straight lines.

Note that opposite angles are equal. Ask students to cross their straight arms and pivot them (or use two metre rules crossed centrally) to illustrate that the opposite angles are always the same.

Point out that, when two straight lines cross, four angles are created. The two acute angles are equal and the two obtuse angles are equal.

Draw several vertically opposite angles and demonstrate how to set out the reasons for the calculation. For example,

$w = 50°$ *because* opposite angles are equal
$x = 130°$ *because* angles on a straight line make 180°.

Plenary

Work through question **5** in Exercise **5b** as a class. Point out the different angle facts which have been used at different stages. Provide model answers with the reasons to justify calculations.

Alternatively, show incorrect reasoning and working out for a similar question and challenge students to identify the errors.

Exercise commentary

Remind students that diagrams are not necessarily drawn to scale. They are expected to calculate the angles not measure them.

Questions 2 and **3** – Students can calculate missing angles using one of two angle facts: angles on a straight line add to 180°, or vertically opposite angles are equal. However, they may prefer to use only vertically opposite angles.

Question 4 – Students can calculate missing angles using one of two angle facts: angles on a straight line add to 180°, or vertically opposite angles are equal.

Answers

1	a	30°	b	150°	c	105°	d	75°
	e	153°	f	27°	g	41°	h	139°
	i	112°	j	68°	k	98°	l	82°

2   $m = 22°, n = 130°, o = 28°$

3   a $r = 120°, s = 60°, t = 120°$
    b $d = 100°, e = 80°, f = 100°$

4   $a = 38°, b = 55°, c = 93°, d = 140°, e = 40°, f = 80°$

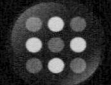

Objectives

- Identify and use angle, side and symmetry properties of triangles and quadrilaterals   (L5)

Key ideas	Resources
1 Triangles can be named from looking at their sides and their angles 2 Some triangles have line symmetry and rotational symmetry	Property of triangles (1130) Straws Geoboards and rubber bands Dictionaries Protractors

Simplification	Extension
The orientation of triangles in question **1** may confuse some students. They can turn the page to give a more comfortable perspective. Three-letter notation for angles may need a reminder. Recall earlier work and refer to the 'journey' from start to finish that 'includes' the angle.	Invite students to measure the angles in the final question of this exercise. Can they generalise about the sum of the angles in a quadrilateral?

Literacy	Links
The vocabulary for triangles and angles is wide and students need to be fluent in it. Angles can be named after their sides or after their angles – and sometimes after both sides and angles. For example, can students draw a right-angled isosceles triangle?	Bring in some dictionaries for the class to use. The word *isosceles* derives from the Greek *isos* meaning 'equal', and *skelos* meaning 'leg'. Ask the class to find other words beginning with *iso* that are related to the word equal. For example, *isobar* – a line on a map linking points with the same atmospheric pressure; *isometric* – having equal dimensions.

Alternative approach

Have straws of various lengths and several of the same length. Straws of different colours help to distinguish different lengths. Arrange the straws into different triangular shapes. Discuss the sides and angles of the triangles and categorise them. Use the words *equilateral, isosceles, right-angled, scalene, equiangular, acute, obtuse, and reflex*.

Cut triangles out of paper. Fold them to show the properties of an isosceles triangle. Fold them to show that an equilateral triangle has three equal angles (and so can be called equiangular).

Use rubber bands on a 3-by-3 geoboard to make different types of triangle. Are there any types that cannot be made on this geoboard? (Equilateral triangle). How many different triangles of each type can be made?

Can students use a geoboard to make a scalene triangle with only acute angles, a scalene triangle with an obtuse angle, a right-angled triangle with an obtuse angle, an isosceles triangle with only acute angles, an isosceles triangle with an obtuse angle, an equilateral triangle with an obtuse angle? Can they give reasons why some of these triangles are impossible?

Checkpoint

1 What name to we give to a triangle that has no equal sides or angles?   (Scalene)

2 If an isosceles triangle has one angle of 40°, what are the sizes of the other two angles? There are two possible answers for this.   (40°, 40°, 100° or 40°, 70°, 70°)

Starter – Triangle bingo

Ask students to draw a 3 × 3 grid and enter nine angles from the following list:

30°, 35°, 40°, 45°, 50°, 55°, 60°, 65°, 70°, 75°, 80°, 85°, 90°, 95°, 100°, 105°, 110°, 115°, 120°, 125°.

Give two angles of a triangle, for example, 80° and 40°. If students have the third angle in their grid (60°) they cross it out. (Keep the arithmetic straightforward.)

The winner is the first student to cross out all nine angles.

Teaching notes

'What am I?' Challenge students to find the shape from the description. Mini whiteboards can be used to draw answers. Here are some possibilities:

- I have three sides and one line of symmetry
- I have three sides and rotational symmetry
- I have three sides, two of which are equal, and one of angle exactly 90°
- I have three sides, two of which are equal in length and one obtuse angle
- I have three sides and three lines of symmetry
- I have three sides and one right angle. None of my sides are equal

In each case draw a diagram of the shape, and mark equal sides and equal angles with mathematical notation.

Invite students to spell key words, using dictionaries where necessary.

Plenary

Draw an isosceles triangle on the board with the top angle labelled 40°. Discuss how to calculate the two missing angles.

Draw an equilateral triangle. Each angle is equal but what is its size?

Ask other questions about the triangle with students responding on mini whiteboards.

Exercise commentary

Questions 1 and **2** – May need to remind students of the notation for a right angle and for sides being equal.

Question 3 – Students measure the sides of the triangles in the students' book. There is no need to measure angles with a protractor (although some students may notice the two right-angled triangles).

Question 4 – List the triangles under headings *Equilateral, Isosceles, Scalene, Right-angled.*

Answers

1	a	equilateral	b	right-angled
	c	isosceles	d	equilateral
	e	right-angled	f	isosceles
	g	isosceles right-angled	h	equilateral

2 a 4 cm   b 71°   c 38°
    d 7 cm   e 60°

3	b	equilateral	c	right-angled
	d	right-angled	e	isosceles
	f	isosceles		

4 ABG, ABO, ABF, ABC, BCO, CDO, DEO, EFO, FAO – isosceles
    ABH, ABI, BCI, BCG, BCF, DCA, EFB, FAC, FAH, FAG – scalene

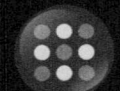

Objectives	
• Know the sum of angles in a triangle and use it to find unknown angles	(L5)

Key ideas	Resources	
1 The angle sum of a triangle is 180°	Angle reasoning	(1080)
	Angle sums	(1082)
	Coloured paper triangles	
	Protractors	

Simplification	Extension
To enable weaker students to engage with angles in a triangle, gain confidence using easier numbers, for example, multiples of 10. Subtraction often proves difficult for students. Encourage use of a jotting diagram and ask students to check work by ensuring the angles add to make 180°.	Extend students to problems that require a combination of a number of geometrical facts.

Literacy	Links
Connections with algebra can be reinforced by setting out the written work. For example, for a triangle with two angles 40° and 80° and an unknown angle, x, write: $$40° + 80° + x = 180°$$ $$120° + x = 180°$$ $$x = 180° - 120°$$ $$x = 60°$$	A geodesic dome is a structure comprised of a network of triangles that form a surface shaped like a piece of a sphere. Geodesic domes are very strong but are lightweight and can be built very quickly. There are famous geodesic domes at the Eden Project in Cornwall and at the Epcot Centre in Florida (with a complete sphere). There are pictures of geodesic domes at http://www.geo-dome.co.uk/ and http://en.wikipedia.org/wiki/Geodesic_dome

Alternative approach

Dissect the triangle by tearing it (with jagged edges) into three pieces, each piece containing one angle. Reassemble the three angles as a straight line. Conclude that the three angles of any triangle add up to a straight angle of 180°.

If students have several identical triangles, they can make a tessellation. By marking the three angles with different labels, it is clear that, within the tessellation, the three angles make many straight angles.

Check the result by each student drawing a large triangle, each one different to any other, and use protractors to measure the three angles. Add the three angles together and collect the totals from all the class. Decide if all the totals are the same and ask why they are not. If all measurements had been accurate, what would the totals have been? Decide that a proof is still needed.

Checkpoint

1   What is the angle at the vertex of any equilateral triangle?   (60°)

2   In a triangle, two angles are known to be 45°, and 60°. What is the size of the third angle?

(180° - 105° = 75°)

Starter – One hundred and eighty!

Ask students to write down their 180 'times table'. Students respond to questions such as:

How many 360s in 1080?	(3)
What is the angle sum of four triangles?	(720°)
How many triangles give an angle sum of 900°?	(5)
How many 180s are there in 3600?	(20)

Teaching notes

Provide each student with a triangle (preferably so that each student has a different triangle). Say that there are many different types and sizes of triangles in the class. Demonstrate with a larger triangle:

- Label each angle A, B and C
- Rip the angles from the triangle
- Arrange the angles so that they fit exactly along the straight line of the whiteboard. Students line their angles against the edge of their book.

Discuss what this shows, recalling that angles along a straight line add to make 180°.

Draw a triangle on the board and measure two angles using a board protractor. Discuss how to **calculate** the missing angle. Demonstrate the working out and reasoning.

Plenary

Draw a triangle with angles labelled 37°, 43° and x. Show three answers:

1) $x = 95°$

2) $37° + 43° = 80°$, $360° - 80° = 280° = x$ because angles in a full turn total 360°

3) $37° + 43° = 90°$, $180° - 90° = 90° = x$ because angles in a triangle total 180°

Discuss misconceptions in each case, and ask for the correct answer.

Exercise commentary

Questions 1 and **2** – Discuss with students that there are two mental methods to choose from: adding on to the smaller angle(s) to make it up to 180°, or starting with 180 and taking away. There is a written method too, but they should attempt am mental method first.

Questions 2 and **3** – The angles are not so straightforward for a mental method. Some students may use a written method instead. (Try to avoid the use of a calculator.)

Question 4 – Use the right angles of the rectangle. Do not use facts about parallel lines.

Question 5 – Students can use line symmetry and fold pairs of angles onto each other, or use rotational symmetry about the centre, or simply use $180° ÷ 3$.

Answers

1	**a**	130	**b**	70	**c**	30	**d**	100
	e	120	**f**	50	**g**	115	**h**	102
	i	78						
2	**a**	59°	**b**	109°	**c**	51°		
	d	$r = 24°, f = 132°$						
3	**i**	d	**ii**	a	**iii**	e		
	iv	b	**v**	f	**vi**	c		
4	$s = 68°, r = 22°$							
5	$\frac{180}{3} = 60$							

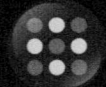

Objectives	
• Derive and illustrate properties of triangles, quadrilaterals, circles, and other plane figures	(L4)
• Describe, sketch and draw using conventional terms and notations: points, lines, parallel lines, perpendicular lines	(L4)

Key ideas	Resources	
1 Identify parallel and perpendicular lines 2 Draw parallel lines	Lines and quadrilaterals	(1102)
	Mini whiteboards	
	Rulers	

Simplification	Extension
Pre-drawn diagrams for question **5** and printed copies of the shapes for question **6** can be used to move the emphasis away from students' drawing/copying to actually completing the actual tasks.	The construction techniques for perpendicular lines could be introduced. Perpendicular bisectors, perpendicular lines from a point on a line and perpendicular lines from a point *to* a line can all be demonstrated and repeated by the students using a ruler and a pair of compasses. Alternatively, geometry software such as GeoGebra could be used.

Literacy	Links
'Parallel' and 'perpendicular' are both key mathematical words and the students could add them to a glossary of key terms by writing their own definitions and checking them with a partner.	The 'New York taxi problem' is an interesting investigation that students could carry out that uses the principles of parallel and perpendicular streets as outlined in the opening notes to this section. The problem and solutions can be found at http://www.gottfriedville.net/mathprob/comb-paths.html

Alternative approach

Ask students to draw two lines, one on one side of their ruler and one on the other side (without moving the ruler from the page). Ask them if they could *ever* get from one line to the other without taking their pencil from the page. Use this as the starting point for discussing the fact that parallel lines never meet and start to work through a precise definition using this fact.

Checkpoint

1   Draw a square. Mark in the arrows to show parallel lines.

(Check students use a pair of single arrows and a pair of double arrows)

2   Draw a trapezium that has two right angles and use a small square to show where they are.

(Check students' drawings)

Starter – How many equal sides?

Quick-fire question and answer, possibly using mini whiteboards: 'How many equal length sides does a... have?' Use square, rectangle, rhombus, equilateral triangle, regular hexagon, etc. to get the students to think about the lengths of the sides.

Teaching notes

Students could refer to the map at the top of the page and through an explanation of the basic definitions of parallel and perpendicular, could start to list the streets which fall into each category. They could do complete lists, or challenge a partner to find streets either parallel or perpendicular to a chosen one.

Formal definitions of parallel and perpendicular are required before students try and draw parallel lines from given information and identify parallel lines in geometrical shapes. Question **6** can be extended to include further quadrilaterals or a shape that has neither parallel nor perpendicular lines (e.g. an equilateral triangle).

Plenary

Play a game such as Barney and Alfie are playing in question **7**. Give the students some geometrical information about a quadrilateral and ask them when they have enough information to identify the shape with certainty, rather than just guessing from a series of options.

Exercise commentary

Questions 1 to 3 – Students may challenge that the diagrams do not show parallel and perpendicular notation. Usually they would but allow for not.

Question 4 – The diagram is given so students can just copy this.

Question 5 – Here the diagram is not given so students may need help drawing the initial line.

Question 6 – Pre-drawn copies of the diagrams could be given to the students to simplify this question.

Question 7 – Discuss all possible answers.

Answers

1 **a** Cross Street **b** Carr Road
   c Rose Street, River Lane **d** No
2 **a** ED   **b** BC   **c** CD
3 **a** EF   **b** AB   **c** GH
   d AB
4 Check students' work
5 Check students' work
6 Check accuracy of students' diagrams
7 Not always, a parallelogram has two parallel sides.

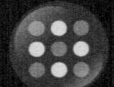

5f Properties of quadrilaterals

Objectives	
• Classify quadrilaterals by their geometric properties	(L6)
• Understand a proof that the angle sum of a quadrilateral is 360°	(L6)

Key ideas	Resources
1 The properties of a quadrilateral define its name 2 The angles of a quadrilateral add up to 360°	Lines and quadrilaterals (1102) A pack of cards giving names and descriptions of quadrilaterals Geoboards and rubber bands A worksheet of the shapes in Question 1

Simplification	Extension
Accurately copying shapes can be problematic for some students. Have them count squares on the gird to get from one corner to another. For example, count 2 squares right and 4 squares up. If they still struggle, provide a pre-drawn worksheet for question **1** for students to label and notate.	In pairs, students give clues to one another to describe different quadrilaterals, for example: Two of my sides are parallel but one is 7 cm and the other is 9 cm. I have two right angles. Mini whiteboards can be used for the second student to sketch the quadrilateral from the description before naming it.

Literacy	Links
There are several spellings that need attention. They include *parallelogram*, *rhombus* and *trapezium*. Venn diagrams can be used to help categorise quadrilaterals. Two intersecting sets of quadrilaterals can be {with all sides equal} and {with all angles equal}. With one set as a subset of another, one set can be {with both pairs of opposite sides parallel} and {with one pair of opposite sides parallel}.	The Trapezium cluster is a bright cluster of stars in the constellation of Orion discovered by Galileo in 1617. The four brightest stars form the shape of a trapezium. There is more information about this cluster at http://en.wikipedia.org/wiki/Trapezium_cluster and at http://www.astropix.com/HTML/B_WINTER/TRAPEZ.HTM

Alternative approach

Use geoboards with rubber bands to create the different quadrilaterals listed on the page of the students' book.

Create new shapes of the same kind. For example, move one corner of a rectangle. What else has to move to keep the shape a rectangle?

Create new shapes of a different kind. For example, a square and a parallelogram can become rectangles by moving two corners; a rectangle can become a trapezium by moving one corner; a kite can become a square by moving one corner. Find which shapes can become an other shape by moving (a) just one cormer, (b) two corners.

Create specific shapes. For example, create a square and rectangle with the same area. Create a kite with one diagonal twice the length of the other diagonal. Create a re-entrant quadrilateral. Create a shape with one pair of opposite angles of 90°, but not the other pair.

Use a 3 × 3 geoboard to find how many of each of the six kinds of quadrilateral can be created on it.

Checkpoint

1 Name the quadrilateral with four equal sides and four right angles. (square)

2 Name the quadrilateral with four equal sides but no right angles. (rhombus)

3 A quadrilateral has angles of 60°, 100° and 140°. What is the size of the fourth angle? (360° − 300° = 60°)

Starter – Quick fire

Recap work of previous chapters on factors, measures, substitution, simplification and fractions. Ask rapid response questions. Students reply by writing on their mini whiteboards. Discuss questions when their answers indicate a need for more support.

Teaching notes

Show various quadrilaterals, their names and descriptions (as in the student book but in a random order). Invite students to match the name with a description, as in question **2** of Exercise **5f**. Demonstrate use of notation of marking parallel lines, lines of equal length and equal angles. Students complete each shape with the appropriate notation. This activity could be done by having shapes and descriptions written on cards which are shuffled and then sorted into pairs.

Ensure that students understand that two lines are parallel if they are straight and equidistant from one another at all points. They will never meet.

Demonstrate on each of the shapes how every quadrilateral can be split into two triangles. Recall that the three angles of a triangle add together to make 180°. Make the case that angles in a quadrilateral must therefore add to 2 × 180° = 360°. Draw a quadrilateral and label three of the angles. Discuss how to **calculate** the missing angle.

Plenary

There are three types of question:

a) Draw a shape and ask questions about its properties.

b) Describe a shape by its properties and students draw the shape.

c) Calculate one angle in a quadrilateral given the other three angles.

Students answer on mini whiteboards and answers are discussed when appropriate.

Exercise commentary

Question 1 – Of the six shapes on the previous page of the students' book, four of them are in this question. Students are required to notate parallel sides and equal lengths and angles.

Question 2 – Refer students to the six basic quadrilaterals on the previous page of their book. It is worth checking that the diagonals of rectangles and parallelograms do not meet at right angles. Students can check this by drawing.

Questions 3 and **4** have students use the basic properties of the rectangle and parallelogram. They focus on notation and labelling conventions of sides and angles.

Question 5 uses the fact that the sum of all angles is 360°. Some students may not spot the right angle in part **c**.

Question 6 – The three points here (about length, intersection and angle) can form the basis of comment on other shapes and their diagonals.

Answers

1 parallelogram; kite; rectangle; parallelogram
2 a Square   b Kite   c Trapezium
   d Rectangle   e Rectangle   f Parallelogram
3 a 3 cm   b 9 cm   c 90°   d no
4 a 7 cm   b 4 cm   c *TS*   d 140°
5 a 60°   b 70°   c 55°
6 Discuss with students

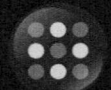

Key outcomes	Quick check
Use the sum of angles at a point and on a straight line to solve problems.	What do the angles on a straight line add up to? (180°) What do the angles at a point add up to? A full turn? (360°)
Recognise vertically opposite angles.	Draw a diagram to show vertically opposite angles.
Classify triangles.	What name do we give to a triangle that has no angles or sides the same? (Scalene)
Use the facts about angles in a triangle to solve problems.	In a traingle two of the angles are 40° and 60°. What is the size of the third angle? (80°)
Recognise parallel and perpendicular lines.	Draw a capital E. Using arrows, show which of the lengths are parallel. Draw a capital T. Using little squares show which lengths are perpendicular.
Classify quadrilaterals.	What is the difference between a square and a rhombus? (A square has equal sides and equal angles. The angles in a square are right angles. A rhombus has two pairs of parallel, equal sides and two pairs of equal angles. These are not 90°.)

⊞ MyMaths extra support

Lesson/online homework	Description
Measuring angles 1081 L5	Learning how to use a protractor. Measuring acute and obtuse angles, estimating angles.

MyReview

Check out

You should now be able to ...

Test it ➡
Questions

✓	Use the sum of angles at a point and on a straight line to solve problems.	⑤ 1
✓	Recognise vertically opposite angles.	⑤ 2
✓	Classify triangles.	⑤ 3
✓	Use the facts about angles in a triangle to solve problems.	⑧ 4
✓	Recognise parallel and perpendicular lines.	④ 5
✓	Classify quadrilaterals.	⑤ 6, 7

Language	Meaning	Example
Angle	A measure of turn, usually given in degrees	90° is a quarter turn or right-angle
Triangle	A 2D shape with three straight sides and three angles	Equilateral, isosceles, scalene and right-angle are special types of triangle
Perpendicular	Lines which meet at right angles	Horizontal and vertical lines are perpendicular
Parallel	Straight lines which are always the same distance apart	Straight railway tracks are parallel
Quadrilateral	A 2D shape with four straight sides and four angles	Squares, rectangles, rhombuses, trapeziums and parallelograms are examples

1 Calculate the missing angles.

a   b
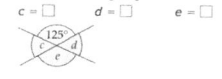

2 Find the missing angles.
$c = \Box$ $d = \Box$ $e = \Box$
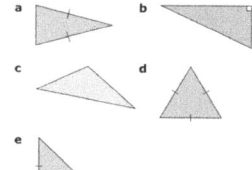

3 Use what you know about triangles to name each of these.

a   b

c   d

e

4 Calculate the missing angle in each of these triangles.

a   b

5 a Draw a line 5 cm long.
  b Draw a second line which parallel to the first and 2 cm away from it.

6 Name these quadrilaterals.

a   b
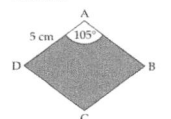

7 Answer these questions about the rhombus.

a Which side is parallel to AB?
b Find the length of side AB.
c Find the size of angle ABC.

What next?

Score		
1 – 3	Your knowledge of this topic is still developing. To improve look at Formative test: 2A-5; MyMaths: 1080, 1082, 1102, 1130 and 1231
4, 5	You are gaining a secure knowledge of this topic. To improve look at InvisiPen: 341, 343, 344 and 345
6, 7	You have mastered this topic. Well done, you are ready to progress!

⬤ **MyMaths**.co.uk

103

Question commentary

Question 2 – Remind students of terminology – vertically opposite

Question 3 – Choosing from scalene, isosceles, equilateral and right-angled

Question 4 – Can check with calculator

Question 6 – Students can explore a non-right- angled trapezium and trapeziums that have right angles. Is it possible to have a trapezium with only one right angle?

Answers

1 a = 107°   b = 95°
2 c = 55°   d = 55°
   e = 125°
3 a isosceles   b right-angled
   c scalene   d equilateral
   e isosceles and right-angled
4 a = 54°   b = 49°
5 a, b two parallel lines, 2 cm apart. One line is 5 cm (length of other does not matter)
6 a trapezium   b parallelogram
7 a DC   b 5 cm
   c 75°

5 MyPractice

1 Use your eye to match each angle with its measurement from the box below.
Name each type of angle.

a   **b**   **c**   **d**

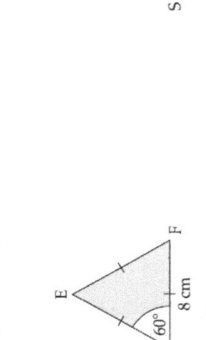

e   **f**   **g**   **h**

| 135° | 360° | 252° | 65° | 90° | 195° | 180° | 25° |

2 The lines in this diagram make a number of angles. State if each angle is acute, obtuse, 90° or reflex.

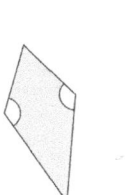

a AB̂C   **b** BĈD   **c** CD̂E   **d** DÊF   **e** EF̂G

3 Find the missing angles.

43° *a*
137° *b*
c 119°
d 61°

4 Find the missing angle in each triangle.

a (33°, 49°, ?)   **b** (94°, 59°, ?)   **c** (39°, ?, □)

5 Copy and complete these statements by using what you know about triangles.

60°   8 cm   E   F   G
R   5 cm   S   71°   T

a This is an _____ triangle.
Side EG is ____ cm long.
Angle GÊF is ____°

b This is an _____ triangle.
Side RS is ____ cm long.
Angle RŜT is ____°

6 Copy this shape.
Mark all the parallel lines with arrows.
Mark all the perpendicular lines with squares.

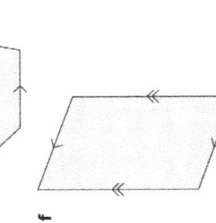

7 Name these quadrilaterals.

a   **b**

c   **d**

e   **f**

Question commentary

Question 1 – Perhaps remind students that acute is less than 90°, obtuse is between 90° and 180°. Reflex is between 180° and 360°.

Question 2 – May need to go over angle notation.

Question 3 – Use vertically opposite or angles on a straight line.

Questions 4 and **5** – Angles in a triangle add up to 180°.

Question 6 – Students need to look for two pairs of parallel lines.

Question 7 – Can give students a list to choose from:

parallelogram, trapezium, square, rhombus, rectangle and kite.

Answers

1	**a** 90°	**b** 25°	**c** 195°	**d** 180°
	e 135°	**f** 360°	**g** 252°	**h** 65°

2 **a** acute **b** reflex **c** obtuse
  d acute **e** 90°

3 $a = 137°$, $b = 43°$, $c = 61°$, $d = 119°$

4 **a** 98° **b** 27° **c** 51°

5 **a** equilateral, 8 cm, 60°
  b isosceles, 5 cm, 71°

6 Check students' sketches

7 **a** kite **b** square **c** rhombus
  d trapezium **e** rectangle **f** parallelogram

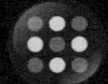
Learning outcomes	
A6 Model situations or procedures by translating them into algebraic expressions or formulae and by using graphs	(L5)
A8 Work with coordinates in all 4 quadrants	(L4)
A9 Recognise, sketch and produce graphs of linear and quadratic functions of one variable with appropriate scaling, using equations in x and y and the Cartesian plane	(L5)
A11 Reduce a given linear equation in two variables to the standard form $y = mx + c$; calculate and interpret gradients and intercepts of graphs of such linear equations numerically, graphically and algebraically	(L5)

Introduction

The chapter starts by looking at plotting coordinates in all four quadrants before moving on to identifying coordinates lying on straight-line graphs. Plotting straight-line graphs using a table of values is covered next before exploring the equation of a straight-line graph for vertical and horizontal lines. Various real-life graphs and conversion graphs are then looked at before the final section which covers the relationship between graphs and formulae.

The introduction discusses how meteorologists use mathematical formulae and graphs to predict future weather patterns. By plotting historical data onto time series graphs, the meteorologists can look for patterns in the data and use this to predict long-term trends. They can then model this going forward in time in order to predict the future patterns that we might experience. Meteorology is far more than the weather man on the evening news and is an extremely complex scientific pursuit. The work of the United Kingdom 'Met Office', along with examples of meteorological data, can be seen at: http://www.metoffice.gov.uk/

A specific example of a time series graph plotting weather patterns can be seen at: http://www.metoffice.gov.uk/climate/uk/summaries/actualmonthly

Prior knowledge

Students should already know how to…

- Substitute whole numbers into simple formulae
- Plot coordinates in the first quadrant of a standard Cartesian grid

Starter problem

The starter problem considers alternative mobile phone tariffs. The best package will obviously depend on the usage by the customer, but the students should recognise that there will be points where one package becomes equivalent to and then better than the previous one.

At 100 minutes usage, package 1 costs £20, as does package 2. Under 100 minutes, package 1 is the cheaper option, but beyond 100 minutes package 2 is cheaper.

Comparing package 3, at 150 minutes usage, package 1 would cost £30 and package 2 would cost £25, so it is still cheaper to have package 2 at this point.

It is only when usage goes above 250 minutes that package 3 finally becomes cheaper than package 2.

Most students will work with informal 'trial-and-improvement' methods but they could be advised to try and work systematically and possibly tabulate the costs at various levels of usage.

Resources

MyMaths

Conversion graphs	1059	Coordinates 2	1093	Drawing graphs	1168
Real life graphs	1184				

Online assessment		**InvisiPen solutions**			
Chapter test	2A–6	The four quadrants	261		
Formative test	2A–6	Plotting straight lines from tables			262
Summative test	2A–6	Drawing graphs	264	Equation of a straight line	265
		Real life graphs	275		

Topic scheme

Teaching time = 7 lessons/3 weeks

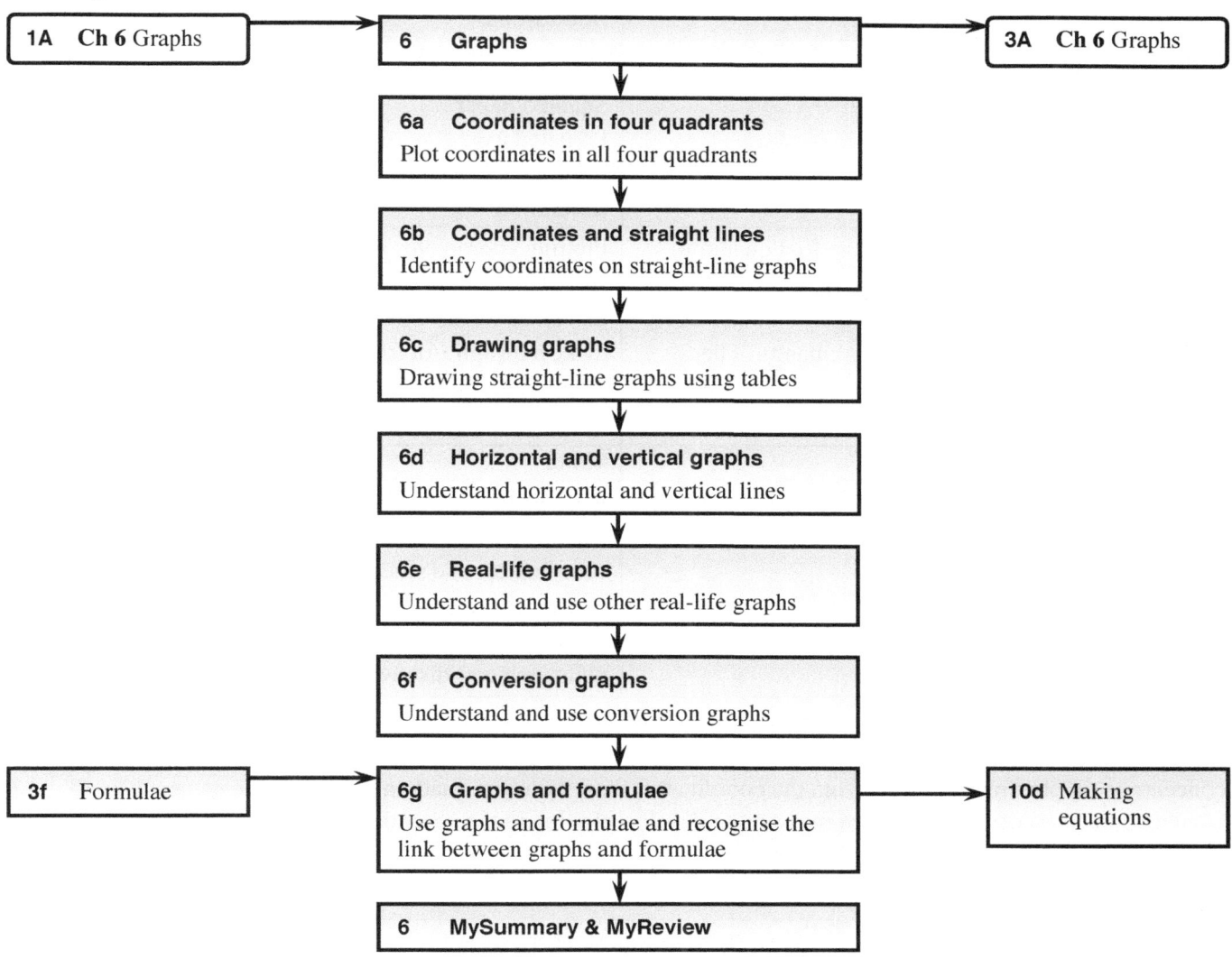

1A Ch 6 Graphs → **6 Graphs** → **3A Ch 6** Graphs

6a Coordinates in four quadrants
Plot coordinates in all four quadrants

6b Coordinates and straight lines
Identify coordinates on straight-line graphs

6c Drawing graphs
Drawing straight-line graphs using tables

6d Horizontal and vertical graphs
Understand horizontal and vertical lines

6e Real-life graphs
Understand and use other real-life graphs

6f Conversion graphs
Understand and use conversion graphs

3f Formulae → **6g Graphs and formulae**
Use graphs and formulae and recognise the
link between graphs and formulae → **10d** Making
equations

6 MySummary & MyReview

Differentiation

Student book 2A 106 – 125	**Student book 2B** 98 – 113	**Student book 2C** 100 – 119
Coordinates in four quadrants	Drawing straight-line graphs	Graphs of linear functions
Coordinates and straight lines	Equation of a straight line	Equation of a straight line
Drawing graphs	Real-life graphs 1	Curved graphs
Horizontal and vertical graphs	Real-life graphs 2	Midpoints of coordinate pairs
Real-life graphs	Time series graphs	Graphs of implicit functions
Conversion graphs		Real-life graphs
Graphs and formulae		Time series

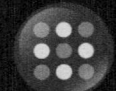

Objectives

- Work with coordinates in all four quadrants   (L5)

Key ideas	Resources
1 Identify coordinates in all four quadrants 2 Plot coordinates in all four quadrants	Coordinates 2 (1093) Squared paper Prepared axes Mini whiteboards

Simplification	Extension
Working with coordinates only in the first quadrant will allow students to re-familiarise themselves with the principles of plotting/identifying coordinates using the 'along the corridor, up the stairs' mantra. Then work through examples which go into the second quadrant, as in question 1.	Plotting coordinates in all four quadrants is the next step. This could be done using a puzzle, or a picture that students have to plot the points for and join up to make a design. Alternatively, the students could be asked to design their own 'word' problem similar to question 4 and challenge a partner.

Literacy	Links
Quadrant Coordinate point	René Descartes is considered the 'inventor' of the standard coordinate system we use today (Cartesian coordinates) and students could do some internet research to find out more about him. They could also investigate more of his mathematical (and philosophical) discoveries.

Alternative approach

The exercise is all about identifying the coordinates from the given grids. An alternative approach would be to concentrate on plotting the points from the coordinates. Start with first quadrant points (students may benefit from prepared sets of axes) and then move on to develop plotting in the other three quadrants. This then links in with the **extension**.

Checkpoint

1 Reflect the point (4, 5) in the y-axis. Give the coordinates of the image.   (-4, 5)

2 Reflect the point (4, 5) in the x-axis. Give the coordinates of the image.   (4, -5)

Starter – Sum to 10

Give the students a number, for example 6, and ask them to write down as quickly as possible the number which would make a sum to 10 (4). Repeat this for other integers between 1 and 10, possibly decimals (to 1 dp) and then negative numbers or numbers greater than 10.

Teaching notes

Emphasise the convention for numbering coordinates (x first) and work through the examples in the student book. Alternatively, have a prepared diagram drawn on graphing software such as GeoGebra to illustrate the principles from the front of the class. Students can respond to quick-fire questions using mini whiteboards or come out to the front to illustrate their answers.

Plenary

Using the example in question **4**, ask the students to spell more words using the letters given and write down the coordinates that spell them. This could be done in pairs, or one person asked to challenge a partner to identify their word(s).

Exercise commentary

This exercise consolidates the point that when coordinates are given, the x-coordinate is first.

Encourage students to use correct notation for coordinate points, i.e. (a, b)

Questions 1 and **2** – These questions give practice in finding points on a grid from given coordinates, and in stating the coordinates of given points on a grid.

Question 3 – Students are asked to give the coordinates of the corners of two rectangles. The coordinates are easily read off a grid, but use the question to discuss reflection of a point in the y-axis. Students should notice that the y-coordinate remains constant, while the x-coordinate changes from positive to negative, and vice versa.

Answers

1	a	M	b	C	c	E	d	A
	e	K	f	S				
2	a	(-3, 1)	b	(4, 5)	c	(-3, 5)	d	(2, 1)
3	a	(2, 4), (6, 4), (6, 1), (2, 1)						
	b	(-2, 4), (-6, 4), (-6, 1), (-2, 1)						
4	a	M	b	A	c	T	d	H
	e	S	f	I	g	S	h	F
	i	U	j	N				

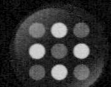

Objectives	
• Generate coordinate pairs that satisfy a simple linear rule	(L4)
• Use coordinates and graphs of simple linear functions to find a simple linear rule	(L5)

Key ideas	Resources	
1 Coordinates of points on a straight line are linked by a rule 2 Knowing a rule allows points to be plotted and a straight line drawn	Drawing graphs Grids with labelled axes Number lines from -10 to 10	(1168)

Simplification	Extension
Drawing and labelling axes can be problematic. Initially, some students may need to have their axes drawn for them.	Ask students to plot the coordinates (1, 6), (2, 5), (3, 4), (4, 3) and describe (a) the positions of the points on the grid, and (b) the numerical relationship between their coordinates.

Literacy	Links
When labelling axes, the usual conventions are: a) just one zero labels the origin when all four quadrants are shown b) the numbers label the grid lines and not the gaps between the grid lines c) the positive axes are labelled x and y and the negative axes are not labelled.	Many patterns and designs can be made by wrapping string around pins nailed into a board. Although all the lines formed by the string are straight, the completed design appears to contain curves. Pictures of designs using string art can be found at http://en.wikipedia.org/wiki/String_art and at http://www.stringartfun.com/

Alternative approach
The aim is for students to 'spot the connection' between the x-value they give and the y-value that the teacher gives them back. A number line from at least -10 to 10 should be visible to all students.
For example, a student says 5, the teacher says 7 and plots the point (5, 7); another student says 3, the teacher says 5 and plots the point (3, 5); then another says -2, the teacher says 0 and plots the point (-2, 0). When students know the 'rule', they write it in words on their mini whiteboards. Eventually, the teacher asks to see their responses.
Repeat for other simple rules.

Checkpoint	
1 Consider the equation $y = 2x$. When $x = 5$, what does y equal?	(10)
2 Does the point (2, 3) lie on the line $y = x + 1$?	(Yes)

Starter – Side to side

On a square grid, draw two axes labelled from -10 to 10. Divide the class into two teams. The aim is for one team to create a snaking line from left to right as the other team creates a line snaking from top to bottom. Members of each team take turns to give the coordinates of a point that can be joined to a previous point which is one square away along the grid (with no diagonals allowed).

The game practises accuracy in giving coordinates in four quadrants.

Teaching notes

Write the coordinates $(1, 1), (5, 6), (4, 4), (10, 10),$ $(11, 11), (3, 3)$ on the board and students pick the odd-one-out. Ask them to give their reason and say what the connection is between the coordinates. Accept 'The y-value is always the same as the x-value'. Discuss how to write this mathematically and accept $y = x$.

Draw the first quadrant for students to plot points at these coordinates. Discuss what they notice; that any coordinate fitting the rule $y = x$ will lie on this line.

Students give coordinates of points that cannot be plotted on the graph as they are too far from the origin. They give decimal values for coordinates and so provide opportunity to discuss that the points can be so close together that they can be joined to make a line. The equation $y = x$ is called 'the equation of the line'.

Repeat with $(1, 2), (5, 6), (4, 5), (10, 11), (12, 13)$ and $(3, 5)$. Students spot the odd-one-out and notice that the y-value is always 1 more than the x-value and give the equation of the line as $y = x + 1$.

Plenary

Give the equation of a line, such as $y = x + 2$. Students use their mini whiteboards to give (a) any point on the line, and (b) the y-value of a point with a given x-value. Include negative x-values.

Give a series of coordinates, such as $(6, 5), (5, 4),$ $(4, 3), \ldots$ and students have to use their mini whiteboards to (a) give another point on the line, and (b) give the equation of the line.

Repeat for other lines.

Exercise commentary

In all questions, students are identifying the patterns in the coordinates and in the points that they are plotting.

Question 1 – This follows the progression: write coordinates, choose whole number coordinates, describe the pattern in words, and write the pattern using an equation.

Question 2 – This question is similar to question **1**, except students have to draw the lines from the given coordinates. Draw the line immediately after plotting points. Do not plot all points and then try to draw the line. Part **d** requires students to use the equation rather than extend the lines.

Question 3 – This question may need further explanation. Students have to identify the equation by looking at the patterns relating x- and y-values of the various sets of coordinates. Students should not simply draw the lines.

Question 4 – This question extends the work informally to simultaneous equations! Students follow a pattern of coordinates to determine whether two lines will cross at a given point. They can check their answer by copying the diagram and extending the two lines.

Answers

1 a i Red $(0, 1)\ (1, 2)\ (2, 3)$
$(3, 4)\ (4, 5)\ (5, 6)$
$(6, 7)\ (7, 8)$
ii Blue $(0, 0)\ (1, 3)\ (2, 6)$
b Red one step to the right and one step up
Blue one step to the right and three steps up
c $y = x + 1,\quad y = 3x$
2 a, b Check students' work
c line A : $y = x + 4$; line B : $y = x$; line C : $y = 4x$
d $(8, 12)$ $y = x + 4$
$(12, 12)$ $y = x$
$(16, 20)$ $y = x + 4$
$(4, 8)$ $y = x + 4$
3 $y = x$: $(0, 0), (1, 1), (2, 2)$
$y = x + 4$: $(0, 4), (1, 5)$
$y = x + 2$: $(0, 2), (1, 3)$
$y = 2x - 2$: $(2, 2), (3, 4), (4, 6)$
$y = x - 1$: $(0, -1), (1, 0)$
4 a Line A: $(3, 11), (4, 12), (5, 13)$
Line B: $(3, 9), (4, 12), (5, 15)$
b No – they cross at $(4, 12)$

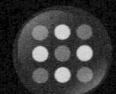

6c Drawing graphs

Objectives

- Recognise, sketch and produce graphs of linear functions of one variable, with appropriate scaling, using equations in x and y and the Cartesian plane
(L5)

Key ideas	Resources
1 Use tables of values to generate coordinate points 2 Plot graphs of simple functions using tables of values	Drawing graphs (1168) Mini whiteboards

Simplification	Extension
Concentrate on examples with just one step such as that in question **1**. Addition of a single value can also be worked on such as $y = x + 2$. Prepared tables and/or axes could also be useful to enable slower workers to get the calculating and plotting parts done quickly.	Examples that include division could be used such as $y = \dfrac{x}{2} + 1$, or examples that have the addition step before the multiplication (e.g. $y = 2(x + 3)$).

Literacy	Links
Emphasise that the 'graph' is simply a visual way of representing the 'function' and try and build in the formal notation for the function in the form '$y =$'	The word *axes* is a heteronym as it can be pronounced in two different ways, each with a different meaning (the plural of axis or the plural of axe). Ask the class to try to list some other heteronyms. Some examples are *minute, lead, wind, buffet, refuse, tear, wind, wound* and *sow*.

Alternative approach

Begin by asking students to find pairs of numbers that 'work' or satisfy a simple function such as $y = x + 4$, having modelled one example. Students can offer their results on mini whiteboards. Select several pairs as appropriate, discussing and checking for accuracy with the whole group. Students should already be familiar with plotting coordinates, but will benefit from the modelling of plotting some of pairs onto a displayed graph.

Checkpoint

1 What is the function machine for the table below?

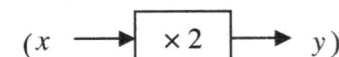

x-coordinate	0	1	2	3	4
y-coordinate	0	2	4	6	8

2 What is the function machine for the table below?

$(x \longrightarrow \boxed{\times 3} \longrightarrow \boxed{+ 2} \longrightarrow y)$

x-coordinate	0	1	2	3	4
y-coordinate	2	5	8	11	14

Starter – Odd-one-out

Which numbers are the odd ones out in these sequences and why?

1, 3, 5, 6, 7, 9 (6: not odd)

1, 4, 9, 16, 24, 36 (24: not square)

The example sequences can be simplified or extended as required to suit the class.

Teaching notes

When drawing tables of values, encourage students to look for a pattern in the numbers or a lack of one that would suggest an error. This is likely to be particularly useful when they start to use negative numbers.

Prepared tables and axes can help speed up the technical work (see **simplification**). In question **3**, the tables could be simplified to make it 'one-step' with the students calculating the values of y directly by applying the function machine to the input x values.

Plenary

Ask students to draw a flow diagram that shows a step by step strategy for drawing a graph from a given equation.

Exercise commentary

Questions 1 and **2** – Students may need help with the equation of the line.

Question 3 – Students may need help filling in the tables.

Question 4 – This could be done in pairs.

Answers

1 **a** 6, 8, 10
   b (3, 6), (4, 8), (5, 10)
   c, d Check students' plots

2 **a** 1, 3, 5, 7, 9   **b** (0, 1), (1, 3), (2, 5), (3, 7), (4, 9)
   c, d Check students' graph

3 **a**

x	0	1	2	3	4	5	6
$x \times 3$	0	3	6	9	12	15	18
+ 1	+ 1	+ 1	+ 1	+ 1	+ 1	+ 1	+ 1
y	1	4	7	10	13	16	19

   b

x	0	1	2	3	4	5	6
$x \times 5$	0	5	10	15	20	25	30
- 5	- 5	- 5	- 5	- 5	- 5	- 5	- 5
y	- 5	0	5	10	15	20	25

4 Blue

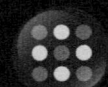
Objectives	
• Recognise straight-line graphs parallel to the *x*-axis or *y*-axis	(L5)

Key ideas	Resources	
1 Lines parallel to the *y*-axis have equations of the form $x = a$. **2** Lines parallel to the *x*-axis have equations of the form $y = a$.	Drawing graphs Grid with axes labelled Graph-drawing software	(1168)

Simplification	Extension
In question **1**, students write the coordinates of several points on each of the lines before deriving their equations. Students write a sentence about each group, using language such as 'The first value is always…' before progressing to use of *x* and *y*. Have some axes prepared for question **2**. Some students may continue to plot (y, x) instead of (x, y). They can devise mnemonics such as: '*x* comes before *y* in the alphabet', 'Across the corridor then up the stairs'.	Students find the equations of four lines that create a square. The square must not be symmetrical about either axis. Students do questions as in Exercise **6d** on axes that extend into negative *x*- and *y*-values.

Literacy	Links
There is a great temptation to confuse the equations of lines parallel to the *x*- and *y*-axes. For example, because the line $y = 6$ runs horizontal across the grid in the direction of the *x*-axis, its equation is often written wrongly as $x = 6$. Similarly, the line $x = 3$ runs vertically up the grid parallel to the *y*-axis and its equation is often written wrongly as $y = 3$.	The word 'horizontal' takes its name from the horizon, the line at which the sky appears to meet the Earth. The part of the sea closest to the horizon when viewed from shore is called 'the offing'. A ship approaching shore would first be seen 'in the offing' from which originated the phrase meaning 'imminent' or 'about to happen soon'.

Alternative approach
Plot points and draw lines using graph-plotting software.   For example, students plot points with coordinates $(8, 1), (8, 5), (8, 0), (8, -2), (8, -4)$. They draw the line through these points by inputting its equation. Have they the correct equation?   Try with points having coordinates $(1, 6), (4, 6), (0, 6), (-3, 6), (-5, 6)$ and draw the line through them.   Students can answer questions **2** and **3** using this software.

Checkpoint	
1 A line goes through the points $(3, 1), (3, 2)$ and $(3, 3)$. What is the equation of the line?	$(x = 3)$
2 A line goes through the points $(0, 5), (1, 5)$ and $(2, 5)$. What is the equation of the line?	$(y = 5)$
3 What is the alternative name for the line $y = 0$?	(The *x*-axis)

Starter – Pigeons and rabbits

Gareth was watching some pigeons and rabbits. He counted the number of heads and feet. There were 12 heads and 38 feet.

Students find how many pigeons and how many rabbits there were.   (5 pigeons, 7 rabbits)

Teaching notes

Invite students to sort these coordinates into two groups: $(1, 7)$ $(3, 6)$ $(4, 7)$ $(11, 7)$ $(3, 9)$ $(3, 4)$ $(2, 7)$

Students give reasons for their grouping:
$(1, 7)$ $(4, 7)$ $(11, 7)$ $(2, 7)$ all have y-values of 7.
$(3, 6)$ $(3, 9)$ $(3, 4)$ all have x-values of 3.

Invite students to describe this mathematically and suggest further coordinates for each group.

Invite students to plot first group and show that they form a **horizontal** line. Repeat for $x = 3$ to get a **vertical** line. Discuss the point at which the lines cross and give the name '**the point of intersection**'.

Students give the coordinates of points for various equations, say $y = 2$ and $x = 6$. They make generalised statements:

Horizontal lines have an equation 'y = a number'.

Vertical lines have an equation 'x = a number'.

Plenary

Show the first quadrant with four lines drawn and labelled A, B, C and D. They are the lines: $x = 4$, $x = 7$, $y = 2$ and $y = 6$. Students write the equation of each line in turn on their mini whiteboards and discuss their responses. Then they write the coordinates of the points of intersection of pairs of lines.

Exercise commentary

Question 2 – Extends beyond the requirements of question 1. Here points are plotted and the lines are drawn first and then the equations are found.

Question 3 – Can students be inventive such that they specify a set of lines which define a shape other than a rectangle or square?

Question 4 – The equations of the axes can cause confusion. There are two ways of seeing them:
(a) plot points on each axis and inspect the x- and y-values, which is the method already used earlier
(b) draw a family of lines, such as $x = 3$, $x = 2$, $x = 1$ and follow the pattern in their positions to draw the line $x = 0$.

Answers

1 **a** A $x = 1$ B $y = 1$ C $y = 6$ D $y = 2$
        E $x = 10$ F $y = 9$ G $x = 4$
    b AB $(1, 1)$, AC $(1, 6)$, AD $(1, 2)$, AF $(1, 9)$
        BG $(4, 1)$, CG $(4, 6)$, DE $(10, 2)$, DG $(4, 2)$
        BE $(10, 1)$, CE $(10, 6)$, FE $(10, 9)$, FG $(4, 9)$
2 **a, b** Check students' plotting
    c set 1 $x = 4$
        set 2 $y = 5$
        set 3 $x = 9$
        set 4 $x = 4$
    d $(4, 7)$ $(9, 7)$ $(4, 5)$ $(9, 5)$
3 **a, b** Check students' plotting
    c Square
    d Check students' plotting
4 **a** $x = 0$ and $y = 0$ **b** y-axis and x-axis

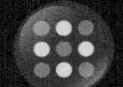

Objectives

- Interpret and draw graphs over time of real-life situations   (L6)

Key ideas	Resources
1 The horizontal axis is always time and each graph has its 'story' to tell 2 The variable may not change over time or it may increase or decrease at different rates	⊕ Real life graphs (1184) Bucket, water and jug Graphs of various 'stories'

Simplification	Extension
There can be difficulties with interpretation. Some students want the *shape* of the graph to have a direct physical connection with the context. Much talk in contexts that can be acted out is needed, such as switching a torch on or slowly opening a blind.	Students investigate the conversion from pounds to dollars (at a straightforward rate such as £1 = $1.50). They construct a conversion graph and use it to change various UK prices into dollars – and vice versa.

Literacy	Links
Being able to read a graph for its 'story' is an essential part of mathematical literacy, but this skill is not easily gained. The graphs of this exercise are all against 'time'. As the graph moves left to right, the story unfolds. The vertical axis describes a variable which either increases, decreases or stays the same. So, present students with many graphs against 'time' and have them talk about how the variable increases, decreases or is steady as time passes. Note that any vertical section of the graph indicates that something has happened 'in no time at all'.	In finance, the exchange rate between two currencies is the price at which one country's currency can be exchanged for another currency. Most of the rates change daily, although some exchange rates are fixed. Current exchange rates and a conversion calculator can be found at http://uk.finance.yahoo.com/currency-converter?u and at http://www.x-rates.com/calculator.html

Alternative approach

Undertake an 'experiment' and have a running commentary over time, with the graph being drawn at the time that the changes take place. For example, pour water into an empty bucket. Have students sketch a graph of depth of water over time on their mini whiteboards, as the teacher talks through what is happening. For example, 'There's no water in the bucket, so the depth is zero. I'm pouring a jugful very slowly, so the depth is increasing slowly. The jug is now empty and the depth in the bucket has stopped rising. Here's another jugful and I'm pouring this in very slowly… at last the jug is empty and the depth is not changing. I'm carrying the bucket to the sink and the surface of the water is wobbling about. At the sink, I pour all the water out very quickly. There's none left'.

Compare graphs. The teacher draws a graph too. Compare graphs with the teacher's. Discuss how speed is shown on the graph.

Repeat with the angle turned through by the classroom door, from 0° when closed to being fully open, with pauses on the way – and then quickly shut.

Checkpoint

1 Sketch a graph that represents a light being turned on quickly, left on for a while and then slowly fading out. Draw the graph with time on the *x*-axis and brightness on the *y*-axis.

(Check students graphs)

Starter – Quick fire

Recap work of previous chapters on factors, measures, substitution, simplification and fractions. Ask rapid response questions. Students reply by writing on their mini whiteboards. Discuss questions when their answers indicate a need.

Teaching notes

Practise informal understanding by asking oral questions. Describe a situation from the building trade. A bricklayer works at a steady rate. If he lays 25 bricks in 15 minutes, how many brick does he lay in 30, 45 and 60 minutes. Point out that, as time doubles, so does the number of brick he lays. After an hour, he rests for 15 minutes and then works for 90 minutes more at the same rate without stopping. He then stops for lunch and has a 30 minute break.

Without labelling axes numerically, students sketch a graph of the number of bricks laid over time. If they have difficulty, construct a table of values for the number of bricks every 15 minutes. Discuss the 'story' of what happens without referring to the scales on the axes. Ask how the graph would change if the bricklayer speeded up or slowed down from his steady rate.

Refer to the graphs in the student book and discuss the stories of each line or curve.

Plenary

Draw a graph which describes a variable over time in a realistic context and label significant points on the graph with A, B, C, …

Tell the 'story' of the graph. Then re-tell it interspersed by saying 'Where are you now on the graph?' Students respond by writing the letter appropriate to that stage of the 'story'.

Exercise commentary

Question 1 – This is a good test of how well students can 'read' the story of a graph. Whereas scenarios B and C are straightforward to match, other scenarios are not so. Much whole-class discussion will be worthwhile.

Question 2 – This will show how well students have understood question **1**.

Question 3 – All students will have different graphs. Telling the 'story' is necessary. Have students show their graph and tell their story.

Question 4 – It could be graph D also. The question does not say that water is flowing at a constant rate.

Answers

1   **a**   D   **b**   F   **c**   A   **d**   B
   e   E   **f**   C

2   **a**   The graph slopes upwards with a gradual increase in gradient
   b   The graph slopes downwards with a sharp negative gradient
   c   The graph shows four peaks of equal height and gradient
   d   There is a very gradual increase in gradient, the graph remains horizontal for a short length of time before a sharp negative gradient

3   Discuss with students

4   **a**   2nd graph as flow is constant but bowl gets wider
   b   1st graph: cylindrical container
       3rd graph: wide base, narrow middle, wide top
       4th graph: gradually getting narrower towards top

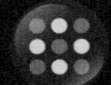

Objectives

- Model situations or procedures by using graphs   (L5)
- Plot and interpret graphs of simple linear functions arising from real-life situations (for example, conversion graphs)   (L5)

Key ideas	Resources
1 Plot conversion graphs 2 Use conversion graphs to convert units	Conversion graphs (1059) Prepared axes and/or tables Mini whiteboards

Simplification	Extension
The conversion graphs used here are simple proportional conversions and therefore should not pose too many problems for the students. However, slower workers may benefit from prepared tables and/or axes so the emphasis can be on using them rather than copying out the tables, etc.	Conversion graphs that include a 'fixed' cost such as energy tariffs or possibly mobile phone tariffs can be looked at. For example, can the students draw a conversion graph for $C = 2x + 20$? Or what about drawing a graph for the relationship between °C and °F (question **5**)?

Literacy	Links
Conversion The idea of converting currencies links into financial literacy and also the development of students' understanding of different currencies and countries.	Students could be asked to find out (or recall) other common conversions (such as inches to cm ($\times 2.5$) and draw a conversion graph of this. Alternatively, they could look up some actual currency conversions ($ to £, for example) and try working with these.

Alternative approach

The approach in question **2** could be used first of all to get the students to think about the conversions numerically before using a graph at all. The graph for miles to km in the student book can be *derived* rather than simply given and the students could then practise reading off the graph once it has been drawn.

Checkpoint

1 A line passes through the points $(0, 4), (1, 4), (2, 4), (3, 4)$
   a What is the same about the coordinates?   (All of the y values are 4)
   b What is the name of the line?   ($y = 4$)
2 A line passes through the points $(2, 0), (2, 1), (2, 2), (2, 3)$
   a What is the same about the coordinates?   (All of the x values are 2)
   b What is the name of the line?   ($x = 2$)

Starter – Simple Substitution

Give the students a simple function such as $y = 3x$ and then quickly generate numbers (possibly using a dice). The students have to substitute the value for x and work out y as quickly as possible. Responses using mini whiteboards can be made quickly. The function could be changed to a two-step one or the values substituted could represent y instead.

Teaching notes

The emphasis at the start is on reading from the graph given in the example. This can be done by quick-fire response on mini whiteboards or by formal exercise. In question **3**, the students have to draw their own conversion graph first so working through the second example more formally may be required to give them the structure to complete their own.

Plenary

£1 = $1.50. Write down ten amounts in £ and their equivalent value in $ as quickly as possible. Encourage 'harder' equivalences. Students can check each other's examples.

Exercise commentary

Questions 1 and **2** – Students are asked to convert between miles and kilometres by using the graph in the student book. This will give practices in reading values accurately.

Question 2 – Advise students to plot all of the coordinates neatly before attempting to draw the line.

Question 5 – This question asks the students to convert temperature by using a formula rather than using a graph. Discuss whether it is easier to work with a formula or a conversion graph.

Answers

1	a	56.25	b	31.25	c	62.5	d	6.25
	e	43.75	f	21.9	g	33.75	h	60
2	a	32	b	96	c	64	d	40
	e	24	f	72	g	88	h	56

3 a

£	0	10	20	40	80	100
€	0	12	24	48	96	120

b, c		Check students' graph					
d	36	e	50	f	100	g	108
h	100.8	i	80				

4 a No   b $80 \times 1.2 = 102$

5 a $9 \times \frac{22}{5} + 32 = 71.6$ so the answers are consistent

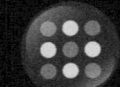

6g Graphs and formulae

Objectives

- Model situations or procedures by translating them into algebraic expressions or formulae and by using graphs   (L5)

Key ideas	Resources
1 Writing formulae from graphs 2 Use the formulae to solve problems	⊕ Conversion graphs (1059) Mini whiteboards

Simplification	Extension
Concentrate on relationships that show proportionality such as those in questions **1** and **2**.	Students could be given further examples of formulae (algebraic) and asked to draw the graphs of them. These do not have to be linear. An example could be $A = x^2$ showing how the area of a square changes with the side length x.

Literacy	Links
The formulae here are all given in 'written' form rather than using algebra but the students could be guided to link the two representations. This will hopefully improve their algebraic literacy as well as their overall literacy.	Questions **3** and **4** look at temperature change over time. Isaac Newton is famous for (among other things) his law on cooling. While the mathematics underpinning the law is far too complex for students at this level, the general principle can be investigated and/or discussed: The rate of change of the temperature of an object is proportional to the difference between its own temperature and the surrounding temperature. Students can also look up some facts about the life and work of Newton as an internet research/homework task.

Alternative approach

Give the students a set of cards with word formulae, tables of values and graphs on them. They can discuss in pairs or small groups which cards go together to make sets of three matching cards. This will stimulate discussion, generate debate and enable the students to develop the links between the three representations.

Checkpoint

1   The table below shows how a liquid changes its temperature as it is heated.

Time (minutes)	0	1	2	3
Temperature (°C)			50	

The temperature starts at 10 °C and adds 20 °C for every minute that it is heated.

a   Complete the table.   (10, 30, 70)

b   Fill in the gaps in the formula: temperature = ___ × number of minutes   + _____

(20 × number of minutes + 10)

Starter – Write algebraically

Give the students some basic operations and ask them to write them concisely using algebra. For example, '2 lots of a number' ($2x$), 'a number plus 7' ($x + 7$), 'double a number plus 3' ($2x + 3$). Examples can be simplified or made harder as appropriate and responses can be via mini whiteboards.

Teaching notes

The first two questions are proportional relationships so students should be able to read off these formulae quite easily. They may need help writing the formulae for the other questions in simple terms. Focus on them being able to continue the pattern or *use* the formula rather than exactly what it reads like when they have written it down. Formalising the algebra can be done if appropriate for the class.

Plenary

The formula for a particular scientific experiment into temperature change is $T = 2x + 7$ where T is the temperature in °C and x is the time in minutes. What is the temperature after:

5 minutes (17)

10 minutes (27)

7 minutes (21)

13 minutes (33)?

Further examples can be provided.

Exercise commentary

Questions 1 and **2** – The students may need help writing formula sentences even though they spot the connection.

Question 3 – This is quite a jump. For every minute the temperature goes up by 15° so the formula sentence is 'the temperature starts at 8 °C then add 15 °C for every minute that it is heated'.

Question 4 – This encourages the jump from the written word to using symbols.

Answers

1   4 times

2 a

Week	0	1	2	3	4
Money saved (£)	0	20	40	60	80

   b   Haziah starts with nothing but saves £20 each week.

   c   Multiple answers possible, e.g. after 3 weeks
       $3 \times £20 = £60$

   d   £120

3 a   The temperature starts at 8 °C and goes up by 15 °C for every minute the water is heated

   b   Multiple answers possible, e.g. when time = 3 minutes, temperature = $8 + 3 \times 15 = 8 + 45 = 53$ °C

   c

Time (minutes)	0	1	2	3	4	5
Temp (0 °C)	8	23	38	53	68	83

4   temperature = $10 \times m + 30$

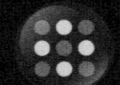

Key outcomes	Quick check
Read and plot coordinates in all four quadrants. L4	Reflect the point (2, 3) in the *x*-axis. Give the coordinates of the image. (2, -3)
Use a table of values to draw a straight-line graph. L5	For the line $y = x + 3$, copy and complete this table of values: **Table:** 	*x*	0	1	2	3	 |---|---|---|---|---|
y	3				 $((1, 4), (2, 5), (3, 6))$
Identify the equations of horizontal and vertical graph lines. L5	Draw axes from -5 to 5 for both *x* and *y*. Draw and label the line $y = 3$ and $x = -2$.
Use real-life graphs and conversion graphs. L5	The conversion rate for US dollars ($) to UK pounds is £1 = $ 1.70 Copy and complete this table by multiplying by 1.7 **Table:** | £	0	10	20	30	40	50 | |---|---|---|---|---|---|---|
$	0	17					 $((20, 34), (30, 51), (40, 68), (50, 85))$
Create and use formulae. L5	The table shows how much money Tilly saved. **Table:** | Week	0	1	2	3	4 | |---|---|---|---|---|---|
Money saved (£)	0	10	20	30	40	 Use the table to write a fomula to connect money saved (M) and the number of weeks (*x*). $(M = 10x)$

⊕ MyMaths extra support

Lesson/online homework	Description
Line graphs and two-way tables 1198 (L4)	Solving problems by reading information from a line graph. Reading information from a two-way table.

MyReview

Check out
You should now be able to ...

		Test it ➡ Questions
✓	Read and plot coordinates in all four quadrants.	④ 1
✓	Use a table of values to draw a straight-line graph.	⑤ 2 – 3
✓	Identify the equations of horizontal and vertical graph lines.	⑤ 4
✓	Use real-life graphs and conversion graphs.	⑤ 5
✓	Create and use formulae.	⑤ 6

Language	Meaning	Example
Coordinates	A pair of numbers that, together, give the position of a point	The coordinates (3, 4) give the position of the point A
Table	Two columns of values that may be plotted as coordinates	x: 1 2 3 4 5 / y: 2 4 6 8 10
Horizontal line	A line on a graph parallel to the x-axis	$y = 1$ or -3 or any constant
Vertical line	A line on a graph parallel to the y-axis	$x = 2$ or -1.5 or any constant
Straight-line graph	A graph with an equation that can be written in the form $y = mx + c$	$y = 2x + 5$, $y = 5x$, $y = -6$ and $2x + 3y = 5$ are all straight lines
Real-life graph	A graph which can be used to illustrate a real-life situation	A graph of distance versus time for your journey to school
Formula	A rule connecting different quantities. You can write a formula in words or symbols	length = width + 3 / $L = W + 3$

1 Give the coordinates of points A, B, C and D.

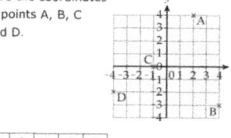

2
x	0	1	2	3
y	6	4	2	0

a Write out the coordinate pairs given in the table.

b Plot the points on the grid.

c Join the points with a straight line.

3

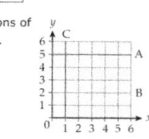

Use the function machine to complete the table of values.

x	1	2	3	4
y				

4 Write the equations of lines A, B, and C.

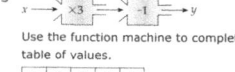

5

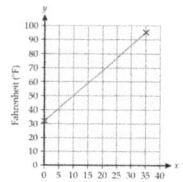

This graph converts centigrade (°C) to Fahrenheit (°F).

a Convert 5 °C to Fahrenheit.

b Convert 68 °F to centigrade.

6 The graph shows how much money Julian has spent by the end of each day of his holiday.

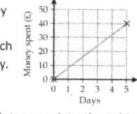

a Use the graph to complete the table.

Day	0	1	2	3	4
Money spent (£)		8			32

b Write a sentence formula for the total Julian has spent each day.

c Julian is staying on holiday for a total of 2 weeks. Use your formula to work out how much Julian will have spent by the end of his holiday.

What next?

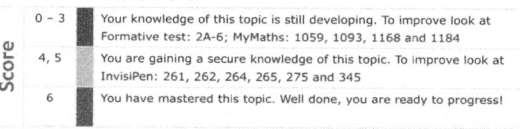

Score		
	0 – 3	Your knowledge of this topic is still developing. To improve look at Formative test: 2A-6; MyMaths: 1059, 1093, 1168 and 1184
	4, 5	You are gaining a secure knowledge of this topic. To improve look at InvisiPen: 261, 262, 264, 265, 275 and 345
	6	You have mastered this topic. Well done, you are ready to progress!

 MyMaths.co.uk

Question commentary

Questions 1 and **2** – Students may need reminding to give the *x*-coordinate first.

Question 4 – Students may need reminding that horizontal lines are $y = c$ and vertical lines are $x = c$.

Question 5 – It is relatively easy to read the values from graph.

Question 6 – Students may notice that the money is going up by £8 each time.

Answers

1 A(2, 4)   B(4, -3)
   C(-1, 0)   D(-4, -2)

2 a (0, 6), (1, 4), (2, 2), (3, 0)
   b, c Check students' plotting

3
x	1	2	3	4
y	2	5	8	11

4 A: $y = 5$ B: $y = 2$
   C: $x = 1$

5 a 41 °F   b 20 °C

6 a
Day	0	1	2	3	4
Money spent (£)	0	8	16	24	32

   b multiply the day by 8
   c £112

6 MyPractice

1 Write the coordinates of the points on the grid.

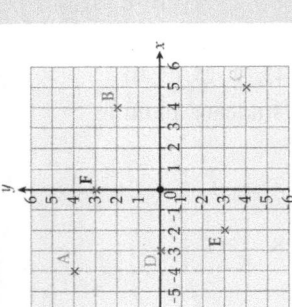

2 Match each equation with the set of coordinates that belong to it.

Set 1	Set 2	Set 3
(0, 0), (1, 3), (2, 6)	(3, 0), (4, 1), (7, 4)	(0, 3), (3, 6), (4, 7)

a $y = x + 3$ b $y = 3x$ c $y = x - 3$

3 Complete the diagrams using the operations shown.

a
x		y
0	→ +7 →	□
3	→ +7 →	□
9	→ +7 →	□
13	→ +7 →	□

b
x		y
0	→ −9 →	□
1	→ −9 →	□
2	→ −9 →	□
3	→ −9 →	□

c
x		y
0	→ ×4 →	□
4	→ ×4 →	□
7	→ ×4 →	□
20	→ ×4 →	□

d
x		y
9	→ ÷3 →	□
15	→ ÷3 →	□
30	→ ÷3 →	□
21	→ ÷3 →	□

4 The red line is called $x = 2$ because all of its x-coordinates are 2.

The yellow line is called $y = 2$ because all of its y-coordinates are 2.

Name the four lines that make the frame of the orange rectangle.

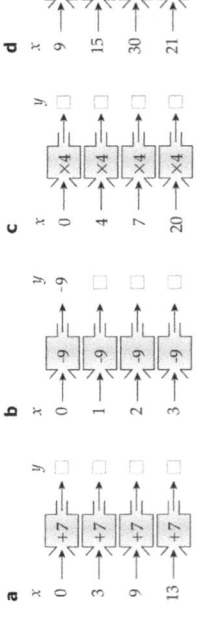

5 Match these graphs with the 'stories' below.

a A car travels at a steady speed.

b A car slows down to stop at a red light.

c A car speeds up while driving.

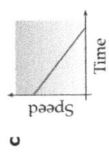
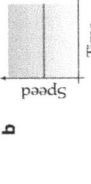

6 The conversion rate from pounds (£) to US dollars ($) is £1 = $1.60.

a Copy and complete this table by multiplying by 1.6.

Pounds (£)	0	10	20	30	40	50
Dollars ($)	0	16				

b Use the values in the table to plot coordinates onto set of axes.

c Carefully join the coordinates to draw an accurate straight line.

d Use your conversion graph to convert:
£25 = $ ____

7 Jo saves £15 for five weeks.

a Complete the table of values below.

Week	0	1	2	3	4	5
Money saved (£)	15	30				

b Complete this formula sentence for Jo's savings.
'The total money saved is the number of weeks
× .... + ...'

c Use the table to draw a graph on axes like these.

d Use any pair of values from your graph to show that your formula works.

e Use your formula to calculate how much Jo will have saved if she continues saving for another five weeks.

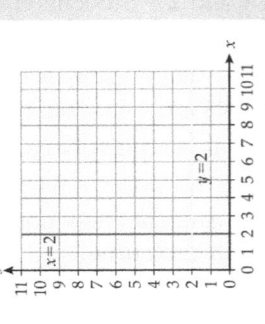

Question commentary

Questions 1 and **2** – Remind students that the *x*-coordinate comes first.

Question 5 – Recognise that 'steady' means unchanging.

Question 6 – Give the students a scale to work with.

Question 7 – The money saved is going up by £15 each week.

Answers

1 **a** (-4, 4) **b** (4, 2) **c** (5, -4)
 d (0, -3) **e** (-2, -3) **f** (0, 3)

2 **a** Set 3 **b** Set 1 **c** Set 2

3 **a** $0 \rightarrow 7$ **b** $0 \rightarrow -9$
  $3 \rightarrow 10$ $1 \rightarrow -8$
  $9 \rightarrow 16$ $2 \rightarrow -7$
  $13 \rightarrow 20$ $3 \rightarrow -6$
 c $0 \rightarrow 0$ **d** $9 \rightarrow 3$
  $4 \rightarrow 16$ $15 \rightarrow 5$
  $7 \rightarrow 28$ $30 \rightarrow 10$
  $20 \rightarrow 80$ $21 \rightarrow 7$

4 $x = 4, y = 5, x = 8, y = 8$

5 **a** b **b** c **c** a

6 **a**

Pounds	10	20	30	40	50
Dollars	16	32	48	64	80

 b, c Check graph is a straight line through (0, 0) and (10, 16)

 d £25 = $40

7 **a**

Week	0	1	2	3	4	5
Money saved (£)	15	30	45	60	75	90

 b $\times 15 + 15$

 c Check graph is a straight line through (0, 15) and (5, 90)

 d Check on any point, e.g. $2 \times 15 + 15 = 45$

 e £165

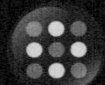

Related lessons		Resources	
Angles	5a	Interior exterior angles	(1100)
Properties of triangles	5c	Sum of angles in a polygon	(1320)
Properties of quadrilaterals	5f	Lines of symmetry	(1114)
Tessellation	9f	Rotation symmetry	(1116)
		Examples of patchwork	
		Isometric paper	

Simplification	Extension
Task **2** parts **b** and **c** could be scaffolded or omitted. Students could work on squared or isometric paper for task **3** to aid their designing. Patterns based on shapes other than the square could be omitted.	Ask students to find the internal angles in regular polygons, from equilateral triangle to dodecagon. (60°, 90°, 108°, 120°, $128\frac{4}{7}$°, 135°, 140°, 144°, $147\frac{3}{11}$°, 150°) Using knowledge of these angles ask students to see how many polygons of one type they can fit exactly around a point. (6 equilateral triangles; 4 squares; 3 hexagons). If you can use two polygons how many possibilities are there now? (2 squares and 3 equilateral triangles (two ways); 1 or 2 hexagons and 4 or 2 equilateral triangles; 2 octagons and 1 square; 2 dodecagons and 1 equilateral triangle) Can you use this knowledge to create six semi-regular tessellations? Can you find the other two semi-regular tessellations? (Based on 1 equilateral triangle, 2 squares and 1 hexagon or 1 square, 1 hexagon and 1 dodecagon)

Links

Students could research the work of the Dutch artist M C Esher and identify any of his work that they think is based on tessellation. Alternatively, they can look at tessellations they meet in everyday life or the Islamic art of the Alhambra Palace in Spain. http://www.alhambra-patronato.es/

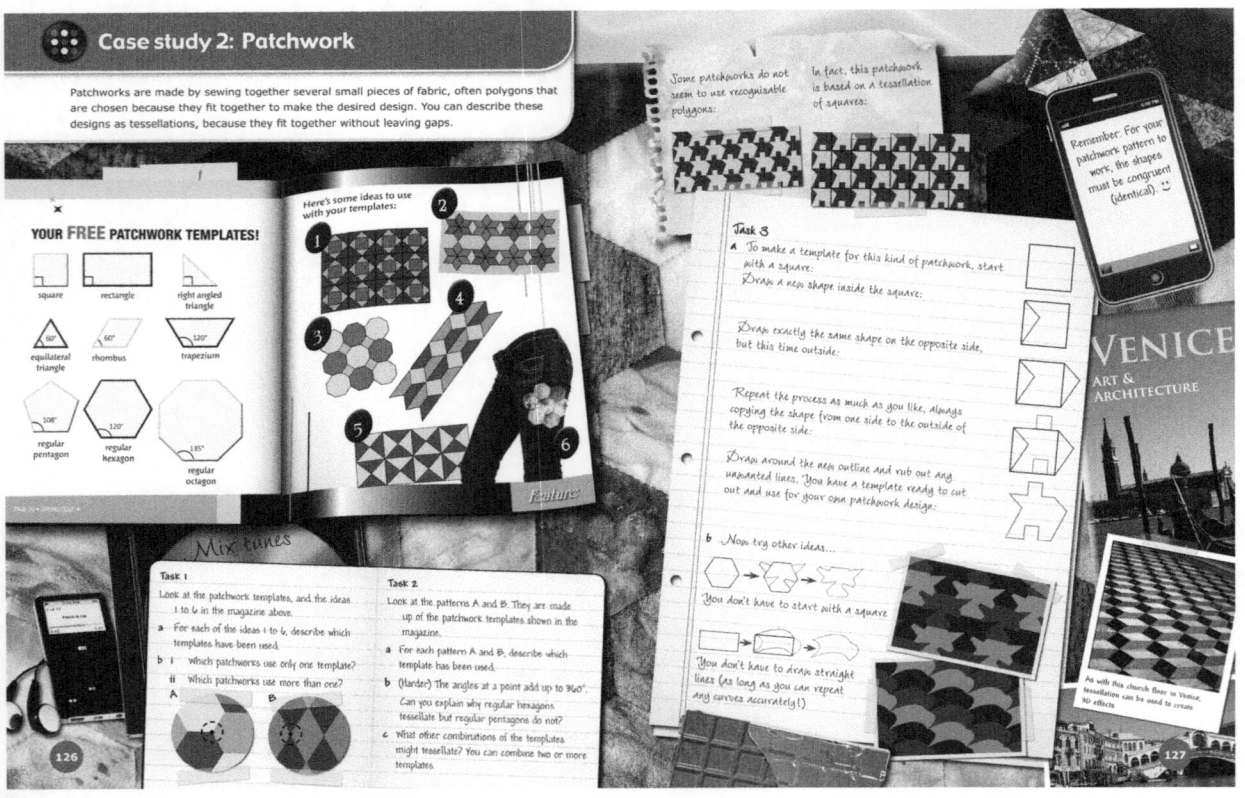

Teaching notes

Patchworks are mainly done as hobbies these days. In times of hardship, patchworks have been used as a way of recycling old clothes to make blankets and such like. Patchworks are often quite geometric in design. A person making the patchwork needs to consider how shapes fit together and often uses a template to make pieces of consistent size and shape. Similar considerations apply to designs using paving stones. This case study uses this geometric nature of patchworks to look at a shapes' internal angles and consider how these determine if a given shape will tessellate.

Introduce the idea of patchworks and remind students about tessellation. Look at the shapes that are used in typical patchworks and discuss what makes the shapes suitable for this purpose.

Look at the case study, focusing initially on the magazine and its free templates. What do you notice about the sizes of the templates? Agree that their dimensions are such that any shape will fit exactly with another.

How long do you think the rectangle is compared with its width? Establish that it is twice as long as it is wide so that it can be used alongside two squares or other shapes. How do you think the lengths of the sides of the trapezium relate to each other? The longer side is twice as long as the shorter sides, which are all the same length as each other. Why do you think the rhombus and the trapezium have both been made with an angle of 60°? Establish that the equilateral triangle has to have an angle of 60° and that if the rhombus and trapezium are going to fit with the triangle, they too have to have an angle of 60°.

Task 1

Now look at the example patchworks and ask students to think about which templates have been used in each patchwork. Give the students a few minutes to note their answers to this before discussing answers. Some students might have considered the lighter spaces in patchworks 2 and 3 as gaps while others might have included them as shapes and named their templates.

Task 2

Use the questions to initiate thinking about the angles in shapes and how these determine whether the shape will tessellate. Ask questions such as why will some shapes tessellate and others not? Is it just to do with the length of their sides or is it also to do with their angles? What is it about the angles of shapes that allow them to be used on their own?

Task 3

To make a template based on a square follow the instructions. Make sure that students understand how the method requires a new shape to be drawn **inside** the shape on one side and **outside** the shape on the other, and that the two shapes are aligned with each other. Look at the two tessellation examples at the end of the instructions to see how the original shape doesn't have to be a square. What shapes could you start with? Establish that the initial shape needs to be one that tessellates.

Answers

1 a 1 Square, right-angled triangle
    2 Isosceles trapezium and rhombus
    3 Regular octagon and square
    4 Square and isosceles trapezium
    5 Right-angled triangle
    6 Regular hexagon
  b i 5, 6   ii 1, 2, 3, 4

2 a **A** Hexagon **B** Rhombus

  b To tessellate, a shape's interior angle must divide evenly into 360, since there are 360° at a point.

Hexagon: $\frac{360}{120} = 3$, therefore hexagons tessellate;

Pentagon: $\frac{360}{108} = 3.333...$, therefore pentagons do not tessellate.

  c Lots of possible answers

3 Students' own answers

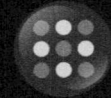

Learning outcomes

N4 Use the four operations, including formal written methods, applied to integers, decimals, proper and improper fractions, and mixed numbers, all both positive and negative   (L4/5)

N5 use conventional notation for the priority of operations, including brackets, powers, roots and reciprocals   (L5)

Introduction

The chapter starts by looking at the order of operations before considering mental techniques for adding and subtracting numbers. Mental methods for multiplication and division are covered before the use of all these methods in a problem-solving context is covered in the final two sections.

The introduction discusses the historical background of calculation and gives a brief history of mechanical calculation devices, including the first mechanical calculator invented by Blaise Pascal in 1642. The development of machines to help perform complex calculations has been a major part of the history of calculation over the last 300 years and eventually led to the development of the high-powered calculators and computers that we use today. Mathematicians such as Ada Lovelace (1815-1852), Charles Babbage (1791-1871) and Alan Turing (1912-1954) are all credited with significant contributions to the development of mechanical calculators and the eventual development of computers as we know them today. Biographies of these eminent mathematicians can be found at:

http://www-history.mcs.st-and.ac.uk/Biographies/Lovelace.html

http://www-history.mcs.st-andrews.ac.uk/Biographies/Babbage.html

http://www-history.mcs.st-andrews.ac.uk/Biographies/Turing.html

Prior knowledge

Students should already know how to…
- Add, subtract, multiply and divide whole numbers
- Use place value

Starter problem

The starter problem is a classic example of a 'Route inspection' problem, often called 'The Chinese Postman' problem (so-called not because of a Chinese postman, but because it was originally studied by a Chinese mathematician, Kwan Mei-Ko, in 1962).

The development of efficient algorithms to solve this kind of problem forms part of a branch of mathematics called 'discrete mathematics'.

Beginning and ending at A, the postman must cover all of the streets at least once. It can be shown that he will not be able to cover each street once only, but that he must walk along some streets more than once. If he repeats streets DE and HF, he can complete the route in the shortest distance. This is equal to the total length of all the streets, plus 0.9 km (DE again) and 1.5 km (HF again). The total distance is therefore 16.7 km.

A possible route would be: AHFHGFEGABCDEDA but there are many others.

More able students could be asked to work out a route which visits each vertex once (the 'Travelling Salesman' problem) or be given more complex examples of these kinds of problems.

Resources

🌐 MyMaths

Doubling and halving	1023	Order of operations	1167
Introducing money	1226	Best buys and value for money	1243
Mixed sums all numbers	1345	Mixed tables 2 to 4	1367
Money problems	1377		

Online assessment

Chapter test	2A–7
Formative test	2A–7
Summative test	2A–7

InvisiPen solutions

Mental methods of addition and subtraction			121
Mental multiplication	122	Mental division	123
Order of operations			124
Written addition and subtraction			125

Topic scheme

Teaching time = 5 lessons/2 weeks

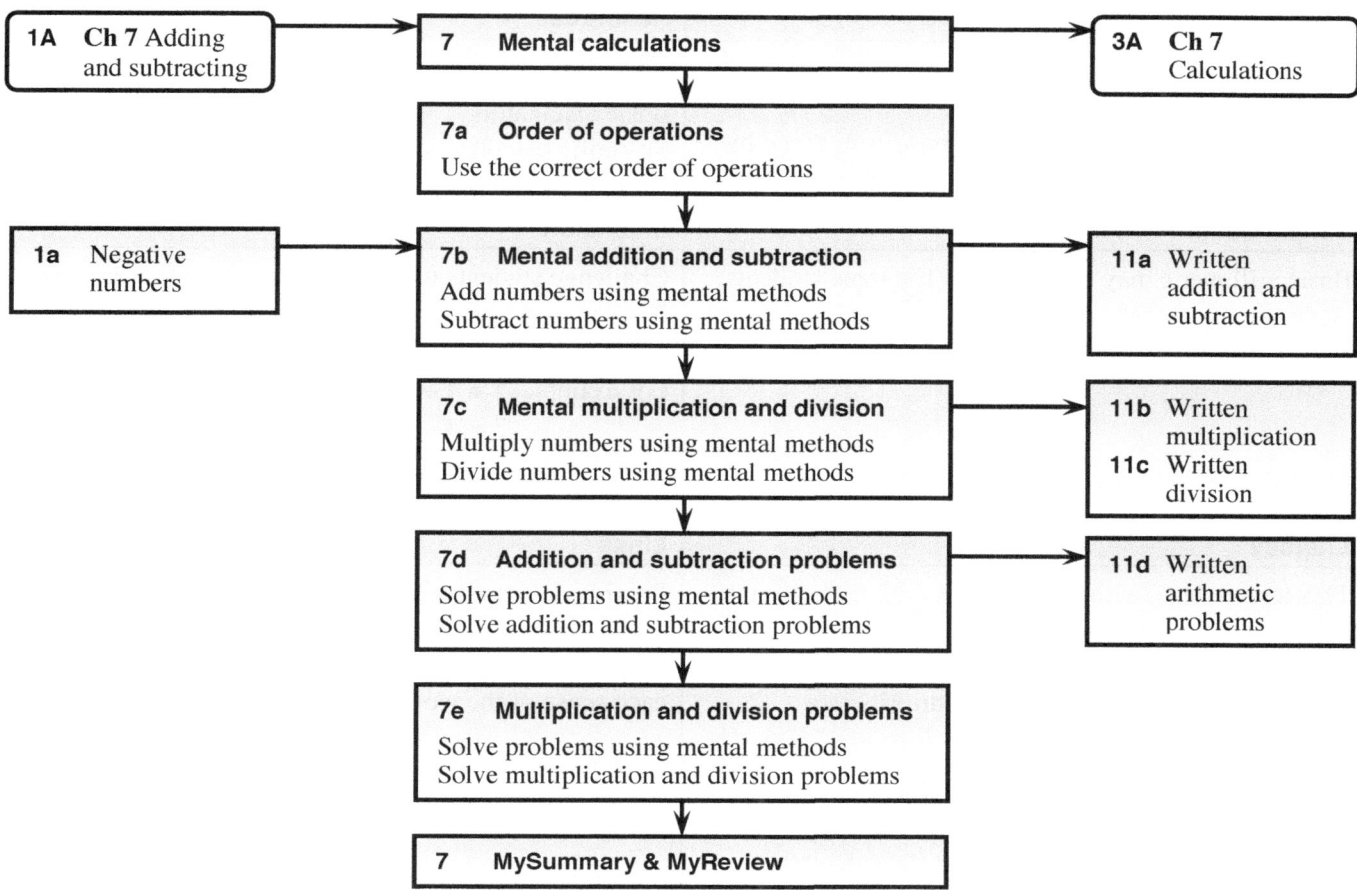

1A Ch 7 Adding and subtracting	

7 Mental calculations

3A Ch 7 Calculations

7a Order of operations
Use the correct order of operations

1a Negative numbers

7b Mental addition and subtraction
Add numbers using mental methods
Subtract numbers using mental methods

11a Written addition and subtraction

7c Mental multiplication and division
Multiply numbers using mental methods
Divide numbers using mental methods

11b Written multiplication
11c Written division

7d Addition and subtraction problems
Solve problems using mental methods
Solve addition and subtraction problems

11d Written arithmetic problems

7e Multiplication and division problems
Solve problems using mental methods
Solve multiplication and division problems

7 MySummary & MyReview

Differentiation

Student book 2A 128 – 143	**Student book 2B** 116 – 133	**Student book 2C** 122 – 135

Order of operations
Mental addition and subtraction
Mental multiplication and division
Addition and subtraction problems
Multiplication and division
   problems
	Rounding
	Mental addition and subtraction
	Multiply and divide by powers
	   of 10
	Mental multiplication and division
	Mental addition and subtraction
	   problems
	Mental multiplication and division
	   problems
		Arithmetic with negative numbers
		Powers of 10
		Mental addition and subtraction
		Mental multiplication and division

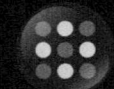

Objectives	
• Use the order of operations, including brackets	(L5)

Key ideas	Resources
1 There is an order of priority for operations in a calculation 2 From high to low, the order of priority is given by the initials: **b i d m a s**	Order of operations (1167) Basic calculators Scientific calculators Dictionaries

Simplification	Extension
Basic arithmetic may be a problem for some students. Have 'times-tables' available but discourage the use of a calculator unless it is essential.	Challenge students to make all the numbers from 1 to 20 using only the number 4 and any of the four basic operations. For example, $1 = 4 \div 4$ $2 = (4 + 4) \div 4$ $\qquad\qquad 3 = 4 - \frac{4}{4}$, etc. Insist on the use of brackets to determine the correct order.

Literacy	Links
This lesson deals with the 'grammar' of mathematics. The made-up word **'bidmas'** is not mentioned explicitly, but it is a useful mnemonic to help get the order correct. It gives the order of priority in a calculation and stands for: **B**rackets **I**ndices **D**ivision **M**ultiplication **A**ddition **S**ubtraction. Brackets are used to make sure that the calculation is approached in the correct order.	Provide dictionaries for the class to use. The word *order* can have several meanings and can be used as a noun or a verb. In which curriculum subject would each sense of the word most likely be used?

Alternative approach

Make sentences that are ambiguous unless given certain emphasis. For example, consider the sentence 'Emma bought a bag of apples and a pack of oranges four times'. If said as 'Emma bought a bag of apples …*pause*… and a pack of bananas four times.' it means something different from 'Emma bought a bag of apples and a pack of bananas …*pause*…four times.' If a is the cost of a bag of apples and b is the cost of a pack of bananas, then the cost of the first sentence is $a + 4b$, whereas the second sentence costs $(a + b) \times 4$.

Similarly with the sentence 'Jim pays £12 and £20 every week for 8 weeks to pay his debt'. It can mean 'Jim pays £12 …*pause*… and £20 every week for 8 weeks to pay his debt.' or it can mean 'Jim pays £12 and £20 …every week for 8 weeks to pay his debt.' The sum repaid is either £12 + (20 × 8) or it is £(12 + 20) × 8. There is a big difference!

Checkpoint

1 Answer these problems:
   a $2 + 4 \times 5$ $(2 + 20 = 22)$
   b $4 - 6 \div 2$ $(4 - 3 = 1)$
   c $6 \times 4 \div 2$ $(24 \div 2 = 12)$
   d $10 - 2 \times 3$ $(10 - 6 = 4)$
   e $(3 + 4) \times 2$ $(7 \times 2 = 14)$

Starter – What is my number?

I am even.
I am a multiple of 9.
I am greater than the number of days in November.
I am less than 8 × 8.
I am 5 more than a square number.   (54)

Students find the number.

This activity can be extended by asking students to make up their own puzzles.

Teaching notes

Provide half the class with basic calculators and the other half with scientific calculators. Invite students to use their calculators to evaluate $3 + 2 \times 5$. Ask for their results and invite students to swap calculators to verify the different answers. Discuss how the same calculation can give two different answers and show that the order in which the operations are performed affects the outcome.

Explain that there is a set of rules to ensure operations are performed in a particular order. The order of priority, from high to low, is:

- Brackets
- Indices
- Division and multiplication
- Addition and subtraction

Introduce students to a calculation with brackets, say $7 + (5 \times 4) \div 2$ and work through how to evaluate it using the correct order. Encourage working just one stage at a time and setting working out accordingly.

Plenary

Give students several calculations. They discuss in pairs whether brackets are required to change the order. Then share views in a whole-class session.

For example,

$3 \times 2 + 1 = 9$ $3 + 5 \div 2 = 4$
$3 + 2 \times 4 = 11$ $4 \times 5 + 5 \times 6 = 240$.

Exercise commentary

All these questions should be completed without the use of a calculator. Have 'times-tables' to hand for some students.

Question 2 – This requires students to evaluate calculations using the priorities of **bidmas**.

Question 3 – This question requires students to calculate the inside of the brackets first (using the **b** of **bidmas**).

Question 4 – Strictly speaking, part **c** does not need brackets as the order in **bidmas** (with × before +) is sufficient to get the right answer. In part **f**, no brackets are needed as – and + have equal priority.

Question 5 – It is essential for students to set out their working at every stage, as in the two suggestions. Later, those with a scientific calculator can check to see if the calculator's logic will be successful.

Answers

1   **a** +   **b** ×   **c** ÷
    d ÷   **e** –   **f** ÷
    g ×   **h** –   **i** ×

2 $5 \times 3 - 8 = 7$ $9 \div 3 + 2 = 5$
    $8 - 4 \times 2 = 0$ $14 - 7 \times 2 = 0$
    $1 \times 9 + 3 = 12$ $6 - 2 \times 3 = 0$
    $5 \times 2 + 2 = 12$ $3 - 2 \times 1 = 1$
    $2 \times 3 + 1 = 7$ $18 - 6 \times 3 = 0$
    $2 + 12 \div 4 = 5$ $4 \times 5 - 19 = 1$

3   **a** 10   **b** 8   **c** 14
    d 14   **e** 5   **f** 8
    g 5   **h** 15   **i** 2

4   **a** $5 \times (3 + 1) = 20$ **b** $(8 - 5) \times 3 = 9$
    c $3 + (2 \times 4) = 11$ **d** $(6 + 4) \div 2 = 5$
    e $(15 - 7) \times 2 = 16$ **f** $20 - (12 + 4) = 4$

5   **a** 38   **b** 10   **c** 2   **d** 9
    e 40   **f** 12   **g** 2

6 $(4 \div 4) + (4 \div 4) = 2$ $4 + (4 + 4) \div 4 = 6$
    $4 - (4 \div 4) = 3$ $4 + 4 - (4 \div 4) = 7$
    $(4 \times 4) \div 4 = 4$ $4 + 4 = 8$
    $4 + (4 \div 4) = 5$ $4 + 4 + (4 \div 4) = 9$
    Other answers possible

7   **a** $25 \times 4 \times 2$ **b** $(7 + 5) \times 4$
    c $25 \times 4 \times (7 + 3) - 3 \times 7$
    Other answers possible

7b Mental addition and subtraction

Objectives

- Strengthen and extend mental methods of calculation, accompanied where appropriate by suitable jottings (L4)
- Make and justify estimates and approximations of calculations (L5)

Key ideas	Resources
1 Mental addition starts with the bigger number 2 Mental subtraction can be done by either 'taking away' or 'adding on'	 Mixed sums all numbers (1345) Blank number lines The 100 square

Simplification	Extension
Jottings and diagrams are essential for those who struggle with accurate mental calculations. Confident students take larger jumps, for example, one jump of 40 as opposed to 4 jumps of 10, but other students may take smaller steps particularly where the values cross over a ten or hundred boundary. For mental calculations below 100, working with a 100 square can be more productive than jottings.	Students consider addition of decimals, starting with 23 + 6.5 (one decimal number) and extending to both numbers being decimal, such as 12.8 + 23.6. Pairs of students set challenging addition questions for one another.

Literacy	Links
To become literate with mental calculations is to become wiser in choosing the right method. For example, the addition 145 + 296 is best *not* done by jumps of 200 (from 145) or 100 (from 296) as a first step. It is best to see 296 as 300, then add the 145 and finally subtract the extra 4 that made the 300. Also, for example, 512 – 189 is best *not* done by 'taking away' 189 from 512, but by starting at 189 and 'adding on' to get to 512, to give 11 + 300 + 12 = 323.	The first person to formally recognise that adding zero to a number does not change the original number was the Indian mathematician and astronomer Brahmagupta who included the result in his work *Brahmasphutasiddhanta* in the year AD 628. There is more information about Brahmagupta at http://en.wikipedia.org/wiki/Brahmagupta

Alternative approach

Mental addition using jumps on a number line should generally start from the bigger number, as with 123 + 465, giving 465 + 100 + 20 + 3.

Mental subtraction presents a choice between:
a) subtraction by 'taking away' as in the students' book with the example 658 – 425; or
b) subtraction by 'complementary addition' as with 307 – 195 where the jumps start at 195 and, adding onto 195, continue as far as 307, giving 5 + 100 + 7 = 112.

Ask students to look out for subtractions like 1002 – 997 for which 'taking away' may be expected, but for which, surely, 3 + 2 = 5 must be easier!

Checkpoint

1 Use partitioning on a number line to answer these problems
   a 42 + 23 (65)
   b 252 + 129 (381)
   c 78 – 43 (35)
   d 124 – 45 (79)

Starter – Quick fire

Recap work of previous chapters and this chapter so far. Ask rapid response questions. Students reply by writing on their mini whiteboards. Discuss questions when their answers indicate a need.

Teaching notes

Write the calculation 428 + 927. Invite students to invent a scenario where this addition is needed; such as the total number of tins of baked beans sold in a shop over two days. Highlight any key word used to describe the scenario: **add, plus, sum, total**.

Highlight the use of **estimation** (using very approximate numbers, such as 400 and 1000) to simplify a calculation and so get a rough answer. This rough answer serves as a check.

Students now mentally calculate 48 + 24 and 51 − 32 (as in the example in the students' book). Again, invent a scenario for this subtraction. Highlight key words such as **difference, take away, minus**. Reinforce the idea of making an initial estimation.

Discuss mental strategies. Model the use of a number line which is jotted down as an aid to students' mental methods. Discuss:

the start number (the bigger of the two numbers) and **partitioning** (adding 10, 10 and 4 to add 24, or subtracting 10, 10 , 10 and 2 to 'take away' 32).

Students consider larger calculations, say 295 + 157, and discuss in pairs the method they used to do this, sharing any jottings they use.

Remind them that a jotting is only a sketch; it is not an accurate drawing. Its purpose is to keep track of the steps that have been taken.

However, 'common sense' must prevail. Consider the calculation 287 + 399. Demonstrate the partition method: start with the bigger number, 399, and take jumps of 100, 100, 10, 10, ... Agree that this is a long complex method.

Ask students for a more appropriate method and use the method of **compensation** (taking 399 as 400 and subtracting 1 at the end to 'compensate'). Discuss how and why you compensate.

Always discuss which method is most appropriate for different calculations.

Plenary

Give students various 2- and 3-digit additions and subtractions. They respond on mini whiteboards and discuss answers as appropriate. Discuss different methods for the same calculation.

Exercise commentary

Question 1 – This question focuses on simple addition and subtraction of 1- and 2-digit numbers. Some subtractions are best done by complementary addition.

Questions 2 and **3** – These questions develop students' partitioning skills. Remind them to start with the bigger number.

Question 3 – Focuses on partitioning numbers and using jottings to help with addition. Remind students to use the largest number as the start position. Part **f** extends past a hundred boundary, so encourage students to take small steps.

Question 4 – Extends to subtraction. Part **f** crosses a hundred boundary. Remind students that they can do a subtraction by 'adding on' to the smaller number. They must choose the best method as they see fit.

Question 5 – Extends calculations to 3-digit numbers. Again, students must choose between the two methods for subtraction.

Question 6 – Requires students add three numbers and extends them into thousands within a worded problem. Students may decide that written methods are the most efficient to achieve correct answers.

Question 7 – Needs a careful reading. Two buses pass by before Yang's bus arrives. She has two answers for each bus.

Answers

1	a	13	b	5	c	16	d	6
	e	17	f	16	g	18	h	5
	i	23	j	12	k	23	l	-1
2	a	61	b	55	c	79		
	d	93	e	53	f	208		
	g	234						

3

+	42	63	97
12	54	75	109
20	62	83	117
31	73	94	128

4	a	24	b	23	c	33
	d	27	e	28	f	52
	g	89				
5	a	397	b	546	c	677
	d	461	e	822	f	361
	g	423	h	250	i	44
	j	260				
6	a	£2352	b	£902		
7	a	39, 11	b	67, 39	c	51, 23

Objectives

- Multiply and divide integers by 10 (L4)
- Recall multiplication facts to 10 × 10 and quickly derive associated division facts (L4)
- Develop mental methods of calculation, accompanied where appropriate by suitable jottings (L4)

Key ideas	Resources
1 The concept of place value is used to multiply and divide by 10 2 Partitioning and compensation are two methods used for multiplication 3 Chunky subtraction and short division are two methods used for division	Doubling and halving (1023) Mixed tables 2 to 12 (1367)

Simplification	Extension
Some students may need a multiplication square. Work with integers before working with decimals in question 3.	More confident students could work on questions involving decimals, such as 2.5 × 4, 3.6 × 3, 12.5 ÷ 5 and work towards 18 ÷ 1.5.

Literacy	Links
Fluency with mental multiplication and division is essential to mathematical literacy. Mental multiplication has a choice of methods: they are partitioning and compensation. Partitioning is likely to be the more common choice. Mental division also has a choice of methods and both are likely to require 'jottings': they are 'chunky' subtraction and short division. Short division is likely to be less prone to error.	The Ancient Babylonians used a number system based on 60. The large number of multiplication facts (60 × 60 of them) made multiplication difficult, so the Babylonians developed multiplication tables. The tables were written in cuneiform script on clay tablets and then baked. There is a picture of a Babylonian multiplication tablet for the 35 times table at http://it.stlawu.edu/~dmelvill/mesomath/tablets/36Times.html

Alternative approach

As an alternative to 'chunky' subtraction, consider $138 \div 6$.

The method of 'short division' is set out as here where 6 into 13 is 2 in the tens (T) column of the answer, leaving 18 in the units (U) column.

$$6\overline{)1\ 3^1 8} \quad \begin{array}{cc} 2 & 3 \end{array}$$

Then 6 into 18 gives 3. The answer is 23.

When teaching this method, a sheet of paper can cover the 8 initially, leaving only the 13 visible. The student then sees 6 divided into 13. The remaining 1 moves into the next column under the sheet of paper to give 18.

This method has less potential for errors than 'chunky' subtraction.

Checkpoint

1 Answer these problems:
- a 24×10 (240)
- b $240 \div 10$ (24)
- c $245 \div 10$ (24.5)
- d 32×3 (96)
- e $122 \div 2$ (61)

Starter – Match the maths

Show students some statements. They group the equivalent statements.

6 + 6 + 6	20 ÷ 5	20 – 5 – 5 – 5 – 5
6 ÷ 3	3 lots of 6	How many 3's in 6?
How many 5's in 20?	6 shared between 3	6 × 3

Teaching notes

Referring to the mental starter, highlight the facts that

- multiplication is repeated addition (linked to 'lots of')
- division is repeated subtraction.

Highlight both processes as opposites of the same idea.

Demonstrate the **partitioning** method with the example 17×6:

17 lots of 6 is equivalent to
10 lots of 6 and 7 lots of 6,
so $17 \times 6 = (10 \times 6) + (7 \times 6)$ which can be found mentally from $60 + 42 = 102$.

Discuss what $144 \div 6$ means. It can be found by asking 'How many sixes go into 144?' or 'How many times can 6 be subtracted from 144?'

| $144 - 6 = 138$ | *once* |
| $138 - 6 = 132$ | *twice...* |

Students can subtract 'chunks' of 6 as $6 \times 10 = 60$, so

$144 - 60 = 84$	*ten times*
$84 - 60 = 24$	*ten times*
$24 - 24 = 0$	*four times*

So, *10 + 10 + 4 = 24 lots of 6 altogether.*
Hence, $144 \div 6 = 24$

An alternative method of division is found under the 'Alternative approach' above.

Plenary

Nine children want to go to an amusement park. Each ticket costs £14. How much will they pay in total?
Discuss how to calculate the total by
a) partitioning 14×9 as 10×9 and 4×9
b) compensation, using 14×10 to get to 14×9.
Discuss the best way to find 21×9, 23×6 and 42×7.

Exercise commentary

Question 1 – Focuses on the inverse relationship between multiplication and division.

Questions 2 and **3** – These questions revise using the place-value grid for multiplying and dividing by 10.

Question 4 – Revises partitioning as a method for mental multiplication.

Question 5 – Requires students to divide using either a chunking method or short division.

Question 6 – Practises mental agility with all four operations.

Question 8 – When dividing by powers of ten, students may need help putting in the decimal point.

Answers

1	a	5	b	3	c	9	d	3
	e	7	f	4	g	8	h	7
2	a	80	b	230	c	60	d	470
	e	340	f	4070	g	1190	h	6730
3	a	6	b	3.5	c	54	d	28.6
	e	10.4	f	65	g	48.5	h	240
4	a	72	b	70	c	54	d	120
	e	72	f	130	g	140	h	112
	i	168	j	216				
5	a	13	b	14	c	12	d	15
	e	17	f	12	g	23	h	23
	i	24	j	35				
6	a	48	b	108				
7	a	6	b	6	c	11		
	d	4	e	14				

8 350; 3 500; 35 000; 350 000; 3 500 000; 35; 3.5; 0.35; 0.035

Objectives	
• Strengthen and extend mental methods of calculation	(L4)
• Make and justify estimates and approximations of calculations	(L5)
• Identify the necessary information to understand or simplify a context or problem	(L5)

Key ideas	Resources	
1 Partitioning and compensation are two mental methods for addition of numbers 2 'Taking away' and complementary addition are two mental methods for subtraction of numbers	Introducing money Mixed sums all numbers Money problems	(1226) (1345) (1377)

Simplification	Extension
Digesting the information given may prove problematic for some students in wordy problems. They can work in pairs and read each sentence aloud to help process the detail and determine a way forward.	Students, in pairs, create a puzzle question similar to question **2** for another pair to solve.

Literacy	Links
The key to being 'literate' with mental computational skills is to be able to draw on a range of methods. The standard mental methods can be supplemented by more flexible approaches that arise in particular cases. There is also the option to switch to a written rather than mental method.	The world record for adding 100 single-digit numbers randomly generated by a computer is 19.23 seconds, held by Alberto Coto Garcia from Spain. Details of other mental calculation World records can be found at http://www.recordholders.org/en/list/memory.html#adding10digits

Alternative approach

The standard methods for mental addition (partitioning and compensation) and for subtraction (taking away and adding on) can be supplemented by more personal methods used for particular problems. Students may well have their own methods. Discuss what methods can be used for particular calculations.

For example,
12 + 24 + 32 + 28 might be best done by counting the 10s first, using bonds of 10 (2 + 8) for any extra 10s and then adding the remaining units.

263 + 305 + 107 might be best done by using the 7 from 107 with the 263 to give 270 + 305 + 100.

Checkpoint

1 a Joe is 158 cm tall and Meg is 15 cm taller than Joe. How tall is Meg? (173 cm)
   b Max is 160 cm tall and his brother, George, is 11 cm shorter than Max. How tall is George? (149 cm)
   c How much taller is Meg than George? (24 cm)

Starter – Estimate

Students estimate an answer by using approximate values found by rounding. For example,

- estimate the number of minutes in the 31 days of July
  - estimate the number of steps taken on a 5 km walk if each pace is about 75 cm
  - estimate the number of units of electricity used from May to September if the daily average is 13 units.

Check using a calculator. How close were the estimates?

Teaching notes

This lesson revisits the mental addition skills that students used earlier in the book. The mental methods include:

Partitioning: counting by jumps on a number line in 100s, 10s and 1s.

Compensating: jumping further ahead to ease the calculation and then subtracting at the end, usually when one of the numbers is close to a multiple of 10 or 100.

Jottings can be used to record steps if a student is not confident at internalising the calculation.

Discuss word problems set in context. Note key words such as 'total', 'sum', 'altogether', 'difference' and whether a problem calls for subtraction or addition. Estimate the answer first by working with approximate values found by rounding.

Plenary

Give students several well-graded additions and subtractions to be done mentally. Set some questions in context. Students use their mini whiteboards to respond. Answers can be discussed as needed.

Exercise commentary

Question 1 – Talk through the mental strategies. Part **a** is best done as 35 + 30 + 25 − 1. In part **b**, Akton to Caulse might be best done as 20 + 20 + 30 and then 5 + 3 + 2.

Question 2 – Get an overall strategy first: Tina and Siobhan are found before Ida and Caleb.

Question 3 – As for question **1**, talk through the mental strategies. For example, in part **a**, the change for £27 when offering a £50 note is best worked out by 'complementary addition' (and not 'taking away').

Question 4 – Order the 2-digit numbers first and then find the differences between various pairs of values.

Answers

1 **a** 89 km
   b Akton to Caulse (80 km against 64 km)
2 **a** Siobhan, 173 cm   **b** 32 cm   **c** 6 cm
3 **a** £27, £23 change
   b £65, £15 change
   c Vincent by £16
4 **a** 19 seconds
   b Cole and David

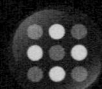

Objectives	
• Strengthen and extend mental methods for multiplication and division	(L4)
• Make and justify estimates and approximations of calculations	(L5)
• Identify the necessary information to understand or simplify a context or problem	(L5)

Key ideas	Resources	
1 Partitioning and compensation are two methods used for multiplication 2 Chunky subtraction and short division are two methods used for division	Doubling and halving Best buys and value for money Mixed tables 2 to 12	(1023) (1243) (1367)

Simplification	Extension
Digesting the information in a word problem may be problematic for some students. They can work in pairs and read each sentence aloud to help process the detail in each problem.	Students tackle problems in various contexts with simple decimals.

Literacy	Links
The key to being 'literate' with mental computational skills is to be able to draw on a range of methods. The standard mental methods can be supplemented by more flexible approaches that arise in particular cases. Where jottings are needed, time should not be spent unduly on neatness; jottings are merely an aid to mental calculation. There is also the option to switch to a written rather than mental method.	The cost of football tickets for all Premiership clubs can be found at http://www.footballticketprices.co.uk/index.php/ premier-league Which club has the most expensive tickets? Which has the least expensive? Find the cost of three adult tickets at each of these two clubs and compare with the cost in the example. Is £115 enough to buy three adult tickets?

Alternative approach

The standard methods for mental multiplication and division are partitioning and 'chunky' subtraction respectively. But the other methods of compensation (for multiplication) and short division (for division) can be preferred. Discuss the choice of methods with students, asking which method they would choose and why.

For example with multiplication,
19×42 might be best done by compensation. Consider 20×42 as 2×420 giving 840. Then compensate for the extra 42 to give $19 \times 42 = 840 - 42 = 798$.

For example with division,
$138 \div 6$ might be best done using short division (with a jotting if necessary).
The method of 'short division' is set out as here where 6 into 13 is 2 in the tens (T) column of the answer, leaving 18 in the units (U) column.
Then 6 into 18 gives 3. The answer is 23.

$$\begin{array}{r} 2\ 3 \\ 6\,)1\,3\,{}^{1}8 \end{array}$$

Checkpoint

1 A group of three adults and four children is going to the cinema. The cost of an adult ticket is £8.50 and the cost of a child ticket is £6.70.
   a Will £60 be enough to cover the cost? $(3 \times 8.5 + 4 \times 6.7 = 52.3.$ Therefore £60 is enough.)
   b If so, how much change will they receive?   (£7.70)

Starter – Quick fire

Recap basic number work so far in this book and this chapter. Include questions on fractions, decimals and percentages and questions using mental computation. Ask rapid response questions. Students reply by writing on their mini whiteboards. Discuss questions when their answers indicate a need.

Teaching notes

Remind students of the **partitioning** method for multiplication. Use the example 17×6. Discuss working out 10×6 and 7×6 as the way to find the answer. Demonstrate and discuss this method with other mental multiplications.

Also remind students of '**chunky subtraction**' as a way to divide. Use the example of $144 \div 6$. It can be found by asking 'How many sixes go into 144?' or 'How many times can 6 be subtracted from 144?'

Students can subtract 'chunks' of 6 as $6 \times 10 = 60$, so

$144 - 60 = 84$	*ten times*
$84 - 60 = 24$	*ten times*
$24 - 24 = 0$	*four times*

So, there are *10 + 10 + 4 = 24 lots of 6 altogether.* Hence, $144 \div 6 = 24$

Set these methods in the context of word problems. Remind students to watch for key words such as 'altogether', 'share', 'total'. Discuss with the whole class and dissect a word problem to get an overall strategy. Then apply the mental methods required.

Other mental methods can be found in 'Alternative approach' above.

Also remind students that, before embarking on accurate calculations, they should firstly get an estimate of the answer by using approximate values found by rounding.
For example,
for 98×21, find an estimate from $100 \times 21 = 2100$ and, for $625 \div 3$, find an estimate from $600 \div 3 = 200$.

Plenary

Provide word problems using an overhead screen. If necessary, read them through and discuss strategies as a whole class. Students then find answers to questions and write them on their mini whiteboards. Discuss the methods used.

Exercise commentary

In all questions, discuss the strategy and the mental methods used by students. They are more important than the answers at this stage.

Question 1 – Requires multiplication by 1-digit or 2-digit numbers followed by a straightforward addition and subtraction.

Question 2 – This is a more complex problem requiring a simple subtraction followed by a division which is best thought of as a multiplication.

Questions 3 to 5 – These questions may each need discussing as a whole class to gain an overall understanding and to adopt a strategy to tackle what is being asked. It is easier to see the overall strategy for question **5** than questions **3** and **4**.

Answers

1   a   No, because cost is £61
   b   Yes, because cost is £185
2   10
3   When he runs (224 beats as opposed to 216 when cycling)
4   a   10
   b   4200 ml or 4.2 litres, 3 cartons
5   Yes

Key outcomes	Quick check	
Use the order of operations, including brackets.	$15 - 2 \times 5$	$(15 - 10 = 5)$
	$12 - 10 \div 2$	$(12 - 5 = 7)$
Use mental methods to add, subtract, multiply and divide.	$73 + 25$	(98)
	$65 - 17$	(48)
	15×6	(90)
	$135 \div 9$	(15)
Solve problems using addition, subtraction, multiplication and division.	Ben wants to buy four books at £7.50 each and two pens at £2.90 each. How much change will he receive from £40? $(4 \times 7.5 + 2 \times 2.9 = 35.8$; so change is £4.20$)$	

⊞ MyMaths extra support

Lesson/online homework			Description
Adding in columns	1020	L3	Adding 2- and 3-digit numbers
Subtraction columns	1028	L3	Subtracting 2- and 3-digit numbers

MyReview

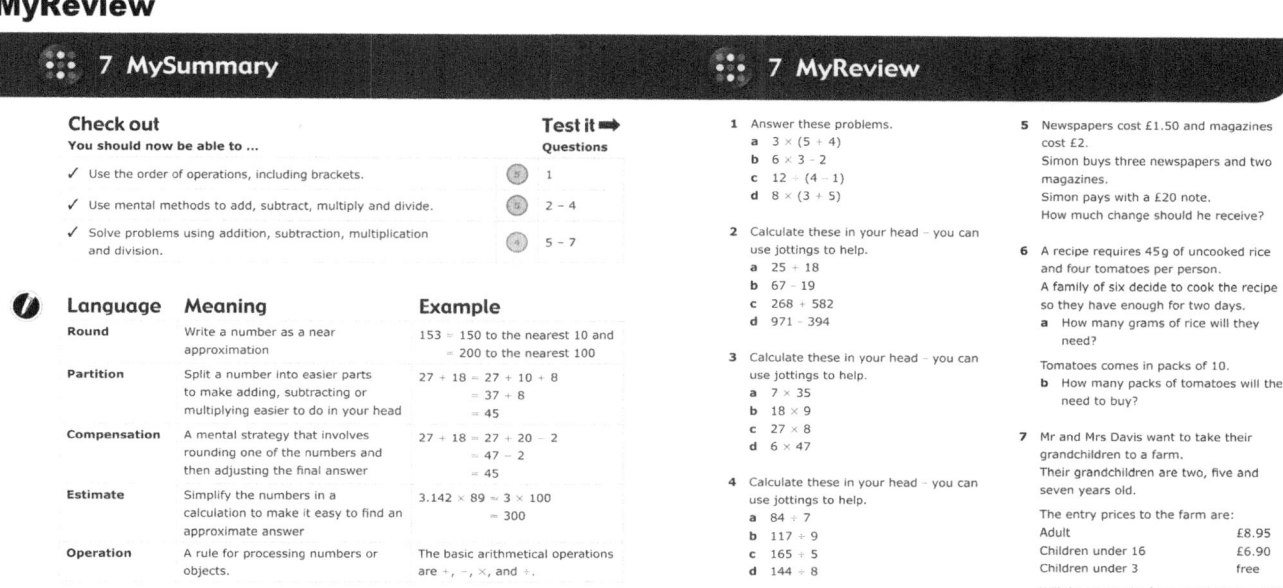

Check out

You should now be able to ...

Test it ➡
Questions

✓ Use the order of operations, including brackets. ③ 1

✓ Use mental methods to add, subtract, multiply and divide. ⑤ 2 – 4

✓ Solve problems using addition, subtraction, multiplication and division. ④ 5 – 7

Language	Meaning	Example
Round	Write a number as a near approximation	153 ≈ 150 to the nearest 10 and ≈ 200 to the nearest 100
Partition	Split a number into easier parts to make adding, subtracting or multiplying easier to do in your head	27 + 18 = 27 + 10 + 8 = 37 + 8 = 45
Compensation	A mental strategy that involves rounding one of the numbers and then adjusting the final answer	27 + 18 = 27 + 20 − 2 = 47 − 2 = 45
Estimate	Simplify the numbers in a calculation to make it easy to find an approximate answer	3.142 × 89 ≈ 3 × 100 = 300
Operation	A rule for processing numbers or objects.	The basic arithmetical operations are +, −, ×, and ÷.

1 Answer these problems.
- **a** 3 × (5 + 4)
- **b** 6 × 3 − 2
- **c** 12 ÷ (4 − 1)
- **d** 8 × (3 + 5)

2 Calculate these in your head – you can use jottings to help.
- **a** 25 + 18
- **b** 67 − 19
- **c** 268 + 582
- **d** 971 − 394

3 Calculate these in your head – you can use jottings to help.
- **a** 7 × 35
- **b** 18 × 9
- **c** 27 × 8
- **d** 6 × 47

4 Calculate these in your head – you can use jottings to help.
- **a** 84 ÷ 7
- **b** 117 ÷ 9
- **c** 165 ÷ 5
- **d** 144 ÷ 8

5 Newspapers cost £1.50 and magazines cost £2.
Simon buys three newspapers and two magazines.
Simon pays with a £20 note.
How much change should he receive?

6 A recipe requires 45 g of uncooked rice and four tomatoes per person.
A family of six decide to cook the recipe so they have enough for two days.
- **a** How many grams of rice will they need?

Tomatoes comes in packs of 10.
- **b** How many packs of tomatoes will they need to buy?

7 Mr and Mrs Davis want to take their grandchildren to a farm.
Their grandchildren are two, five and seven years old.
The entry prices to the farm are:
Adult	£8.95
Children under 16	£6.90
Children under 3	free

Will the trip to the farm cost less than £35?

What next?

Score		
0 – 3		Your knowledge of this topic is still developing. To improve look at Formative test: 2A-7; MyMaths: 1023, 1167, 1226, 1243, 1345, 1367 and 1377
4, 5		You are gaining a secure knowledge of this topic. To improve look at InvisiPen: 121, 122, 123, 124 and 125
6, 7		You have mastered this topic. Well done, you are ready to progress!

Question commentary

Question 1 – Students may need a reminder of BIDMAS.

Questions 2 – 4 – Students may evolve different but equally valid methods of answering these questions. Perhaps they could work in pairs or small groups to discuss strategy.

Questions 5 – 7 – Students may need guidance in setting out solutions.

Answers

1 **a** 27   **b** 16
     c 4   **d** 64

2 **a** 43   **b** 48
     c 850   **d** 577

3 **a** 245   **b** 162
     c 216   **d** 282

4 **a** 12   **b** 13
     c 33   **d** 18

5 £11.50

6 **a** 540 g   **b** 5 packs

7 Yes

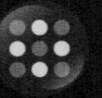

1 Answer these problems.

Step 1	Step 2	Step 3
Do all calculations in brackets.	Do multiplication and division.	Do addition and subtraction.

Remember to follow the **order of operations**.

a $(5 \times 3) - 6$
b $10 - (2 \times 4)$
c $3 \times (4 + 2)$
d $(6 \times 3) - 5$
e $(6 \times 4) \div 3$
f $8 - (8 \div 2)$
g $12 \div (3 \times 2) + 5$
h $5 \times (10 \div 2) - 10$
i $(4 \times 2) + (9 \div 3)$
j $(7 + 2) \div (18 \div 6)$

2 Answer these addition problems.

a $43 + 35 =$
b $54 + 28 =$
c $128 + 231 =$
d $234 + 316 =$
e $593 + 237 =$

3 Answer these subtraction problems.

a $58 - 26 =$
b $82 - 28 =$
c $288 - 154 =$
d $318 - 154 =$
e $405 - 256 =$

4 Do these calculations in your head.
Multiply each number by 10.

a 7
b 23
c 45
d 6.9
e 4.3
f 15.8

5 Do these calculations in your head.
Divide each number by 10.

a 50
b 180
c 270
d 45
e 78
f 188

6 Here are two items for sale in a supermarket.

Pint of milk	£0.49	Jar of coffee	£2.79

Alice buys a jar of coffee and a pint of milk.
Alice pays with a £5 note. How much change will she receive?

7 Kylie works in a shop.
She worked from 2 pm to 7 pm on Friday and from 1 pm to 4 pm on Saturday.
The table shows her pay for each hour worked.

	Hourly pay
Weekdays, 9 am to 5 pm	£6.80
Weekdays, after 5 pm	£7.90
Saturday	£7.90

How much was Kylie's pay for this week?

8 a Jimi downloads 34 albums, at £11 each.
How much does he spend?

b Marie goes for a Christmas lunch with 14 other people in her office.
They each pay the same amount of money.
The total cost of the lunch is £345.
How much does Marie pay for her Christmas lunch?

Question commentary

Question 1 – Students have to apply BIDMAS. Encourage students to write down steps.

Questions 2 and **3** – Use partition methods.

Questions 4 and **5** – Students may need to be reminded where to place the decimal point.

Question 6 – Use partition methods.

Questions 7 and **8** – Encourage students to make jottings if they wish. Perhaps explore different ways of tackling the questions. There are several steps involved.

Answers

1	**a** 9	**b** 2	**c** 18	**d** 13
	e 8	**f** 4	**g** 7	**h** 15
	i 11	**j** 3		
2	**a** 78	**b** 82	**c** 359	**d** 550
	e 830			
3	**a** 32	**b** 54	**c** 134	**d** 164
	e 149			
4	**a** 70	**b** 230	**c** 450	
	d 69	**e** 43	**f** 158	
5	**a** 5	**b** 18	**c** 27	
	d 4.5	**e** 7.8	**f** 18.8	
6	£1.72			
7	£59.90			
8	**a** £374	**b** £23		

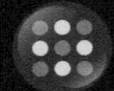
Learning outcomes

S1 Describe, interpret and compare observed distributions of a single variable through: appropriate graphical representation involving discrete, continuous and grouped data; and appropriate measures of central tendency (mean, mode, median) and spread (range, consideration of outliers)   (L5)

S2 Construct and interpret appropriate tables, charts, and diagrams, including frequency tables, bar charts, pie charts, and pictograms for categorical data, and vertical line (or bar) charts for ungrouped and grouped numerical data   (L4/5)

Introduction

The chapter starts by looking at planning a survey and the methods of data collection we might employ. Grouped frequency tables are covered before bar charts and pie charts. Mode, median, range and mean are all covered. Finding averages from grouped frequency tables precedes work on comparing data sets and writing statistical reports.

The introduction discusses the principle of a census. This is where everyone living and working in the country is asked a number of questions about their lifestyles, etc. in order to build up a complete picture of the population of the country. This is as opposed to a sample where only a selection of people is asked. Censuses are useful for governments since they have to make important decisions that affect all of our lives. Understanding attitudes, behaviours and the needs of the population help them to make the correct decisions.

Censuses in the UK take place every ten years and the last UK census took place in 2011. Details can be found at: http://www.ons.gov.uk/ons/guide-method/census/2011/index.html

Prior knowledge

Students should already know how to...

- Add, subtract, multiply and divide whole numbers
- Draw simple diagrams representing discrete data

Starter problem

The starter problem poses three statistical questions for students to consider. In all cases, these questions could be answered (partially at least) from surveying the students in the class. This also provides a good opportunity to discuss how representative such a survey is. How might it be improved? How could we collect a more representative sample from the school year, or the whole school, or the local area?

The idea of a hypothesis, rather than a question, could also be discussed. This is where a statement is made about what you expect to find. For example, the first question could be converted into a hypothesis by saying that you believe 'most students travel to school by bus.' The third question could likewise be converted into a hypothesis such as 'boys take less time to get to school than girls.'

The methods of analysis available once the data is collected could also be discussed. The data cycle could be completed by using this analysis to reach a conclusion.

Resources

MyMaths

All averages	1192	Frequency tables and bar charts	1193
Mean and mode	1200	Median, mode from freq tables	1202
Median and range	1203	Pictograms and bar charts	1205
Reading pie charts	1206	Drawing pie charts	1207
Introducing data	1235	Types of data	1248

Online assessment

Chapter test	2A–8
Formative test	2A–8
Summative test	2A–8

InvisiPen solutions

Organising data in tables	411	Planning an enquiry	414
Questionnaires	415	Bar charts	422
Pie charts	423	Mean of a list	441
Frequency table averages	442	Comparing data sets	445
Writing a statistical report	448		

Topic scheme

Teaching time = 10 lessons/4 weeks

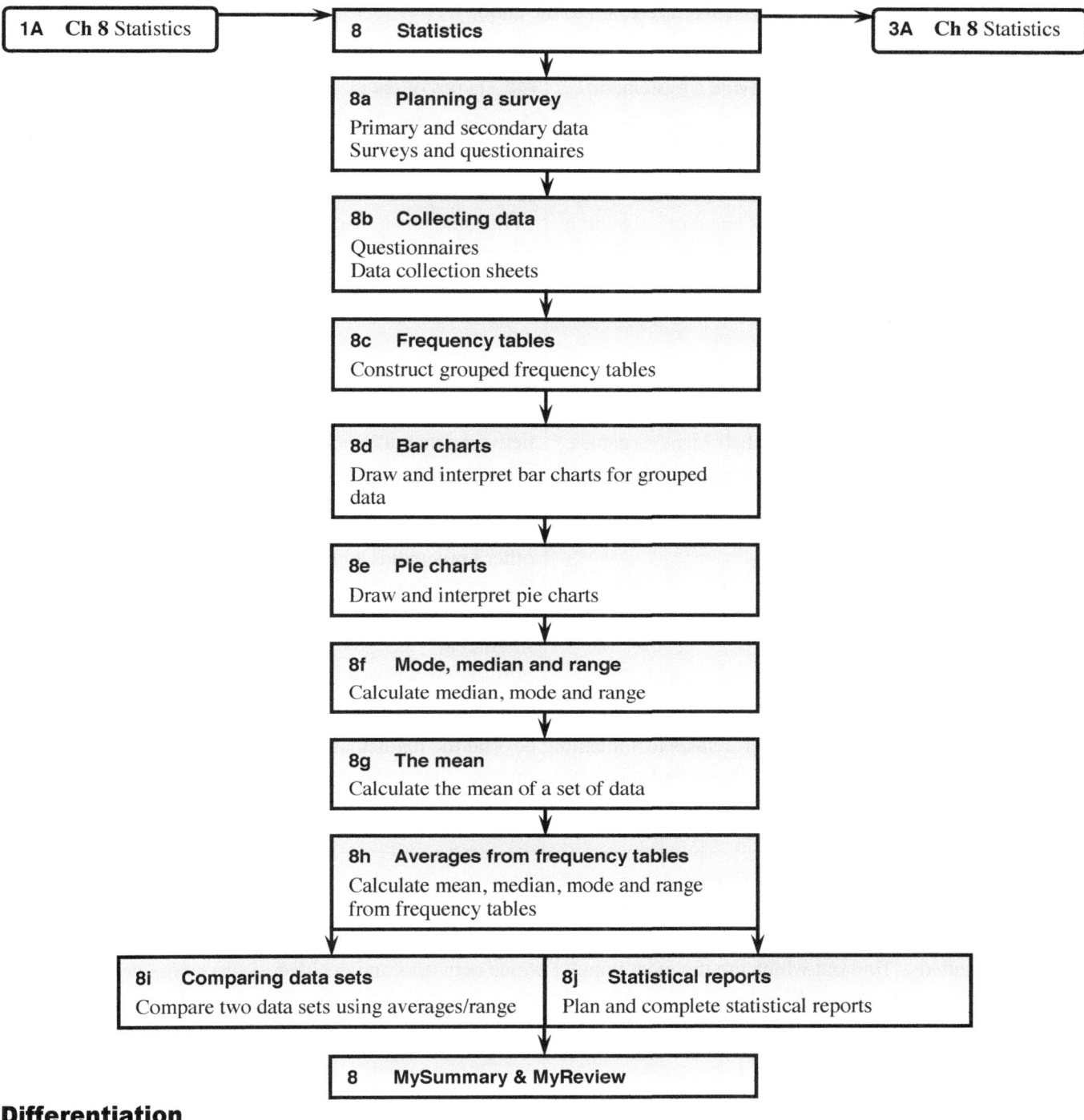

| 1A   Ch 8 Statistics | → | 8   Statistics | → | 3A   Ch 8 Statistics |

8a   Planning a survey
Primary and secondary data
Surveys and questionnaires

8b   Collecting data
Questionnaires
Data collection sheets

8c   Frequency tables
Construct grouped frequency tables

8d   Bar charts
Draw and interpret bar charts for grouped data

8e   Pie charts
Draw and interpret pie charts

8f   Mode, median and range
Calculate median, mode and range

8g   The mean
Calculate the mean of a set of data

8h   Averages from frequency tables
Calculate mean, median, mode and range from frequency tables

8i   Comparing data sets
Compare two data sets using averages/range

8j   Statistical reports
Plan and complete statistical reports

8   MySummary & MyReview

Differentiation

Student book 2A   144–169
Planning a survey
Collecting data
Frequency tables
Bar charts
Pie charts
Mode, median and range
The mean
Averages from frequency tables
Comparing data sets
Statistical reports

Student book 2B   134–155
Planning a data collection
Collecting data
Pie charts
Bar charts and frequency diagrams
Averages
Averages from frequency tables
Scatter graphs and correlation
Stem-and-leaf diagrams

Student book 2C   136–159
Planning a statistical
         investigation
Collecting data
Frequency tables
Constructing diagrams
Averages 1
Averages 2
Interpreting statistical diagrams
Scatter diagrams and correlation
Comparing distributions

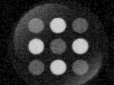

Objectives

- Discuss an area of enquiry that can be addressed by statistical methods and identify ways to explore it (L5)
- Identify possible sources of data that are relevant to the enquiry   (L5)

Key ideas	Resources
1 A data-handling cycle helps provide a systematic approach to an enquiry 2 Both primary and secondary data can be used	⊞ Types of data (1248) A poster of the data-handling cycle Access to the Internet

Simplification	Extension
Consider students' relative skills of speaking, listening, reading and writing when forming pairs or groups for shared tasks. Pairs and groups need to discuss each question first before committing to paper their final answer.	Invite students to use IT to design an appropriate survey for Paul in question **4** and consider how he could collect his data efficiently.

Literacy	Links
This exercise involves much discussion. It gives ample opportunity for students to gather their ideas, organise them and articulate them in pairs, groups and whole-class sessions. Their speaking and listening skills will be very evident.	The Internet is a worldwide system of computer networks that allows the user to access information from any other computer (with permission). It was developed by the US government in 1969 to allow researchers to access information on computers at other universities and was first known as the Advanced Research Projects Agency Network or ARPANET. There is a timeline showing the development of the Internet at http://www.webopedia.com/quick_ref/timeline.asp

Alternative approach

This topic comes more alive when it relates to something beyond the mathematics classroom. Other subjects may be embarking on an investigation. The school might have an issue that needs exploration. The work of the textbook can run alongside a 'real-life' context from outside the classroom.

Checkpoint

1 State whether the following is *primary* or *secondary* data.
   a Asking the people who live in your road which phone network they use.   (Primary)
   b Looking on the Internet to find out which are the most popular phone networks.   (Secondary)

2 If you wanted to find out which are the most popular phone networks and decided to survey the people in a supermarket at 2 pm on a Monday, what would be limiting about this?   (Many people will be at work, etc.)

Starter – Today's number is …36

Ask questions based on 'Today's number'; for example,

> What is double 36? (72)
> What are the factors of 36?
> (1, 2, 3, 4, 6, 9, 12, 18, 36)
> How many of the factors are square numbers? (4)
> What is 10% of 36? (3.6)

Teaching notes

Choose a hypothesis such as, 'France is the most popular holiday destination'. Ask for students' opinions. Invite students to articulate why they agree or disagree with the statement. Discuss how to test the hypothesis.

Describe the data-handling cycle and ask students how data could be collected to act as evidence to support the hypothesis or not. Discuss each aspect of the cycle.

Primary data is data you collect yourself. Accept suggestions that students could survey the class about their holiday destination. Discuss the advantages (such as immediacy of responses and questions tailored to the exact enquiry) and disadvantages of this approach (a small data group and different types of bias, etc.)

Secondary data is data collected by someone else. Research on holiday destinations might be found on the Internet. Again, discuss the advantages and disadvantages, such as the huge amount of data, the reliability of the data, etc.

Throughout this lesson, students will benefit from working in pairs and groups to discuss their ideas. They need to take notes to feedback their thoughts in a whole-class plenary session.

Plenary

Invite groups to feedback on topics such as those suggested in question **2** in Exercise **8a**. Point out good features, such as relevant questioning and the benefits of closed questions. The class agrees the best features of a survey.

Exercise commentary

Throughout this exercise, students will benefit from working in pairs or groups to discuss their ideas.

Question 1 – Distinguishes between primary and secondary data.

Question 2 – Focuses on appropriate survey questions to investigate a given enquiry.

Question 3 – Asks about the sources of primary and secondary data.

Question 4 – Requires students to improve a plan of an enquiry.

Question 5 – Students list the advantages and disadvantages of primary and secondary data.

Answers

1. a secondary b primary
   c secondary d primary
2. Feed back students' suggestions and discuss
3. Various answers possible. Here are some suggestions:
   Search the internet for data
   Conduct a survey in Year 8
   Contact Age Concern for information
4. a Not all pets (e.g. goldfish) get taken for a walk
   b He would be better conducting a survey across a random cross-section of the population of his town

5.

	Primary data	Secondary data
Advantages	You have control over how the data is collected	Quicker to get hold of and easier if you want a large sample
Disadvantages	Time consuming to collect	May not always target the specific population you want

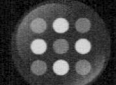

Objectives		
• Plan how to collect and organise small sets of data from surveys and experiments		(L5)
• Design data collection sheets or questionnaires to use in a simple survey		(L5)
• Suggest possible answers, given a question that can be addressed by statistical methods		(L5)

Key ideas	Resources
1 Questionnaires and data-collection sheets can be used to collect data 2 Their design is crucial to the quality of the data	Examples of data collection sheets and questionnaires

Simplification	Extension
Exercise **11b** is quite wordy and, if literacy is problematic for some students, it is worth considering students' relative strengths when grouping students. Groups should discuss each question first before committing to paper their final answer.	Students could consider an enquiry of their own to investigate in their year group. Invite them to create a questionnaire and data collection sheet to collect information.

Literacy	Links
New words are required for aspects of statistics that are connected with collecting data; words such as *survey, sample, biased sample, questionnaire, data-collection sheet, data-capture sheet, open questions, closed questions*. These words and their purpose need explaining as they appear.	People who carry out surveys and market research over the telephone are called 'telemarketers'. The data collected is usually used by companies to target sales and to develop new products. It can also give companies information about customers and how satisfied they are with their service. There is a job description for telemarketing at http://www.careerplanner.com/Job-Descriptions/Telemarketers.cfm

Alternative approach

There are issues with selecting those who are given the questionnaire or who are interviewed for the data-collection sheet. Questions to ask students include:

Who will receive the questionnaire? How are they to be selected to give an unbiased sample?
Does the age, the gender, the place of residence, the occupation, etc. have a bearing on who receives a questionnaire?
When interviewing for the data-collection sheet, does the time of day and the place of first contact affect the sample?
Are there any other points that need to be taken into account?

Checkpoint

1 To survey how long students spend on their homework each day, how would you structure the question?

(The answer should have sections such as: Up to and including half an hour; More than half an hour but less than or equal to one hour, etc. Check for no ambiguity in categories.)

Starter – Numbered cubes

Ask students to imagine a bag containing ten cubes numbered 1, 2 or 5. Cubes are drawn out of the bag and replaced each time. The results are recorded, for example as:

5, 1, 5, 5, 2, 2, 2, 5, 2, 5, 2, 2, 2, 2, 5, 2, 2, 2, 5, 2

Students estimate how many of each number there are in the bag. (For example, one 1, six 2s, three 5s)

Teaching notes

Refer to the hypothesis from last lesson that 'France is the most popular holiday destination'. Note the use of questionnaires (which are quick to give to many people but take longer to collate data) and data-collection sheets (where collation is immediate but is time-consuming at the point of collection).

Discuss what questions could be asked. Use inappropriate questions to stimulate discussion. For example, is the question 'Do you stay in a hotel/tent/apartment/with family?' relevant? Students reach agreement on appropriate questions and how best to record the data if using a data-collection sheet.

As before, students will benefit greatly from whole-class, group and paired discussion. They need to articulate their own arguments whilst listening to the opinions and ideas of others. Notes need to be taken if there is any feedback in a plenary session.

Plenary

Invite groups to give feedback on their discussion. Point out good features of questionnaires and data-collection sheets. The class agrees the best features to incorporate into any future designs.

Exercise commentary

Throughout this exercise, students will benefit from working in pairs or groups to discuss their ideas.

Questions 1–4 – Focus on designing and improving questions in various surveys.

Question 5 – This focuses on open questions. Students can consider which questions are necessary to 'close'.

Answers

1 Question 1: put age categories on the tick boxes
  Question 2: change 3rd box to 3 or more
  Question 3: add another box, titled 'Other'

2 **a** He will only take his sample from people that use the canteen – there are likely to be other people who don't use the canteen because they do not like the food

  b Obtain a sample of all the students in the school, perhaps by placing data sheets in registers for randomly selected students

3 Question 8. Re-write as:
  Recycling. Please tick one of these boxes to tell us how much of your rubbish you recycle

None	☐	Some but less than 10%	☐
More than 10% but less than 25%	☐	More than 25%	☐

4 Her family is hardly likely to be representative of the entire population. A better approach may be to ask the Association of British Travel Agents for information

5 Discuss students' answers with class

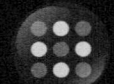

Objectives

- Construct frequency tables for gathering discrete data, grouped where appropriate in equal class intervals   (L4)
- Collect small sets of data from surveys and experiments   (L4)

Key ideas	Resources
1 Data can be collated using tally charts and represented in frequency tables 2 Frequency tables can have data that is not grouped together or grouped into classes	Frequency tables and bar charts (1193) Introducing data (1235) Tabloid and broadsheet newspaper s

Simplification	Extension
The task in question **3** is quite complex and some students may require a more manageable and shorter extract. Alternatively, students could work in groups and tally one line each before combining their results.	Students compare the word lengths from two paragraphs from different sources, such as a tabloid newspaper and broadsheet newspaper.

Literacy	Links
New words for this lesson include: *tally* (plural: *tallies*), *tally chart*, *frequency*, *frequency table*, *class intervals*, *analysis* and the verb *analyse*. Some of these have spellings that will need attention.	Jane Austen was an English novelist who lived from 1775 to 1817. She wrote six completed novels, all published anonymously, about the life of women in the social circles of the early 19th century. All six novels have been adapted for television and film productions including *Pride and Prejudice*. Students could compare sentence lengths from an extract from a Jane Austen novel and an extract from a modern bestseller. There is more information about Jane Austen at http://en.wikipedia.org/wiki/Jane_Austen

Alternative approach

This topic has more purpose when it relates to something beyond the mathematics classroom. Other subjects or the school itself may be embarking on an investigation that needs data to be collected. Science is often a fertile area for data-handling.

Checkpoint

1 Complete a tally chart for the following list of goals scored in 18 football matches

2 4 0 3 2 3

2 0 1 1 4 3

0 1 1 2 0 1

Number of goals	Tally	Frequency
0		
1		
2		
3		
4		

(Check students' tallies. Should give the following frequencies from 0 to 4: 4, 5, 4, 3, 2)

Starter – Student survey

Draw a Venn diagram for two different attributes; for example, 'brown eyes' and 'cereal for breakfast'.

Students frame possible questions to collect data to include in the diagram, with classmates answering by a show of hands. Enter the data and then ask questions, such as, 'How many students have brown eyes but did not have cereal for breakfast?'

The activity can be extended to three attributes.

Teaching notes

Students give their shoe size and each value is listed for all the class to see. Invite students to suggest a more efficient way of collecting this data, such as 'Raise your hand if your shoe size is X.'

Use tallies and a tally chart to construct a frequency table. Note that tallies are grouped into 5s for ease of counting. The data is now organised and can be analysed. Conclusions can be drawn, such as: the least common, the most common, the smallest, the largest shoe size is ...'

A further activity is to have students measuring their heights. Discuss how to record this information in a frequency table. Note that, in this case, there are too many values for each to have its own place in the frequency table. Discuss how to group them. Demonstrate recording and organising the data using equal class intervals.

Plenary

Refer to question **4** and the discussion about the differences in word length that had been noted. Also discuss the results of the extension activity with two newspapers. Ask in what kind of sources students might expect to see significant differences in word length.

Exercise commentary

Encourage students to draw a tally for each number as they go through, crossing out the numbers as they go.

Questions 1 and **2** – These two questions involve creating frequency tables for ungrouped data (in question **1**) and grouped data (in question **2**).

Question 3 – This is a more substantial task that may be shared by several pairs of students working on different lines of text.

Question 4 – This question lends itself to a whole-class discussion about the comparison of the distributions of two data sets.

Answers

1 a, b

Goals scored	Tally	Frequency
0	IIII	4
1	HHH I	6
2	HHH IIII	9
3	HHH IIII	9
4	I	1
5	I	1

2

Number of emails	Tally	Frequency
0 – 9	HHH	5
10 – 19	HHH HHH II	12
20 – 29	HHH HHH HHH HHH	20
30 – 39	II	2

3

Length of word	Tally	Frequency
1 – 2	HHH HHH IIII	14
3 – 4	HHH HHH HHH IIII	19
5 – 6	HHH HHH II	12
7 – 8	HHH I	6
9 – 10	III	3
11 – 12	II	2

4 They are very similar, but discuss with students.

Objectives

- Construct, on paper and using ICT, bar charts to represent data, including bar-line charts   (L4)

Key ideas	Resources
1 Bar charts can represent discrete data 2 Comparative bar charts compare the distributions of two sets of data on the same chart	Frequency tables and bar charts (1193) Pictograms and bar charts (1205) Copies of charts from the students' book Pre-prepared axes Examples of comparative bar charts

Simplification	Extension
Constructing axes may cause problems for some students. They can refer back to the examples in their book to consider what each axis should represent. Some weaker students will benefit from pre-prepared axes for each question.	In pairs, students challenge one another with questions based upon their bar charts. For example, in question **1**, how many pets did the vet see in total? In question **2**, place the numbers in order from most common to least common, etc.

Literacy	Links
Bar charts only use discrete data. There is quantitative (numerical) data and qualitative or categorical (non-numerical) data. Examples of these types of data are runs in cricket, goals in soccer (quantitative); eye-colour and types of pets (qualitative). The columns on a bar chart are separated by gaps; they do not touch. Two distributions of data can be shown together on the same bar chart. The columns of a bar chart can run horizontally rather than vertically. A bar chart can have vertical lines rather than columns. Such a chart is called a 'bar-line chart'.	There is a bar chart showing the holiday destinations for UK residents in 2003 at http://www.statistics.gov.uk/cci/nugget.asp?id51108 Which country was the most popular to visit? (Spain) What percentage of those people taking a holiday abroad visited Spain? (30%) Does the graph show how many people visited Spain? (No; the total number of people taking holidays abroad is not given) How many of the class visited Spain last year? Express this as a percentage and compare with the figure on the graph.

Alternative approach

Bar charts can be constructed in different ways. Here are two other, very contrasting, ways.

The simplest way, often used with young children in primary school, is to give each child a square which they stick to form columns on blank paper with a horizontal axis labelled with their current interest; such as favourite type of pet.

An electronic method is to use a spreadsheet with a column for the names of the categories and the adjacent column for their frequencies. The categories and frequencies are highlighted and the toolbar is used to draw a bar chart.

Checkpoint

1 The frequency chart shows the shoe sizes of students in a Year 8 class. There are 30 students in the class.

Shoe size	3	4	5	6	7	8	9
Frequency	2	7	?	4	2	4	2

How many students have shoe size 5?   (9)

Starter – Temperatures

Write a list of times and temperatures:

6 am	9 am	12 noon	3 pm	6 pm	9 pm
9 °C	16 °C	21 °C	23 °C	17 °C	14 °C

Give students quick-fire questions; for example, 'What is the biggest temperature difference over 3 hours?' 'By how much did the temperature change between 9 am and 12 noon?'

This activity can be differentiated by the choice of temperatures.

Teaching notes

Introduce students to the terms **quantitative data** (numerical data) and **qualitative/categorical data** (non-numerical).

Refer to the data from the previous lessons: colour of eyes; number of goals scored in a match; word length; etc. Students say which type of data each one is. They then give other examples of data for each type. Note that quantitative (numerical) data can include grouped data.

Refer to diagrams in the students' book to highlight:

– A bar chart uses vertical (or horizontal) bars of equal width to show the frequency of data in each category
– Bar charts show exact values. They allow comparison of one category with another
– A bar-line chart uses a line instead of a bar
– Two distributions can be shown alongside each other on the same bar chart.

Plenary

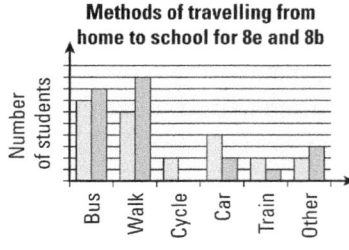

Methods of travelling from home to school for 8e and 8b

Show a comparative bar chart and discuss what it shows.

Note that without labelled axes and a title it has no meaning.

Note that this type of chart allows for comparison of two pieces of data on the same axes. Discuss any additional information and highlight the necessity of a **key**. Has this chart got a key?

Exercise commentary

Students may need advice on the size of the bar charts.

Question 1 – Students construct a bar chart to represent given qualitative (categorical) data.

Questions 2–4 – Students use quantitative (numerical) data; compare with question **1**. In question **4**, the data is grouped and students can refer to the previous page in their book for an example on how to label the axes.

Question 5 – This is a substantial piece of work that takes the students from the list of raw data, through the use of tally charts (not mentioned here) and into drawing of bar charts for grouped data.

Answers

1 Check students' bar chart

2 a

Shoe size	Tally	Frequency
3	II	2
4	IIII	4
5	HHH III	8
6	HHH	5
7	HHH II	7
8	II	2
9	II	2

b Check students' bar chart

3, 4 Check students' bar-line chart and bar chart

5 a

Items of post	Tally	Frequency
0 – 4		0
5 – 9	HHH	5
10 – 14	HHH	5
15 – 19	HHH HHH	10
20 – 24	IIII	4
25 – 29	II	2
30 – 34	I	1

b Check students' bar chart

c

Items of post	Tally	Frequency
0 – 9	HHH	5
10 – 19	HHH HHH HHH HHH I	15
20 – 29		6
30 – 39		1

d Discuss with students

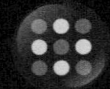

Objectives

- Interpret pie charts that represent data   (L5)
- Construct, on paper and using ICT, simple charts to represent data   (L5/6)

Key ideas	Resources
1 A pie chart uses sectors of a circle to represent different categories of data **2** The angles of the sectors are proportional to the frequencies of the categories	Reading pie charts (1206) Drawing pie charts (1207) Class-size protractor Protractors and rulers Calculators Computer spreadsheet

Simplification	Extension
Constructing pie charts can be problematic for students as it involves calculating the various angles and using a protractor to draw the angles. Students should initially consider which sectors will be biggest and smallest as this will later help them check their work. A revision of how to use a protractor may be necessary. It may be beneficial to pair weaker students with students more confident with protractors.	Using more confident students to 'teach' less confident students provides a natural extension, requiring students to articulate their understanding. A further extension is to have less straightforward angles in the pie charts.

Literacy	Links
The *pie chart*, sometimes known as a *circle diagram*, is divided into *sectors*. Words that include *sect-*, such as 'bisect, dissect, insect, section', all come from a Latin word meaning 'cut'. In France, a pie chart is called a *camembert* after the round shape of the cheese.	The first known use of a pie chart was in 1801 by William Playfair. Playfair was a Scottish engineer who also invented the bar chart. There is copy of one of his pie charts at http://en.wikipedia.org/wiki/Image:Playfair-piechart.jpg

Alternative approach

An alternative way of calculating the angles of the sectors is to work with fractions. For example, if there are three categories with frequencies of 6, 15 and 9 (which total 30), then the three sectors are $\frac{6}{30} = \frac{1}{5}$, $\frac{15}{30} = \frac{1}{2}$ and $\frac{9}{30} = \frac{3}{10}$ of the circle, finding equivalent fractions. As the full circle is 360°, then the angles are $\frac{1}{5} \times 360°$, $\frac{1}{2} \times 360°$ and $\frac{3}{10} \times 360°$, giving 72°, 180° and 108° (which total 360°). Awkward numbers will need a calculator. When drawing the circle, be sure to make the radius just over 5 cm. School protractors will then fit easily.

To draw a pie chart using a computer spreadsheet, construct it with two columns for the names of the categories and their frequencies. The categories and frequencies are highlighted and the toolbar is used to draw a pie chart.

Checkpoint

1 30 people are asked how they get to work. The results are as follows:

Transport	Number of people
Walking	10
Cycle	5
Bus	15

    a If you were to draw a pie chart, how many degrees would one person represent?   (360° ÷ 30 = 12°)

    b What is the angle of the sector that represents 'Walking'?   (Walking: 10 × 12° = 120°)

Starter – Quick fire

Recap work of previous chapters and this chapter so far. Especially include revision of number work with fractions, decimals, percentages and mental computational skills. Ask rapid response questions with students responding on mini whiteboards. Discuss answers when there is a need.

Teaching notes

Show a bar chart displaying categorical data; draw a circle and discuss how to present the same information in a pie chart.

Refer to the examples in the student book and discuss how to divide the circle into 360 parts. Ensure students understand:

360° represents the *total* number of all the items of data. Use proportion to find the number of degrees for each category. Having found the angles for each sector, demonstrate:

- using a compass to construct the circle, noting the centre point
- drawing a start line from the centre of the circle
- using a protractor to measure the first angle
- placing the protractor on the new line to measure the second angle and so on.

Plenary

Show a simple frequency table with four categories and a total frequency of 360, 180 or 90. Students work out the angle for each category, writing their angles on mini whiteboards. Discuss their results.

Exercise commentary

Question 1 – The opening question is straightforward, especially when, in part **c**, the student realises that the sector is nearly a quarter of the circle.

Questions 2–4 – Here the focus is on constructing a pie chart from given data. The questions present different degrees of challenge in calculating the angles of the sectors.

Question 5 – Raw data has to be collated and tabulated before the calculation of angles can begin.

Question 6 – This extends students as the number of degrees to represent one 'unit' is not an integer value.

Answers

1 a Strawberry **b** Vanilla **c** 25%
2 a Check sectors are labelled and have the following angles:

Red	135°
Silver	90°
Black	90°
Other	45°

3 a 48 **b** 6
   c Check sectors are labelled and have the following angles:

Cars	225°
Vans	90°
Lorries	45°

4 Check pie chart is appropriately labelled and has the following sector angles:

Roll/sandwich	120°
Hot meal	100°
Salad	140°

5 Check sectors are labelled and have the following angles:

Good	180°
Normal	108°
Underdeveloped	72°

6 $10 + 3 + 1 = 14$

so Red $= \frac{10}{14} \times 360° \approx 257°$

Silver $= \frac{3}{14} \times 360° \approx 77°$

Green $= 360° - 257° - 77° = 26°$

Objectives	
• Calculate statistics for small sets of discrete data: find the mode, median and range	(L4)

Key ideas	Resources
1 An average is a typical value for the data set. It can be the mode or the median 2 The range is a measure of the spread of the data about the average	Mean and mode (1200) Median and range (1203) A computer spreadsheet

Simplification	Extension
Work together to provide a clear worked example. Initially, use a data set with an odd number of items. Ordering a data set is straightforward. Having ordered, the mode and range are found easily. For the median, have students strike out items in pairs from each end of the distribution.	Students find three data sets where: 1) the mode is 3 2) the mode is 5 but the median is 6 3) the mode is 6, the median is 5 and the range is 11.

Literacy	Links
Statistics are everywhere and to understand them is part of being numerate – and especially to understand when they are being misused in order to mislead. Advertisers and politicians often use and misuse statistics to their own advantage. For example, '9 out of 10 dieters said they lost weight' says nothing about the sample size or how much weight was lost. Remind students that: - the 'mode' is 'the most common' (with all the o's) - the 'median' is in the 'middle' (with the m and d).	The word *average* comes from the French word *averie* which means 'damage sustained at sea'. Costs of losses at sea were shared between the ship owners and the cargo owners and the calculations used to assess the individual contributions gave rise to the modern sense of the word *average*.

Alternative approach

A computer spreadsheet can help with handling data.
- Enter the items of the data set in a column of the spreadsheet and highlight it.
- Use the *data* and *formulas* tabs on the toolbar to place the data in order of size.
- Then find the mode, median and range.
This method is quicker than ordering data with pen and paper.

Checkpoint

1 The ages of 11 children at a playground were recorded
   3 4 3 5 7 4 3 2 5 6 3
   a Place the ages in order, smallest first. $(2, 3, 3, 3, 3, 4, 4, 5, 5, 6, 7)$
   b What is the modal age?   (3)
   c What is the median age?   (4)

Starter – Today's number is …25

Ask questions based on 'Today's number', for example:

What is 50% of 25? (12.5)
What is the closest prime number to 25? (23)
What is 60 subtract 25? (35)
Is 25 a multiple of 3? (No)
What is 200% of 25? (50)

Teaching notes

Ask students for their shoe size and record the data as a list (and include your shoe size if there is an even number of students in the class). Discuss what value students would use as the average, recalling that an average is a value that can be taken as typical of the data. Accept notions of 'middle value' and 'most common'. Introduce:

- the most common value, called the **mode**
- the middle value when arranged in order, called the **median**.

Demonstrate that, to find the middle, the data must first be ordered from smallest to biggest. Show how to cross off one value from each end of the data until only the middle value is left.

Amend the data set so that there is an even number of values. Show that, when there are *two* middle values, the median is the midpoint between them.

Refer to the shoe sizes of the class and introduce the range of data. Emphasise that the range tells us how much difference there is between the highest and lowest values. The range is not an average. The **range** gives some idea of how spread out the data is.

Plenary

Write a data set in order: 2, 2, 2, 7, 8, 8, 9, 10, 11. They could be shoe sizes of a group of friends or the ages of dogs kept by students in a class.

Students find the mode and median. Discuss which of these two averages is the most representative or typical of the data. Ask students to justify their choice.

Note that statistics in everyday life, for example in newspapers and advertisements, often misrepresent the bigger picture. It is important to consider which average has been used and why.

Exercise commentary

Question 1 – Note Jen has 'two modes' in her data set (bimodal data) and Jo has none.

Questions 2 and **3** – Both questions require the median to be found. Note that not all data sets are ordered and that some data sets have an even number of items.

Question 4 – When finding the range of a data set, it is not essential to arrange the data in order of size.

Question 5 – This asks students to find the mode and the median of a data set. In each data set, there is only one modal value and the data set has been ordered.

Question 6 – The examples asked for are not as straightforward as they might appear at first glance. This question would be good for pair work.

Answers

1	a	Amy	7	Selma	12
		Jen	6	Jo	6
	b	Amy	5	Selma	6
		Jen	4 and 9	Jo	No mode
2	a	James			
	b	Kalid	5	Emily	4
		Dan	6.5	Steph	6
		James	8		
3	a	Sandra	4	Abbie	5
		Lizzie	4	Jill	6
		Maya	4		
	b	Sandra	5	Abbie	7
		Lizzie	4.5	Jill	8
		Maya	4.5		

4 a 8   b 6
   c 9   d 4.2 kg
5 a 4, 3   b 8, 8   c 5, 5
6 a 1 2 3 3 4 5   b 1 1 2 3 4
   c 1 2 2 4 5 6   d 1 1 1 2 3 4 5
Other answers possible

8g The mean

Objectives

- Calculate the mean for sets of discrete data: use a calculator or spreadsheet for large data sets   (L5)

Key ideas	Resources
1 The mean is another type of average of a data set 2 The mean is the sum of all the items of data divided by the number of items of data	Mean and mode (1200) A computer spreadsheet Calculators

Simplification	Extension
Some students may have difficulty with the division when finding a mean. They may need to use a calculator for this activity. The alliteration of the three averages can confuse. A useful mnemonic is that the 'mode' is 'the most common' result (with all the o's), the 'median' is the 'middle' result (with the **m** and **d**) and the '**mean**' is 'mean' because you have to work it out.	Students make a data set where the mode is 4, the mean is 6 and the median is 5. (4, 4, 4, 5, 5, 9, 11)

Literacy	Links
When the word 'average' is used in everyday life, it can refer to just a typical event in a general way ('I'm having an average sort of day today.'). Sometimes it is given a numerical value but doesn't say which type of average it is ('Some teenagers earn an average of £20 with Saturday jobs.'). In this case, the word 'average' usually refers to the **mean**.	Human heights are known to range from 22.5" (57 cm) to 8' 11.1" (272 cm). However, these heights are exceptional and are usually caused by a medical condition. In Britain, the average height for men is 5' 9" (175 cm) and for women is 5' 4" (162 cm). Your height depends on both the genes that you inherit from your parents and your health and nutrition; that is, how well you eat. More information on human heights can be found by searching the Internet.

Alternative approach

In the previous lesson, a computer spreadsheet helped with finding the mode, median and range. It can also help with finding the mean of a data set.

As before, enter the data set in a column of the spreadsheet. Highlight the empty cell below the column of data and use *Insert function* in the tool bar. Select AVERAGE (as even the computer doesn't use the word 'mean'!). The mean appears in the empty cell.

Note that there was the choice of selecting SUM which gives the total of all the items of data. This SUM divided by the number of items will also give the mean.

Checkpoint

1 The ages of seven children in a playground were recorded.
1 3 3 4 5 6 6
What is the mean age? $(28 \div 7 = 4)$

Starter – Favourite crisps

A pie chart represents the favourite crisps of 36 students.

The flavours and angles (not in the same order) are: chicken, onion, plain, salt & vinegar; 120°, 90°, 100° and 50°.

25% of students preferred plain. Twice as many preferred salt & vinegar to chicken. A third preferred onion.

Ask students to match the angles with the flavours. How many students prefer each flavour?
(9, 90°, plain; 10, 100°, salt & vinegar; 5, 50°, chicken; 12, 120°, onion)

Teaching notes

Discuss the average amount of pocket money for a 13-year-old. Is it better to work it out as the mode or the median?

Introduce another average, the **mean**. Introduce it as the **fair** or **levelled** average if the money of all respondents was shared out equally. On a bar chart, it is the height of the bars if all of them were 'levelled out'.

To find the mean:
– add all the individual values to get a total
– divide the total by the number of values in the data set.

Work through several examples to gain confidence in calculating the mean and also to recall the mode and median from the previous lesson.

Plenary

Ask students to calculate the mean eye-colour and the median eye-colour of students in the class. Note that the mode is the only average that can be used for **categorical** (**non-numerical**) data sets.

Thinking of the three types of average, discuss:
- which type of average shoe size might a shoe shopkeeper be interested in
- which type of average bag weight might the pilot of a plane be interested in
- which type of average height might a photographer of students at schools be interested in.

Exercise commentary

Questions 1–3 – Students calculate the mean from small data sets in questions **1** and **2**, which give whole number answers, but need a calculator for question **3**, which includes decimal values and gives decimal answers that will need discussion of when to round.

Question 4 – All three averages, mean, median and mode, are required.

Questions 5 and **6** – These require calculating the mean from a large data set in a context. Students should be encouraged to:
- either use a calculator and devise a strategy for checking their calculations (such as, add and check each column in turn)
- or use a computer spreadsheet where values can be checked after they have all been entered.
Discuss the advantages and disadvantages of these two methods.

Question 7 – This can be done in pairs.

Answers

1	a	5	b	8	c	6

2	5

3	a	22.25	b	27.38	c	4264.83

4		Mean	Median	Mode
	a	12.3	9	9
	b	11.1	6.5	28
	c	108.9	109	109

5	165 cm

6	48.5

7		Mean	Median	Mode	Most representative
	a	10.25	7	7	Median/mode
	b	55.75	41	34	Median
	c	44.7	29	2	Median

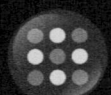

8h Averages from frequency tables

Objectives

- Calculate statistics for small sets of discrete data:
  - the median and the modal class for grouped data   (L4)
  - the mean, including from a simple frequency table   (L6)

Key ideas	Resources
1 There are three common averages 2 For a given set of data, one average may be more typical of the data than the other averages	Median, mode from freq tables (1202) Calculators Computer spreadsheets

Simplification	Extension
Calculation of the mean and median from frequency tables can be confusing. Re-write the data as a string of numbers in the raw form before it was tabulated. For the mean, discuss shortcuts to find the total. For the median, discuss how to find the middle item of data.	More confident students to articulate their understanding to struggling students. Direct them to avoid 'telling' but instead focus on asking questions to draw out the information – how can we find the total number of eggs? etc.

Literacy	Links
A common misconception with frequency tables is that students see the number of classes in the table as the full data set; for example, the table below has only 6 items of data because there are only 6 classes. To avoid this, students need to create frequency tables from raw data and find averages from **both** the raw data **and** its frequency table.	The number of eggs laid by a female bird varies from species to species. Many species of albatross only lay one egg every other year. Their low reproductive rates mean that the birds are under threat of extinction. There is more information about albatrosses at http://animals.nationalgeographic.co.uk/animals/birds/albatross.html

Alternative approach

In the previous two lessons, a computer spreadsheet helped with finding the mode, median, the mean and range of a data set of individual items. It can also help to find the mean from a frequency table.

Consider the number of brothers and sisters that the 11 members of a class have. The data is given in this table.

	Children	Frequency	$f \times c$
Labels cells A1, B1 and C1 with *Children*, *Frequency* and $f \times c$. In columns A and B, enter the number of siblings from 0 to 5 with their frequencies. In cell C2, create the formula C2 = B2*A2. Drag the formula down for all the siblings and frequencies. Insert the *AutoSum* function in cell B8 to calculate the total of all frequencies. This should be 11 as we know there are 11 students. Repeat for cell C8 to give the total number of all siblings (22). The mean number of siblings is 22 ÷ 11 = 2.	0 1 2 3 4 5 Total	2 2 4 1 1 1 11	0 2 8 3 4 5 22

Use a spreadsheet to check answers in Exercise **8h** that were found using a calculator.

Checkpoint

1 The table shows the number of people recorded in cars driving through a set of traffic lights at 8 am one day.

Number of people	1	2	3	4
Frequency	8	10	12	3

  a How many cars had 3 people in them?   (12)
  b How many cars were there altogether?   (33)
  c What is the total number of people in the survey?   (76)
  d What is the mean number of people in a car?   (76 ÷ 33 = 2.3)

Starter – DVDs

Ask students to calculate the mean and range of the playing times of the following DVDs:

Harry Potter and the Chamber of Secrets

	2 hours 34 minutes
Toy Story 2	1 hour 29 minutes
Billy Elliot	1 hour 45 minutes

(Mean = 1 hr 56 min; Range = 1 hr 5 min)

Teaching notes

Each student in class says how many siblings they have. The raw results are written as a string of numbers. Use the data to create a tally chart and a frequency table.

Discuss the average number of siblings, recalling from previous lessons, the mode, median and mean.

Highlight how clearly the modal value can be found from the frequency table, but ensure students recognise that the modal value is the *value* of the data and *not* the frequency.

Discuss how to calculate the mean and median values. These are not easy from the table, so return to the string of raw data. Discuss the efficiency of using the raw data and find shortcuts that can be used.

Model a more efficient method, drawing on the shortcuts and based on finding 'frequency × value'. A third row (or column) can be added to the table. Gain as much as possible from students themselves.

If the class is particularly able, discuss an efficient way to find the median from a frequency table.

Work through other examples.

Plenary

Allow plenty of time to work through each of the questions in the student book. Invite students to demonstrate each step to the whole class with reference to the frequency tables.

Exercise commentary

Questions 1 and **2** – Parts **a** and **b** can create misunderstandings. For question **1**, it could be time well spent to write out the raw data as a string of numbers. Relate the raw data to the frequency table and the answers to parts **a**, **b** and **c** will follow. The same approach could be taken for question **2**, but the string of numbers in the raw data is very long.

Question 3 – Part **d** is the easiest part; part **c** is the hardest. The whole data set is not too large to write out as raw data. This approach is likely the best method for part **c**.

Question 4 – This is far easier than question **3**.

Question 5 – This is straightforward.

Question 6 – This can be done by calculator or spreadsheet. Discuss the relative merits of each method.

Answers

1	a	23	b	36	c	1.6 (1 dp)
2	a	38	b	55	c	1.45
3	a	45	b	2.25
	c	2	d	1
4	a	16

    b   mean = 2.9, median = 3, mode = 3

    c   range = 6

5 The highest value with a non-zero frequency recorded take away the lowest value with a non-zero frequency recorded

6 Check students' work

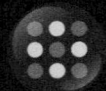
Objectives

- Compare two simple distributions using the range and one of the three averages: mode, median or mean   (L5)

Key ideas	Resources
1 The comparison of two distributions is made by considering the relative values of their averages and their ranges	All averages (1192) Reading pie charts (1206) Rulers Calculators Examples of comparative bar charts.

Simplification	Extension
Students work in pairs as discussion about each question will help their understanding. Students often forget to order data when calculating the median. They could *always* order the data, whichever average they want to find, as ordered data helps with calculating all three averages.	Students can use the Internet to visit the BBC weather website and compare the five-day forecasts of two cities in the UK.

Literacy	Links
When making a comparison between two distributions, students need to write a short paragraph. The two distinctive features of a distribution are its central or typical value (which the averages can describe) and whether results are tightly or loosely ranged about the central value (which the ranges can describe). So the paragraph says how different the averages are and how tightly or loosely the data is spread about the averages.	Like people, plants need to consume the right types of food to grow strong and healthy. If the soil is deficient in a nutrient, then plants do not grow as well as they could. For example, a lack of nitrogen leads to stunted growth; whilst a lack of copper can cause yellowing of leaves. Farmers use fertilizers to help supply the essential chemical elements that plants need. There is more information at http://en.wikipedia.org/wiki/Fertilizer

Alternative approach

A comparative bar chart can be drawn for two frequency tables using a computer spreadsheet.

Input the frequencies for the classes of two distributions; one set in column A and the other set in column B. Highlight the two sets.

Use the toolbar for *Insert* and then *Bar*. Select the most appropriate of the many bar charts on offer. Choose the one that shows the two data sets most clearly.

Compare the two distributions using the mode and the range.

Checkpoint

1 Nine students took a Maths test that is marked out of ten and, then again, took a similar test two weeks later. Had their marks improved? Use the median and the range to compare the two data sets.

Student	A	B	C	D	E	F	G	H	I
1st test	5	7	7	5	8	8	9	5	8
2nd test	6	9	7	7	7	9	9	8	10

(1st test: median 7 and range 4. 2nd test: median 8 and range 4. Yes, the results have improved.)

Starter – Missing numbers

Students find:

- three numbers with a total of 24 and give the range
- four numbers with a total of 60 and a range of 7 (12, 14, 15, 19 and other answers)
- four numbers with a mean of 10 and a range of 8 (6, 8, 12, 14 and other answers).

Teaching notes

Split the class into two even-sized groups (include yourself if there is an odd number of students). The aim is to compare the hand-spans of group A and group B.

Both groups measure the span of their hands and record the results in a list.

Students compare groups A and B by discussing the largest and smallest values and the **range** of the two distributions.

Find the three averages for each group and discuss the average hand-span of each group taking each average in turn.

Write a short report on the conclusions.

Plenary

Show several comparative bar charts similar to those in question 1. Ask for comments which compare the two distributions using the mode and the range.

Exercise commentary

This exercise involves much discussion in pairs that can be fed back to the whole class in a plenary session.

Question 1 – This uses a comparative bar chart. Both classes have the same mode (C) and the same range (A to E), and yet clearly one class did better than the other.

Question 2 – This needs much discussion, especially for part **b**. Students may not appreciate that the larger segment will not necessarily mean a larger total frequency.

Question 3 – There are only 5 boys and 5 girls. So the raw data can quickly be written in order. Finding the median and the range are both straightforward.
This is the first question asking for a comparison. Two sentences need to be created; one to describe the relative value of the medians as typical values and the other to describe the ranges as measures of spread.

Question 4 – This requires a similar approach as that for question **3**.

Question 5 – This comparison extends to comparing data using all three averages. The ranges could be included in the final discussion.

Answers

1 The classes are roughly the same sizes (8W–29, 8Y–30), but 13 people got A's or B's in Class 8Y compared to only 7 in Class 8W. The number of grade C's was roughly equal in each class, so Class 8Y had the better results with a far higher proportion of good grades.

2 **a** Order of popularity in Week 1 was S, O, V, C. In Week 2 it was V, C, S, O.

   b The chocolate segment for Week 2 is larger but without knowing the total sales per week you cannot say whether or not more was sold.

3 **a**

	Median	Range
Boys	21	10
Girls	18	4

   b The boys ate more on average, but there was much more variability between individual boys than girls.

4 **a**

	Median	Range
Test 1	6.5	7
Test 2	3.5	6

   b Test 2 was harder as the scores were much lower on average (and overall).

5 **a**

	Median	Mean	Mode
Test 1	10	9.7	11
Test 2	11	9.4	11

   The medians are very similar with Test 2 being higher.
   There is no appreciable difference in the means.
   The modes are identical.

   b The scores are not comparable. A percentage score may be a more meaningful way to compare tests.

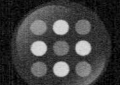

Objectives

- Write a short report of a statistical enquiry, including appropriate diagrams, graphs and charts   (L5)
- Justify the choice of presentation   (L5)

Key ideas	Resources
A statistical report is written at the end of a project and includes the purpose of the project and how data is gathered, analysed and represented in graphs or charts. It will draw any conclusions from the analysis and compare them with the original aims.	Pictograms and pie charts (1205) Reading pie charts (1206) A poster of the data-handling cycle Protractors and compasses Worksheets with circles split into 10° intervals (with 36 parts) for question **2**

Simplification	Extension
Students have difficulty choosing the most appropriate type of chart to represent data. For example, in question **2**, they need to find: 1) how many students do *some* recycling (this includes values from three categories) 2) how many students do *no* recycling. Students decide which graph shows the combination of the first three categories more clearly. If a pie chart, then some students need a circle split into 10° intervals.	Students can undertake a project with a clearly stated aim; such as surveying the amount of pocket money the members of the class receive. They can decide what data is needed, how to gather it and analyse it, how to represent it and analyse it. They can then draw their conclusions and say whether they have achieved their aim.

Literacy	Links
This lesson is as much about making good judgements as it is about drawing graphs. Students working in pairs will help generate discussion, promote understanding and help make good decisions. Their skills of presenting their ideas to their partner and reaching agreement together with their skills of clear writing and presentation enhance their literacy.	Most companies publish an annual report. If possible, bring in some examples. How many bar charts and pie charts are used in each report? How easy are they to read? Does the report have a clear conclusion or summary section? There are examples of annual reports at http://www.rail-reg.gov.uk/upload/pdf/rss_report_06.pdf and at http://www.lawsociety.org.uk/aboutlawsociety/whatwe do/researchandtrends/statisticalreport.law

Alternative approach

The report can also include any limitations that students may have encountered and any further or future lines of enquiry that may be needed.

Rather than just work in pairs, the discussions and outcomes of each pair can be presented to the whole class. Combining the efforts of everyone through whole-class discussion may well lead to an even better report.

Checkpoint

1 Would you choose a pie chart or a bar chart to illustrate the following data?

60 people were asked to choose a number between 1 and 9 inclusive.

Number	1	2	3	4	5	6	7	8	9
Frequency	4	5	5	5	8	11	13	6	3

(Bar chart – as there are many categories)

Starter – Quick fire

Recap basic number work. Include questions on fractions, decimals and percentages and questions using mental and written computation. Work of this chapter can also be included. Ask rapid response questions. Students reply by writing on their mini whiteboards. Discuss questions when their answers indicate a need.

Teaching notes

Refer to the data-handling cycle and recap the stages covered so far throughout this chapter.

Discuss that, at the end of any investigation, you need to conclude what your data shows and how it relates to the original aims of the enquiry.

Introduce the example from the student book: Freya wants to investigate students' methods of travelling to school. Work through each stage of the handling data cycle:

- discuss how she could collect this information, recalling surveys and questionnaires, primary and secondary data, and open and closed questions
- decide how to collate the data and represent it in tables and diagrams
- decide if averages and range are needed as part of the investigation
- draw conclusions and relate them back to the original aims of the enquiry.

Students' final report provides details of the process and also the final conclusions and whether they have met the overall aims.

Plenary

Referring to question **4** of Exercise **8j**, introduce a data set to highlight how extreme data values can skew an average. Consider the data set:
5, 5, 10, 10, 15, 15, 50, 50, 60, 60, 350.

Alternatively, obtain feedback, via a whole-class plenary session, on the reports written by pairs of students. Identity good features. Discuss where shortcomings lie.

Exercise commentary

This exercise creates the need for much discussion in paired work and in whole-class sessions.

Question 1 – The focus is on constructing a bar chart and highlighting key features.

Question 2 – This requires students to construct a pie chart from a frequency table and to see the justification for taking the first three categories together when comparing them with the fourth category. It also compares the appropriateness of bar charts and pie charts.

Question 3 – This requires students to consider the size of the sample of data.

Question 4 – This question directs students to consider the merits and shortcomings of each of the three averages. See also the notes under 'Plenary'.

Answers

1   a   Difficult, because all 4 sectors look roughly the same size
    b   Check students' bar charts
        The bar chart is easier to use because you can see which bar is tallest
2   a   Because it is not easy to see if less than half the students never recycle
    b   Check pie chart sectors are correctly labelled and have angles:
        Every day $40°$
        Most days $80°$
        Sometimes $50°$
        Never $190°$
    c   Can easily see that the 'Never' sector is more than $180°$
3   a   Position 2 has a higher average wind speed
    b   No. On a different day the wind speed might be greater at position 1
4   Sometimes one of the averages is more appropriate than the others, e.g. the median is more appropriate than the mean when one or two extreme values are present. The mode would be more appropriate if we were dealing with clothing sizes.

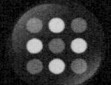

Key outcomes		Quick check
Plan a survey and collect data.	L4	If you wanted to conduct a survey to find out how students travelled to school, how would you phrase the question. (Go through possibilities)
Use frequency tables.	L4	Draw a tally chart and frequency table for the following data. Twenty people were asked how many brothers and sisters they had. 1 2 2 1 3 0 1 4 3 2 / 2 1 0 6 4 3 3 2 1 1 *Answer (check students' tallies)*

Number of brothers and sisters	Tally	Frequency
0		2
1		6
2		5
3		4
4		2
5		0
6		1

Key outcomes		Quick check
Draw bar charts and pie charts.	L5	If you were to draw a pie chart for the data in the previous question, what would be the angle in the sector represnting three brothers and sisters? $(4 \times 36° = 144°)$
Find the mean, mode, median and range of a list of numbers.	L5	Find the mean, median and mode number of brothers and sisters in the previous two questions. (Mean 4.2 Median 2 Mode 1) What is the range? $(6 - 0 = 6)$
Find the mean, median and mode for data in a table.	L5	Twenty people were asked how many dogs they owned. The data is below

Number of brothers and sisters	Frequency
0	3
1	8
2	5
3	4

Find the mean, median and mode.

(Mean 3 Median 1 Mode 1)

⊕ MyMaths extra support

Lesson/online homework	Description
Line graphs and two-way tables 1198 L4	Solving a problem by reading information from line graphs and two-way tables

MyReview

Check out
You should now be able to ...   **Test it ➡**
                                                                     Questions

✓ Plan a survey and collect data.   ④ 1, 2

✓ Use frequency tables.   ④ 3

✓ Draw bar charts and pie charts.   ⑤ 4, 5

✓ Find the mean, mode, median and range of a list of numbers. ⑤ 6

✓ Find the mean, median and mode for data in a table.   ⑤ 7

Language	Meaning	Example
Primary data	Data which you collect yourself	The results of a survey or experiment that you carried out
Secondary data	Data which you did not collect yourself	Information from a book or the internet
Bar chart	A graph using the heights of bars to represent frequencies. The bars should be equal width and have gaps between them	There are examples of bar charts on page 152
Pie chart	A circular chart divided into sectors	There are examples of pie charts on page 154
Average	A value that represents the typical values in a data set	Examples are the mode, median and mean
Mode	An average, defined as the data value that occurs most often	Data: 3, 2, 5, 8, 5, 6, 2, 5 Ordered: 2, 2, 3, 5, 5, 5, 6, 8
Median	An average defined as the middle value when the data are listed in numerical order	Mode = 5 Median = (5 + 5) ÷ 2 = 5
Mean	An average defined as the sum of all of the data values divided by the number of data values	Mean = (2 + 2 + ... + 8) ÷ 8 = 4.5
Range	A measure of the spread of data. It is defined as the largest value minus the smallest value	For the data above Range = 8 − 2 = 6

1 Decide whether each source of data is primary or secondary.
   a Data from a survey you carry out at a shopping centre.
   b Data from the records of patients at a doctors' surgery.

2 What is wrong with this questionnaire?

> **Question 1:**
> How many pets do you have?
> 1-2 ☐   2-4 ☐   4+ ☐
>
> **Question 2:**
> Do you agree that dogs are the best animal?
> yes ☐   no ☐

3 Jenny counts the number of daisies in 1 m × 1 m squares in her garden.
   3 2 0 1
   4 3 2 2
   3 1 2 3
   5 3 3 2
   Draw a tally chart and frequency table for this set of data.

4 Draw a bar chart for the set of data in question 3.

5 Students in year 8 at a school can either bring a packed lunch, go to the canteen, or go home for lunch. The table shows how many students do each.

Lunch	Packed	Canteen	Home
Number	60	85	35

Draw a pie chart for this set of data.

6 The number of goals in games played by the school football team was recorded.
   3 5 2 1 1
   0 4 3 3 2
   Calculate
   a the mode
   b the median
   c the mean
   d the range.

7 Students were asked how many pens they had with them.

Number of pens	Frequency
0	5
1	20
2	10
3	2

Calculate
   a the mode   b the median
   c the mean   d the range.

What next?

Score		
0 – 3		Your knowledge of this topic is still developing. To improve look at Formative test: 2A-8; MyMaths: 1192, 1193, 1200, 1202, 1203, 1205, 1206, 1207, 1235 and 1248
4, 5		You are gaining a secure knowledge of this topic. To improve look at InvisiPen: 411, 414, 415, 422, 423, 441, 442, 445 and 448
6, 7		You have mastered this topic. Well done, you are ready to progress!

 MyMaths.co.uk

Question commentary

Question 1 – Remind students of primary and secondary data, if necessary.

Question 2 – The students could also be asked to provide improved questions.

Questions 3 and **4** – These questions are linked and are quite straightforward.

Question 5 – You may need to remind students to work out number of degrees for each student, i.e. 360° ÷ 180.

Question 6 – Can also ask which average is the most representative.

Question 7 – Some students may find it easier to list out the data in order.

Answers

1 a primary   b secondary

2 Question **1** needs a box for 0 pets and the other boxes need to change as the quantities overlap.

   Question **2** is a leading question and too emotive, also people may agree with just part of the statement.

3

Number of daisies	Tally	Frequency
0	I	1
1	II	2
2	ⅢⅢ	5
3	ⅢⅢ I	6
4	I	1
5	I	1

4 Check students' bar charts

5 Check pie chart sectors are correctly labelled and have angles:
   Packed   120°
   Canteen   170°
   Home   70°

6 a 3   b 2.5
   c 2.4   d 5

7 a 1   b 1
   c 1.24 (2 dp)   d 3

1 Gail wants to investigate mobile telephone costs.
She wants to find out how much money people spent on their mobiles, and what sorts of contracts they choose.

a Suggest one source of primary data that Gail could use in her project.

b Explain how Gail could use secondary data in her project.

2 Explain what is wrong with the following survey questions, and write a better version of each one.

a Are you young or old?

b Do you eat a healthy diet?

c Do you take lots of exercise?

3 Georgie records the colours of 20 cars passing her house.

R R SG Gn Bl SG SG R Bk SG Bl
SG SG Gn Bl W W Bk Bl Bl W

Code: R = Red
SG = Silver or Grey
Gn = Green
Bk = Black
Bl = Blue
W = White

Draw a frequency table for this set of data.

4 Jenny decides to check the contents of her pencil case.
She finds that it contains 5 pencils, 11 gel pens, 2 ballpoint pens and 3 crayons.
Draw a bar chart for this set of data.

5 Ten people enter a talent competition.
There are 5 singers, 2 comedians, 1 impressionist and a juggler.
Show this information on a pie chart.

6 Find the median, mode and range of each of these sets of numbers.

a 11, 13, 13, 16

b 2, 3, 4, 4, 5, 5, 5, 8, 9

c 4, 7, 4, 3, 9, 6, 3, 5, 1

7 Find the mean of each of these sets of numbers.

a 5, 6, 4, 8, 3, 5

b 10.4, 5.9, 8.7, 4.6, 8.9

c 105, 124, 183, 89, 73

8 Find the mean, median and mode of the data in the table which gives the number of spelling mistakes per page in a 20-page booklet.

Mistakes	0	1	2	3
Frequency	17	2	0	1

9 The numbers of goals scored by two hockey teams in 12 matches were as follows.

Team A: 0, 2, 1, 0, 0, 3, 1, 0, 2, 3, 2, 1
Team B: 3, 2, 2, 3, 1, 0, 4, 3, 5, 1, 2, 2

Compare the number of goals for the two teams, using the range and a suitable average.

10 Gerry wanted to test the statement, 'Girls spend longer on homework than boys'.
He asked ten boys and ten girls to record the number of minutes they spent on homework one evening.

Boys: 65, 35, 25, 45, 55, 70, 45, 35, 30, 40
Girls: 45, 55, 65, 35, 20, 45, 40, 65, 55, 35

a Draw a suitable chart to represent this data.

b Calculate a suitable average for each set of data.

c What conclusion should Gerry reach? Explain your answer.

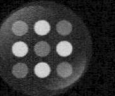

MyMaths.co.uk

Question commentary

Questions 1 and **2** – These questions can be done in pairs.

Questions 3 and **4** – Should be straightforward.

Question 5 – Students may need help working out the size of the sectors.

Question 6 – Part **c** needs to be written in order first.

Question 7 – Calculators are useful here.

Question 8 – Some students may find it easier to list the data.

Question 9 – Students may find all three averages first and then discuss which best represents the data.

Question 10 – Encourage students to order the data first.

Answers

1 **a** She could conduct a survey in the town centre on a Saturday, or a postal survey of people drawn randomly from the electoral roll (although under 18's would be omitted)

    b She could obtain information from mobile phone companies

2 **a** What age are you? (And give groups to choose from)

    b How many portions of fruit and veg do you eat a day? (Plus other questions on fat intake, alcohol consumption, sugar and salt consumption, etc.)

    c How many hours exercise do you take per week? (And give options, e.g., < 5, 5–9, 10–14, etc.)

3

Colour	Tally	Frequency
R	III	3
SG	++++	5
GN	II	2
BK	II	2
BL	++++	5
W	III	3

4 Check students' bar chart

5 Check pie chart sectors are correctly labelled and have angles:

    Singers   200°

    Comedians   80°

    Impressionist 40°

    Juggler   40°

6   Median   Mode   Range

   a 13   13   5

   b 5   5   7

   c 4   4 or 3 8

7 **a** 5.2

   b 7.7

   c 114.8

8 Mean = 0.25

   Median = 0

   Mode = 0

9 On average (comparing medians), Team B scores more goals than Team A (2 compared to 1). However, there is greater variability in Team B's scores with a range of 5 as opposed to 3.

6 **a** Depends on groupings used. As an example:

Time in Minutes	No. of boys	No. of girls
20 – 29	1	1
30 – 39	3	2
40 – 49	3	3
50 – 59	1	2
60 – 69	1	2
70 - 79	1	0
	10	10

   b The mean time spent by boys is 44.5 min

       The mean time spent by girls is 46 min

   c On average, girls spend slightly longer than boys on their homework, but not to a significant extent

MyAssessment 2

These questions will test you on your knowledge of the topics in chapters 5 to 8.
They give you practice in the types of questions that you may eventually be given in your GCSE exams. There are 70 marks in total.

1 a Using what you know about angles, find the missing angles. (4 marks)

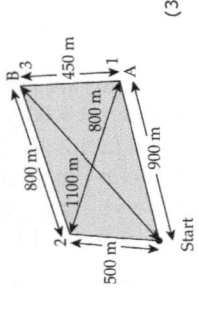

  b What name do we gives this particular triangle? (1 mark)

2 What names do we give shapes with these properties?
  a All four sides are the same length, and opposite angles are equal but not 90°. (1 mark)
  b Only one pair of the four sides are parallel. (1 mark)

3 a Find the missing angles in this quadrilateral. (2 marks)
  b What is the size of missing angle 'c'? (1 mark)

4 a Use centimetre squared paper to draw x and y axes between -5 and +5 (1 mark)
  b Plot these four points: A(2, 4), B(2, -3), C(-5, -3) and D(-3, 3). (4 marks)
  c What quadrant is point C in? (1 mark)
  d What are the equations of the lines joining A to B and C to B? (2 marks)
  e Join the points A to C. What are the coordinates of the two points where this line intersects the x and y axis? (2 marks)

5 The table shows the charges made by a self-drive van hire company

Number of days	0	1	2	3	4	5
Charge (£)	100	150	200	250	300	350

  a Draw a graph to represent this information. (4 marks)
  b What is the initial cost of hiring a van? (1 mark)
  c How much does it cost to hire a van per day? (1 mark)

6 a Use centimetre squared paper to draw an x-axis from 0 to 30 and label this 'kilometres'. Draw a y-axis from 0 to 15 and label this 'miles'. (4 marks)
  b Construct a conversion graph that converts kilometres to miles. Use the conversion 1 mile ≈ 1.6km. Plot at least 4 points on your graph. (5 marks)

7 Use jottings or partitioning to answer these problems. Give an estimate of your answer first.
  a 86 + 46 (1 mark) b 63 - 47 (1 mark) c 739 + 132 (1 mark)
  d 629 - 327 (1 mark) e 27 × 8 (1 mark) f 165 ÷ 5 (1 mark)
  g 83 × 7 (1 mark) h 108 ÷ 6 (1 mark)

MyAssessment 2

8 Part of an orienteering course is shown.
Competitor A runs from the start to control 1 then to control 2 and back to the start.
Competitor B runs from the start to control 3 then to control 2 and back to the start.
Which competitor went the further distance and by how much? (3 marks)

800 m, 450 m, 800 m, 1100 m, 900 m, 500 m, B, 3, 1, A, 2, Start

9 Two packets of crisps costing 63p each and three bottles of fizzy drink costing £0.96 each was bought in a local shop by three children.
  a Work out the total cost of the items bought in the shop. (2 marks)
  b The children decided to share the costs between each of them. How much did they each pay? (2 marks)

10 Here is part of a questionnaire about families.
  a Explain how each of these questions could be improved. (3 marks)
  b Construct two more possible questions that could be asked. (2 marks)

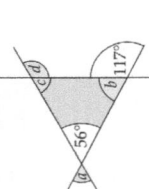

Q1. Do you use the internet
Sometimes ☐ Occasionally ☐ Often ☐
Q2. How old are you
Young ☐ Middle aged ☐ Old ☐
Q3. Do you have a
Boyfriend ☐ Girlfriend ☐ Neither ☐

11 The pie chart shows the area of the oceans in millions of square kilometres. The total ocean area is taken to be 360 million square kilometres.
  a Estimate the area of the Atlantic Ocean. (2 marks)
  b Estimate the area of the Arctic Ocean. (2 marks)

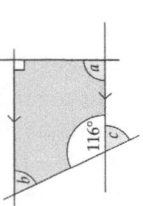

Antarctic, Arctic, Pacific, Indian, Atlantic

12 The table shows the number of goals scored for a hockey team over the course of a season.

Number of goals	0	1	2	3	4	5
Frequency	5	3	6	1	4	2

  a How many matches were played altogether? (1 mark)
  b Draw a bar chart to represent this information. (3 marks)
  c For the number of goals scored, calculate
    i the mean ii the median iii the mode iv the range. (7 marks)

MyMaths.co.uk

Mark scheme

Questions 1 – 5 marks
a 4 $a = 56°, b = 63°, c = 61°, d = 119°$
b 1   scalene

Questions 2 – 2 marks
a 1   rhombus; not quadrilateral
b 1   trapezium

Questions 3 – 3 marks
a 2 $a = 90°, b = 64°$
b 1 $c = 64°$

Questions 4 – 10 marks
a 1   Ensure correct axes drawn
b 4   Check all four points correctly plotted; -1 each error or omission
c 1   3rd quadrant
d 2 $AB : x = 2, CB : y = -3$
e 2   (0, 2) and (-2, 0)

Questions 5 – 6 marks
a 4   Ensure correct axes drawn (1 mark) and correct points plotted (2 marks); line must be drawn (1 mark)
b 1   £100
c 1   £50 per day

Questions 6 – 9 marks
a 4   Ensure correct axes drawn (2 marks); correct points plotted and labelled (2 marks)
b 5   At least 4 points correctly plotted (4 marks); straight line must be drawn (ruler) (1 mark)

Questions 7 – 8 marks
a 1   140, 132; must see evidence of estimate for marks to be given in all answers.
b 1   10, 16
c 1   850, 871
d 1   300, 302
e 1   240, 216
f 1   30, 33
g 1   560, 581
h 1   20, 18

Questions 8 – 3 marks
3   2200 m, 2400 m, B by 200 m; 1 mark each part

Questions 9 – 4 marks
a 2 $(0.63 \times 2) + (0.96 \times 3) = £4.14$
b 2 $£4.14 \div 3 = £1.38$

Questions 10 – 5 marks
a 1   Question too vague, should have boxes for once a day, twice a day, 3 times a day or never
    1   Question too vague, should be more specific 3–12, 13–19, 20–40, 41–65, 66+
    1   Question is asking personal information and so should be avoided. Ask about eye colour instead
b 2   Are you male or female? What is your favourite sport? Or other viable suggestions

Questions 11 – 4 marks
a 2   80° hence $\sim$ 80 million km^2; accept $\pm$ 1°
b 2   15° hence $\sim$ 15 million km^2; accept $\pm$ 1°

Questions 12 – 11 marks
a 1   21 matches
b 3   Ensure correct bar chart drawn, correct height and labelled
c i   3 $44 \div 21 = 2.1$; need to see working
    ii   2   median is 11th match, median goals is 2
    iii 1   2
    iv   1 $5 - 0 = 5$

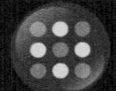

Learning outcomes	
G5	Describe, sketch and draw using conventional terms and notations: points, lines, parallel lines, perpendicular lines, right angles, regular polygons, and other polygons that are reflectively and rotationally symmetric
	(L5)
G8	Identify properties of, and describe the results of, translations, rotations and reflections applied to given figures
	(L5)

Introduction	Prior knowledge
The chapter starts by looking at reflection, reflection symmetry, rotation and rotational symmetry before moving on to look at translations and tessellation.	Students should already know how to… • Recognise the symmetry properties of simple shapes

Introduction

The chapter starts by looking at reflection, reflection symmetry, rotation and rotational symmetry before moving on to look at translations and tessellation.

The introduction discusses the idea of symmetry in art. Buddhist sand mandalas are the main focus but it also mentions Islamic and Hindu art as well as contemporary artists such as M C Escher. Symmetry in the natural world is also considered. There are many great examples of traditional and contemporary art that uses extensive symmetry to create what is referred to as 'formal' art, designed to affect the viewer through the appreciation of the patterns, rather than the emotions that the art stirs.

The following websites provide a wealth of examples that could be used to illustrate these art forms:

http://patterninislamicart.com/

http://www.mysticalartsoftibet.org/mandala.htm

http://en.wikipedia.org/wiki/Rangoli

http://www.mcescher.com/

Prior knowledge

Students should already know how to…

• Recognise the symmetry properties of simple shapes

Starter problem

The starter problem invites students to make a tile to carry out a tessellation with. Escher-style tiles are made by taking a simple square or rectangle and removing a small section from one of the edges. This removed piece is then added to the opposite edge of the tile. This process can be repeated for the other pair of edges so that the tile now no longer has any obvious symmetry. It will, however, tessellate the infinite plane a bit like the pieces from a jigsaw puzzle.

Investigating regular and semi-regular tessellations made from regular polygons also provides a good way to introduce the concepts of symmetry and tessellation to students.

This website provides an excellent, simple introduction to all of the key ideas:

http://www.mathsisfun.com/geometry/tessellation.html

Resources

MyMaths

Lines of symmetry	1114	Rotating shapes	1115	Rotation symmetry	1116
Translating shapes	1127	Symmetry	1230		

Online assessment

InvisiPen solutions

Chapter test	2A–9	Reflection and rotation symmetry			361
Formative test	2A–9	Reflection	362	Translation	363
Summative test	2A–9	Rotation	364	Tessellations	365

Topic scheme

Teaching time = 6 lessons/2 weeks

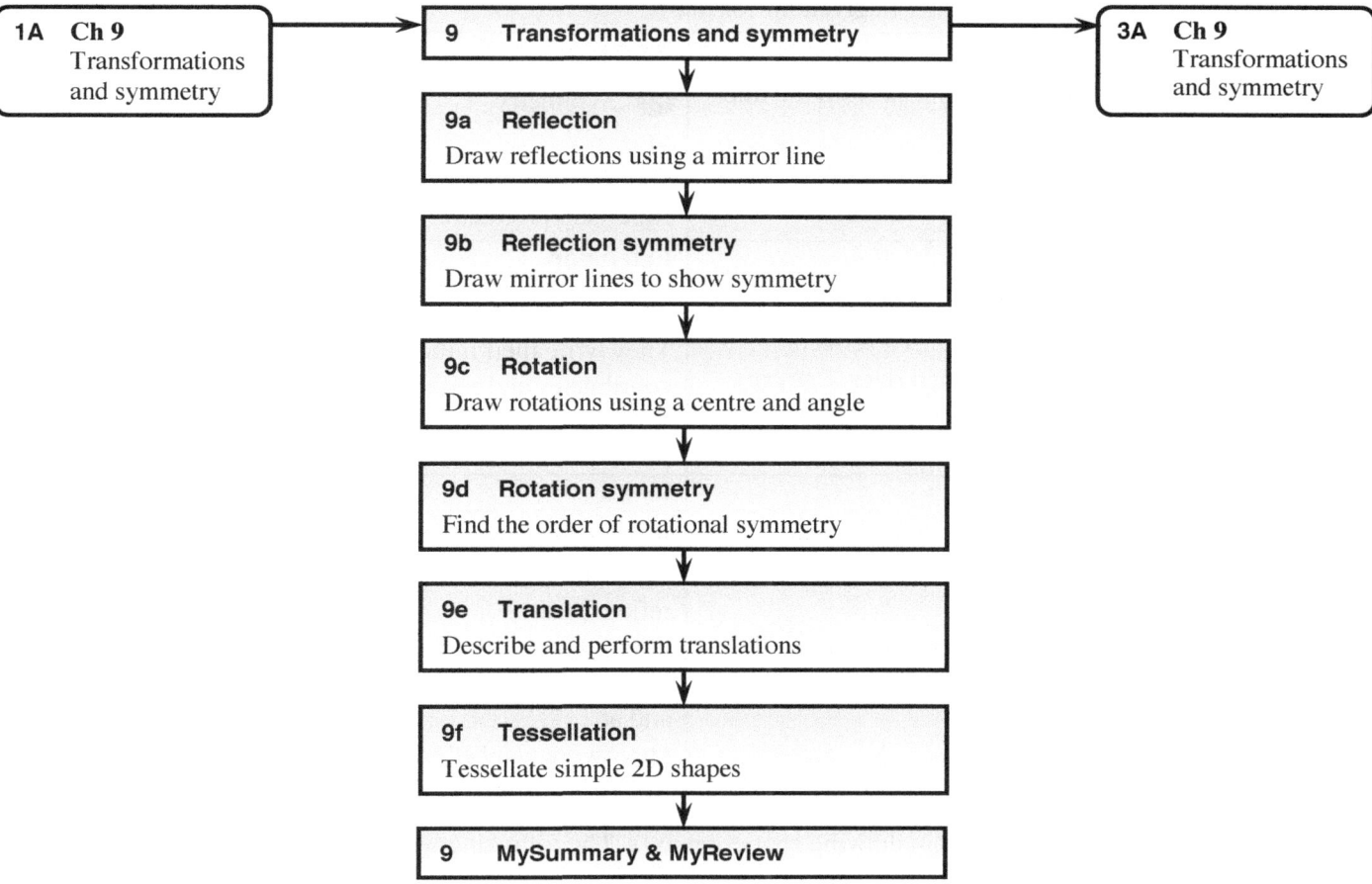

| 1A Ch 9 Transformations and symmetry | → | 9 **Transformations and symmetry** | → | 3A Ch 9 Transformations and symmetry |

9a Reflection
Draw reflections using a mirror line

9b Reflection symmetry
Draw mirror lines to show symmetry

9c Rotation
Draw rotations using a centre and angle

9d Rotation symmetry
Find the order of rotational symmetry

9e Translation
Describe and perform translations

9f Tessellation
Tessellate simple 2D shapes

9 MySummary & MyReview

Differentiation

Student book 2A   172 – 189

Reflection
Reflection symmetry
Rotation
Rotational symmetry
Translation
Tessellation

Student book 2B   158 – 173

Transformations
Combinations of transformations
Symmetry
Enlargements 1
Enlargements 2

Student book 2C   162 – 177

Transformations
Combinations of transformations
Symmetry
Enlargements 1
Enlargements 2

Objectives	
• Understand and use the language and notation associated with reflections	(L4)
• Transform 2D shapes by reflecting in given mirror lines	(L4)

Key ideas	Resources	
1 The object and image are equidistant from the line of reflection	⊞ Symmetry	(1230)
	Mirrors	
2 The line joining object and image is perpendicular to the line of reflection	Squared grid paper	
	Ruler and protractor	

Simplification	Extension
Restrict examples to simple geometrical shapes such as rectangles and triangles. Students check reflections with a mirror and equidistance with a ruler. Use only horizontal and vertical lines of reflection; leave sloping lines of reflection until later.	Students reflect shapes in lines sloping at 45°. They write their initials using straight lines and distinct coordinates and reflect them.

Literacy	Links
The *line of reflection* is also less formally known as the *mirror line*. Other words used in this topic are: *corresponding* meaning 'in a similar position', and *perpendicular* meaning 'at right angles to'.	Reflections are used in photography to add interest to a photograph. There is a collection of photographs using reflection at http://photography.nationalgeographic.com/photograph y/photos/patterns-nature-reflections.html and at http://www.danheller.com/mirrors.html

Alternative approach
Investigations can free the topic from drawing shapes on axes. The following website provides various investigative activities: http://nrich.maths.org/public/leg.php?group_id=12&code=131#results Computer-generated transformations add further interest. Have students ever stood between two parallel mirrors and seen their multiple reflections running away from them, or stood between two mirrors at right-angles to each other? What happens if the two mirrors are at other angles to each other? Place two mirrors vertically at various angles on a sheet of paper and count the number of images that can be seen.

Checkpoint		
1 a Draw x- and y-axes from 0 to 10. Draw the line $x = 3$.		
b Plot the point $(1, 2)$ and reflect it in the line. Give the coordinates of the image.		$(5, 2)$
c Plot the point $(4, 5)$ and reflect it in the line. Give the coordinates of the image.		$(2, 5)$

Starter – Quick fire

Recap work of previous chapters and especially number work. Ask rapid response questions. Students reply by writing on their mini whiteboards. Discuss questions when their answers indicate a need.

Teaching notes

Show two incorrect reflections:

- the nearest points to the mirror line are equidistant but the shape has not been 'flipped'
- the shape is 'flipped' but the points are not equidistant.

Students discuss what is wrong and demonstrate that reflecting each point separately ensures equidistance from the mirror line; only then are points joined together. This method naturally 'flips' the shape.

Draw the line $y = x$ and join points $(1, 2)$, $(2, 3)$ and $(1, 5)$ to create a triangle. Discuss where this shape will be after reflection in the mirror line. Again, demonstrate by taking each point separately and counting the *diagonal* distances of each corner in turn to the mirror line to achieve equidistance.

Plenary

On axes labelled from 0 to 11, draw an object and its image and discuss where the mirror line will be. Students decide first if the mirror line is horizontal, vertical or diagonal. Then they calculate points on the mirror line by halving the total distance between corresponding points on object and image. These points can be used:

$(4, 1), (4, 5), (1, 1)$ and $(8, 1), (8, 5), (11, 1)$ $(x = 6)$
$(4, 1), (4, 2), (1, 2)$ and $(4, 4), (1, 4), (4, 5)$ $(y = 3)$
$(3, 5), (1, 5), (1, 4)$ and $(5, 1), (4, 1), (5, 3)$ $(y = x)$

Exercise commentary

Questions 1–3 – These questions all involve reflecting shapes in horizontal and vertical mirror lines. Question **1** has no axes and the shapes are reflected corner by corner. The points on the axes in question **2** are followed by the shapes on axes in question **3**.

Question 4 – Students have to draw two reflections using both axes. The question can be extended by asking students how the shape can be reflected to a position in the final empty quadrant.

Question 5 – The basic principles stay the same. Counting squares to position an image point is done by counting diagonals of squares at right angles to the line of reflection. This is quite a jump though, and students might find it easier to move the page so the mirror line is either horizontal or vertical.

Answers

1 **a, b, c, d**   Check students' drawings
2   R' $(12, 2)$ S' $(18, 3)$ T' $(15, 5)$ U' $(19, 6)$ V' $(16, 7)$
3 **a, b, c**   Check students' drawings
   d A' $(6, 5)$ B' $(3, 6)$ C' $(2, 5)$ D' $(3, 2)$
4 **a, b**   Check students' drawings
5 **a** $(4, 8)$ **b** $(6, 9)$ **c** $(9, 8)$ **d** U' $(8, 4)$

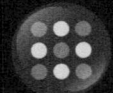

Objectives	
• Recognise and visualise the reflection symmetries of a 2D shape	(L5)

Key ideas	Resources	
1 A shape with reflection symmetry has at least one line of symmetry 2 Some shapes have several lines of symmetry	Lines of symmetry Mirrors Paper cut-outs of various 2D shapes Tracing paper	(1114)

Simplification	Extension
Students find horizontal and vertical lines of symmetry easier to recognise than diagonal lines of symmetry. Turning the page into a different orientation may help. Lines of symmetry can be found (and can be checked after being found) by using mirrors.	Students research on the Internet where symmetry is found in everyday life; for example, in architecture, art, nature, religious symbols. Students can present their findings to the class as an alternative plenary session.

Literacy	Links
The word *symmetry* comes from a combination of Latin and Greek meaning 'measured together'. Other words where '*sym-*' means 'together' are sympathy and symphony. A *line of symmetry* is also less formally known as a 'mirror line'. *Reflection symmetry* is also called 'line symmetry'.	The flags of all the world's countries can be found at https://www.cia.gov/library/publications/the-world-factbook/docs/flagsoftheworld.html The Austrian flag has two lines of symmetry. Can students identify other flags with lines of symmetry? Does the flag of the United Kingdom have a line of symmetry?

Alternative approach

Tracing a shape is another simple method of searching for a line of symmetry. Fold the tracing and see if one half of it can be made to lie exactly on top of the other half. If it can, then the crease is the line of symmetry. Particularly explore the lines of symmetry of the rectangle and parallelogram. Both these shapes have the potential to cause some confusion.

A kaleidoscope is a good instrument for seeing symmetrical shapes. With squared grid paper, students can imitate a kaleidoscope by using coloured pencils to shade squares and make patterns that are designed to have one or two lines of symmetry. Shading triangles on isometric paper can give shapes with three lines of symmetry.

In addition, websites such as http://nrich.maths.org/1840 provide investigative approaches.

Checkpoint

1 Reflection symmetry can be checked in various ways. Investigate the following with students:
   a Ask students to place a mirror on a shape so that the reflection of what is in front of the mirror is exactly the same as what is behind the mirror.
   b Cut a shape out of card. Ask students to fold the card in half so that one half lies exactly on top of the other half.
   c Students trace a shape. Ask them to fold the tracing so that half of it lies on the other half. Where is the mirror line? (Along the crease)

Starter – Moving triangles

This activity extends the previous lesson to reflections in all four quadrants. Students draw a triangle with vertices at $(1, 1), (2, 1), (1, 5)$. Then students draw its reflection in the y-axis and write down the coordinates of the new triangle.　　　　$((-1, 1), (-2, 1), (-1, 5))$
Do students notice any relation between the two sets of coordinates?
Repeat by reflecting in the x-axis.

Teaching notes

Show how a square can be folded exactly in half in four different ways. State that it has *reflection symmetry* and that each fold line is a *line of symmetry*. Demonstrate how a mirror placed along a line of symmetry reflects half the shape to create the full shape.

Provide students with various 2D shapes cut out of paper or thin card; for example, rectangles, various types of triangles, parallelograms. They find as many ways as they can to fold each shape exactly in half.

Students demonstrate their lines of symmetry of the different shapes, using the correct name for each shape. Record answers using dotted or coloured lines to illustrate lines of symmetry.

Plenary

Students create shapes with two, three or four lines of symmetry:

How many different shapes can they create for each criterion?

See also the 'Extension' activity.

Exercise commentary

This topic lends itself to much practical activity, often with students working in pairs to share tasks and confer on findings.

Questions 1 and **2** – Students should check their answers using mirrors, particularly for question **1e** and all of question **2**.

Question 3 – This extends reflection symmetry to regular polygons. Can students generalise their findings? What is the number of lines of symmetry of a 100-sided and a 1000-sided regular polygon? Discuss the symmetry of a circle?

Question 4 – This addresses a common misconception relating to the symmetry of a parallelogram.

Questions 5 and **6** – The use of a mirror is recommended.

Answers

1. **a** Vertical line through centre `
   b Vertical line through centre
   c Horizontal line through centre
   d Horizontal line through centre
   e Diagonal line from bottom left to top right through centre
2. **a** Vertical and horizontal lines through centre and diagonals through centre
   b Vertical and diagonal lines through centre
   c Vertical and horizontal lines through centre and diagonals through centre
   d Vertical and horizontal lines through centre
   e Vertical and horizontal lines through centre and diagonals through centre
3. The number of sides = the number of lines of symmetry
4. **a** Only if a rectangle
   b None (if not a rectangle)
5. C, W, D, E, A, X
6. Check students' work

Objectives

- Understand and use the language and notation associated with reflections   (L4)
- Transform 2D shapes by rotating about a given point   (L4)

Key ideas	Resources
1 A rotation maintains the shape and size of an object but alters its position	Rotating shapes (1115)
2 A rotation is defined by an angle and direction of rotation and a centre of rotation	Tracing paper Photocopies of the shapes in question **2** Graphing software

Simplification	Extension
Some students will intuitively 'see' the rotation but all should check their work using tracing paper. Students who have more difficulty rotating 90° than 180° should watch horizontal lines become vertical, and vice versa.	Students rotate a more complex shape, such as a pattern of their initials. They rotate clockwise through 90°, 180° and 270°. They can change the centre of rotation to see how this affects the final outcome.

Literacy	Links
Rotations need not always be studied on grids with axes. For example, a tessellation of regular hexagons can be created using only rotations of one hexagon onto another. Other tessellations are based on reflections of the previous exercise. See Escher's work at http://www.mcescher.com/ and find which of his paintings are based on rotations or reflections or combinations of both.	The London Eye is also known as the Millennium Wheel as it was built to mark the start of the new millennium. It takes about 30 minutes for the wheel to complete one complete rotation. There is more information about the London Eye at http://www.londoneye.com/

Alternative approach

Here are several different approaches.

1) Rather than looking at lots of shapes and different rotations, it can be more interesting to take one irregular shape and see how it moves for different positions of the centre of rotation. The centre can be a point outside the shape, a point on the edge of the shape or a point within the shape.

2) Polar graph paper may be used to plot and rotate shapes. Shapes can be likened to images seen on a radar screen.

3) Interlocking cog wheels with different numbers of teeth can be investigated for the number of turns taken for different numbers of teeth. Discuss gearing on bicycle wheels where the number of turns one wheel makes is different to the turns on the other wheel.

4) If the centre of rotation is known, a compass can be used to draw an arc from a point on the object shape to the corresponding point on the image. Computer-generated rotations often show the path traced out by a point as it rotates; for example, a rotation and a reflection can be seen happen at http://www.s-cool.co.uk/gcse/maths/transformations/revise-it/transformations

Checkpoint

1 Draw an isosceles triangle that has a base of 4 squares long and is 6 squares high.
Rotate the triangle 90° clockwise about the centre of its base.
(Check students' drawings. Students can work in pairs and compare their answers.)

Starter – Quick fire

Recap work of previous chapters on number, computation and algebra. Ask rapid response questions. Students reply by writing on their mini whiteboards. Discuss questions when their answers indicate a need.

Teaching notes

Show a clock face with a hand pointing to 12 and discuss where it will be after a turn or **rotation** of 90°. Highlight that the direction of turn is important and note the directions of clockwise and anticlockwise.

Discuss where the hand will be after 90°, 180°, 270° and 360° turns clockwise and anticlockwise. Students understand that 90° = quarter turn, 180° = half turn, 270° = three-quarter turn and 360° = a full turn.

Draw a shape. Rotate it clockwise 90° about one of its vertices. Take a tracing of the original shape, use a sharp point to keep a fixed centre of rotation, and note that horizontal lines become vertical lines and vice versa.

Repeat with different centres of rotation both inside and outside the shape.

Note that rotation preserves a shape and size; it is the shape's position that changes.

Emphasise that to specify any rotation, you need a centre, a direction and an angle.

Plenary

Draw line A from point (2, 2) to point (2, 5), and line B from (4, 2) to (7, 2). Students have to give details of the rotation from line A to line B. Students may intuitively give the direction (as clockwise) and the angle (as 90°) before devising ways to find the centre of rotation at the point (3, 1).

Exercise commentary

Question 2 – This question requires students to rotate a given shape. A photocopy of the shapes in this question would be beneficial, time-saving and reduce the likelihood of students' drawing in the book! Notice that shape F has a centre of rotation *inside* the shape. Tracing paper really helps.

Question 3 – This extends students to carry out rotations with the centre of rotation outside the shape. Some students will find this easier than when the centre is inside the shape.

Answers

1 **a** 180° clockwise **b** 90° anticlockwise
   c 270° anticlockwise **d** 90° anticlockwise
   e 270° clockwise **f** 180° anticlockwise
2 Check students' diagrams
3 Check students' diagrams

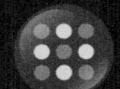
Objectives

- Recognise and visualise the rotational symmetries of a 2D shape   (L5)

Key ideas	Resources
1 A shape with rotation symmetry will fit onto itself at least once before it completes a full turn about a point	Rotational symmetry (1116) Tracing paper Paper cut-outs of various 2D shapes

Simplification	Extension
Students may identify rotational symmetry when, in fact, it is line symmetry. How tracing paper is used can emphasise the difference between rotational and line symmetry: either the tracing paper is rotated about a point or it is folded so one half fits on the other half.	Students can research on the Internet where rotational symmetry is found in everyday life: for example, in architecture, in art, in religious symbols. Students can present their findings to the class as an alternative plenary session.

Literacy	Links
Whereas reflection (or line) symmetry has just a mirror line (or line of symmetry), rotational symmetry has a centre of rotation *and* an **order** of rotational symmetry. The order of rotational symmetry is the number of times a shape fits onto itself in one full turn. So, *every* shape has rotational symmetry of order 1, because every shape fits onto itself at the end of a full turn. So, really, a shape of order 1 means it has no true rotational symmetry!	The patterns seen in a kaleidoscope all have rotational symmetry. The kaleidoscope was invented in 1816 by David Brewster in Scotland. They are usually thought of as toys but are also used by designers and artists. There are instructions for making a simple kaleidoscope at http://www.zefrank.com/dtoy_vs_byokal/index.html and an interactive kaleidoscope at http://www.kaleidoscopesusa.com/makeAscope.htm

Alternative approach

A kaleidoscope is a good instrument to see symmetrical shapes. With squared grid paper, students can imitate a kaleidoscope by using coloured pencils to shade squares and make patterns that are designed to have rotational symmetry of order 2 or 4. Shading triangles on isometric paper can give shapes with rotational symmetry of order 3.

In addition, websites such as http://nrich.maths.org/1868 provide investigative approaches.

Checkpoint

1 What is the order of rotational symmetry of the following shapes?
   a Square   (4)
   b Isosceles triangle   (1)
   c Rectangle   (2)

Starter – Shape pairs

Write the following two lists of shapes and numbers for the class to see.

Regular octagon, regular hexagon, regular pentagon, equilateral triangle, isosceles triangle, rectangle, square

1   2   3   4   5   6   8

Students match the name of each shape to the number of its lines of symmetry, writing their answers on their mini whiteboards. Each shape is then drawn with its lines of symmetry.

Teaching notes

Write up the words: MUM, HAH and POP and challenge students to spot the odd one out. POP has no reflection symmetry. Repeat with MOW, SOS and SOW. Two of these words have symmetry but not reflection symmetry. Students describe what they notice.

Demonstrate with the words MOW and SOS, written on paper, that they can be rotated through 180° and look identical. These have **rotational symmetry of order 2** as in a full turn they fit exactly onto themselves twice.

Use tracing paper to demonstrate how to determine the order of rotational symmetry of a rectangle.

- Trace the shape.
- Place a dot in a top corner to indicate when it has rotated a full turn.
- Use a pencil to hold the copy of the shape on tracing paper at the centre of the shape.
- Rotate the tracing paper one full turn.
- Count how many times there is a 'fit' in 360°.

Provide students with various paper shapes, such as rectangles, various kinds of triangle, parallelograms, and tracing paper. The students find the centre and order of rotational symmetry for each shape.

Plenary

Students draw a 3 × 4 grid of 12 squares. They shade squares to create shapes with rotational symmetry of order 2 and then of order 4. Their partner tests them using tracing paper. How many different shapes can they create for each criterion?

Exercise commentary

Questions 1 and **2** – Students are asked for the orders of rotational symmetry of several shapes and signs on sight (without tracing). Discuss what the order is for shape **1a** and whether or not it has rotational symmetry.

Question 4 – Dotty squared paper will help to keep the rotations accurate.

Answers

1 **a** 1   **b** 4   **c** 3   **d** 1
2 **a** 1   **b** 0   **c** 2   **d** 0
3 The number of sides = its order of rotational symmetry
4 Check students' work

Objectives

- Understand and use the language and notation associated with translations (L4)
- Transform 2D shapes by translation (L4)

Key ideas	Resources
1 A translation maintains the shape, size and orientation of a shape but changes its position **2** A translation moves an object onto its image by a slide defined by the number of squares moved on a grid	Translating shapes (1127) Individual axes of all four quadrants (extension) Axes of first quadrant – both axes 0-16

Simplification	Extension
Some students include the start point when counting. They should count the 'moves' (that is, the gaps between the grid lines) and not the grid lines themselves. If the square gird is a centimetre grid, they can measure the 'moves' using a ruler. Copies of labelled axes may be useful in question **3** for some students.	Students can combine transformations in all four quadrants by: • joining points $(1, 2)$, $(1, 5)$ and $(2, 5)$ to make triangle A • reflecting A in the y-axis, labelling the image triangle B • rotating B by 90° anticlockwise about $(0, 0)$, labelling the image triangle C • translating C using the instruction (8 left, 2 down). What are the new coordinates of the final triangle?

Literacy	Links
The words *transformation* and *translation* are often confused. Thinking of *translation* as moving 'sideways' from one language to another helps to make the distinction. Although the word *vector* is not used in this lesson, the two movements, left/right and up/down, define a vector. The notation $\begin{pmatrix} x \\ y \end{pmatrix}$ for horizontal movement for vertical movement. is easily confused with the notation (x, y) for the coordinates of a point. The words *object* and *image* can be introduced and the notation A' for the image of A.	When solving a sliding puzzle, the pieces are translated from one position to another until the final image is completed. There are examples of sliding puzzles at http://ngm.nationalgeographic.com/your-shot/slide-puzzles

Alternative approach

Investigations can free the topic from drawing shapes on axes. The website http://nrich.maths.org/9350 provides various investigative activities involving different transformations. Computer-generated transformations add further interest.

The moves on a traditional 'snakes and ladders' board can be written using the 'right/left, up/down' notation.

The work of M C Escher's at http://www.mcescher.com/ can be analysed to see which of his drawings involve translations.

Checkpoint

1 Draw x- and y- axes from 0 to 10.
  a Plot the points $(2, 2)$, $(4, 2)$ and $(3, 6)$ and join to make an isosceles triangle.
  b Translate the triangle 4 units to the right and 2 units up.
  c Give the coordinates of the vertices (corners) of the image . $((6,4), (8, 4)$ and $(7, 8))$

Starter – Order 4

Ask students to draw:

- shapes that have rotation symmetry of order 4 but no reflection symmetry
- shapes that have rotation symmetry of order 4 and do have reflection symmetry.

Ask students how many lines of symmetry these shapes have.

Teaching notes

Draw the two triangles with corners $(1, 3), (4, 4), (1, 9)$ and $(8, 1), (11, 2), (8, 7)$. Discuss whether a reflection or rotation has taken place. Notice that the image has been neither 'flipped' (in a reflection) nor turned (in a rotation). Invite suggestions to describe how it has changed. Elicit that the shape has moved position by *sliding* without any rotation.

Students suggest how to describe the move by giving two numbers: one for horizontal movement and another for vertical movement. Introduce the vector notation using brackets as on the previous page of the students' book, where the upper number denotes horizontal movement (right/left) and the lower number vertical movement (up/down).

Draw a shape on a squared grid without axes and demonstrate a translation. Impress that the count is of movement across the squares. Demonstrate by counting the movement for each corner of the shape in turn, to show that the translation applies to the whole shape.

Plenary

Discuss how to simplify the notation even further, prompting students to consider how to differentiate between left and right and between up and down, without using the words themselves. Make the link with coordinates but impress that coordinates are *always* found by starting the count at the origin. For a translation, the count starts at any point on the object shape.

Students give the translation instructions for all three questions in Exercise **9e** using this simplified notation.

Exercise commentary

Question 1 – Students are asked to complete a statement. They can also write their answers using the vector notation on the previous age.

Question 2 – Students translate a shape, corner by corner. Be sure they count the movement across the grid and not the grid lines themselves.

Question 3 – The object shapes are drawn on labelled axes. Mention the notation of the 'dash' for indicating an image. So A' is the image of A. Also the use of the words *object* and *image* can be used.

Answers

1 **a** 5 right, 2 up **b** 4 left, 3 down
   c 6 right, 0 up or down
2 **a, b, c**   Check students' drawings
3 **a, b, c, d**   Check students' drawings
   e Shape A: $(7, 7)$ $(10, 11)$ $(7, 11)$
       Shape B: $(5, 4)$ $(8, 4)$ $(7, 1)$ $(4, 1)$
       Shape C: $(10, 6)$ $(11, 4)$ $(10, 2)$ $(9, 4)$

Objectives

- Explore these transformations and symmetries (using ICT)   (L5)

Key ideas	Resources
1 A tessellation is a repeated pattern of a shape that covers an area without any gaps or overlaps 2 Some tessellations can use more than one repeated shape	Construction kits Paper, scissors, tracing paper Squared grid paper Appropriate computer software

Simplification	Extension
Rather than copying a shape repeatedly using tracing paper or a square grid, students can use small tiles made of card or plastic.	Students can use the Internet to research where tessellations can be found in everyday life, such as in art, design, architecture, nature, etc. They can present their findings to the class.

Literacy	Links
The words *tessellate* and *tessellation* come from the Latin word 'tessella' which was a small square piece of stone or pottery used as a tile in mosaics. The Romans made many beautiful mosaic floors and pictures which can still be seen today. Use a search engine for 'images of Roman mosaics'.	Islamic art does not use images of living things, but instead uses geometric patterns and tessellations. The Alhambra palace in Granada, Spain, is richly decorated with Islamic art. For more information about the palace see: http://en.wikipedia.org/wiki/Alhambra Examples of patterns in the Alhambra are found at: http://www2.spsu.edu/math/tile/grammar/moor.htm

Alternative approach

Ideas and resources for tessellations are many and varied. They provide for interesting work in class for students working alone or in pairs.

Tessellations sometimes use more than one basic shape. Students can tessellate with regular hexagons and triangles and with squares and triangles. A 3-shape tessellation uses regular hexagons, squares and triangles where all shapes have the same length of side.

Some construction kits have various regular shapes that can be used to create tessellations.
The work of the Dutchman, M C Escher, either from a book or from http://www.mcescher.com/ provides many ideas for creating designs.

Students can use computers to make tessellations. Investigate possibilities at http://nrich.maths.org/6069 and http://www.mymaths.co.uk/indexLog.asp?h=97109

Checkpoint

1   Give three examples in everyday life where you see tessellations. What are the shapes used in the tessellations?   (Floor tiles, bathroom tiles, paving stones, brick work, ...)

Starter – Quick fire

Recap basic number work. Include questions on fractions, decimals and percentages and questions using mental and written computation. Ask rapid response questions. Students reply by writing on their mini whiteboards. Discuss questions when their answers indicate a need.

Teaching notes

Show students some tessellations and invite them to provide a definition of 'tessellation'. It is a 2D-pattern made from repetitions of a shape (or shapes) with no gaps or overlaps. The shape can be reflected, rotated or translated but it always stays the same size and shape. That means that all the tiles are congruent.

Students are given congruent shapes or they make their own from paper or card. They need about ten copies. They see if their shape tessellates and share their results with the class.

Alternatively, they draw repeated shapes on squared or isometric paper to make a tessellation.

Plenary

Draw a tessellation of several squares. Label all the angles at any one point.

Repeat with equilateral triangles and hexagons. Label all the angles at any one point.

Students notice that the total of all the angles at a point within a tessellation is 360°.

Draw regular pentagons to meet at a point (or fit pentagonal tiles together) and label each angle 108° degrees. Discuss why this shape will not tessellate. Seek the response that 108 is not a factor of 360, so they cannot fit around a point in such a way that there will be no gaps. What other shape is needed with regular pentagons to make a tessellation?

Exercise commentary

This topic provides good opportunity for creative activity for students alone, in pairs or small groups.

Questions 1 and **2** –Multiple copies of the basic shapes are needed or, as the book suggests, use square grid paper.

Question 3 – Students could design one shape that will tessellate and another that will not. They should avoid shapes already considered in questions **1** and **2**.

Question 4 – Explores whether some irregular shapes will tessellate. Tracing paper can be helpful here.

Question 5 – Focuses on where tessellations are seen in the real world. This question can be extended for confident students, see 'Extension' and 'Links'.

Question 6 – This question is described in the notes on 'Plenary'.

Answers

1 Check students' answers as they may all show different tessellations

2 Check students' answers as they may all show different tessellations

3 Check students' answers as they may all show different tessellations

4   **a** no   **b** yes   **c** no   **d** yes

5 Multiple answers possible – discuss students' answers

6 Multiple answers possible – discuss students' answers

Key outcomes		Quick check
Find reflections in mirror lines.	L5	Draw x- and y-axes from 0 to 10. Draw a triangle by plotting $(2, 2)$, $(6, 2)$ and $(4, 5)$. Draw the line $x = 5$ and reflect the triangle in the line. Give the coordinates of the reflected image. $\qquad$ $((8,2), (4, 2)$ and $(6, 5))$
Recognise reflection and rotational symmetry.	L5	How many lines of symmetry has a square? $\qquad$ (4) What is the order of rotational symmetry of an equilateral triangle? (3)
Rotate shapes on a square grid through different angles.	L5	Draw a square. Choose a corner and rotate it about $180°$.
Translate shapes.	L5	Draw a square and translate it by 3 left and 4 down.
Make tessellating patterns.	L5	Choose a trapezium and show how it can tessellate.

⊕ MyMaths extra support

Lesson/online homework			Description
Reflecting shapes	1113	L6	Reflect shapes through lines on a set of axes
All transformations	1125	L6	Understanding the transformations rotation, reflection, translation and enlargement

MyReview

Check out

You should now be able to ...

Test it →
Questions

✓ Find reflections in mirror lines.	(s)	1
✓ Recognise reflection and rotational symmetry.	(s)	2, 3
✓ Rotate shapes on a square grid through different angles.	(s)	4
✓ Translate shapes.	(s)	5
✓ Make tessellating patterns.	(s)	6

Language	Meaning	Example
Reflection symmetry	Shapes have reflection symmetry if they have a line of symmetry	An isosceles triangle has reflection symmetry
Reflection	A transformation which flips an object over a mirror line	See page 174
Rotation	A transformation that turns an object through a given angle about a given centre of rotation	See page 178
Rotational symmetry	A shape has rotational symmetry if it fits exactly over its original position more than once in a full turn	An equilateral triangle has rotational symmetry order 3
Translation	A transformation which slides an object	See page 182
Tessellation	A tiling pattern of repeated shapes that doesn't have any gaps or overlaps	Here is part of a tessellation made from parallelograms

1 Copy the shapes on squared paper and reflect the shapes in the mirror lines.

a b

2 Describe
  a the reflection symmetry
  b the rotational symmetry of this shape.

3 Describe
  a the reflection symmetry
  b the rotational symmetry of this shape.

4 Copy the triangle on squared paper and rotate the triangle 90° anticlockwise about the point.

5 Copy the diagram and translate the triangle $\binom{3 \text{ right}}{4 \text{ down}}$

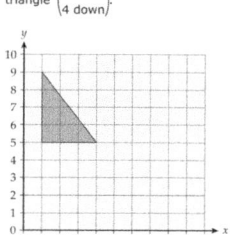

6 Copy the shape on square grid paper and tessellate it six times.

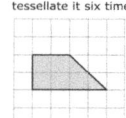

What next?

Score		
	0 – 3	Your knowledge of this topic is still developing. To improve look at Formative test: 2A–9; MyMaths: 1114, 1115, 1116, 1127, 1230 and 6001 (Tessellations tool)
	4, 5	You are gaining a secure knowledge of this topic. To improve look at InvisiPen: 361, 362, 363, 364 and 365
	6	You have mastered this topic. Well done, you are ready to progress!

Question commentary

Question 1 – Students can use tracing paper.

Questions 2 and **3** – Students can work in pairs or you may wish to hold a class discussion.

Question 4 – Encourage use of tracing paper.

Questions 5 and **6** – Straightforward questions on translation and tessellation.

Answers

1

a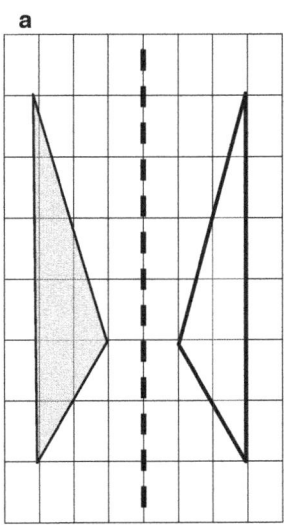

b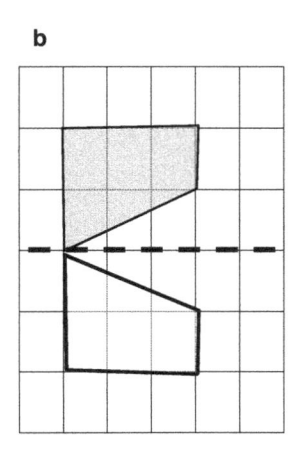

2 a 4 lines of symmetry   b order 4

3 a 0 lines of symmetry   b order 2

4

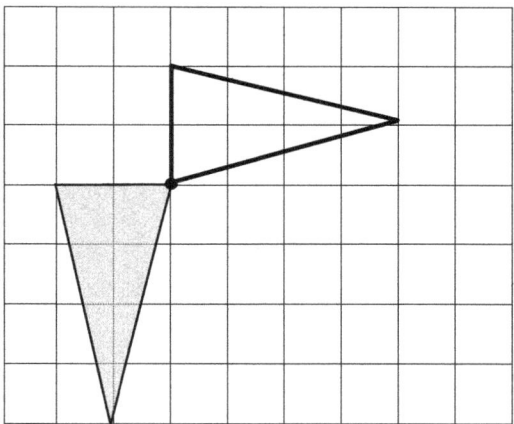

5 Translated triangle with vertices at coordinates (4, 5), (4, 1) and (7, 1)

6 Check students' answers as they may all show different tessellations

9 MyPractice

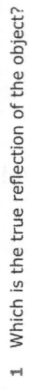

9a

1 Which is the true reflection of the object?

Object

A   B   C   D   E

2 The letters in these two words have reflective symmetry. When reflected, what words will you see?

H I D E   C O D E

9b

3 How many lines of symmetry has each of these shapes?

a   b   c   d

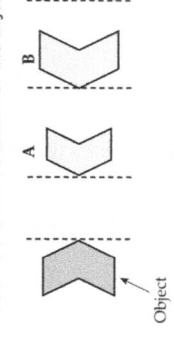

9c

4 Describe these rotations by stating the direction of turn (clockwise or anticlockwise), and the angle of turn. The centre of rotation is marked ×.

a   b   c   d

5 Copy the triangle on the grid.

  a Rotate it 90°, anticlockwise about the centre of rotation, marked ×. Label it A.

  b Next, rotate it 90° clockwise about the centre of rotation. Label it B.

M986W

6 Give the order of rotational symmetry for each shape.

  a   b   c

9d

7 Copy each shape and translate it.

  a Translation: (5 left, 3 down)

  b Translation: (6 right, 3 up)

  c Translation: (3 left, 4 up)

9e

8 Describe each of these translations.

  a   b   c

9 Carry out the following transformations on these shapes. Copy each shape and...

  a reflect shape A in the mirror line.

  b rotate shape B 90° clockwise.

  c translate shape C (6 right, 5 down)

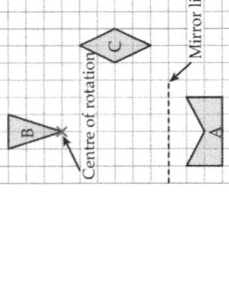

Centre of rotation

Mirror line

9f

10 Tessellate this shape on square grid paper so that your pattern contains six shapes.

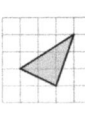

Question commentary

Question 1 – Students may need to measure the lengths of the shapes.

Question 2 – Should be straightforward.

Question 3 – If necessary, draw and cut out shapes and check by folding.

Questions 4–6 – Tracing paper can really help.

Questions 7–9 – Students need to count squares not lines in translations.

Question 10 – If necessary cut out six of these shapes to show how they can tessellate.

Answers

1 D
2 HIDE CODE
3 **a** 1   **b** 4   **c** 2   **d** 4
4 **a** 180° clockwise   **b** 90° anticlockwise
   c 270° clockwise   **d** 90° anticlockwise
5 Check students' diagrams
6 **a** 3   **b** 4   **c** 2
7 **a, b, c**   Check students' diagrams
8 **a** $\begin{pmatrix} 6 \\ -2 \end{pmatrix}$ **b** $\begin{pmatrix} -5 \\ 2 \end{pmatrix}$ **c** $\begin{pmatrix} -4 \\ -4 \end{pmatrix}$

9 Check students' diagrams
10 Check students' answers as they may all show different tessellations

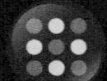

Related lessons		Resources	
Real-life graphs	6e	Add and subtract decimals	(1007)
Bar charts	8d	Real life graphs	(1184)
Written addition and subtraction	11a	Examples of graphs from newspapers	

Simplification	Extension
Students may need structured guidance working through the table in task **1**.	Students could be asked to look at the percentage changes of wheat production, consumption and stocks and the percentage change of the price of wheat and the production of biodiesel.
	Further research could also be carried out into misleading graphs that appear in the press or online.

Links

Students should be encouraged to look in more detail at the range of crops that are being used for various purposes and research the effects this is having worldwide on food prices and levels of availability. There is much useful data on the internet, for example www.hgca.com or www.ukagriculture.com/crops/crops.cfm.

Students could be organised to research different aspects to bring together as a class.

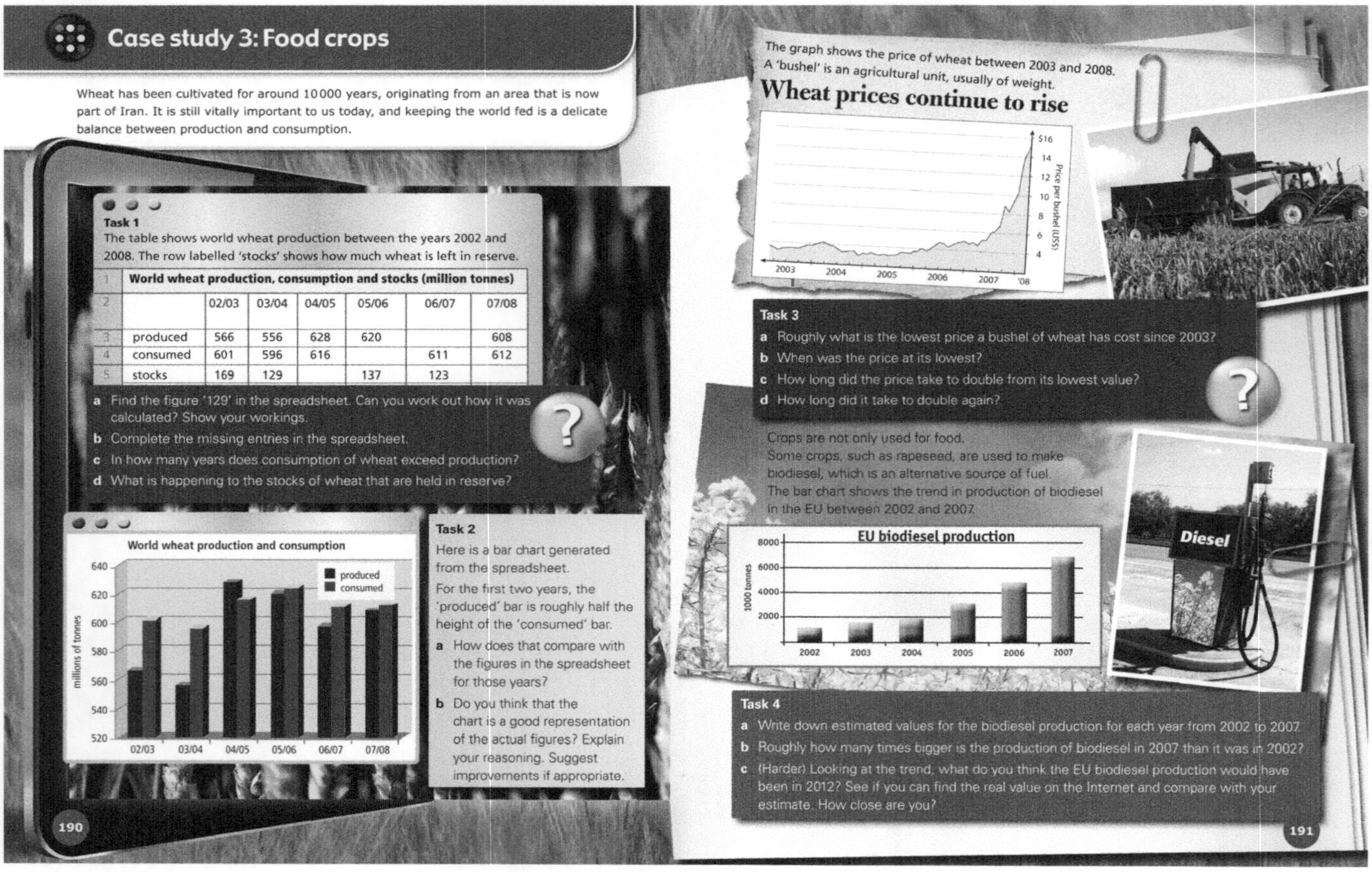

Case study 3: Food crops

Wheat has been cultivated for around 10 000 years, originating from an area that is now part of Iran. It is still vitally important to us today, and keeping the world fed is a delicate balance between production and consumption.

Task 1

The table shows world wheat production between the years 2002 and 2008. The row labelled 'stocks' shows how much wheat is left in reserve.

World wheat production, consumption and stocks (million tonnes)						
	02/03	03/04	04/05	05/06	06/07	07/08
produced	566	556	628	620		608
consumed	601	596	616		611	612
stocks	169	129		137	123	

a Find the figure '129' in the spreadsheet. Can you work out how it was calculated? Show your workings.

b Complete the missing entries in the spreadsheet.

c In how many years does consumption of wheat exceed production?

d What is happening to the stocks of wheat that are held in reserve?

Task 2

World wheat production and consumption

Here is a bar chart generated from the spreadsheet.

For the first two years, the 'produced' bar is roughly half the height of the 'consumed' bar.

a How does that compare with the figures in the spreadsheet for those years?

b Do you think that the chart is a good representation of the actual figures? Explain your reasoning. Suggest improvements if appropriate.

The graph shows the price of wheat between 2003 and 2008. A 'bushel' is an agricultural unit, usually of weight.

Wheat prices continue to rise

Task 3

a Roughly what is the lowest price a bushel of wheat has cost since 2003?

b When was the price at its lowest?

c How long did the price take to double from its lowest value?

d How long did it take to double again?

Crops are not only used for food. Some crops, such as rapeseed, are used to make biodiesel, which is an alternative source of fuel. The bar chart shows the trend in production of biodiesel in the EU between 2002 and 2007.

EU biodiesel production

Diesel

Task 4

a Write down estimated values for the biodiesel production for each year from 2002 to 2007.

b Roughly how many times bigger is the production of biodiesel in 2007 than it was in 2002?

c (Harder) Looking at the trend, what do you think the EU biodiesel production would have been in 2012? See if you can find the real value on the Internet and compare with your estimate. How close are you?

Teaching notes

Many students will be aware of the rising use of biofuels through hearing about cars that run on chip fat and other oils. Some may have experienced it or know adults who use biofuels. Running cars in this way is often portrayed as being 'alternative' and 'green'. Students might also be aware that prices for wheat and other crops have recently been rising quite rapidly, and know that there is a shortage of food crops in some parts of the world.

This case study focuses on production figures for wheat and biodiesel to raise the possibility that there could be a partial link between the increasing use of biodiesel and the increasing price and shortage of wheat.

Task 1

Introduce the case study and look at the spreadsheet shown at the top left. Discuss what is meant by 'produced', 'consumed' and 'stocks' and look at the first two columns to see how the figures relate to each other. Discuss how you have to find the surplus or deficit of production compared with consumption and then adjust the stocks level accordingly. Give the students a few minutes to work out the missing values on the spreadsheet and answer the related questions.

Task 2

When the students have considered the questions relating to this bar chart, discuss their opinions about the reasonableness or otherwise of the vertical scale. For example, the differences would be very hard to determine if the vertical axis started at zero. However, starting the axis at 520 million tonnes means that the shortfall between wheat production and consumption appears exaggerated. In the first two columns the production appears to provide only about half the amount of wheat that is needed.

Task 3

Look at the graph showing wheat prices for the past few years. What do you notice about the graph? The most obvious thing is that the prices rise very rapidly in the last two years shown on the graph. Students should then work through the questions about the graph.

Task 4

Look at the final graph on the spread that shows figures for biodiesel production in Europe. Do you notice anything familiar about this graph? Elicit that the shape is very similar to the shape of the wheat price graph, increasing only slowly for a while and then increasing much more rapidly. Conclude by considering whether the production of biofuels could be having an influence on the cost of wheat and other crops.

Answers

1 a $169 - (596 - 556)$

b

	02/03	03/04	04/05	05/06	06/07	07/08
Produced	566	556	628	620	597	608
Consumed	601	596	616	624	611	612
Stocks	169	129	141	137	123	119

c 5 years

d Decreasing trend

2 a Appears to be half the height but should be 95% of the height.

b Students' answers. The suppressed zero makes the size of the difference misleading, but allows it to be seen.

3 a Just over $3

b May, 2004

c $2\frac{1}{2}$ years

d $\frac{1}{2}$ year

4 a 1300, 1800, 2000, 3200, 4800, 6600

b 5

c Students' own answers

10 Equations

Learning outcomes

A3 Understand and use the concepts and vocabulary of expressions, equations, inequalities, terms and factors (L5)

A6 Model situations or procedures by translating them into algebraic expressions or formulae and by using graphs (L5)

A7 Use algebraic methods to solve linear equations in one variable (including all forms that require rearrangement) (L5)

Introduction

The chapter starts by looking at one-step equations and then moves on to equation puzzles, solved by balancing. Equations that require two steps to solve are then covered before the final section that looks at making equations from a written context.

The introduction discusses how biologists use equations to model things like population growth among species of animal. This concept uses a form of equation known as an exponential equation, where the growth (or decline) in a population is related to the population present at the time (among other factors). There are many other things that behave according to these kinds of rule. Bacteria growth can be modelled using exponential equations, for example. Radioactive substances that 'decay' over time can also be modelled using the concept of exponential decay. Each radioactive substance has what is called a 'half-life': the length of time it takes for the radioactivity to halve. Carbon-15 has a half-life of 2.449 seconds so its rate of decay is very fast, whereas titanium-44 has a half-life of close to 63 years. The longest half-life known is that of the isotope tellurium-128 which has a half-life of 2.2×10^{24} years – over 100 000 000 000 000 times longer than the universe has been in existence!

Prior knowledge

Students should already know how to…

- Perform simple arithmetic operations on positive and negative whole numbers

Starter problem

The starter problem is a puzzle that requires students to carry out two series of operations on a single chosen number.

The first result, P, is obtained by multiplying by two and then adding two: $2x + 2$.

The second result, Q, is obtained by multiplying by four and then subtracting four: $4x – 4$.

Students are invited to find out when P is equal to Q. Most will proceed by trying numbers to see when there is equivalence.

An algebraic approach would be to set the two numbers equal to each other and solve the resulting equation. While this is outside the scope of the covered material, it is interesting to see what result(s) it gives:

$2x + 2 = 4x – 4$

$6 = 2x$

$x = 3$

There is just a single answer which students should be able to work out quite quickly.

Resources

MyMaths

Simple equations	1154	Solving equations	1182

Online assessment / **InvisiPen solutions**

Chapter test	2A–10	Making equations	231	Balancing equations	233
Formative test	2A–10	One-step equations	234		
Summative test	2A–10				

Topic scheme

Teaching time = 4 lessons/2 weeks

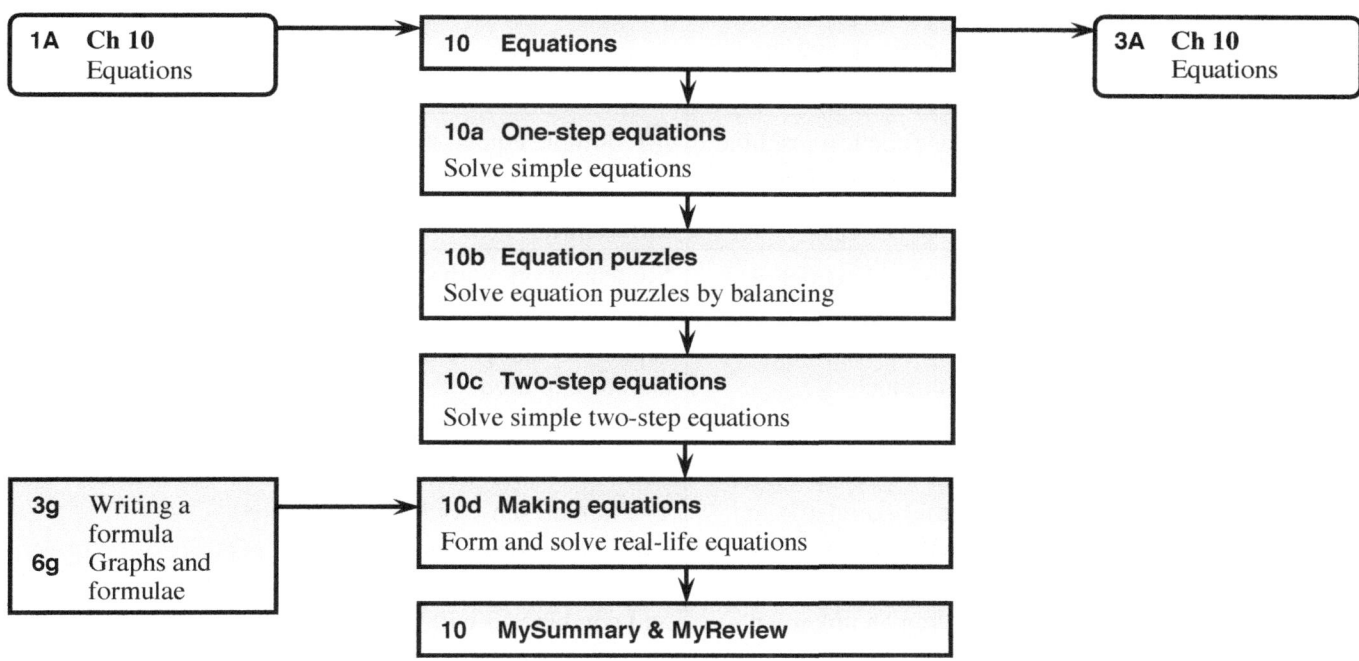

1A   Ch 10 Equations

10   Equations

10a   One-step equations
Solve simple equations

10b   Equation puzzles
Solve equation puzzles by balancing

10c   Two-step equations
Solve simple two-step equations

3g   Writing a formula 6g   Graphs and formulae

10d   Making equations
Form and solve real-life equations

10   MySummary & MyReview

3A   Ch 10 Equations

Differentiation

Student book 2A   192 – 205

One-step equations
Equation puzzles
Two-step equations
Making equations

Student book 2B   176 – 189

Solving one-step equations
Solving multi-step equations
Equations with brackets
Real-life equations

Student book 2C   180 – 195

Linear equations 1
Linear equations 2
Equations with fractions
Trial-and-improvement 2
Real-life equations

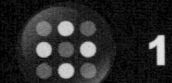

Objectives

- Know the meaning of the word equation   (L5)
- Solve simple linear equations with integer coefficients (with the unknown on one side only) using an appropriate method, such as inverses operations   (L5)

Key ideas	Resources
1 An equation can be thought of as function machine 2 Solving an equation uses the inverse operation	Simple equations (1154)

Simplification	Extension
Often students can intuitively solve simple equations but find the layout of the working problematic. Allow them to gain confidence initially with one type of operation (say, addition as in the introductory example).	Students work with equations following formal algebraic conventions; for example, $2x = 14$ and $\frac{x}{4} = 7$. Equations that give decimal and negative answers can also be explored.

Literacy	Links
The 'language' of mathematics in this exercise is to use a diagrammatic representation, the function machine, which is equivalent to an algebraic representation, the equation, involving an unknown value. An 'inverse operation' is an operation that reverses the effect of the original operation.	The human sense of balance is called equilibrioception. The brain collects information from a series of organs in the inner ear called the labyrinth, and combines it with information from the other senses such as sight and touch, to help prevent the body from falling over. A disturbance to the sense of balance can cause the person to feel giddy or unsteady. There is more information about equilibrioception at http://en.wikipedia.org/wiki/Equilibrioception

Alternative approach

In subsequent exercises in this chapter, equations are represented by balances with two scale pans. This approach can also be used in this exercise.

For example, in question **5a**, the equation $x + 9 = 12$ is represented by a balance with an unknown weight x and 9 kg in the LHS pan and a weight of 12 kg in the RHS pan. Taking 9 kg out of each pan keeps the two pans still in balance and leaves the weight x alone on the LHS with 3 kg on the RHS. The solution of the equation is thus $x = 3$. This answer is clearly the case because $3 + 9 = 12$. Students sometimes see the introduction of scales and balances as unnecessary for such a simple problem. They can be reassured that the notion of 'keeping a balance' is a useful ploy when equations become more complex.

The worked example of the students' book where $m - 7 = 5$ is solved by adding 7 to both scale pans. The -7 thus becomes 0 and the solution is $m = 12$. The reasoning is the same as in the students' book but the mental picture is different.

Checkpoint

1 Solve these equations using inverse operations.
    a $x + 6 = 20$ ($x = 14$)
    b $y - 5 = 10$ ($y = 15$)
    c $k \times 3 = 21$ ($k = 7$)
    d $p \div 5 = 2$ ($p = 10$)

Starter – Calculate 100

Challenge students to see who can get the closest to 100 using the digits 1 to 9 and any operation(s), for example, $123 - 4 - 5 - 6 - 7 + 8 - 9 = 100$.

Follow this by further recap of number work of previous chapters. Ask rapid response questions. Students reply by writing on their mini whiteboards. Discuss questions when their answers indicate a need.

Teaching notes

'I have a number, I add 5 and the answer is 7'. Discuss how to write this mathematically and show $x + 5 = 7$. Say that x is used to represent the unknown number.

Students 'solve' the equation and justify their answer. Students will often offer two ways:
a) counting on from 5 to make 7
b) subtracting 5 from 7.

Say that both methods are valid. It is the second method that introduces the idea of using the *inverse* operation to *undo* what has been done. Demonstrate the use of a flow chart.

Repeat with other equations such as $x - 4 = 6$, $2x = 24$ and $\frac{x}{4} = 5$. Draw function machines and use inverse operations.

Plenary

Give a variety of simple one-step equations both orally and in writing. Students write their answers on mini whiteboards. Discuss answers as necessary.

Depending on the success of the one-step equations, give oral problems of the type 'I have a number. I double it then add 3. The answer is 5. Find the number.' Students respond as before on mini whiteboards.

Exercise commentary

Question 1 – Uses students' mental number skills to solve simple one-step problems.

Question 2 – Uses two function machines; one the inverse of the other. The output of the first becomes the input of the second.

Question 3 – Requires students to solve equations informally when written as incomplete calculations. Some students will revert to 'common sense' methods rather than use inverses. Accept all valid methods.

Question 4 – Requires solving formal equations using inverses. Students will benefit from having a worked example to refer to in order to perfect their working out as in question **2**.

Question 5 – Applies the skill of solving equations to a real-life context. Students may solve the problem without writing equations. Discuss how equations can be written for this scenario.

Answers

1	a	4	b	7	c	10			
	d	50	e	5	f	15			
2	a	12	b	-9	c	10			
	d	23	e	150	f	-4			
3	a	3	b	22	c	9			
	d	19	e	45	f	5			
	g	10	h	4					
4	a	3	b	30	c	5	d	20
	e	20	f	20	g	6	h	10
	i	3	j	21	k	7	l	0
	m	567	n	4	o	9	p	19
5	a	£6.50	b	£25					
6	26								

Objectives

- Know the meaning of the word equation   (L5)
- Solve linear equations with integer coefficients and with unknowns on either or both sides   (L5)

Key ideas	Resources
1 An equation can be thought of as a balance with two scale pans 2 To maintain a balance, the same operation must act on both sides	Simple equations (1154) Solving equations (1185) Old-style kitchen scales Tubes and counters

Simplification	Extension
Provide students with tubes and counters to represent the known and unknowns and allow them to remove objects physically. They can draw sketch diagrams to illustrate each stage. Provide copies of balances in Exercise **10b**, so that students can cross out what they take away from both sides.	Students consider the progression to algebraic symbolism by writing an algebraic equation. They can mirror their 'instructions' for each stage of the solution using algebra, as suggested in the plenary activity.

Literacy	Links
Equations have their particular vocabulary. There is both formal and informal language. *To solve an equation* is not unlike solving a crime: something previously unknown has been found out and there is *a solution*. To find the solution, you have to *balance* all the facts of the case. You can adjust the balance by *doing to one side what you do to the other*. The aim of the adjusting is to *simplify both sides*. You can check the solution by *substitution* into the original equation.	Equations are used in Chemistry to describe reactions. The chemicals that react are on one side of the equation and the chemicals that they produce are on the other. A balanced equation has equal numbers of each type of atom on each side of the equation. There is a game to balance chemical equations at http://funbasedlearning.com/chemistry/chemBalancer/ques2.htm

Alternative approach

To see and use old-style kitchen scales adds more than even good diagrams can provide. Use a pair of kitchen scales with two pans to illustrate objects in balance becoming unbalanced when something is 'taken away' from one side. Show that the balance returns when the same amount is taken away from the other side. A sketch diagram can be drawn to represent the scales and their contents.

To solve Bob and Jane's scenario in 'Teaching notes', there are three levels of increasing symbolism:
a) place the tubes and loose sweets in the two scale pans
b) draw a sketch of the pans, writing $2t + 1$ in the LHS pan and $t + 10$ in the RHS pan
c) write the equation $2t + 1 = t + 10$.
Now start taking away from both sides. The first step is to take one tube, t. The three representations are altered and recorded. The second step is to take one sweet, 1, from both sides. Again, the three representations are recorded. At all stages, the pans, the sketch and the equation run in parallel.

Checkpoint

1 Find the value of y

   $y + y + y + 2 + 2 = y + y + 2 + 2 + 2$ $(y = 2)$

2 Find the value of p

   $p + p + p + 3 = p + 3 + 3 + 3 + 3 + 3$ $(p = 6)$

Starter – Algebraic products

Draw a 4 × 4 table on the board. Label the columns with the terms: a b 2a 7 and label the rows with the terms: a 3a b c.

Ask students to fill in the table with the products. For example, the top row in the table would read a^2, ab, $2a^2$, $7a$.

This activity can be differentiated by the choice of terms.

Teaching notes

Write on the board 'Bob and Jane have the same number of sweets. Bob has 2 tubes and 3 loose sweets and Jane has 1 tube and 10 loose sweets.'

Draw a diagram of two scale pans holding tubes and loose sweets to represent both parties. The problem is to find how many sweets are in a full tube.

Discuss what mathematical sign can be placed between the two containers to show that they have the same number of sweets. Say that the equals sign acts like a set of scales and each side must balance. Discuss what could be done to both sides to maintain this equilibrium.

Demonstrate each action by an illustration:
– Take one tube from both sides
– Take 3 loose sweets from both sides

We now know how many sweets are in a tube (7). Check the number 7 by replacing each tube in the original statement with 7 loose sweets. Bob and Jane both have 17 sweets.

Extend this approach to a similar example but with a final step of division. For example, Bob has 3 tubes and 3 loose sweets; Jane has 1 tube and 11 loose sweets.

Plenary

Bob has 2 tubes and 5 loose sweets and Jane has 1 tube but 17 loose ones. Find how many sweets are in each tube.

Write diagrams and instructions alongside formal algebraic working. Discuss how to write the original statement, how to choose each operation and how to write the next statement. Write formal working-out alongside any diagrams:

$$2x + 5 = x + 17 \qquad (-5)$$
$$2x = x + 12 \qquad (-x)$$
$$x = 12$$

Introduce the word 'solve' by saying that the students have solved an equation.

Exercise commentary

Questions 1 and **2** – Students solve equations informally from picture representations of balancing scales. Students write what happens to both sides and redraw the subsequent picture at each step. This will progress to setting out clear algebraic working later.

Question 3 – Begins the move to symbolic equations. Students can copy these equations in full and cross out what they take away from both sides before writing the next step.

Answers

1	a	1	b	4	c	2		
	d	3	e	3	f	3		
	g	5	h	17				
2	a	10	b	5				
3	a	5	b	2	c	4	d	4

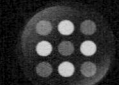

Objectives

- Solve simple linear equations with integer coefficients and the unknown on one side only using the method of 'balancing' (L5)

Key ideas	Resources
1 An equation can be represented by two scale pans balancing 2 Any operation on one side must be balanced by the same operation on the other side	Solving equations (1182) Old-style kitchen scale pans

Simplification	Extension
Ensure the arithmetic is straightforward so that the focus is on solving equations rather than doing the arithmetic. Students solve one-stage problems before moving on to simple two-stage problems. Restrict examples to those using multiplication and addition.	Extend students to two-step equations involving division and subtraction. Students solve equations with decimal or negative solutions.

Literacy	Links
The layout of the worked example in the students' book has $$3x + 6 = 18$$ $$3x + 6 - 6 = 18 - 6$$ $$3x = 12$$ $$3x \div 3 = 12 \div 3$$ $$x = 4$$ Once the process of inverse operations is understood, the working can be condensed by doing the inverse operation mentally. The written layout now becomes: $$3x + 6 = 18$$ $$3x = 12$$ $$x = 4$$ with the associated oral patter of 'Subtract 6 from both sides' and 'Divide both sides by 3' going unwritten.	In Africa, India and the Far East, seeds were traditionally used as standard weights in balance pans to weigh small amounts. Carob seeds were often used because of their uniform size. The weight of an average carob seed is 200 milligrams. The carat is the unit used to weigh gold and diamonds today and originates from the weight of a carob seed. The weight of one carat is precisely 200 milligrams, or 0.2 grams. There is more information about the history of weighing at http://www.averyweigh-tronix.com/main.aspx?p51.1.3.4

Alternative approach

An alternative is to have a set of scales where objects and weights can accompany the oral explanation of the written symbols. Even if no physical scales are available, a metre rule balanced on a pencil might suffice.

Three representations can then be seen to run in parallel: namely, the physical scales, diagrams of the scales and the working of an algebraic equation.

Checkpoint

1 Solve these equations (find the value of the letters), showing all the steps.

    a $3x + 2 = 14$ $(3x = 12, x = 4)$

    b $3 + 6y = 21$ $(6y = 18, y = 3)$

Starter – £20 more

A CD player and batteries together cost £23. The CD player cost £20 more than the batteries. How much do the batteries cost?   (Not £3! They cost £1.50)

Ask students to explain their methods.

Teaching notes

Write a one-step equation, say $x + 4 = 9$. Students explain how to solve it. Recall from previous lessons the use of flowcharts and their inverses and the formal way of setting out working. Mention that the equals sign acts like a set of scales – both sides must balance – and, if we want to **undo** what has been done, we must perform the same operation on **both** sides to retain the balance.

Now extend this approach to two-step equations, such as $2x + 5 = 11$. Remind students that $2x$ means $2 \times x$. Demonstrate constructing a flowchart for this equation, and then construct the inverse flowchart using inverse operations. Highlight how the order is reversed, linking the order to a real-life scenario such as 'You walk forwards and turn on the light. To get back to the start, you turn off the light and walk backwards.'

Repeat with different equations.

Plenary

Students solve simple two-step equations such as $5x + 2 = 17$, writing their working on their mini whiteboards. Discuss any misunderstandings that arise.

As an extension and if appropriate, discuss the difference between $2x + 6 = 16$ and $2(x + 6) = 16$. Students suggest how this equation might be solved.

Exercise commentary

Question 2 – Students copy the blank function machines, complete the first using the information provided, and then construct the inverse machine.

Question 3 – Students decide what they can take off both sides. In part **a**, it may be necessary to highlight that a 10 kg unit is equal to ten 1 kg units.

Question 4 – Students meet formal two-step equations. Students should be aiming to use the balance method here. If necessary, they can sketch a diagram of a balance with two scale pans.

Question 6 – Requires students to construct and solve a two-step equation from a real-life problem.

Question 7 – This is a prequel for the Exercise **10d**.

Answers

1	**a** 11	**b** 24	**c** 120	**d** 75
2	**a** 6	**b** 32	**c** 4	**d** 72
3	**a** 2	**b** 5	**c** 1	
4	**a** 5	**b** 5	**c** 5	**d** 2.8
	e 6	**f** 3	**g** 3	**h** 3
	i 1	**j** 2	**k** 5	**l** 2

5   10 kg

6   10.8 litres

7   **a**   **i** $5x = 10$ **ii** $x - 15 = 20$ **iii** $x \times x - 3 = 22$

   b   **i** 2   **ii** 35   **iii** 5

Objectives	
• Construct simple linear equations in different situations and solve them	(L5)

Key ideas	Resources	
1 Equations can arise in different situations and can be solved using inverse operations or by 'balancing' both sides of an equation	Solving equations	(1182)

Simplification	Extension
The wordy nature of this lesson may be problematic for some students. Offer students scenarios where the written language follows the pattern of the equation, as in the worked example about straws in the students' book. Let students choose their preferred method of solution; function machines or balances. It may be beneficial for students to work on problems with a familiar context (such as those in questions **1** and **2**).	Working in pairs, students create their own word problems to give to a partner. They must consider the solution is viable; for example, you cannot have 4.5 sweets in a tube!

Literacy	Links
As mentioned above in 'Simplification', early work on this topic can have sentences constructed so that the flow of words is the same flow as that needed to write the equation. For example: 'Jane has two packets of biscuits and an extra 5 loose biscuits and, altogether, she has 29 biscuits.' This sentence becomes $2x + 5 = 29$ with the algebra 'following' the words.	The equals sign was first used by the Welsh mathematician and physician Robert Recorde in 1557 in his book 'The Whetstone of Witte'. He used two parallel lines in the symbol because 'noe 2, thynges, can be moare equalle'. However, other symbols for 'is equal to' were still used until the 1700s, including the Latin abbreviation *ae* or *oe* (for *aequalis* or 'equal') There is more information about Robert Recorde at http://en.wikipedia.org/wiki/Robert_Recorde

Alternative approach
The two approaches used in the introduction to equations have already been explored; namely, using inverse function machines and using the notion of 'balance' with scale pans. These two methods can run independently. But they both have the same basic concept of 'undoing what has already been done' and the order of the doing and undoing is crucial. In creating equations from a context, an introductory approach is mentioned above of writing the scenario in such a way that the algebra flows from the words. As students get more skilled, then the language need not be constrained in this way.

Checkpoint
1 Four bags of sugar and 250 g weigh the same as 2.25 kg. **a** Letting b stand for the weight of a bag of sugar, write an equation to represent the above statement. <div align="right">$(4b + 250 = 2250)$</div> **b** Solve your equation to find the weight of a bag of sugar. <div align="right">$(4b = 2000, b = 500$; therefore a bag of sugar weighs 500 g$)$</div>

Starter – T, S or F

Present these statements and students respond on mini whiteboards with 'Always **T**rue', '**S**ometimes true' or 'Always **F**alse':

$x + 6 = 6 + x$	(T)
$2 + x = 2x$	(S, if $x = 2$)
$x - 5 = 5 - x$	(S, if $x = 5$)
$x + 3 = 7$	(S, if $x = 4$)
$x + x - x = x$	(T)

Students justify their answers.

Teaching notes

Introduce the scenario where Bob and Jane have the same number of sweets, but Bob has 2 tubes and 6 loose ones, whereas Jane has 14 loose ones. The problem is to find how many sweets are in a tube.

Emphasise an **equation** as a mathematical sentence with an equals sign. Discuss what is equal in this scenario and note that each person has the same **unknown**; that is, the number of sweets in a tube. Discuss how to solve this equation by using:

- a flowchart method
- a balance method.

In context, students ask, 'What can we take away from both Bob and Jane and still keep them equal?' More abstractly, students ask, 'What operations have happened to the unknown and in what order shall we *undo* them?'

Work through some further examples, creating equations and solving them, such as:

I have two bags of pens and four loose ones. I know that in total there are 42 pens.

John has six tubes of sweets and four loose ones. He has a total of 46 sweets.

I have three weeks' pocket money and an extra £2. In total, I have £23.

Plenary

Offer contexts in which equations arise. For example,

- a rectangle has a perimeter of 30 cm. It is 9 cm long. Find its width, x
- an isosceles triangle has sides of x, x, and 5 cm. Its perimeter is 17 cm. Find the length, x.

Students write an equation on their mini whiteboards and discuss it. They then solve the equation and discuss their answers.

Exercise commentary

Questions 1–3 – Require students to construct and solve two-step equations, starting with the familiar context of sweets in a tube as in question **1**.

Question 4 – The comment in the box is the starting point. Students can then take the first two sentences and write an equation, with the two sentences providing the two sides of the equation. A diagram of the situation might help. The equation does not include any units.

Question 5 – There is no hint in a box to give the starting point, but the diagram indicates that the score of each of the four judges should be the unknown.

Answers

1. **a** 2 packets + 7 sweets = 25 sweets
   b Let p = Number of sweets in a packet
   c $2p + 7 = 25$
   d $p = 9$
2. **a** 2 packets + 7 sweets = 31 sweets
   b $2p + 7 = 31$
   c $p = 12$
3. **a** $3m + 4 = 52$
   b $m = 16$
4. Let b = the volume of a beaker. Then
   a $3b + 50 = 275$ **b** 75 cl
5. Let x = score given by each of the first 4 judges. Then
   a $4x - 5 = 23$ **b** 7

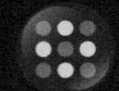

Key outcomes	Quick check
Solve one-step equations using inverses and balancing. L5	Find the value of m in each case $5 + m = 17$ $(m = 12)$ $m - 7 = 21$ $(m = 28)$ $5 \times m = 30$ $(m = 6)$ $m \div 5 = 10$ $(m = 50)$
Form equations from word problems. L5	Write down the equation from this word problem. Start with a number, call it n. Multiply it by 5 and add 2. The result is 37. $(5n + 2 = 37)$
Solve two-step equations. L5	Solve the equation you have just formed. $(5n = 35, n = 7)$
Make equations from real situations. L5	4 apples and 60 g weigh 300 g. Let a stand for the weight of an apple. Form an equation. $(4a + 60 = 300)$ Solve your equation to find the weight of an apple. $(4a = 240, a = 60$; therefore an apple weighs 60 g$)$

⊞ MyMaths extra support

Lesson/online homework	Description
Function machines 1159 L4	Using function machines to solve equations

MyReview

10 MySummary

Check out
You should now be able to ...

		Test it ➡ Questions
✓	Solve one-step equations using inverses and balancing.	⑤ 1, 2
✓	Form equations from word problems.	⑤ 3
✓	Solve two-step equations.	⑤ 4, 5
✓	Make equations from real situations.	⑤ 6

Language	Meaning	Example
Equation	A mathematical statement, written in algebra and including an equals sign, which is true for one or more values of the unknown	$2x + 1 = 7$ is an equation
Solution	The value(s) of the unknown that the equation is true for	$x = 3$ is the only solution of the equation above
Inverse	An operation that reverses the effect of a given operation	The inverse of $+ 5$ is $- 5$ The inverse of $\times 3$ is $\div 3$
Operation	A rule for processing number or letters.	The basic operations are $+, -, \times$ and $\div$.

10 MyReview

1 Solve these equations.
  a $a + 3 = 13$ b $b + 7 = 7$
  c $c - 5 = 8$ d $d - 11 = 15$
  e $e \times 5 = 35$ f $f \times 10 = 60$
  g $g \div 2 = 20$ h $h \div 10 = 30$

2 Find the weight of each box by balancing.
  a
  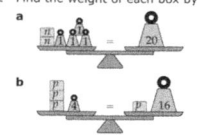
  b

3 Find the starting numbers in these statements.
  a Start with a number, multiply it by 4 and add 1. The result is 45.
  b Start with a number, multiply it by 5 and subtract 2. The result is 38.
  c Start with a number, divide it by 2 and add 3. The result is 7.
  d Start with a number, add 1 and divide by 2. The result is 13.

4 Solve these equations.
  a $2x + 9 = 13$
  b $3x + 6 = 27$
  c $5x - 10 = 45$
  d $6x - 12 = 36$

5 a Write an equation for these scales.

  b Solve the equation to find the value of m.

6 The total number of students travelling on a school trip is 85. They fill 2 coaches, leaving 7 to travel in a minibus.
  a Write an equation linking the total number of students and the numbers travelling by coach and by minibus. Use c for the number of students in each coach.
  b Solve your equation to calculate the number of students in each coach.

What next?

Score		
0 – 3		Your knowledge of this topic is still developing. To improve look at Formative test: 2A-10; MyMaths: 1154 and 1182
4, 5		You are gaining a secure knowledge of this topic. To improve look at InvisiPen: 231, 233 and 234
6		You have mastered this topic. Well done, you are ready to progress!

Question commentary

Encourage use of the balance method.

Questions 1 and **2** – Straightforward.

Question 3 – Parts **c** and **d** involve division. Show students how to write this.

Question 4 – Parts **c** and **d** involve subtraction for the first time in a two-step equation. Students may need reassuring as how to proceed.

Questions 5 and **6** – Should be straightforward. In **6** students do not need a letter for the mini bus.

Answers

1	**a**	10	**b**	0
	c	13	**d**	26
	e	7	**f**	6
	g	40	**h**	300
2	**a**	8	**b**	6
3	**a**	11	**b**	8
	c	8	**d**	25
4	**a**	2	**b**	7
	c	11	**d**	8
5	**a**	$3m + 6 = 24$	**b**	6
6	**a**	$2c + 7 = 85$	**b**	39

10 MyPractice

1 Work out the value of the letters in each of these inverse function machines.

a $k \rightarrow +7 \rightarrow 5$ $k \rightarrow -7 \rightarrow 5$

b $n \rightarrow +15 \rightarrow 10$ $n \rightarrow -15 \rightarrow 10$

c $t \rightarrow \div 2 \rightarrow 30$ $t \rightarrow \times 2 \rightarrow 30$

d $p \rightarrow \times 4 \rightarrow 36$ $p \rightarrow \div 4 \rightarrow 36$

e $b \rightarrow -5 \rightarrow 27$ $b \rightarrow +5 \rightarrow 27$

f $m \rightarrow \times 6 \rightarrow 48$ $m \rightarrow \div 6 \rightarrow 48$

2 Dave and Emma are selling raffle tickets for the school fête.
Dave has three books and two loose tickets.
Emma has one book and twelve loose tickets.
They have the **same number of tickets**.

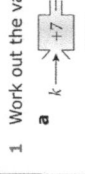

How many tickets are there in one whole book?

3 Solve these equations using inverse operations. Calculate the value of the letters.

a $x + 7 = 11$ b $x + 40 = 90$

c $n - 45 = 60$ d $k - 3 = 33$

e $g - 53 = 7$ f $b - 9 = 1$

g $u \times 3 = 15$ h $x \div 2 = 6$

i $l \times 4 = 24$ j $y \div 10 = 4$

k $s \times 4 = 60$ l $z \div 21 = 21$

4 Solve these equations. Find the values of the letters.

a $4s + 6 = 46$ b $5x + 10 = 25$

c $3t + 3 = 30$ d $5a + 4 = 14$

e $5p + 7 = 47$ f $8k + 5 = 21$

g $7y + 8 = 29$ h $6x + 11 = 41$

i $7m + 1 = 50$ j $9d + 7 = 25$

k $5z + 7 = 32$ l $15d + 20 = 50$

5 There are ten loose sweets and three full packets shown here. Altogether there are 34 sweets.

a Write a sentence to link the two amounts of sweets.

b Think of a symbol to represent the number of sweets in a packet.

c Use the symbol to make an equation linking the number of sweets in the picture and the total of 34.

d Solve the equation to find the number of sweets in a packet.

6 You have three full packets and ten loose sweets, but this time the total number of sweets is 31.

a Write a sentence linking 31 sweets, ten loose sweets and three full packets.

b Write your sentence as an equation using your symbol.

c Solve your equation to find the new number of sweets in a full packet.

Question commentary

Question 1 – Parts **a** and **b** involve negative answers.

Question 2 – Let the number of tickets in a book be represented by the letter b.

Question 3 – In part **l**, reassure students that $z = 0$ is a valid solution.

Question 4 – These equations all lead to integer solutions.

Questions 5 and **6** – Encourage clear working.

Answers

1	a	-2	b	-5	c	60		
	d	9	e	32	f	8		
2	5							
3	a	4	b	50	c	105	d	36
	e	60	f	10	g	5	h	12
	i	6	j	40	k	15	l	0
4	a	10	b	3	c	9	d	2
	e	8	f	2	g	3	h	5
	i	7	j	2	k	5	l	2

5　a　3 packets + 10 sweets = 34 sweets

　　b　Let p = number of sweets in a packet

　　c　$3p + 10 = 34$

　　d　8

6　a　3 packets + 10 sweets = 31 sweets

　　b　$3p + 10 = 31$

　　c　7

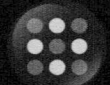
Learning outcomes

N4 Use the 4 operations, including formal written methods, applied to integers, decimals, proper and improper fractions, and mixed numbers, all both positive and negative (L4/5)

N5 Use conventional notation for the priority of operations, including brackets, powers, roots and reciprocals (L5)

N15 Use a calculator and other technologies to calculate results accurately and then interpret them appropriately (L5)

Introduction

The chapter starts by looking at written methods for addition, subtraction, multiplication and division (including decimal numbers) before a section focusing on written arithmetic problems. The final two sections cover calculator skills, including brackets, powers and roots, and interpreting the calculator display.

The introduction discusses the different ways in which cultures write. The right to left conventions of the Arabic and Hebrew cultures and the top to bottom conventions of the Chinese and Japanese cultures mean that different cultures have very different ways of setting out text. Obviously, since mathematics is a 'universal' language, we have to agree to a convention in which everyone follows the same method. The use of left to right conventions in setting out mathematical calculations, the use of BIDMAS and some other standard methods are the same throughout the world.

However, different cultures still have different methods for carrying out calculations, many of which are as efficient as the ones we are used to using in a typical mathematical classroom. Chinese multiplication, for example, is a nice alternative to our standard method and can be used to show the students a different way.

http://www.youtube.com/watch?v=n97nmGGlBf4

Prior knowledge

Students should already know how to...

- Add, subtract, multiply and divide numbers using mental methods
- Add, subtract, multiply and divide whole numbers

Starter problem

The starter problem is a classic 'Countdown' type puzzle where the students have to use the six given numbers (and standard operations) to make target numbers.

While there are no right or wrong answers (assuming the calculation works!), students will need to check that they get the operations in the correct order.

The first one can be solved by making 300 and then adding the seven. 300 can be made from doing $(40 \div 4) \times 10 \times 3$.

The second number could be recognised as 25 squared and therefore students could be asked to make 25 from the other five numbers. $7 \times 3 + 4 = 25$ so this works.

Extensions could be to change the target number, or get students to pick their own. Also, you could insist they use all of the numbers, or a specified subset of the numbers.

Resources

MyMaths

Adding in columns	1020	Multiply double digits	1025	Subtraction columns	1028
Long division	1041				

Online assessment

Chapter test	2A–11
Formative test	2A–11
Summative test	2A–11

InvisiPen solutions

Written multiplication	126	Written division	127
Calculator methods			129
Adding and subtracting decimals			131

Topic scheme

Teaching time = 6 lessons/2 weeks

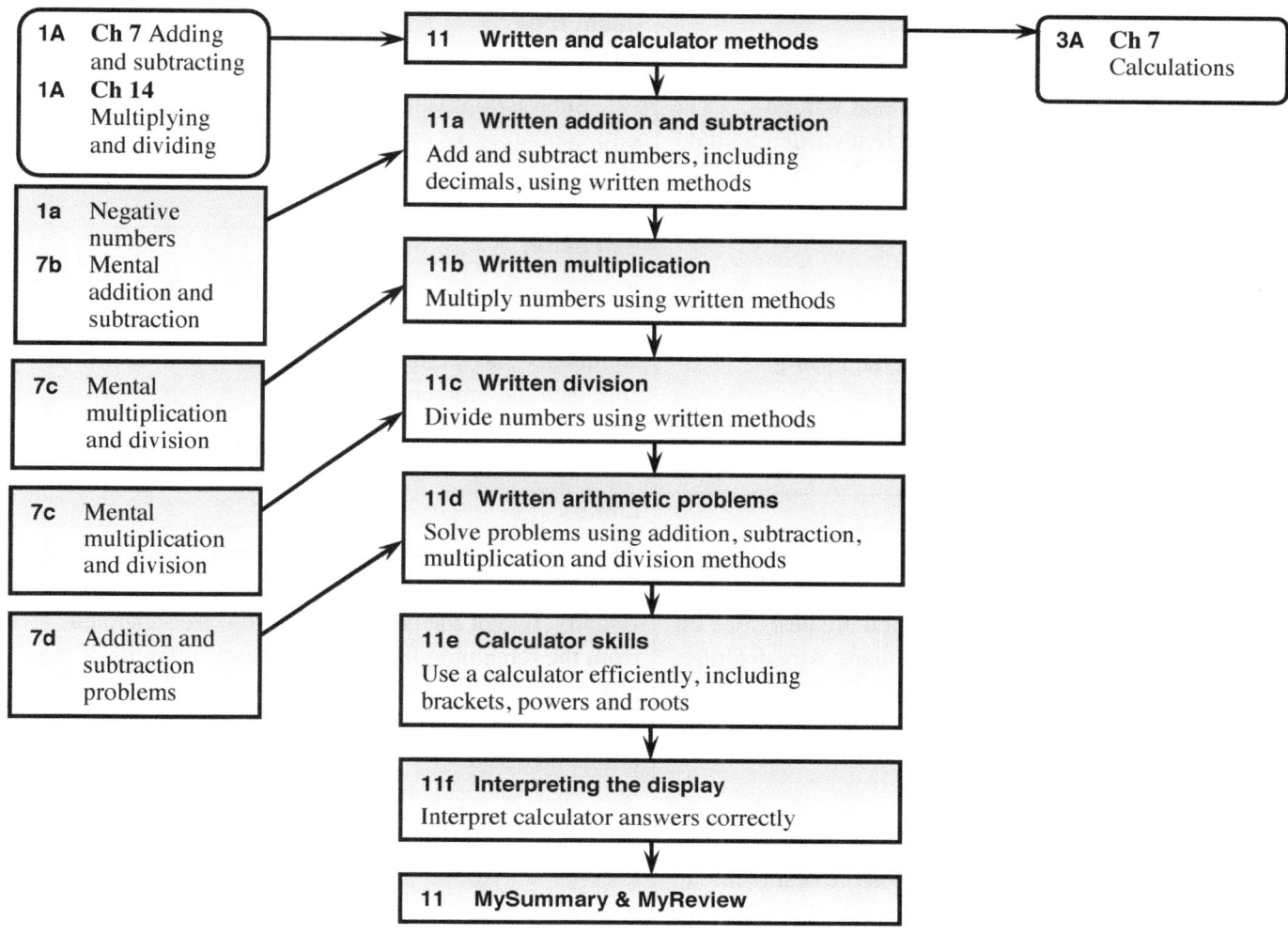

1A Ch 7 Adding and subtracting
1A Ch 14 Multiplying and dividing

1a Negative numbers
7b Mental addition and subtraction

7c Mental multiplication and division

7c Mental multiplication and division

7d Addition and subtraction problems

11 Written and calculator methods

3A Ch 7 Calculations

11a Written addition and subtraction
Add and subtract numbers, including decimals, using written methods

11b Written multiplication
Multiply numbers using written methods

11c Written division
Divide numbers using written methods

11d Written arithmetic problems
Solve problems using addition, subtraction, multiplication and division methods

11e Calculator skills
Use a calculator efficiently, including brackets, powers and roots

11f Interpreting the display
Interpret calculator answers correctly

11 MySummary & MyReview

Differentiation

Student book 2A   206 – 223
Written addition and subtraction
Written multiplication
Written division
Written arithmetic problems
Calculator skills
Interpreting the display

Student book 2B   190 – 209
Written addition and subtraction
Written methods of multiplication
Written methods of division
Order of operations
Addition and subtraction problems
Multiplication and division
    problems
Calculation methods

Student book 2C   196 – 215
Multiplication
Division
Calculator skills
Calculators in context
Order of operations
Written addition and subtraction
Multiplication and division
    problems

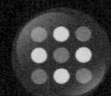

Objectives

- Use efficient methods to add and subtract whole numbers and decimals (L4)

Key ideas	Resources
1 Addition and subtraction can be performed using a variety of methods, both mental and written 2 The 'column method' is an efficient written method for both addition and subtraction of integers and decimals	Adding in columns (1020) Subtraction columns (1028) Mini whiteboards

Simplification	Extension
Subtraction is weaker than addition for most students. Typically they will reverse the digits when mentally subtracting within a column, rather than using decomposition. For example, 5 6 2 – 1 4 7 is seen as $7 - 2$ in the units column, and not $12 - 7$.	Provide students with examples that have been worked incorrectly. They correct them and write 'teacher comments', highlighting errors and explaining how to approach the problem correctly.

Literacy	Links
As with writing in English, so writing in mathematics is most easily understood if it is well set out. Written calculations using the column method are best done on squared paper with one digit to a square. Any decimal points can either have their own column or be positioned on a grid line.	An abacus is a mechanical calculator and consists of a frame containing rows of beads threaded onto wires. Usually, two of the beads in each row are separated from the remaining five by a crossbar. Versions of the abacus are still widely used in the Far East and Africa. There is more information about the abacus and an online abacus at http://www.educalc.net/144267.page

Alternative approach

Before doing a calculation, decide on the best method:

- for additions, the choice is between a mental or written method
- for subtractions, if a mental method is chosen, the next choice is between 'taking away' from the larger number or 'adding onto' the smaller number
- for subtractions, if a written method is chosen, the next choice is whether to use the column method with possible decomposition (as expected in this exercise) or to use 'complementary addition' starting from the smaller number.

Checkpoint

1 Use a written method to work out:
  a $167 + 89$ (256)
  b $167 - 89$ (78)
  c $16.7 + 8.9$ (25.6)
  d $16.7 - 8.9$ (7.8)

Starter – Pocket money

Anwar receives £5 pocket money each week.

Bryony's pocket money started at £3 and increased by 50p each week, so she got £3 in week 1, £3.50 in week 2, £4 in week 3, etc.

Charlie said he was happy, because his pocket money started with 10p and it doubled each week: 10p, 20p, 40p, etc.

Students find who would get the most money after 5 weeks (Anwar) and after 10 weeks? (Charlie)

Teaching notes

Recall previous lessons on mental addition, mental subtraction and the use of jottings. Discuss when these mental methods are not appropriate.

Note that, for a three-digit calculation, say 376 + 218, a written method is often more appropriate than a mental method.

Carry out this addition incorrectly using a written method. Invite students to point out what has gone wrong. Highlight errors and misconceptions, such as:

Digits lined up incorrectly in place value columns:

```
  3 7 6
  2 1 8
  2 5 5 6
```

Tens have not been carried over (6 + 8 = 14):

```
  3 7 6
  2 1 8
  5 8 14
```

Now consider subtractions. Emphasise the points:

- line up digits in correct place-value columns
- work from right to left
- always subtract the **bottom** digit **from** the **top** digit, and never the other way round
- use decomposition to get an extra 10 from the T column on the left when a subtraction is not possible.

Plenary

Give students some additions and subtractions to do on their mini whiteboards. Check results and discuss them as necessary.

Also, look at question **7** as a class. At each stage, discuss what operation is necessary and whether a written method is necessary or whether a mental method would be more appropriate.

Exercise commentary

Questions 1–3 – These questions give practice in written methods for simple addition and subtraction. Ensure that students 'carry' when digits run into the next column with additions and 'regroup' by decomposition as necessary with subtractions. Question **3** extends to 4-digit numbers.

Questions 4–6 – Extend to decimals. Ensure that students line up the decimal points vertically.

Question 7 – This poses a convoluted word problem requiring repeated addition and subtraction. Students may notice that a mental method is more appropriate.

Answers

1	a	218	b	453	c	280
	d	339	e	420	f	313
2	a	263	b	115	c	89
	d	135	e	209	f	78
3	a	3832	b	4367	c	4374
	d	3645	e	3125	f	2754
4	a	241.7	b	68.4	c	420.3
5	a	224.0	b	324.5	c	303.0
6	a	42.5	b	74.5	c	53.0
	d	43.0	e	246.2	f	323.9
7	12					
8	474					

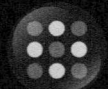

Objectives

- Make and justify estimates and approximations of calculations   (L5)
- Multiply three-digit by two-digit whole numbers   (L5)

Key ideas	Resources
1 Long multiplication is the most efficient written method for multiplying two numbers 2 It is good practice to estimate an answer first	Multiply double digits (1025) Multiplication squares (as support)

Simplification	Extension
For some students, focus first on 2-digit × 2-digit multiplications and, later, progress to 3-digit by 2-digit multiplications. Use digits which are 5 or less to begin with, as these times-tables are more likely known; for higher times-tables, a multiplication square may be needed by students with weak recall of multiplication facts.	Extend to multi-step problems with multiplications set in a variety of different real-life contexts. Extend to multiplications involving decimal numbers; for example, 342 × 2.3 and 34.2 × 23

Literacy	Links

There are several methods for multiplying two numbers. 'Long multiplication' is likely to be the most efficient. There are two ways to set out the working, depending on the order in which the digits of the second number are taken. In any class, there are likely to be students with backgrounds using both ways. For example,
 	
  2 1 3   and   2 1 3
  × 3 1   × 3 1
  2 1 3   6 3 9 0
6 3 9 0   2 1 3
6 6 0 3   6 6 0 3
 	
A policy of working on squared grid paper with 'one digit to one square' helps keep work lined up in columns.
	Number 10 Downing Street in London is the official residence of the First Lord of the Treasury, who is usually also the Prime Minister of Great Britain. The first prime minister to live at Number 10 was Robert Walpole in the early 1700s and most prime ministers have lived there since. The house is mainly comprised of offices and the Prime Minister's apartment at the top of the building was created from rooms originally used by servants. There is more information about Number 10 at
	http://www.number10.gov.uk/history-and-tour

Alternative approach

The grid method is based on the area of a rectangle found from *length × width*. Both numbers are partitioned and then the results of the partitioning added together. Its disadvantages are that it is quite time-consuming and there are many opportunities for errors. Consider 213 × 31.

×	200	10	3
30	6000	300	90
1	200	10	3

213 × 31 = 6000 + 200 +300 + 10 + 90 +3 = 6603

Checkpoint

1   Consider long multiplication for 213 × 31.
    a   Which number goes 'on top' and which 'on the bottom'?
                                                (213 on top because it is bigger; 31 on the bottom)
    b   When you multiply by 31, will you start with the 1 or the 3?   (Either)
    c   When you multiply by the 3, which place-value column is the 3 in and so what do you need in your working?   (It is in the T column, so there needs to be a 0 in the row of the working)

Starter – Quick-fire products

Students use mini whiteboards to answer quick fire questions:

3×10	32×10	41×10
23×10	4×100	12×100
1.5×10	2.7×10	3.1×100, etc.

Teaching notes

Referring to the starter, discuss what it means to multiply by 10 and 100, and extend to decimal values, such as 1.2×10 and 4.3×100.

If students are prone to simply 'add one or two zeros', point out that it does not always work. For example, with 1.2×10, 'adding a 0' gives 1.20 which means there are no hundredths and it is the same as 1.2. Demonstrate, using the place-value columns, that each digit moves one place or two places to the left when multiplying by 10 or 100.

Invite students to calculate 12×18. If students have previously met the partitioning method, discuss the calculation 12×18 and note that both numbers need to be partitioned. Demonstrate the use of a grid to find the answer.

Turn to the standard method of 'long multiplication'. Point out that (a) it is usually easier if the larger number (18) is on the 'top row', (b) there is a choice of starting the working with the 1 or the 2 of the second number, 12. Once this choice is made, it is suggested that all the class make the same choice and keep to it thereafter.

For those students who have met both methods, ask them which method they think is quicker and less prone to errors.

Extend the method to multiply 3-digits by 2-digits and, later, 3-digits by 3-digits. Ask which method is more efficient. Ask students to estimate their answers before starting their calculation. Approximate each number by rounding and then estimate the answer. For example, 12×18 can be estimated as $10 \times 20 = 200$.

Plenary

Ask questions in context. Students use their mini whiteboards to calculate answers. They choose between a mental method and a written method. Discuss the working where necessary. For example,

Dylan sends 14 text messages. Each one costs 9p. What is the total cost? (A mental method could be chosen; 10×14 then 9×14)

I have 12 tubes of sweets. In each tube there are 23 sweets. How many sweets altogether?

Exercise commentary

Questions 1–4 – These provide a gradual build-up of complexity. Remind students that they need to estimate the answer before starting the calculation.

Question 1 – Focuses on 2-digit by 1-digit multiplications.

Questions 2 and **3** – Require students work with 2-digit by 2-digit multiplications.

Question 4 – Extends to three digits. So when rounding, use 1 significant figure.

Question 5 – Sets questions in various contexts.

Question 6 – Is a problem-solving activity based on products of consecutive numbers. It can be attempted in pairs or small groups.

Answers

1	**a**	105	**b**	117	**c**	96	**d**	136
	e	234	**f**	133	**g**	280	**h**	161
	i	176	**j**	222	**k**	261	**l**	344
2	**a**	132	**b**	182	**c**	180	**d**	238
	e	195	**f**	240	**g**	234	**h**	228
	i	289	**j**	342	**k**	294	**l**	476
3	**a**	832	**b**	1012	**c**	722	**d**	999
	e	2668	**f**	2340	**g**	2064	**h**	3393
	i	4624	**j**	6952	**k**	8554	**l**	9801
4	**a**	1512	**b**	1582	**c**	1962	**d**	2074
	e	2448	**f**	3770	**g**	4844	**h**	5394
	i	7524	**j**	11 662	**k**	24 034	**l**	26 961
5	**a**	616 MB	**b**	1920 min	**c**	1316		
6	**a**	33, 34	**b**	52, 53				

c The last two digits multiplied together give the end digit

d Find the square root of the product and use the two whole numbers either side of this.

Objectives

- Divide three-digit whole numbers by two-digit whole numbers (L5)
- Multiply and divide integers and decimals by 10, 100, and explain the effect (L5)

Key ideas	Resources
1 Short and long division are two methods of dividing integers	Long division (1066) Multiplication square (as support)

Simplification	Extension
In the first instance, concentrate on short division by a single-digit number without remainders. Progress to having remainders. Then divide by straightforward 2-digit integers (such as 11, 12, 20, 21) using short division without remainders. Progress to having remainders. Long division can come much later, if at all. The layout can mystify. Using short division, even when dividing by 2-digit numbers such as 23 or 31, can be less problematic than long division.	Students tackle further problems in real-life contexts. For example, a restaurant bill of £138 is to be split between eight diners. How much will they each pay? Highlight that there can be no 'remainder' – the whole bill must be paid!

Literacy	Links
The students' book suggests that short division can be used even where long division is a clear choice of method. The example given is $35 \div 1.4$, multiplied by 10 to make the whole number calculation $350 \div 14$. As the layout of long division is problematic for some students, using short division in this way could be quite a relief! Adopting the policy of writing computations on squared grid paper with 'one digit to one square' keeps the working in columns more controlled.	The Island of Cyprus is divided into two. Turkey invaded Cyprus in 1974 and occupied one-third of the island, setting up the Turkish Republic of Northern Cyprus. Southern Cyprus is a member of the EU and the population has links with Greece. The border between the two parts is called the Green Line and is patrolled by UN soldiers. There is more information at http://news.bbc.co.uk/cbbcnews/hi/find_out/guides/world/Cyprus/newsid_3031000/3031897.stm

Alternative approach

Short division is not as confusing on paper as long division. However, when dividing by a number beyond the 'times tables', students need to make 'jottings on the side' to work out multiples. For example, $701 \div 17$, when set out using short division, becomes:

$$\underline{\quad 4\ 1\ \text{r}\ 4\quad}$$
$$17\ )\ 7\ 0^2 1$$

and jottings on the side are the multiples $17, 34, 51, 68$, showing that $70 \div 17 = 4\ \text{r}\ 2$

Checkpoint

1 Work the following out
   - a $128 \div 8$ (16)
   - b $12.8 \div 8$ (1.6)
   - c $12.8 \div 0.8$ ($128 \div 8 = 16$)
   - d $1.28 \div 0.8$ ($12.8 \div 8 = 1.6$)

Starter – Quick-fire quotients

Students use mini whiteboards to answer quick fire questions:

$30 \div 10$	$320 \div 10$	$450 \div 10$
$400 \div 100$	$32 \div 10$	$450 \div 100$, etc.

Teaching notes

Referring to the starter, discuss what it means to divide by 10 and extend the discussion to decimal values; for example, $12 \div 10$, $430 \div 100$. Note that 'deleting one or two zeros' does not always work as, for example, there is no zero to delete when dividing 12 by 10.

Demonstrate, using the place-value columns, that each digit moves one or two places to the right when dividing by 10 or 100.

Discuss what the calculation $325 \div 14$ means. Finding how many 14s go into 325 can be done in stages, starting with the highest place-values. Subtractions tell how much is still let to be divided. Write the division as $14\,)\,\overline{3\,2\,5}$ on square grid paper and follow the step-by-step explanation given in the students' book. The division does not result in an integer answer. The remainder is denoted by the letter 'r'. At a later stage, show students that the answer can be written without a remainder by using a fraction in the answer.

Division by a decimal can be avoided by re-writing the division using integers. By using a different notation, the division can be thought of as a fraction. An equivalent fraction is found by multiplying 'top' and 'bottom' by 10, which leads to a division involving only integers. For example,
$35 \div 1.4 = 35/1.4 = 350/14 = 350 \div 14$.

See 'Alternative approach' above for comments on short division.

Plenary

Students choose between long and short division for straightforward calculations such as $301 \div 13$ where only low multiples of 131 are required. They do their working on mini whiteboards and check it using the teacher's answers.

Exercise commentary

Questions 1 and **2** – Explain that as the answers are given, then the inverse operation × is required to find the original starting numbers.

Questions 3 and **4** – These divisions of 3-digit by 1- or 2-digit numbers are best done by short division. Ask students to choose between long and short division and to justify their choice. Question **3** has no remainders and question **4** does have remainders.

Questions 5 and **6** – These questions are not only set in various contexts, but also they involve decimals. Question **5** involves divisions by decimals and question **6** involves divisions of decimals.

Question 7 – There are two points to note. The shredding has taken place horizontally across the long divisions, not vertically. Also, it may help to know that parts **a** and **e** are not fractions.

Answers

1	**a** 6	**b** 17	**c** 45	**d** 279			
2	**a** 285	**b** 119	**c** 350	**d** 48.4			
3	**a** 21	**b** 42	**c** 23				
	d 34	**e** 31	**f** 16				
4	**a** 25 r 2	**b** 25 r 3	**c** 20 r 3				
	d 12 r 5	**e** 22 r 6	**f** 23 r 5				
5	**a** 22	**b** 22	**c** 15	**d** 15			
6	**a** £4.65	**b** 3.2 m	**c** 3 min 5s				
7	Check students' work						

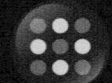

Objectives
• Use the 4 operations, including formal written methods, applied to integers, decimals, proper and improper fractions, and mixed numbers, all both positive and negative   (L4)

Key ideas	Resources
1 Calculate, using written and mental methods, the answers to real-life problems	Multiply double digits (1025) Long division (1041) Mini whiteboards Highlighters Poster paper and pens

Simplification	Extension
Where students experience difficulty, support them in the analysis of the questions. Offer highlighters to help pick out key points from (copies of) individual questions and encourage dialogue with other students.	More able students can be challenged to produce high quality explanations and justifications of their thinking that could be used as model strategies.

Literacy	Links
Reading a problem with comprehension is essential. Encourage reading out loud; highlighting or underlining key pieces of information, and reviewing solutions in context.	The division symbol ÷ is called an obelus. The symbol was originally used in manuscripts to mark passages containing errors but first appeared as a division symbol in a book called *Teutsche Algebra* by Johann Rahn in 1659. In Denmark, the obelus was used to represent subtraction. Students could be asked to investigate the history of other mathematical symbols as a homework task.

Alternative approach
Differentiate problems in terms of level of challenge, either by labelling or using colour-coding, and group students appropriately, with the task of producing team solutions to each of their problems. This could make nice display work for the classroom. Make it clear that the presentation of solutions with choice of approach is important to include and also encourage checking devices.

Checkpoint

1 Amina goes shopping with £50 and buys a book for £7.89, chocolate at £2.49, and a computer game for £30.99.
  a How much does she spend?   (£41.37)
  b How much has she left?   (£8.63)

Ask students to add up numbers you read out that are **not** multiples of 7.

For example, 16, 21, 3, 7, 28, 30, 15, 8, 35, 11, 5, 14, 12, 49, 17 (117).

Can be differentiated by choice of multiple and numbers.

Teaching notes

The four operations are all used throughout this lesson so ensure that students have a clear understanding of how to set out the various calculations before proceeding. Further examples without context may be needed or these skills can be checked using a quick test or some mini whiteboard work at the start of the lesson.

Plenary

Refer students back to questions **3** and **4**. Ask them to choose one part of one of these questions and to explain to a partner how they worked out their answer.

Exercise commentary

Question 1 – Check that students align the numbers. Some may like to add up the numbers by doing two at a time.

Question 2 – Encourage students to break the problem down and to organise their solution.

Questions 3–5 – Students can work in pairs to discuss the strategy for solving the problem. Each student could write down their solution and pass it to the other to see how clear it is to understand.

Answers

1 Risotto 453.5 g
   Spiced rice 667.6 g
2 **a** 9.4 m   **b** 157.2 m
3 **a** £22   **b** 14 miles
4 Yes, because 14 minibuses can hold 252 people
5 **a** 47.5 km Ayton → Isoy → Hodear → Gewizzle → Eckershit
   b 22.9 km Hodear → Crikey → Drat

Objectives

- Carry out calculations with more than one step using brackets and the memory (L5)

Key ideas	Resources
1 Brackets can be used to ensure the right priority is given to operations within a calculation	Calculators

Simplification	Extension
Students can become confused when a calculator shows a decimal answer for money. For example, 0.4 for 40 pence and 1.6 for £1.60 (not £1.06) are common misunderstandings. Remind students of these errors before embarking on money problems.	Students create 'word problems' that would lead to the calculations of question **2**.

Literacy	Links
The same calculation arising in different contexts can have different answers. Consider $32 \div 5 = 6.4$. Finding the cost of one article if 5 of them cost £32, uses $32 \div 5 = 6.4$ and the cost of one article is £6.40. A car can carry 5 passengers and there are 32 people to transport. How many trips are needed? 6.4 is not a sensible answer. The number of trips is 7 (with a few spare places on the last trip). A bottle holds 5 litres. How many of these bottles can be completely filled from 32 litres? Again, 6.4 is not a sensible answer. There can be only 6 full bottles (with 2 litres of liquid left over). So the same calculation, $32 \div 5$, has given three different answers: 6.40, 7 and 6. Understanding the context is essential.	The first real scientific pocket calculator was the Bowmar 901B, patented in 1971. It could add, subtract, divide and multiply whole numbers and decimals. It wasn't long before the first scientific calculator came along – the Hewlett–Packard HP35 in 1972, and then the rest followed thick and fast until within a few years they became commonplace. The International Vintage Electronics Museum in Hove, West Sussex has the website http://s206301103.websitehome.co.uk/museum/pocket.calc.htm

Alternative approach

Question **4** in Exercise **11e** can be used to test the efficiency of two methods when using a calculator with complex calculations. Have some students calculate by using brackets to enter the entire calculation. Have other students calculate the contents of the brackets first, make jottings of these parts of the calculation, and then use their jottings to find the final answer. Explore how long each method takes and which method more often gives the correct answer. The piecemeal approach may take longer but may be less prone to error.

Checkpoint

1 Use your calculator to work these out:

   a $8 + 4 \times 6$ (32)

   b $(8 + 4) \times 6$ (72)

   c $8 \div 4 \times 6$ (12)

   d $8 \div (4 \times 6)$ (1/3)

Discuss why the answers are different.

Starter – Make 1000

Ask students to draw two rows of three boxes to representing two 3-digit numbers. Throw a dice six times and, after each throw, ask students to enter the score into one of their six boxes.

The students add their two 3-digit numbers together mentally or using a written method, but not a calculator. The student with the total closest to 1000 wins.

The activity can be adjusted by changing the target number.

Teaching notes

Each student has a calculator, preferably the same make for each student, although different makes with different logics are useful too.

Give students a series of operations to calculate, such as $12.4 + 3.9 \div 7.93$, etc.

Find how many different answers there are in the class and ask where they think the errors have occurred. They suggest keying errors and different logics. State that, even though a calculator 'does the work for you', mistakes are common and highlight the need to make an initial approximation every time before doing a calculation on a calculator.

Design calculations to use the more important keys on the calculator, including the 'clear' key. Many keys can be left until later.

Work through stages in the student book to gain confidence with more complex calculations. Always insist that they make an estimate to check against each answer.

As a footnote, ensure that, when using a calculator which has no bracket keys, students know that any brackets must be calculated first.

Plenary

Give students calculations to work out. They write their answers and any written working on their mini whiteboards. Discuss any errors.

Give worded problems and repeat.

Exercise commentary

Question 1 – Students do mental methods first. Discuss whether some of these brackets are strictly needed at all. BIDMAS gives the priorities for mental calculation and should do so for scientific calculators too.

Questions 2 – Students make estimates first. As in question **1**, BIDMAS should operate with scientific calculators and some of these brackets may be unnecessary.

Question 3 – Parts **a** to **d** can be checked by using the inverse function keys.

Question 4 – This is a particularly challenging question for those students with good estimation skills.

Question 5 – These worded problems could first be answered using written methods of computation which are then checked by calculator.

Answers

1	**a** 3	**b** 28	**c** 3.5	**d** 7
	e 11	**f** 23		
2	**a** 39	**b** 17.76	**c** 21	
	d 39	**e** 25.4	**f** 84	
	g 36			
3	**a** 15	**b** 24	**c** 529	
	d 3136	**e** 5.8	**f** -2.05	
	g $\frac{5}{6}$	**h** $\frac{11}{7}$		

4 $\sqrt{2.9 \times (81 - 2.5) + 3.8}$

5   **a** £41.47   **b** £78   **c** £52

6   Discuss with students

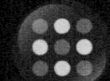

Objectives	
• Enter numbers and interpret the display in different contexts	(L5)
• Make and justify estimates and approximations of calculations	(L5)

Key ideas	Resources
1 Find an estimate of an answer before finding the answer on a calculator 2 Answers displayed on a calculator often need rounding	Calculators

Simplification	Extension
Rounding numbers with many decimal places can be confusing. Remind students that most of the decimal places are irrelevant. If, for example, they want an answer to 2 decimal places, then they are only concerned with the third decimal place to indicate whether the second decimal place rounds up or down.	Students can create word problems that would lead to the calculations in question **5**.

Literacy	Links
All rational numbers can be written as one of two types of decimal: terminating or recurring. Terminating decimals come to an end, such as 0.25, whereas recurring decimals run on forever in a repeating pattern, such as 0.3333... or 0.123123... Rather than use repeated dots as above to indicate a recurring decimal, a notation is used where a dot is placed above a single recurring digit, such as 0.3̇, or above the first and last of several recurring digits. The initials 'dp' are used so that 'to 2 decimal places' is written as 'to 2 dp'.	Continuing the theme from the previous Links, the first widely available hand-held battery-operated calculator was the Sharp LC-8 (also known as the EL-8) which was introduced in January 1971. The calculator measured 100 mm × 163 mm × 67 mm and was advertised as the world's smallest electronic calculator. Ask the class to compare the size of their own calculator. There is a video of an advertisement for the LC-8 at http://www.boreme.com/boreme/funny-2007/sharp-lc-8-p1.php and at http://www.youtube.com/watch?v5nCcgoTc8AQc

Alternative approach

a) A loose sheet of paper can be useful to help rounding a decimal. If a decimal needs rounding to (say) 2 decimal places, use the paper to cover up all place values after the second decimal place. What is seen is the required answer, but it may need changing if the first hidden digit revealed by moving the paper to the right (that is, the third decimal place) has a value of 5 or more.

b) An interesting investigation of decimals is to change all fractions of the form $1/x$ for $x = 2$ to $x = 26$ into decimals using a calculator. List the answers in two columns: terminating decimals and recurring decimals. Can students see a pattern in the x-values of the terminating decimals? Values of x that are multiples of 2, 5 and 10 terminate; other values of x give recurring decimals. Test this conclusion with x values above 26.

Checkpoint

1 Use your calculator to do the following and give your answer correct to 1 decimal place.
   a $11 \div 7$ (1.6)
   b $36 \div 16$ (2.3)
   c $199 \div 10$ (20.0)

Starter – 9999

Students make as many integers as possible between 1 and 20 inclusive, using four nines and any operations; for example, $1 = 99 \div 99$.

Hint: The square root of 9 is 3.

Teaching notes

Invite students to use a calculator to evaluate £20 ÷ 8 and £10 ÷ 3. Discuss the answers. To put the answer into context it needs units, in this case £, and therefore two decimal places.

For £20 ÷ 8, explain that a zero can be inserted as a second decimal place, as it indicates 'no hundredths'.

For £10 ÷ 3, mention that 'tidying up' the recurring decimal answer can use a dot above the first decimal place to represent all other recurring digits. However, for the monetary context of this answer, there is a need to round the answer to 2 decimal places. Use a number line with extremes labelled £3.30 and £3.40 and discuss where 3.3333… sits. Students recall that a digit less than 5 rounds *down* and a digit 5 or more rounds *up*.

Provide further questions for work in pairs before discussing them as a whole class.

For example, £36 ÷ 16 (units), £25 ÷ 8 (appropriate rounding), £40 ÷ 6 ('tidying' and rounding).

Plenary

Students tackle questions on time. For example;
- a 12-hour job is split equally between eight people. How much time is spent per person?
- the BBC transmits 96 programmes in 24 hours. What is their average length?

Discuss how to interpret the answer in each case.

Exercise commentary

Questions 1 and **2** – Both these questions practice rounding, either to 1 decimal place or 2 decimal places.

Questions 3 and **4** – Students could be asked to find answers using mental methods and to check them on a calculator.

Question 5 – Students should not simply substitute each operation in turn until they find the correct one. They should estimate the answer for each operation in turn and then check their choice using a calculator.

Question 6 – Students by now should recognise 0.33333… as a third and know that a third of an hour is 20 minutes.

Answers

1	a	4.6	b	12.2	c	22.6		
	d	9.1	e	7.3	f	8.7		
2	a	1.29	b	2.29	c	2.83		
	d	2.84	e	1.76	f	8.10		
3	a	£6.30	b	£3.40	c	£6.90	d	£2.60
4	a	4 m 70 cm			b	3 m 40 cm		
	c	10 m			d	3 m 20 cm		
5	a	×	b	+	c	−		
	d	÷	e	×	f	÷		
6	a	Recurring			b	5 hours 20 minutes		

Key outcomes	Quick check	
Use the column method to add and subtract whole numbers and decimals.	Add together 1.78 and 2.34	(4.12)
	Subtract 2.56 from 11.84	(9.28)
Use the standard method to multiply whole numbers.	Find	
	23 × 67	(1541)
	245 × 34	(8330)
	414 ÷ 9	(46)
	Can you set this out in both short and long division?	
Use written methods to solve problems.	A tin of baked beans costs £0.66. What is the cost of 8 tins? Give the answer in pounds.	(£5.28)
Use a calculator to work out longer calculations.	Use your calculator to find	
	16 − 3 × 4 + 8	(12)
	24 ÷ 9 and give your answer to 1 dp	(2.7)

MyMaths extra support

Lesson/online homework			Description
Factors and primes	1032	L4	Finding factors of whole numbers and identifying prime numbers
Multiples	1035	L4	Finding multiples of numbers, testing for divisibility, finding the LCM
Odds, evens, multiples	1218	L2	Looking at odd and even numbers and multiples of 2, 5 and 10 using a 100 square

MyReview

Check out

You should now be able to ...

Test it ➡
Questions

✓ Use the column method to add and subtract whole numbers and decimals. — (4) 1, 2

✓ Use the standard method to multiply whole numbers. — (s) 3

✓ Use long and short division. — (s) 4, 5

✓ Use written methods to solve problems. — (4) 7

✓ Use a calculator to work out longer calculations. — (s) 8, 9

Language	Meaning	Example
Long multiplication	A method you can use when multiplying two numbers with two or more digits	453 $\times$ 34 13590 1812 15402
Long division	A written method, suitable for dividing by a two-digit number	20 r 17 23)477 46 17
Divisor	In a division, the number you are dividing by	463 ÷ 3 = 154 r 1
Remainder	In a division, what is left when two numbers do not divide exactly	3 is the divisor 1 is the remainder
Short division	An alternative method to long division	6 8 r 1 14)9 ⁵5 ¹¹3
Estimate	An approximate answer	An estimate for 170 ÷ 38 is 160 ÷ 40 = 4

1 Calculate these additions.
a 2 2 0   b 9 6 9
  + 1 0 8   + 5 1 8

c 7 9 0.5   d 79.4 + 53.7
  + 3 7.7

2 Calculate these subtractions.
a 7 3 3   b 5 8 4
  – 5 0 2   – 4 1 8

c 6 3.9   d 9410 – 393
  – 5 3.8

3 Calculate these using the standard written method.
a 11 × 71
b 64 × 95
c 54 × 508
d 667 × 58

4 Calculate these. There are no remainders.
a 270 ÷ 6
b 384 ÷ 8
c 204 ÷ 12

5 Calculate these. Give the remainder.
a 107 ÷ 7
b 220 ÷ 9
c 217 ÷ 11

6 Jake's shopping trolley contains the following items.
Grapes £1.86
Potatoes £2
Chicken £5.50
Cheese £3.36
Disposable BBQ £13.95
How much change will he get from £30?

7 Ali buys 14 burritos at a total cost of £19.46. What is the cost of one burrito?

8 Calculate these using your calculator.
a 14 + 3 × 8
b 9 – 3 ÷ 3
c (11 + 3) × 5
d 25 – 4 × (2 + 3)

9 Work these out using your calculator and round your answers to 2 dp.
a 19 ÷ 7
b 13 ÷ 3.7
c 44 ÷ 9
d 884 ÷ 0.76

What next?

Score		
0 – 4	Your knowledge of this topic is still developing. To improve look at Formative test: 2A-11; MyMaths: 1020, 1025, 1028 and 1041	
5 – 7	You are gaining a secure knowledge of this topic. To improve look at InvisiPen: 126, 127, 129 and 131	
8, 9	You have mastered this topic. Well done, you are ready to progress!	

⊕ **MyMaths**.co.uk

Question commentary

Questions 1 and **2** – Students may need reminding of 'carrying' and 'borrowing'.

Question 3 – Remind students to put the smaller number under the larger number to make it easier.

Questions 4 and **5** – Straightforward, only one digit is carried.

Question 6 – Just check potatoes at £2 goes in the right column.

Question 7 – Students need to recognise division.

Question 8 – Check for use of brackets.

Question 9 – May need to remind students of 2 dp.

Answers

1	a	328	b	1487
	c	828.2	d	133.1
2	a	231	b	166
	c	10.1	d	9017
3	a	781	b	159
	c	27432	d	38686
4	a	45	b	48
	c	17		
5	a	15 r 2	b	24 r 4
	c	19 r 8		
6	£3.33			
7	£1.39			
8	a	38	b	8
	c	70	d	5
9	a	2.71	b	3.51
	c	4.89	d	1163.16

11 MyPractice

1 In the number 125, the 2 stands for 20. Write down what the bold digit stands for in each number.

a 2**0**4

b 1**4**83

c 5**0**69

d 6**1**71

e 4**3**8

2 Copy and complete these additions.

a 241 + 137

b 302 + 245

c 156 + 340

d 356 + 43

e 61 + 228

f 136 + 118

g 352 + 340

h 217 + 453

i 183 + 620

j 467 + 153

3 Copy and complete these subtractions.

a 358 − 215

b 574 − 313

c 278 − 158

d 364 − 160

e 495 − 205

f 480 − 115

g 362 − 216

h 638 − 252

i 547 − 187

j 416 − 370

4 Complete these multiplication problems using long multiplication.

a 23 × 14

b 15 × 24

c 16 × 34

d 21 × 26

e 42 × 23

f 56 × 31

5 Complete these division problems using a mental or written method.

a 90 ÷ 6 =

b 104 ÷ 4 =

c 105 ÷ 3 =

d 170 ÷ 5 =

e 276 ÷ 12 =

f 294 ÷ 14 =

g 352 ÷ 16 =

h 252 ÷ 21 =

6 Use a mental or written method to solve each of these problems.

a Betty uses a route finder to travel from Gorley to Poole. On the way she stops for a coffee at Iredale and does some shopping at Darby. What is the total distance she travels?

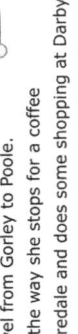

Poole — 9.79km — Darby — 15.65km — Iredale — 26.8km — Gorley

b In an iron works, Michel mixes metals together to make alloys with special properties. He makes a batch of wear-resistant alloy using 3.2kg of carbon, 0.95kg of manganese, 16.8kg of chromium, 2.783kg of molybdenum and 76.5kg of iron. What is the total weight of the alloy?

c In the school discus competition, Titus throws the discus 52.86m. He beats the school record by 9.375m. What was the old school discus record?

52.86M

7 Use a calculator to answer these written problems.

a Kirsty is weighing four parcels. The weights are: 2.46kg, 0.85kg, 4.08kg and 10.6kg. What is the total weight of parcels?

b Carlo has a length of chain; it is 6.3 metres long. He cuts 2.75 metres from the length of chain. How much chain is left over?

c A coach can carry 52 soccer supporters. Eight full coaches travel to an away match. How many supporters are on these coaches?

d Nine workers share a bonus of £3861. How much does each worker get?

e Three friends share £14.71. How much does each one get? Round your answer to 2dp.

8 Maurice works out how long it takes him to cycle to the beach on average, using a calculator. He gets this answer on the display, in hours.

How many minutes does it take Maurice to cycle to the beach, to the nearest minute?

0.8333333

MyMaths.co.uk

Question commentary

Questions 1–5 – These questions cover the arithmetical processes. Students should be encouraged to show clear working.

Questions 6 and **7** – Students need to recognise how to solve the problem. Again, help with setting out the solutions may be required.

Question 8 – The answer is a decimal fraction of an hour. Students may need help changing this to minutes.

Answers

1	a	200	b	80	c	9		
	d	6000	e	400				
2	a	378	b	547	c	496	d	399
	e	289	f	254	g	828	h	670
	i	803	j	620				
3	a	143	b	261	c	120	d	204
	e	290	f	365	g	146	h	386
	i	360	j	46				
4	a	322	b	360	c	544		
	d	546	e	966	f	1736		
5	a	15	b	26	c	35	d	34
	e	23	f	21	g	22	h	12
6	a	52.24 km			b	100.233 kg		
	c	43.485 m						
7	a	17.99 kg	b	3.55 m	c	416		
	d	£429	e	£4.90				
8	50 minutes							

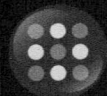

12 Constructions

Introduction	Prior knowledge
The chapter starts by getting the students to accurately measure and draw angles and line segments. Using a ruler and protractor to construct triangles is then covered. The final section covers scale drawing.	Students should already know how to… • Measure lengths and angles using a ruler and protractor

Introduction

The chapter starts by getting the students to accurately measure and draw angles and line segments. Using a ruler and protractor to construct triangles is then covered. The final section covers scale drawing.

The introduction discusses how supermarket companies make use of geometrical construction methods to find ideal sites to locate things like warehouses. For example, if there are three supermarkets located in a particular area, it would make sense for the distribution warehouse to be an equal distance from each one. This can be done by using a map (drawn to scale) and constructing the perpendicular bisectors of each pair of supermarkets. The rules of triangulation tell us that these three lines should cross at a single point and this should be our warehouse location.

The idea of triangulation as a method of location goes beyond this practical use. Map makers, navigators and manufacturers of mobile phone location apps and GPS all use triangulation methods to help them. In GPS, for example, the phone (or satnav) transmits a signal to three masts (or towers) or satellites, and the distance the signal travels to each one can be used to calculate (accurate to a few metres) the location of the device.

Prior knowledge

Students should already know how to…

• Measure lengths and angles using a ruler and protractor

Starter problem

The starter problem requires the students to construct a triangle from given lengths of sides. Using a pair of compasses and a ruler is the standard way of completing this but it is beyond the scope of this book. Students might alternatively pursue a trial-and-improvement method using just a ruler.

If they generate lengths of their own, a similar approach can be taken but they may 'stumble across' combinations that do not work.

The triangle inequality states that the sum of the lengths of the two shorter sides must be greater than the length of the longer side in order to create a triangle. If, for example, the students choose 3 cm, 4 cm and 8 cm, the triangle is not possible.

Resources

MyMaths

Measuring angles	1081	Constructing triangles	1090	Map scales	1103
Scale drawing	1117	Measuring lengths	1146		

Online assessment		InvisiPen solutions			
Chapter test	2A–12	Measuring lines and reading scales			331
Formative test	2A–12	Measuring and classifying angles			341
Summative test	2A–12	Constructing a triangle	371	Scale drawings	372

Topic scheme

Teaching time = 4 lessons/2 weeks

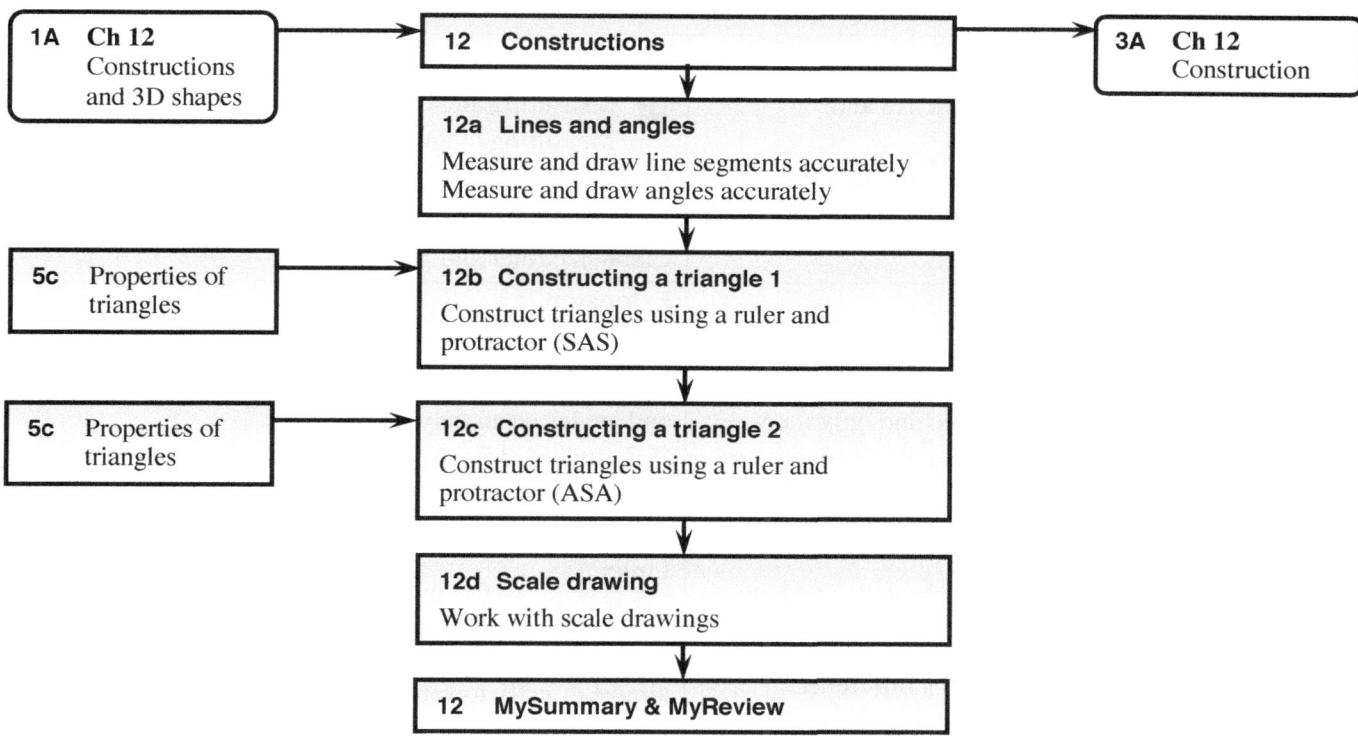

Differentiation

Student book 2A 224 – 237

Lines and angles
Constructing a triangle 1
Constructing a triangle 2
Scale drawing

Student book 2B 210 – 229

Constructing triangles 1
Constructing triangles 2
Bisectors
Constructing perpendiculars
Loci
Scale drawings
Bearings

Student book 2C 216 – 233

Constructing triangles 1
Constructing triangles 2
Bisectors and perpendiculars
Scale drawings
Loci
Bearings

Objectives

- Use a ruler and protractor to measure and draw lines to the nearest millimetre and angles to the nearest degree (L5)

Key ideas	Resources
1 A ruler measures lines in centimetres and millimetre 2 A protractor measures angles in degrees either clockwise or anticlockwise	Measuring angles (1080) Measuring lengths (1146) Rulers Protractors Class-size ruler and protractor

Simplification	Extension
Students often have difficulty using a protractor. To overcome this, students should name the type of angle they are measuring, estimate its size and only then decide which scale on the protractor to use to measure the angle. Pairing more confident students with less confident ones will help.	Students construct a triangle with base 5 cm and base angles 42° and 73°. They measure the remaining sides and angles accurately. (5.3 cm, 65°, 3.7 cm)

Literacy	Links
'Angle' has two aspects. The dynamic aspect is concerned with turning, such as turning a door handle. The static aspect is concerned with a difference in direction, such as the angle between two crossroads at a junction. The word *protractor* comes from Latin words meaning 'to draw forward'. To measure and draw angles of over 180°, you can use a 360° protractor in the shape of a full circle.	Before the days of satellites, sailors used a sextant to find their position on the ocean. The earth's axis points almost directly towards the North Star and so the star never appears to move in the sky. Sailors used the sextant to measure the angle of the star above the horizon so that they could then calculate their latitude. There is more information about sextants at http://en.wikipedia.org/wiki/Sextant

Alternative approach

Measurement of length and angle takes on a more interesting dimension when set in a context. A natural context is the use of measurement with maps. For example, having a map with a scale of 1 cm for 1 km is easy to use.

- Suppose there are three villages A, B and C. Draw lines AB and BC, such that their lengths are greater than 5 cm (which is the usual radius of school protractors). Measure the distances AB and BC in centimetres, writing them in kilometres due to the scale of the map. Also measure the angle ABC (in degrees). Imagine two railway lines, one from A to B and the other from A to C. Then angle ABC is the difference in their two directions and is an example of the static notion of angle.

- Suppose you can see villages Y and Z from a hilltop H. Measure the distances HY and HZ. Measure the angle YHZ, which is the angle you turn through from looking at Y to looking at Z. This is an example of the dynamic notion of angle.

Checkpoint

1 Using a sharp pencil, draw a line 4 cm long. Draw an angle of 55° on the right end of the line. Check your answer with your neighbour.

2 Draw another line 4 cm long. Draw an angle of 120° on the left end of the line. Check your answer with your neighbour.

Starter – Quick fire

Recap work of previous chapters and especially number work including mental and written computational skills. Ask rapid response questions. Students reply by writing on their mini whiteboards. Discuss questions when their answers indicate a need.

Teaching notes

Students draw a line 4.6 cm long and then swap books with a partner to check the length of the line. Discuss accuracy and the need to have a sharp pencil and measure from 0 (not the end of the ruler or the mark for 1).

Draw an angle on the board. Discuss the type of angle and recall key terms: **acute, right, obtuse, straight** and **reflex.** Students name the angle and hence estimate the size of the angle. Demonstrate how to measure the angle using a protractor, ensuring first that the lines of the angle extend beyond the protractor's edge. Emphasise that:

- the central cross of the protractor should be exactly on the point of the angle
- the base line of the protractor must line up with the angle base line
- the scale to choose has its zero on the angle's base line and counting starts at this zero.

Highlight there are two measurements at every point and discuss how to decide which to use.

Students draw an angle of 62°, swap angles with their partner and check each other's angles.

Draw an angle of 50° and calculate the reflex angle of 310°. Ask how an angle of 340°, 290°, … can be drawn.

Plenary

Students are shown various angles. On mini whiteboards, they give the type of each angle and an estimate of its size. Each angle is measured.
They are shown an angle and they calculate the reflex angle at that point. They are asked to draw angles of various sizes which are checked by a partner.

Exercise commentary

Questions 1 and **2** – Students undertake accurate measurement of distances and then accurate construction of lines. Their pencils need to be sharp.

Questions 3 and **4** – Students undertake accurate measurement of angles and then accurate construction of angles.

Question 5 – Students practise reading the correct scale accurately.

Question 6 – This offers a simple application where accurate measurement of two lines is key to the illusion.

Answers

1   **a**   85 mm   **b**   34 mm   **c**   3 mm
   d   68 mm
2   **a–e** Check students' drawings
3   $a = 32°$ $b = 24°$ $c = 105°$
  $d = 147°$
4   Check students' drawings
5   **a**   65°   **b**   155°   **c**   45°
5   Both same length

Objectives	
• Use a ruler and protractor to construct a triangle, given two sides and the included angle (SAS) (L5)	

Key ideas	Resources
1 A triangle can be constructed if certain information about it is known 2 One construction is based on knowing the length of two sides and the angle between them	Constructing triangles (1090) Protractors Rulers Class-size ruler and protractor

Simplification	Extension
Some students may continue to have difficulty constructing and measuring angles accurately. Pairing more confident students with less confident ones will help.	Students can construct more complex shapes, such as a quadrilateral made up of two triangles with specified dimensions (SAS).

Literacy	Links
There are three common ways of giving sufficient information to draw a triangle accurately. The SAS method of this exercise is one way. The other two ways are the ASA method, described in the next lesson, and the third method is SSS where all three sides are known.	A hexaflexagon is a flat hexagon-shaped paper toy that can be folded or flexed along its folds to reveal and conceal its faces alternately. It was invented in 1939 in the USA by Arthur Stone and its construction is based on equilateral triangles. There are instructions to make a hexaflexagon at http://hexaflexagon.sourceforge.net/ and at http://www.flexagon.net/flexagons/hexahexaflexagon-c.pdf

Alternative approach
An application of the SAS method adds interest. A gardener has two lengths of fence AB = 8 m and BC = 10 m. He decides to fix them in place so that angle ABC is either 30°, 60° or 90°. Draw three triangles for these three angles and find the distance between A and C. He has a third length of fence which is 16 m long. Which of the three triangles gives the best fit for this 16 m length of fence? (Angle ABC = 60°)

Checkpoint

1 Construct the isosceles triangle that has two angles of 50° and only one side of length 6 cm.
  a What is the size of the third angle?   (80°)
  b What is the length of the two equal sides?   (4.7 cm)

Starter – Clock angles

Ask students to give the angle between the hour and minute hands at the following times:

3.00, 4.00, 6.00, 8.00, 12.30, 1.30 and 4.30

Remember that the hour hand moves as well as the minute hand!

(Answers: 90°, 120°, 180°, 240°, 165°, 135° and 45°)

Teaching notes

Sketch an angle on the board labelled 60° and arms labelled 8 cm and 5 cm. Recall from the previous lesson how to draw this accurately and make the distinction between a **sketch** and a **construction**. Students now construct the triangle, adding the third side.

Refer students to their book and point out that they have constructed the triangle described there.

Sketch another triangle and provide the information needed for the SAS construction. The students make the construction, exchange it with a partner and check each other's work.

Plenary

Show various sketches of triangles only some of which have the information for the SAS method of construction. Students write on their mini whiteboards whether each triangle qualifies for the SAS construction.

Show a sketch of a triangle with a base of 8 cm and base angles of 40° and 60°. Discuss how this sketch differs from the SAS sketches. Ask whether it would be possible to draw a unique triangle from this information.

Exercise commentary

Questions 1 and **4** – Students construct SAS triangles.

Question 2 – Students accurately measure the lengths and angles of triangles before constructing them.

Question 3 – Extends to SSS triangles. Students consider which triangles will exist. The sum of two sides must always be larger than the third.

Question 4 – Consolidates names of triangles.

Answers

1   a   7.9 cm   b   6.0 cm   c   7.5 cm
    d   7 cm
2   Check students' work for accuracy
3   Set **b**. The sum of the two shortest sides is less than the longest side.
4   a   isosceles   b   equilateral
    c   right-angled

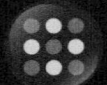

Objectives

- Use a ruler and protractor to construct a triangle, given two angles and the included side (ASA)   (L5)

Key ideas	Resources
1 A triangle can be constructed if certain information about it is known 2 One construction is based on knowing the sizes of two angles and length of the side between them	⬚ Constructing triangles (1090) Protractors Rulers Class-size ruler and protractor

Simplification	Extension
Pair more confident students with less confident ones to provide help with using the protractor.	Students construct quadrilaterals and they decide how to split them into triangles.

Literacy	Links
The construction of triangles using SAS is the basis of map-making using triangulation. For example, if two points A and B are accessible and the distance between them can be measured, then a third inaccessible point P can be fixed on a map by measuring the distance AB and the two angles PAB and PBA. By fixing several points from A and B, a whole area of ground can be mapped without visiting any other points.	A Sierpinski triangle is a mathematical construction named after the Polish mathematician Walter Sierpinski. To draw a Sierpinski triangle, begin by drawing an equilateral triangle. Join the midpoints of the three sides to form four smaller equilateral triangles. Remove (or shade) the central triangle. Now repeat the process to split each remaining triangle into four smaller triangles and remove (or shade) the three central triangles. Repeat the process again. This process can be repeated an infinite number of times! There is an animation showing the construction of a Sierpinski triangle at http://en.wikipedia.org/wiki/Sierpinski_triangle

Alternative approach

Constructing triangles takes on a more interesting dimension when set in a context. A natural context is their use with maps. As written in 'Literacy' above, triangulation uses SAS triangles to fix points when map-making. Use a simple scale such as 1 cm = 1 km.

Decide on a base line joining two points such as hilltops or village churches. Give students two angles to be drawn at each end of the line and thereby fix the position of the desired place on the map. Repeat for as many places as need to be mapped.

Having fixed several points on the map, the distances between these points can be measured. Make explicit to students that, by merely measuring angles at the end of the base and never visiting these points, the distances between them can be found. This method is invaluable to map-makers.

Checkpoint

1 Draw a line 5 cm long. Draw a right angle at the right end of the line. At the other end (the left end), draw an angle of 55°.
   Measure the third angle. Why should it be 35°?   (Angles in a triangle add up to 180°)

Starter – Quick fire

Recap work of previous chapters and especially number work, including mental and written computation. Ask rapid response questions. Students reply by writing on their mini whiteboards. Discuss questions when their answers indicate a need.

Teaching notes

Sketch a triangle, given two angles and the included side. Students say how they would start this construction – with the base length. Students and teacher together construct their own triangle by:

1) using a ruler to construct the base accurately

2) drawing the left-hand angle. Remind students to:
   - line up the base line of the angle with the base line of the protractor
   - line up the centre of the protractor with the point of turn of the angle (on the left in this case)
   - count from 0 (not 180) to ensure use of the correct scale
   - extend the arm of the angle.

3) drawing the right-hand angle.

Students construct the third angle of the triangle by finding the point of intersection of the two arms of the angles.

Plenary

Show students several triangles with different data on their sides and angles. Students identify whether the triangles can be constructed using SAS, ASA, SSS or none of these. They show their choices using mini whiteboards. Discuss the triangles where none of these three constructions are possible.

Exercise commentary

Questions 1–3 and **5** – These questions use ASA constructions. Question **3** involves the three-letter angle notation.

Question 4 – This illustrates the incorrect use of a protractor. What would happen if the lines were continued downwards?

Answers

1 a equilateral   **b** right-angled
   a isosceles
2 Check students' constructions
3 Check students' constructions
4 Ricky has constructed angles of 120° at the base, i.e. used the protractor in the wrong direction
5 triangular pyramid

Objectives	
• Use scales to make and interpret scale drawings	(L5)

Key ideas	Resources	
1 A scale drawing is an accurate plan of a life-sized object 2 The scale can be written, for example, either using units as 1 cm : 10 m or without units as 1 : 1000	Map scales Scale drawing Map of local area Rulers	(1103) (1117)

Simplification	Extension
Initially, use simple scales such as 1 cm : 1 m or 1 cm : 10 m. Remind students that, when using a ruler, the ruler lines up at the 0 (zero) mark and not at the end of the ruler.	Students complete a scale drawing of the classroom and furniture arrangement using a more complex scale, for example, 2 cm : 1 m.

Literacy	Links
Maps have been in use for thousands of years. They have existed in some form from Babylonian times. In Britian, today's maps have many uses. Road atlases have scales of about 1 : 200 000 (1 cm = 2 km). Maps for outdoor activities have scales of 1 : 50 000 (1 cm = 500 m) or 1 : 25 000 (1 cm = 250 m). Street maps have scales of about 1 : 10 000 (1 cm = 100 m).	Model railways are available in different gauges. This means that they are built to different scales. The OO gauge means that the model is built to a scale of 1 : 76; that is, 1 cm on the model represents a distance of 76 cm in real life. On an N-gauge model 1 cm represents a distance of 146 cm. If an N-gauge model locomotive is 5 cm long, how long is the real-life locomotive? There are pictures of different gauge model locomotives at http://ngaugesociety.com/modelling/scales/scales.htm

Alternative approach
Many people are not used to imagining themselves travelling along a map. So, before using a map for finding distances and lengths, have students describe a journey on foot using a street plan. Use language such as 'Start at A and walk along B street, take the second right onto C road, go straight across D street and take the third right turn …'. Students can write their final position on their mini whiteboards. Start with journeys that move away from the map-reader (most likely northwards), so that the map-reader has their own left and right orientated similarly to the journey's left and right. Later, describe journeys that travel sideways across the map and, finally, describe journeys that come towards the map-reader (when some map-readers may want to turn the map upside down to follow instructions). Once confident with following instructions, have students give instructions to others in the class.

Checkpoint	

1 A plan of a room is drawn on a scale of 1 cm to 1 m.
  a This scale can be written as 1 cm : 1 m or 1 : ?
The room is rectangular. It measures 4.2 m by 3.5 m.
  b Draw a scale diagram of the room.
	(100)
	
	(Diagram should measure 4.2 cm by 3.5 cm)

Starter – Quick fire

Recap work of previous chapters and especially number work, including mental and written computation. Ask rapid response questions. Students reply by writing on their mini whiteboards. Discuss questions when their answers indicate a need.

Teaching notes

Look at the A-Z pages of the local area. Pose questions to highlight key points:

Why isn't this map the real size of the area?

Why is it important that this map is precise? Introduce the idea of scale and point out the scale of the map. Emphasise that the scale gives the relationship between the scale drawing (that is, the map) and real-life distances and allows the calculation of real distances.

Students suggest jobs that use scale drawings (beside map-makers). Mention fashion designers, architects, engineers, town planners, scientists, builders.

Discuss how to draw a scale drawing of the classroom and the furniture arrangement. Students suggest a suitable scale. Point out the need to use the same scale for every measurement so that the proportions remain the same and a shape, such as a rectangular desk, will keep its shape.

Plenary

Refer back to the map of the local area. Students find two places of local interest, use a ruler to find the distance between them (rounded to an approximate number of centimetres) and then, by using the scale, find the approximate real-life distances between the two places. Repeat for other places.

Exercise commentary

Question 1 – Requires students to calculate real distances from a simple scale drawing using a scale of 1 cm : 1 m.

Question 2 – Students construct a scale drawing from a sketch using the scale 1 cm : 1 m.

Question 3 – Extends to use of a scale of 1 cm : 1 km.

Answers

1 **a** 10 m   **b** 6.9 m   **c** 8.3 m   **d** 1.9 m
   e 6.3 m   **f** 2.8 m   **g** 1.9 m   **h** 2.2 m
   i 2.7 m   **j** 1.7 m

2 Check drawing is a copy of diagram with key measurements
   1 cm, 1 cm, 6.5 cm and 4 cm

3 16.5 km

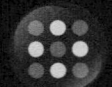

Key outcomes	Quick check
Measure and draw lines and angles accurately.	Draw a line 4 cm long. Using a protractor draw an angle of 45° at an end of the line. Draw an angle of 90° at the other end. Join the two lines to make a triangle. Measure the third angle. Why is it 45°?
Construct a triangle given two sides and the included angle.	Draw a line of 6 cm long. On the right end of the line, draw an angle of 40° with a line 5 cm long. Join to make a triangle. Measure the other side of the triangle. (3.9 cm)
Construct a triangle given two angles and the included side.	Draw a line 4 cm long. Using a protractor draw an angle of 45° at an end of the line. Draw an angle of 60° at the other end. Join the two lines to make a triangle. Measure the third angle. Why is it 75°?
Draw and use simple scale drawings.	A map is drawn on a scale of 1 cm to 1 km. This can be written as 1 cm : 1 km or 1 : ? (1 : 100 000) The length of a short road is 800 m. What length is drawn on the map to correspond to this? (0.8 cm)

MyReview

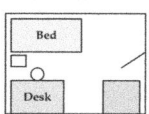
Check out

You should now be able to ...

Test it ➡
Questions

✓	Measure and draw lines and angles accurately.	⑤ 1, 2
✓	Construct a triangle given two sides and the included angles.	⑤ 3
✓	Construct a triangle given two angles and the included side.	⑤ 4
✓	Draw and use simple scale drawings.	⑤ 5, 6

Language	Meaning	Example
Construct	To draw a shape accurately using a ruler, protractor and pair of compasses	See pages 228–231
Scale drawing	A diagram which is used to accurately represent real-life objects	Architects' plans are scale drawings of buildings
Protractor	An instrument for measuring angles	See pages 226–231

1 Draw these angles accurately using a ruler and protractor.
   a 37°   b 174°

2 Draw lines of these lengths using ruler.
   a 2.5 cm   b 10.8 cm

3 Construct these triangles accurately using a ruler and protractor.
   a
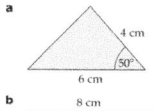
   b
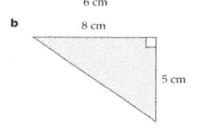

4 Construct these triangles accurately using a ruler and protractor.
   a   b
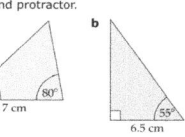

5 This is a scale drawing of a room using a scale of 1:100.
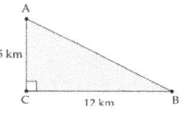

   What are the real life dimensions of
   a the room
   b the bed
   c the desk?

6 Three town A, B and C are positioned as shown in the diagram.
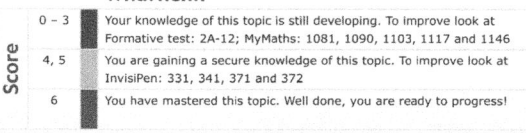

   a Construct a scale drawing of this triangle using a scale of 1 cm to represent 1 km.
   b Calculate the real life distance of town A from town B.

What next?

Score		
	0 – 3	Your knowledge of this topic is still developing. To improve look at Formative test: 2A-12; MyMaths: 1081, 1090, 1103, 1117 and 1146
	4, 5	You are gaining a secure knowledge of this topic. To improve look at InvisiPen: 331, 341, 371 and 372
	6	You have mastered this topic. Well done, you are ready to progress!

Question commentary

Questions 1–4 – Students can work in pairs, checking each other's angles and lines.

Questions 5 and **6** – Straightforward questions on scale drawing.

Answers

1 a angle of 37°   b angle of 174°
2 a line of 2.5 cm   b line of 10.8 cm
3 a Check SAS 6 cm, 50°, 4 cm
   b Check SAS 8 cm, 90°, 5 cm
4 a Check ASA 45°, 7 cm, 80°
   b Check ASA 90°, 6.5 cm, 55°
5 a 4 m × 3 m   b 2 m × 1 m
   c 1.5 m × 1 m
6 a Check lengths are 5 cm, 12 cm and 13 cm
   b 13 km

12 MyPractice

12a

1 Draw these lines accurately using a ruler.

a	3 cm	b	3 cm 2 mm	c	4 cm 3 mm
d	8 cm 8 mm	e	12 cm 1 mm	f	7 cm 5 mm
g	10 cm 9 mm	h	8 cm 7 mm	i	3.5 cm
j	2.8 cm	k	5.3 cm	l	8.3 cm

2 Measure the lengths AB, BC, CA in this triangle.
Give your answers to the nearest millimetre.
What type of triangle is this?
Explain how you know.

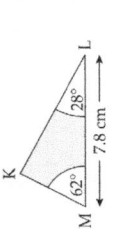

3 Write the angle shown in each question.

a

The angle is between 90° and 100°.

b

The angle is between 20° and 30°.

c

The angle is between 110° and 130°.

4 Measure these angles and then draw them accurately using a protractor.

a

b

12b

5 Measure this triangle and make an accurate copy of it.
You have been given one angle, and the length of two sides.

7.5 cm, 28°, 8.5 cm (triangle R S T)

12c

6 Measure this triangle and make an accurate copy of it.
You have been given two angles, and the length of one side.

62°, 28°, 7.8 cm (triangle K L M)

12d

7 Measure the distances on this plan of James' garden.
Use the scale 1 cm : 1 m to give the measurements for the real garden.

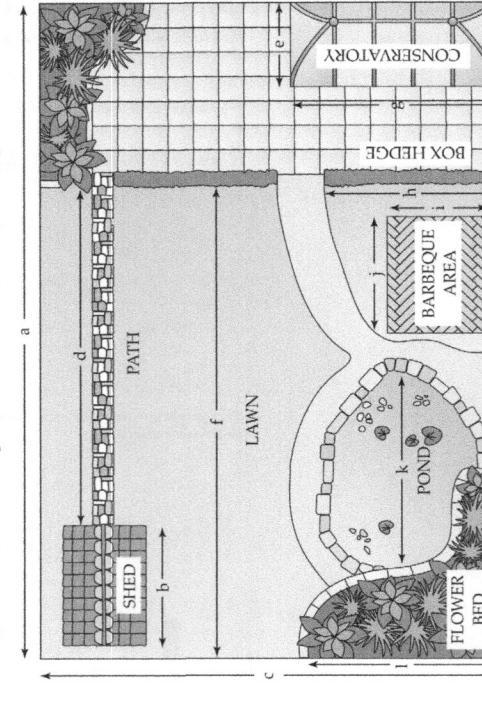

a How many metres long is the garden?
b What is the length of the shed?
c How many metres wide is the garden?
d What is the length of the path?
e What is the width of the conservatory?
f What is the length of the lawn?
g What is the length of the conservatory?
h What is the length of the box hedge?
i How wide is the barbeque area?
j How long is the barbeque area?
k What is the width of the pond?
l What is the width of the flower bed?

MyMaths.co.uk

Question commentary

Question 1 – Can ask students to check each other's work which consolidates measuring and drawing. Encourage sharp pencils for accurate work.

Questions 2–4 – Students can work in pairs.

Question 5 – Students can check with each other that they have the same result for the length of RS.

Question 6 – Students could predict the third angle and then measure to check the accuracy of their diagram.

Question 7 – The garden is the entire diagram.

Answers

1   Check students' work for accuracy
2   AB = 3.7 cm   BC = 6.5 cm   CA = 4.6 cm
     Scalene – all lengths are different
3   a   95°
     b   25°
     c   125°
4   a   55°
     b   120°
5   Check students' work for accuracy
6   Check students' work for accuracy
7   a   13.4 m   b   2.5 m   c   9 m   d   7.3 m
     e   1.7 m   f   9.7 m   g   4.1 m   h   3.4 m
     i   2 m   j   2.4 m   k   4 m   l   4.7 m

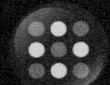
Related lessons		Resources	
Properties of triangles	5c	Lines and quadrilaterals	(1102)
Properties of quadrilaterals	5f	Properties of triangles	(1130)
		Examples of folded figures	
		Prepared squares of paper	
		Other examples of origami from books, etc.	

Simplification	Extension
Prepared origami squares can be used to help students get started with the activities. Pre-folded templates can also be given to students.	Students could be challenged to make further origami shapes from instructions in books or found on the internet. Some students may already be able to make origami patterns and these students could be used as 'experts' to teach others.

Links

Links could be made to design technology, considering the practical uses of folding. For example, there has been much research on effective ways of folding a map so that adjacent sections can be made visible without unfolding the whole map and one such fold has been used with large solar panel arrays on satellites where the panel opens up once the satellite is in orbit. See:

http://math.serenevy.net/?page=Origami-ApplicationLinks

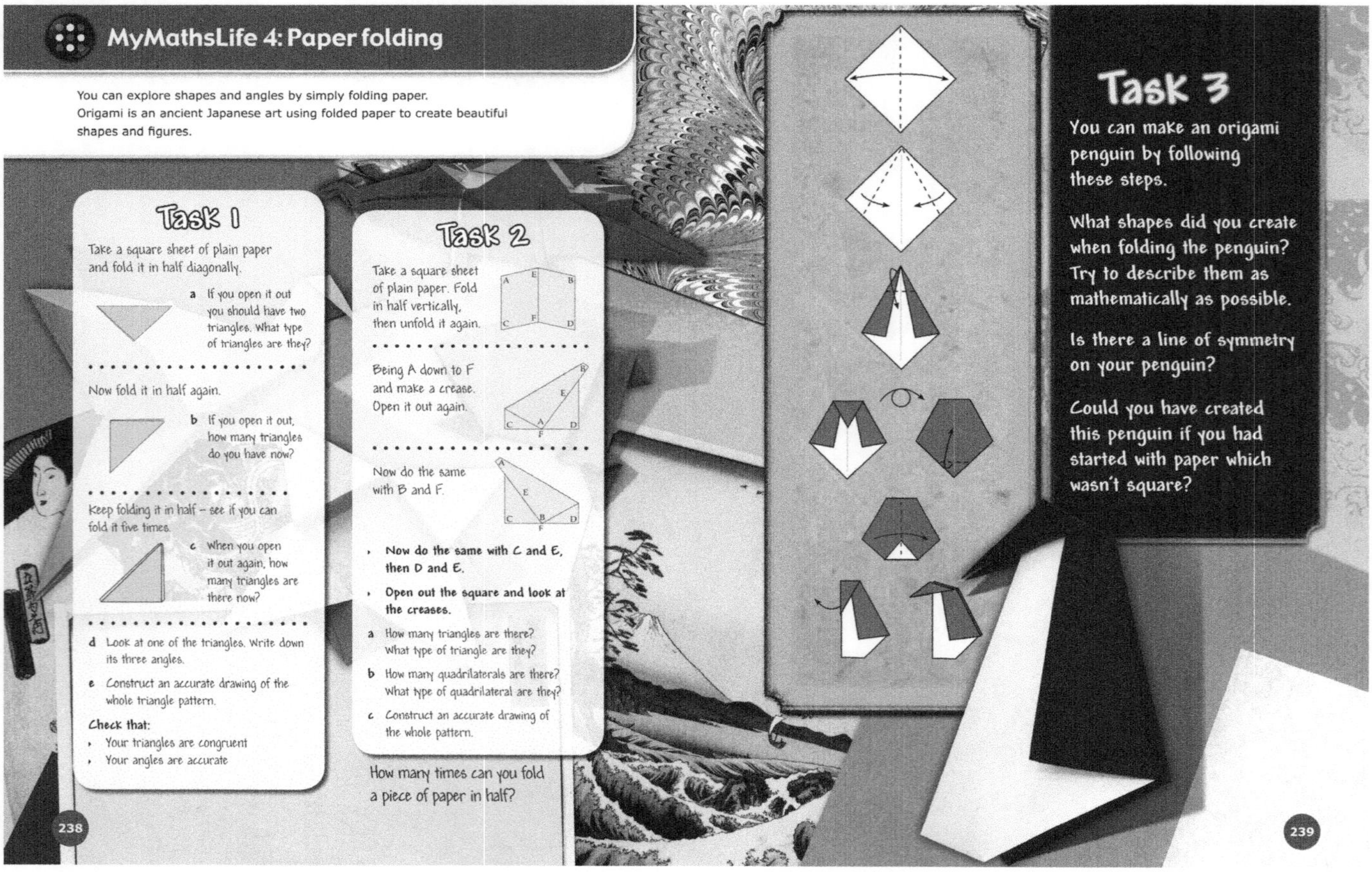

MyMathsLife 4: Paper folding

You can explore shapes and angles by simply folding paper.
Origami is an ancient Japanese art using folded paper to create beautiful shapes and figures.

Task 1

Take a square sheet of plain paper and fold it in half diagonally.

a If you open it out you should have two triangles. What type of triangles are they?

Now fold it in half again.

b If you open it out, how many triangles do you have now?

Keep folding it in half – see if you can fold it five times.

c When you open it out again, how many triangles are there now?

d Look at one of the triangles. Write down its three angles.

e Construct an accurate drawing of the whole triangle pattern.

Check that:
› Your triangles are congruent
› Your angles are accurate

Task 2

Take a square sheet of plain paper. Fold in half vertically, then unfold it again.

Being A down to F and make a crease. Open it out again.

Now do the same with B and F.

› Now do the same with C and E, then D and E.
› Open out the square and look at the creases.

a How many triangles are there? What type of triangle are they?

b How many quadrilaterals are there? What type of quadrilateral are they?

c Construct an accurate drawing of the whole pattern.

How many times can you fold a piece of paper in half?

Task 3

You can make an origami penguin by following these steps.

What shapes did you create when folding the penguin? Try to describe them as mathematically as possible.

Is there a line of symmetry on your penguin?

Could you have created this penguin if you had started with paper which wasn't square?

Teaching notes

Origami is the art of paper folding and has been practised in Japan since the 17th century. It uses a combination of folds and creases to produce designs from paper, without cutting or sticking. This case study looks at several such designs and gives students the opportunity to consider the shapes within them.

Task 1

Encourage students to fold their paper using sharp creases. This will mean that the triangles formed are easy to see. Can the students see other sizes of triangle as well as the small ones created from the repeated folding?

Task 2

Again, stress the importance of sharp folds. Students should be encouraged to compare their patterns with others to check the constructions and also to enable discussion of the end results.

Task 3

Look at the pictures showing how to make a penguin. Check that the students understand how they show the stages for folding the paper. Ask them to use the instructions to make a penguin, stressing the importance of making sharp folds. When they have made their penguins, ask them to answer the questions in the panel. To answer the last question, they might want to try folding a penguin from a rectangular piece of paper. When they have had sufficient time, discuss their answers.

Answers

1   a   Isosceles

     b   4

     c   32

     d   45°, 45°, 90°

     e   Students' own drawings

2   a   4; Isosceles

     b   8; Trapeziums

     c   Students' own drawings

3   Discuss task with students

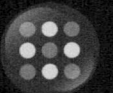

MyAssessment 3

These questions will test you on your knowledge of the topics in chapters 9 to 12.
They give you practice in the types of questions that you may eventually be given in your
GCSE exams. There are 60 marks in total.

1 Copy this shape onto square grid paper.

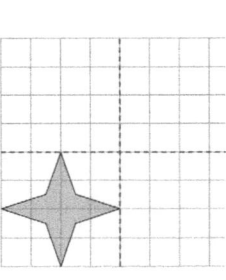

  a Draw all the lines of symmetry. (2 marks)

  b Reflect the shape along the dotted
    vertical line, then reflect both shapes
    about the horizontal mirror line. (2 marks)

  c What is the name of the polygon formed
    at the centre of these reflections? (1 mark)

2 Copy each of these shapes on square
  grid paper.

  a Rotate shape A 180° clockwise about
    the centre of rotation shown by the dot. (2 marks)

  b Rotate shape B 270° anticlockwise
    about the centre of rotation shown by
    the dot. (2 marks)

3 Copy this shape on square grid paper.

  a Transform the shape using (4 left
                         3 down) (2 marks)

  b If the coordinates of the shape were
    (6, 6), (6, 4), (5, 4), write down the
    coordinates of the transformed shape. (2 marks)

4 Solve these equations using inverse operations.

  a $d + 4 = 7$ (1 mark)   b $e - 3 = 11$ (1 mark)

  c $4f + 2 = 14$ (2 marks)   d $14g - 9 = 61$ (2 marks)

5 A garden fish pond is being filled with water. The pond holds 240 litres of water.
  The pond already contains 160 litres when 20 more buckets of water added.

  a Using the symbol 'b' for bucket write an equation for this problem. (2 marks)

  b Solve your equation to find how much water the bucket holds. (2 marks)

6 23 students go on a school expedition. They fill two minibuses and there are 7 left over.

  a Using 's' as the number of students in each minibus, write an equation linking
    the total number of students with those travelling by bus. (2 marks)

  b Solve the equation to calculate the number of students on each minibus. (2 marks)

7 Use standard column procedures to solve these problems.

  a $3484 + 1842$ (1 mark)   b $629.4 + 79.9$ (1 mark)

  c $1945 - 679$ (1 mark)   d $529.7 - 201.8$ (1 mark)

8 Use an appropriate method to solve these problems.
  Show all your working.

  a 163×28 (2 marks)   b $225 \div 8$ (2 marks)

  c $12 \div 0.8$ (2 marks)   d $84 \div 4.2$ (2 marks)

9 Use your calculator to solve these problems to 1 dp (if required).
  Remember to give an estimate of the answer first.

  a $(25 \times 3) \div 7.2$ (2 marks)   b $(45.1 - 16.9) \times 3.6$ (2 marks)

  c $9.2 \times (6.1 + 13.7)$ (2 marks)   d $(13.1 + 4.7) \div (9.3 + 8.5)$ (2 marks)

10 Using ruler and protractor construct these angles accurately.

  a $73°$ (1 mark)   b $161°$ (1 mark)

11 Construct these triangles accurately using ruler and protractor.

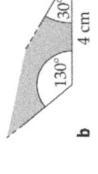

  a   b (6 marks)

12 The diagram shows a rough plan of a
  garden. The garden contains a small
  rectangular pond and a flower border
  along three sides of the garden.
  Redraw the plan as accurately as possible
  using straight lines and a scale
  of 1 cm = 1 m (1 : 100). (5 marks)

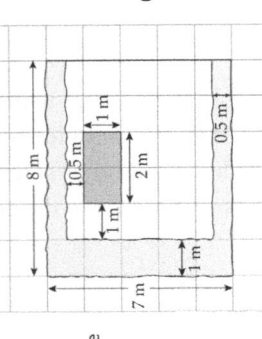

Mark scheme

Questions 1 – 6 marks

a   2   4 lines of symmetry in total

b   2   Correct reflections; 4 in total including original figure

c   2   Regular octagon; -1 mark if 'regular' is missing

Questions 2 – 4 marks

a   2   Check correct rotation about correct centre

b   2   Check correct rotation about correct centre

Questions 3 – 5 marks

a   2   Ensure correct translation undertaken in both directions

b   3 $(2, 3), (2, 1), (1, 1)$; -1 mark each error

Questions 4 – 6 marks

a   1 $d = 3$

b   1 $e = 14$

c   2 $f = 3$

d   2 $g = 5$

Questions 5 – 5 marks

a   3 $20b + 160 = 240$; -1 mark each error or omission

b   2 $20b = 80, b = 4$ litres

Questions 6 – 4 marks

a   2 $2s + 7 = 23$

b   2 $2s = 16, s = 8$ students

Questions 7 – 4 marks

a   1   5326

b   1   709.3

c   1   1266

d   1   327.9

Questions 8 – 4 marks

a   1   4564

b   1   28 r 1

c   1   15

d   1   20

Questions 9 – 8 marks

a   2   10, 10.4

b   2   100, 101.5

c   2   200, 182.2

d   2   1, 1

Questions 10 – 2 marks

a   1   Correct angle; ±1°

b   1   Correct angle; ±1°

Questions 11 – 6 marks

a   3   Correct angles to within ±1° , correct base length to within ±1 mm

b   3   Correct angles to within ±1° , correct base length to within ±1 mm

Questions 12 – 5 marks

    5   Correct scale used; correct size of flower border on all sides; correct size of pond; pond in correct position

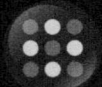

Learning outcomes

A14 Generate terms of a sequence from either a term-to-term or a position-to-term rule   (L4)
A15 Recognise arithmetic sequences and find the nth term   (L4)
A16 Recognise geometric sequences and appreciate other sequences that arise   (L5)

Introduction

The chapter starts by looking at the term-to-term and position-to-term rules for arithmetic and other sequences before looking at sequences in context. Triangular numbers are covered in the final section.

The introduction discusses the presence of sequences inside the human body, specifically related to the sequence of bases in DNA which determine the physical characteristics of each cell in the body. The use of DNA sequencing can help us to treat specific diseases and also in the solving of crimes by using DNA profiling of both the physical evidence and the suspects in the crime. This kind of profiling is known as DNA fingerprinting since each person has a unique genetic sequence in their DNA.

The study of the human genome has been a huge part of modern scientific research and scientists have spent many years developing their techniques to allow them to determine the sequence of chemical base pairs which make up human DNA. There are 3 billion bases of genetic information found in human cells and it has therefore been a massive undertaking. Information on the human genome project, its uses and future developments can be found at:

http://www.wellcome.ac.uk/Our-vision/Research-challenges/Genetics-and-genomics/index.htm?gclid=CMyQu9Xagr0CFerpwgod62cAOw

Prior knowledge

Students should already know how to…

• Recognise patterns in sequences of numbers

Starter problem

The starter problem considers a specific sequence of 'growth' of a 'dog' made up of coloured squares. Students should quickly recognise that the neck of the dog (coloured blue) grows by one square each evolution and that the legs of the dog (coloured red) both grow by one square each evolution. This should enable them to quickly draw the next one or two evolutions. The fourth evolution will have a neck three squares long and legs four squares long.

Students could be invited to come up with a simple rule (either written down or using mathematical language) which describes each evolution. They could also be invited to come up with their own 'mad scientist' design that has similar growth patterns.

The idea of evolution in sequences started with work done by John Conway in 1970. He developed a 'Game of life' simulation in which successive iterations of an initial cellular structure (drawn on a square grid) evolved according to a very simple rule structure. An online applet showing how the 'Game of life' works can be found at: http://www.bitstorm.org/gameoflife/

The rules which make up the 'Game of life' are:

For a space that is 'populated':
• Each cell with one or no neighbours dies, as if by loneliness.
• Each cell with four or more neighbours dies, as if by overpopulation.
• Each cell with two or three neighbours survives.

For a space that is 'empty' or 'unpopulated'
• Each cell with three neighbours becomes populated.

Resources

Topic scheme

Teaching time = 4 lessons/2 weeks

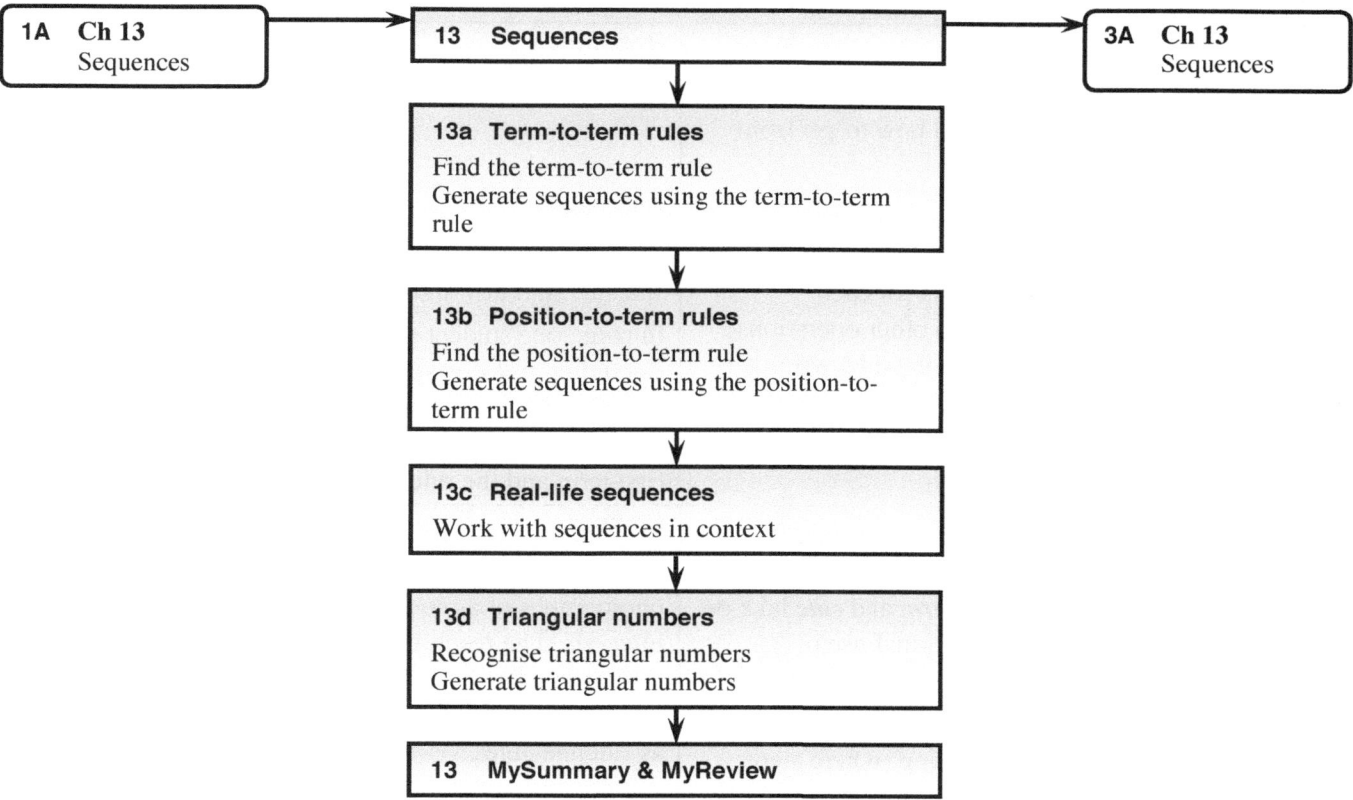

1A   Ch 13
Sequences

13   Sequences

3A   Ch 13
Sequences

13a   Term-to-term rules

Find the term-to-term rule
Generate sequences using the term-to-term rule

13b   Position-to-term rules

Find the position-to-term rule
Generate sequences using the position-to-term rule

13c   Real-life sequences

Work with sequences in context

13d   Triangular numbers

Recognise triangular numbers
Generate triangular numbers

13   MySummary & MyReview

Differentiation

Student book 2A	242 – 255
Term-to-term rules	
Position-to-term rules	
Real-life sequences	
Triangular numbers	

Student book 2B	234 – 247
Term-to-term rules	
Position-to-term rules	
Sequences in context	
Geometric sequences	

Student book 2C	238 – 251
General term of a sequence	
Sequences in context	
Geometric sequences	
Recursive sequences	

Objectives

- Describe integer sequences $\qquad$ (L4)
- Generate sequences from number patterns and geometrical contexts $\qquad$ (L5)

Key ideas	Resources
1 A sequence is defined by a rule **2** The rule gives the first term and how to get from one term to the next term	⊞ Sequences $\qquad$ (1173)

Simplification	Extension
Some students may initially consider only additive rules and check that their rule works for each consecutive term. When moving to other operations, remind students to give the operation when writing a rule.	Students find sequences that include negative numbers; such as, start at 7 and subtract 4; start at -15 and add 2. In pairs, one student gives a sequence of numbers (including negatives) for which their partner derives the rule. As an extension, one student gives the 2nd, 3rd and 4th term from which their partner derives the first term and the rule.

Literacy	Links
The students' mathematical vocabulary is extended in this lesson. The words *sequence, term* and *rule* take on technical meanings beyond their normal use in everyday English. For example, the word *sequence*, from the Latin for 'follow', is used in 'sequence dancing' where steps follow a repeated pattern.	Chronophotography is the art of taking a series of photographs of a moving object at regular time intervals. The resulting photographs form a sequence, similar to a flip book. Chronophotography was made popular during Victorian times by photographers such as Étienne-Jules Marey and Georges Demeny. There are examples of chronophotography at http://www.sequences.org.uk/chrono1/0000.html and at http://www.elearning-art.net/art-net_courses/Moving_Images_Workshop_(Eng)/1SHO RTHISTORY/1Zoopraxinoscope.htm

Alternative approach

Setting sequences in context adds a greater purpose to analysing them. For example, in saving up to buy an item costing (say) £75, a child starts with birthday-present money of £45 and saves £4 each week from pocket money. How many weeks does it take to save £75?

Other examples could be finding
- how long it takes for £92 in a bank account to be used up if the account holder draws £12 out of the account each week
- how long it takes for the tank holding heating oil to be used up if, at the start of November, there are 350 litres of oil in the tank and the heating requirements of a house use 30 litres a week.

Checkpoint

1 Find the next two terms in each of the following sequences:

a $3, 7, 11, 15, \ldots$		$(19, 23)$
b $20, 16, 12, 8, \ldots$		$(4, 0)$
c $64, 32, 16, \ldots$		$(8, 4)$
d $2, 20, 200, \ldots$		$(2000, 20\,000)$

Starter – Connections

If $x = 2$ and $y = 6$, students write ten algebraic rules connecting x and y. Give some examples to start with, such as $y = \frac{1}{2}x + 5$, $y = 4x - 2$, $x + y = 8$.

The activity can be extended by using a negative value for x or y.

Teaching notes

Give students a start number, say 13, and a rule, say add 3. Ask students in turn for the next number. Write responses which generate the sequence. Explain key terms: **sequence, number pattern, term,** and **rule**

Show students a simple picture sequence (or use sequences in the students' book):

Students give each term a number and discuss the rule to find the number of lines for the fourth term. Emphasise that the term-to-term rule is the start number (3) and how to get from one term to the next (+ 3).

Give students some numerical examples. Note that it is often useful to find the difference between terms to help find the rule. They describe a sequence 3, 5, 7, 9 as 'start at 3 and add 2' and the sequence 17, 14, 11, 8 as 'start at 17 and subtract 3'.

Challenge them with more demanding sequences by asking for the first five terms of the sequence with the rule (a) start at 14, subtract 5; (b) start at 3 and double.

Plenary

Give students several numerical sequences. On their mini whiteboards, they write the term-to-term rule for each sequence by giving the first term and the rule to get from one term to the next. Discuss their answers where appropriate.

Show students the first four terms of a sequence of straws and discuss how many straws are required to make the 5th and 6th terms in the sequence. Ask how they would find the number of straws for 32nd term. Discuss the limitations of a term-to-term rule.

Exercise commentary

Throughout these questions, when stating the term-to-term rule, remind students that they need to give the starting number as well as how to get from one term to the next term.

Questions 1–3 – These questions all use geometric patterns to give a sequence. In question **1**, students should recognise the 3-times table. In questions **2** and **3**, students first find the differences between consecutive terms.

Question 4 – Remind students to test their rules on *all* the numbers given, not just the first few terms.

Question 5 – Students match a rule with its numerical sequence. Students will have to look at more than the first two terms to decide between the rules.

Question 6 – Students need only use a few numbers in each sequence and they can use the same number several times in different sequences.

Answers

1 a Check drawings – should be a 3 × 4 and a 3× 5 lattice
   b 3, 6, 9, 12, 15   c add 3
2 a 4, 7, 10, 13
   b Start with 4 to move to the next term add 3
   c 16
3 a 4, 7, 10, 13
   b Start with 4 to move to the next term add 3
   c 19
4 a i   add 5   ii   subtract 4
      iii divide by 2   iv   multiply by 2
      v   add 1.5   vi   add 15
   b i   22   ii   3
      iii 15   iv   16
      v   7.5   vi   62
5 add 7
   add 3
   subtract 6
   subtract 50
   divide by 2
   multiply by 2
6 Multiple answers possible, check students' work

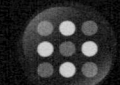

Objectives

- Generate sequences from number patterns or geometric patterns   (L3)
- Generate terms of a simple sequence knowing the relation between the position of a term in a sequence and the value of the term.   (L5)

Key ideas	Resources
1 Each term has a position number which gives the position of the term in the sequence 2 The position-to-term rule works out the term if its position in the sequence is known	*n*th term (1165)

Simplification	Extension
Students often become confused between the two types of rule: term-to-term and position-to-term. Use the example in the students' book and also questions **1** and **2** to use each rule in parallel.	Show students four position-to-term rules, such as × 5, × 3 + 9, × 2 + 10 and × 4 + 4. They calculate the 25th term under each rule and then place the rules in ascending order depending on the value of this 25th term.

Literacy	Links
Note that, whereas the term-to-term rule requires the first term of the sequence to be stated in the rule, the position-to-term rule does not.	The 'Look and say' sequence is a famous non-linear sequence that sometimes appears in puzzle books. The first eight terms are 1, 11, 21, 1211, 111221, 312211, 13112221, 1113213211. What is the rule for moving from one term to the next? (Say the previous term out loud in words, and then write what is said in numbers. For example, 'one one' becomes 11; 'two ones' becomes 21; 'one two, one one' becomes 1211, etc.) Try starting the sequence with 2 or 3 instead of 1.

Alternative approach

To illustrate the difference between the two rules, draw a geometric sequence (such as the one in the worked example of the students' book) and separate the board or screen beneath it into a LHS and a RHS.

On the LHS, write the numeric terms of the sequence 5, 8, 11, 14, … and a series of *horizontal* arrows labelled + 3 from one term to the next. Write the term-to-term rule as 'Start at 5; add 3'.

On the RHS, write the numeric terms of the sequence 5, 8, 11, 14, … and, above the terms, write ordinal numbers 1st, 2nd, 3rd, 4th, … Then write a series of *vertical* arrows from the ordinals to the terms, labelled '× 3 then + 2'. Write the position-to-term rule as 'Multiply by 3, then add 2'.

If several examples are done in this way, students may notice that the number added *horizontally* for the term-to-term rule is the same number that multiplies *vertically* for the position-to-term rule.

Checkpoint

1 The position-to-term rule is '× 5, then + 2'.
  a Find the first term.   (7)
  b Find the tenth term.   (52)
  c Write down the first four terms of the sequence.   (7, 12, 17, 22)
  d Write down the 'term-to-term rule'.   (Add 5)

Write the following sequences on the board:

50, 48, 44, 38, 30, …   J, F, M, A, M, …
3, 6, 12, 24, 48, …   2, 5, 10, 17, 26, …
S, M, T, W, T, …   A, Z, B, Y, C, …

Students find the next term in each sequence.

(The next terms are: 20, J for June, 96, 51, F for Friday, X.)

Teaching notes

Write the sequence 3, 5, 7, 9, … for the class to see. Students describe it using the start number and the term-to-term rule. Students give the 5th, 6th, 7th terms.

Above each term, write its position. Students now begin the task of finding the 25th term (which is 51). Write each of their answers and discuss the problems with this task – it is laborious and mistakes are made.

Write the sequence 2, 4, 6, 8, … and students find the 25th term in this sequence. Point out that the term-to-term rule is 'Start with 2; add 2' but that a quicker more efficient rule links **position** and **term**. Students articulate the rule as 'The term = the position × 2'.

Refer back to the initial sequence. Students make the link between 2, 4, 6, 8 and 3, 5, 7, 9. They notice that each term of 3, 5, 7, 9 is 'one more than' the corresponding term of 2, 4, 6, 8. So they derive the rule for 3, 5, 7, 9 as 'The term = the position × 2 and then + 1'.

Rewrite using a function machine as in the students' book and demonstrate each position as **input** and term as **output**. Use 25 as the input to check if any student correctly calculated the 25th term.

Plenary

Provide several position-to-term rules in the form of a multiplication followed by an addition. Students find the term for a given position and write it on their mini whiteboards. Discuss where appropriate.

For a given sequence, have students find the first four terms of the sequence using the position-to-term rule. Repeat for other sequences. Have students recognise that the difference between consecutive terms is the same as the multiplication within the position-to-term rule.

Exercise commentary

Questions 1 and **2** – Students describe a sequence first as a series of numbers, then as a term-to-term rule (remembering to include the start number) and then as a function machine for the position-to-term rule.

Questions 3 and **4** – Students generate sequences using position-to-term rules. In question **4**, students may ask if the two equal terms must have the same position – which is not the case.

Question 5 – Can students see the answer from the rules without the need to calculate any of the terms in the sequence? (The common difference of the sequence is 3, so the flow diagram with × 3 is the correct one.)

Answers

1 a 5, 8, 11, 14   b add 3
   c i $(1 × 3) + 2 = 5$ ii $(4 × 3) + 2 = 14$
2 a 4, 6, 8, 10, add 2
   b e.g. $(1 × 2) + 2 = 4, (2 × 2) + 2 = 6$
3 a 6, 11, 16, 21   b 0, 4, 8, 12   c 10, 15, 20, 25
   d 2.5, 3, 3.5, 4
4 6
5 Rule **c**

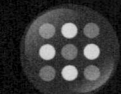

Objectives

- Use linear expressions to describe the *n*th term of a simple arithmetic sequence, justifying its form by referring to the activity or practical context from which it was generated   (L5)

Key ideas	Resources	
1 Investigating a simple situation systematically, recording, analysing observations, generalising and testing conclusions	*n*th term	(1165)
	Sequences	(1173)

Simplification	Extension
Encourage students having difficulty to make full use of diagrams and tables for structure.	More able students can be stretched with the investigation of a rule for triangular numbers (as in the handshakes investigation in question **4**).

Literacy	Links
Quality of written communication, particularly of reasoning and testing, should be encouraged in this session. Students can work together and challenge each other as to whether points made are clear, results clearly presented in tables, diagrams used to illustrate or clarify, and so on.	All human cells contain DNA. DNA stands for Deoxyribonucleic Acid and DNA molecules hold the instructions for building living things. DNA molecules are made up of four building blocks called bases or nucleotides. The order or sequence of the bases along the molecule gives the genetic information for characteristics such as hair and eye colour.

Alternative approach

Students may work in pairs on an investigation which has the capability of resulting in linear relationships, and perhaps others. Matchstick growth patterns are a good source, and these could be used as a starting activity to develop the work covered in the exercise.

Checkpoint

1 Lillian buys a new bike. She travels 30 miles on the first day. After that she averages 20 miles a day.

a Fill in the table to show how many miles she has travelled since she has had her new bike.

Number of days	1	2	3	4	5
× 20	20				
Number of miles	30	50			

b Copy and complete this position-to-term rule:
Number of miles = _____ × number of days + _____   ($m = 20d + 10$)

c How many will she have travelled after the first week?   ($m = 20 \times 7 + 10 = 150$)

Starter Strange sequences

Write the following sequences on the board:

50, 48, 44, 38, 30, ...   J, F, M, A, M, ...
3, -6, 12, -24, 48, ...   2, 5, 10, 17, 26, ...
S, M, T, W, T, ...

Ask students for the next term in each sequence.

Answers: 20, J (June), -96 (multiply previous term by -2), 37, F (Friday).

Can be extended by students making their own 'strange sequences'.

Teaching notes

A focus in this section is to demonstrate the use of sequences in a real-life context. Students can be encouraged to describe the rules with which they are working in words and using symbols. Collaborative approaches can be encouraged here in order to develop student confidence and to promote purposeful mathematical discussion.

Having initiated whole-class discussion through the worked examples, invite students to discuss how sequences might appear in real-life contexts.

Plenary

Challenge students to write a sequence problem of their own, using the examples in the exercise as a model.

Exercise commentary

Questions 1–4 – The position-to-term rule will take some consolidation. Encourage students to use the multiplicative factor given by the differences in the terms, and then look for the number that adjusts the rule. Working in pairs may help.

Answers

1 a 9, 11
   b i   6, 8, 10   7, 9, 11
      ii 2 × number of weeks + 1
   c 25
2 a 52, 60   b Start with 20 and add 8 each week
   c 8, 16, 24, 32, 40   20, 28, 36, 44, 52
   d Number of pounds = 8 × number of weeks + 12
   e £332
3 a 130, 150   b 20 × number of days + 30
   c 430   d 630
4 a 3   b 6, 10, 15
   c The sequence is triangular numbers: 1, 3, 6, 10, 15, 21, etc.
   d Add number of people – 1 (i.e. to get from handshakes for 5 people to 6 people add (6 – 1) = 5)
   e The jumps between terms change every time. The actual rule is number of handshakes = $(n – 1)(n)/2$

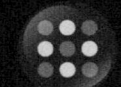

13d Triangular numbers

Objectives

- Recognise the first few triangular numbers (L4)
- Generate sequences from numerical patterns and geometrical contexts (L5)

Key ideas	Resources
1 Counters can be arranged into triangular patterns by adding extra rows. The total number of counters in each pattern in a triangular number	Squares and triangles (1054) Diagrams of sequences of square numbers and triangular numbers About 20 identical spheres Counters as support

Simplification	Extension
Drawing diagrams of triangular numbers may be difficult for some students. They can follow the right-angled triangle image and the ascending number of dots in each row. Sometimes, using counters to establish the pattern before copying it can help.	Link triangular numbers to the song 'Twelve days of Christmas'. Challenge students to calculate the total number of gifts received from 'my true love' over the twelve-day period of Christmas!

Literacy	Links
Now knowing that triangular numbers and square numbers exist, students could ask the question 'What about pentagonal numbers? Or hexagonal numbers or heptagonal, or octagonal…?' They can research these other numbers using the Internet and see the geometric patterns that they create.	The game of snooker begins with 15 red balls arranged in a triangle. Snooker was invented in 1875 as one of many variants of the game of billiards. It was first played by British army officers in India and later became popular in the UK. There is more information about snooker at http://en.wikipedia.org/wiki/Snooker and at www.worldsnooker.com/

Alternative approach

From the diagram of triangular numbers, each triangular number can be written as the sum of the numbers in each row. For example,

$1 = 1$
$3 = 1 + 2$
$6 = 1 + 2 + 3$
$10 = 1 + 2 + 3 + 4$

The relation that generates the next triangular number is clear: for the nth triangular number simply add n to the previous triangular number. For example, the 5th triangular number = the 4th triangular number + 5 $= 10 + 5 = 15$.

$15 = 1 + 2 + 3 + 4 + 5$

Also, adding two adjacent triangular numbers generates a square number.

So, $4^2 = 16 = 10 + 6 = 1 + 2 + 3 + 4 + 3 + 2 + 1$
and $5^2 = 25 = 15 + 10 = 1 + 2 + 3 + 4 + 5 + 4 + 3 + 2 + 1$, and so on.

Checkpoint

1 The 3rd triangular number is 6.
   a Can you find the 4th triangular number by drawing? (Draw a triangle of dots with four rows to give 10.)
   b Can you find the 4th triangular number from the 3rd?   (4th number = 3rd number + 4 = 6 + 4 = 10)

Starter – Quick fire

Recap work of previous chapters and especially number work, including mental and written computation. Ask rapid response questions. Students reply by writing on their mini whiteboards. Discuss questions when their answers indicate a need.

Teaching notes

Recap the square number sequence.

Show a diagram of the sequence of triangular numbers and discuss how it develops; that is,

– the ascending number of dots in each row

– the term-to-term pattern, such as: for the sixth term, add a row of 6 to the previous term; for the seventh term add a row of 7 to the previous term.

– Overall, starting with the first triangular number 1, the term-to-term pattern is $+2, +3, +4, \ldots$

Note that the sum of any term and the previous term is the same as the square number for that position; for example, the third triangular number + the second triangular number = the third square number.

Demonstrate visually how the diagram of a square number can be divided into diagrams for two consecutive triangular numbers. Show the diagram for the fifth square number and students suggest where to draw a line to show how the square can be split into the two triangular numbers.

Plenary

Discuss students' approaches to question **6**. Use several small spheres or balls to show how a pattern of tetrahedral numbers (3D triangular numbers) builds up. Students look at and then predict how many spheres are in each successive layer of the pyramid of spheres and, from the layers, find the 1st, 2nd and 3rd tetrahedral numbers. Can they predict the number of spheres in the next layer and then predict the 4th tetrahedral number? And the 5th?

Exercise commentary

Question 1 – The focus is on the array pattern of triangular numbers. In fact, the diagram for question **2** can be used for question **1**.

Questions 2 and **3** – These questions deal with how the sequence of triangular numbers develops from one term (or row) to the next.

Questions 4 and **5** – Focus on the relationship between triangular and square numbers as discussed in the introductory activity on the previous page.

Question 6 – Extends students to consider a three-dimensional number pattern. This is discussed in the plenary.

Question 7 – There are several ways of solving this problem. Perhaps the easiest is to take the statement in question **3** that the 20th triangular number is 210 and use the pattern already discovered that the nth triangular number is the $(n-1)$th number + n, and work up to 325.

Questions 8–10 – These questions are suitable for pair work.

Answers

1 $1 + 2 + 3 + 4 + 5 = 15$ Check triangle drawn

2   **a**   Add a row of 7 dots to the base

     b   28   **c**   7

3   **a**   45   **b**   120   **c**   190, 231

4   **a**   square can be split into two triangles

     b   10 and 15

     c $10 + 15 = 25$

5 $15 + 21 = 36$

6   **a**   56   **b**   91

7   25

8   190, 210

9   36

10 Discuss with students

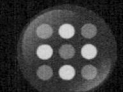

Key outcomes		Quick check
Find and use rules that describe sequences of numbers.	L4	What are the next two terms in the following sequence? 4, 9, 14, 19, … (24, 29) What is the term-to-term rule? (Add five)
Use position-to-term rules to generate sequences.	L4	Write dowm the first four terms of the sequence generated by the position-to-term rule '× 3 then − 2'. What is the term-to-term rule? (Add 3)
Understand the connection between triangular numbers and square numbers.	L5	Write down the first seven triangular numbers. (1, 3, 6, 10, 15, 21, 28) Write down the first seven square numbers. (1, 4, 9, 16, 25, 36, 49) Add together the third and fourth triangular numbers. Which square number is this equal to? ($6 + 10 = 16 =$ 4th square number)
Use sequences to solve real-life problems.	L5	Sam is saving to go on holiday. He starts with £50 and saves £30 each week. How much will he have saved after 5 weeks? (£170) Copy and complete this position-to-term rule: Amount saved = ____ × number of weeks + ____ (Amount saved = $30 \times$ number of weeks + 20)

⊞ MyMaths extra support

Lesson/online homework			Description
Counting 4	1349	L4	Sequences with whole numbers, decimals and negatives

MyReview

Check out
You should now be able to ...

Test it ➡
Questions

✓	Find and use rules that describe sequences of numbers.	④ 1
✓	Use position-to-term rules to generate sequences.	③ 2
✓	Understand the connection between triangular numbers and square numbers.	⑤ 3
✓	Use sequences to solve real life problems.	⑤ 4

Language	Meaning	Example
Sequence	A set of numbers, called *terms*, which follow a pattern	2, 5, 8, 11, ... is a sequence
Term-to-term rule	An instruction how to get from one term in a sequence to the next term	For the sequence above the rule is start at 2 and +3
Position-to-term rule	A rule which works out the value of any term from its position in the sequence	For the sequence above, the position-to-term rule can be given by this diagram: 
Triangular number	A number that falls in the sequence: 1, 3, 6, 10, 15, 21, 28, ...	36 and 45 are both triangular numbers.

13 MyReview

1 For each sequence, find the term-to-term rule and write the next two terms.
   a 4, 9, 14, 19, ...
   b 18, 14, 10, 6, ...
   c 3, 11, 19, 27, ...
   d 0.5, 1, 1.5, 2, ...
   e 5, 10, 20, 40, ...
   f 400, 200, 100, 50, ...

2 Write the first four terms of the sequence generated by each of these position-to-term rules.

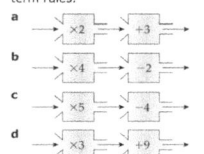

3 a What are the first 4 triangular numbers?
   b The 9th triangular number is 45. What is the 10th triangular number?
   c The 20th triangular number is 210. What is the 19th triangular number?

4 Jerome is paying back money to his cousin for a concert ticket. He starts by giving his cousin £5 and agrees to pay back £2 each week.
   a Jerome records the amount of money that he has paid back.
      5, 7, 9, ...
      Write the next two terms in Jerome's sequence.
   b Write a term-to-term rule for this sequence.
   c Copy and complete this table of values.

Number of weeks	1	2	3	4	5
×2					
Amount paid back (£)	5	7	9		

   d Copy and complete this position-to-term rule.
      Amount paid back =
      ___ × number of weeks + ___
   e Use the rule to find out how much Jerome will have paid back after 12 weeks.
   f The concert ticket cost £30. How long will it take Jerome to pay back his cousin?

What next?

Score		
0 – 2	Your knowledge of this topic is still developing. To improve look at Formative test: 2A–13; MyMaths: 1054, 1165 and 1173	
3	You are gaining a secure knowledge of this topic. To improve look at InvisiPen: 281, 284 and 285	
4	You have mastered this topic. Well done, you are ready to progress!	

 **MyMaths**.co.uk

Question commentary

Question 1 – Encourage students to write down differences.

Question 2 – Straightforward

Question 3 – Students hopefully remember how triangular numbers are formed from the previous lesson.

Question 4 – A practical application of sequences.

Answers

1 a *start with 4 and add 5*; 24, 29
   b *start with 18 and subtract 4*; 2, -2
   c *start with 3 and add 8*; 35, 43
   d *start with 0.5 and add 0.5*; 2.5, 3
   e *start with 5 and double*; 80, 160
   f *start with 400 and halve/÷2*; 25, 12.5

2 a 5, 7, 9, 11   b 2, 6, 10, 14
   c 1, 6, 11, 16   d 12, 15, 18, 21

3 a 1, 3, 6, 10   b 55   c 190

4 a 11, 13   b *start at 5 and add 2*
   c middle row: 2, 4, 6, 8, 10; bottom row: 11, 13
   d 2, 3   e £27   f 14 weeks

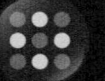

13 MyPractice

1 a Add the next two patterns in this sequence.

b Write the number of arrows in each drawing as a number sequence.

c What is the term-to-term rule for the number sequence?

2 a Write the term-to-term rule for each of these sequences.

   i 4, 9, 14, 19, ...   Start at ...... and add on ......

   ii 21, 32, 43, 54, ...

   iii 160, 80, 40, 20, ...

   iv 1, 3, 9, 27, ...

   v 2.5, 3.0, 3.5, 4.0, ...

   vi 3, 11, 19, 27, ...

b Write the next term in each sequence above.

3 Write a sequence for each of these position-to-term rules.

a position → ×2 → −1 → term

b position → ×4 → −4 → term

c position → +3 → ×2 → term

4

a Write the number sequence for this pattern.

b Complete this sentence:

To move onto the next drawing in the pattern you need to .... more matches.

c Complete the calculations below.

Sequence: 1st   2nd   3rd   4th

          3   5   7   9

$(1 \times 2 + 1 = 3)$ $(\square \times 2 + 1 = \square)$ $(\square \times 2 + 1 = \square)$ $(\square \times 2 + 1 = \square)$

d Write the position-to-term rule for the number sequence.

position → □ → term

> The rule has two operations.

5 Here are the first three triangular number patterns.

a How many *more* dots will you need to draw the next pattern?

b Draw the next two patterns.

c Write the numbers in a sequence.

6 There are 36 dots in the square number pattern.

a 36 = ... × ....

b Copy the pattern onto paper.

The square can be divided into two triangular numbers.

Draw rings around the two triangles.

c Which two triangular numbers add together to make 36 (6^2)?

7 Hamida is saving to go on holiday.

She starts with £50 and saves £15 each week.

a Complete the sequence of Hamida's savings.

50, 65, ... , 95, 110, ... , ...

b Write the term-to-term rule for this sequence.

c Copy and complete this table of values.

Number of weeks	1	2	3	4	5	6
× _____						
Amount saved	50	65		95	110	

d Copy and complete this position-to-term rule:

Amount saved = _____ × number of weeks + _____

e Hamida wants to save at least £300.

Will she have reached her goal after 20 weeks?

Question commentary

Questions 1–3 – Should be straightforward.

Questions 4 and **5** – Students can work in pairs. They may need help interpreting what is being asked of them.

Question 7 – A practical application. Part **d** is potentially the most difficult; finding what to multiply by (15) and finding what to add (35).

Answers

1   **a**   Check students' work
     b $2, 4, 6, 8, 10$ **c**   add 2

2   **a**   **i**   add 5   **b**   **i**   24
          ii   add 11   **ii**   65
          iii   divide by 2   **iii**   10
          iv   × by 3   **iv**   81
          v   add 0.5   **v**   4.5
          vi   add 8   **vi**   35

3   **a** $1, 3, 5, 7, \ldots$
     b $0, 4, 8, 12, \ldots$
     c $8, 10, 12, 14, \ldots$

4   **a** $3, 5, 7, 9$
     b   add 2
     c $(2 \times 2 + 1 = 5)$ $(3 \times 2 + 1 = 7)$ $(4 \times 2 + 1 = 9)$
     d   position $\rightarrow \times 2 \rightarrow +1 \rightarrow$ term

5   **a**   4
     b   Check triangles drawn; one with 10 dots and one with 15
     c $4, 9, 15, 22$

6   **a** 6×6 **b**   Check students' work
     c $15 + 21$

7   **a** $50, 65, 80, 125, 140$
     b   Start at 50, add 15
     c   middle row: $15, 30, 45, 60, 75, 90$;
       bottom row: $80, 125$
     d   Amount saved = 15(number of weeks) + 55
     e $20 \times 15 + 35 = 335$. Yes

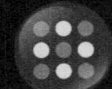

Learning outcomes

G1 Derive and apply formulae to calculate and solve problems involving: perimeter and area of triangles, parallelograms, trapeziums, volume of cuboids (including cubes) and other prisms (including cylinders) — (L4/5)

G15 Use the properties of faces, surfaces, edges and vertices of cubes, cuboids, prisms, cylinders, pyramids, cones and spheres to solve problems in 3D — (L5)

Introduction

The chapter starts by looking at 3D shapes in general: naming the shapes and looking at the number of faces, edges and vertices that each shape has. The second section covers isometric drawings of 3D shapes before a section on nets. Surface area and volume of a cuboid are then covered.

The introduction discusses how companies use an appreciation of surface area and volume to design environmentally-friendly packaging for their products. If you look around the supermarket, you can see packaging designed as cubes, cuboids, cylinders and other prisms, each of which is designed to suit the purpose of the packaging and also to add some aesthetic value while being only as big as necessary to safely package the goods. The use of efficient packaging can also help companies to reduce costs since customers do not buy the products for the packaging alone. The cost incurred from the packaging is a 'throw away' cost to the company since the packaging is rarely useful to the consumer and almost always gets thrown away or at best recycled.

Higher level mathematics can help companies solve what are referred to as 'optimisation' problems. Mathematicians use what is called differential calculus to find the minimum surface area for a given volume, or to solve similar problems. This type of mathematics will be covered in A level.

Prior knowledge

Students should already know how to…

- Carry out simple arithmetic
- Recognise simple 3D shapes
- Work out the areas and perimeters of plane figures

Starter problem

The starter problem requires students to work with the volume of a cuboid formula in order to reduce the surface area of a given package, for the fixed volume stated. Trial-and-improvement is clearly going to be the method of choice for most students and they should easily be able to determine that a package measuring 10 cm by 6 cm by 6 cm will work. Here the surface area is $4 \times 10 \times 6 + 2 \times 6 \times 6 = 312 \text{ cm}^2$ as opposed to the original of $2 \times 12 \times 6 + 2 \times 12 \times 5 + 2 \times 6 \times 5 = 324 \text{ cm}^2$.

There is an interesting link to prime factorisation. There are many possible (whole number) combinations of side length for the cuboid and some will be better than the original and some worse. By finding the prime factorisation of 360 we can actually work out how many combinations there will be and also what these combinations are. We *could* therefore try them all.

$360 = 2^3 \times 3^2 \times 5$ so if we split this prime factorisation into three parts, lots of different ways, we can find all the combinations. The one given in the question is $2 \times 2 \times 3, 2 \times 3$ and 5. The one stated above is $2 \times 5, 2 \times 3$ and 2×3. An alternative could be $2 \times 2 \times 2, 3 \times 5$ and 3 and more able students could be invited to come up with others and check their surface areas.

Resources

Topic scheme

Teaching time = 5 lessons/2 weeks

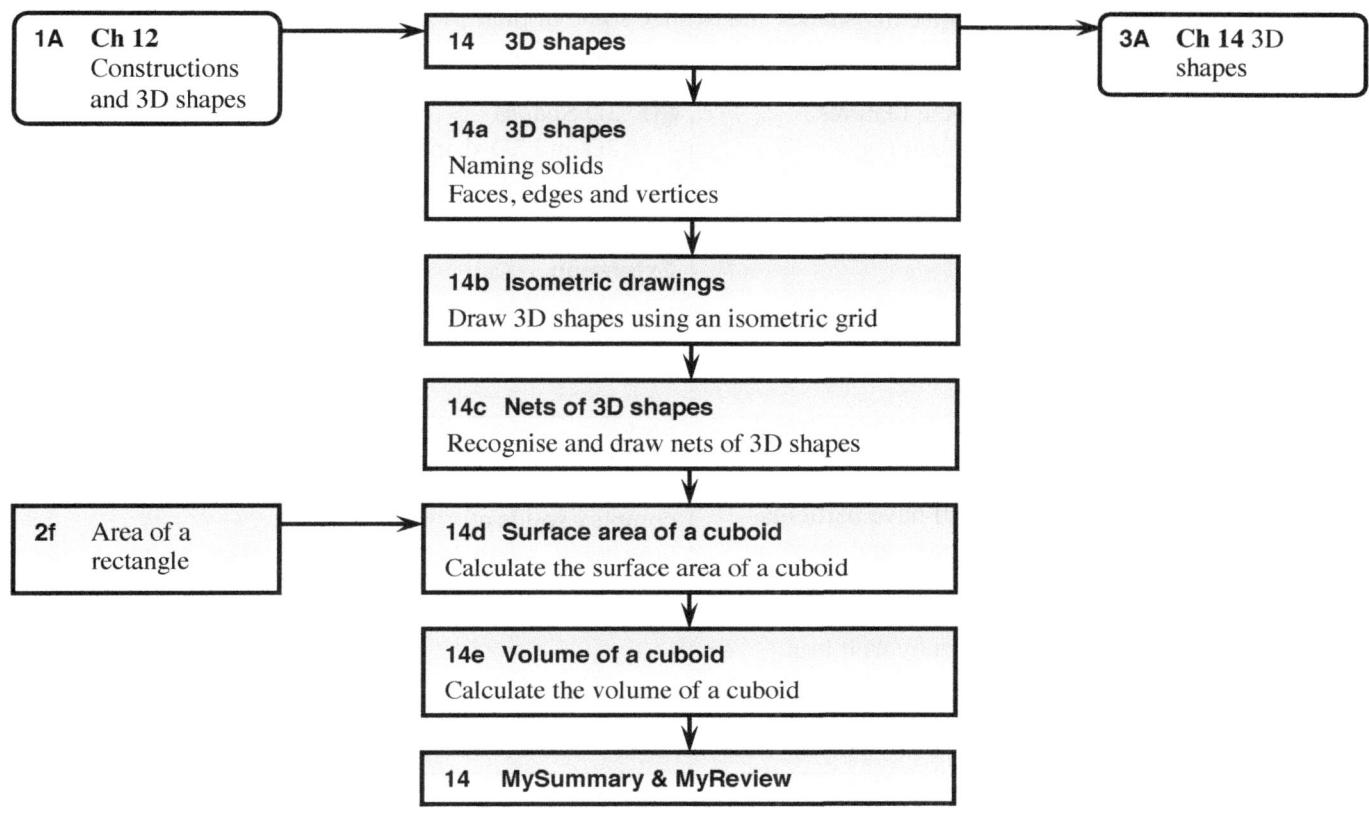

Differentiation

<table>
<tr><td>Student book 2A   256 – 271</td><td>Student book 2B   248 – 263</td><td>Student book 2C   252 – 265</td></tr>
<tr><td>3D shapes
Isometric drawings
Nets of 3D shapes
Surface area of a cuboid
Volume of a cuboid</td><td>3D shapes
Plans and elevations
Surface area of a cuboid
Volume of a cuboid
Prisms</td><td>3D shapes
Plans and elevations
Surface area of a prism
Volume of a prism</td></tr>
</table>

Objectives

- Name 3D shapes (L4)
- Use 2D representations to visualise 3D shapes and deduce some of their properties (L4)

Key ideas	Resources
1 Name 3D shapes by looking at the features 2 Identify 3D shapes from given features	3D Shapes (1078) 2D and 3D shapes (1229) Examples of 3D shapes Card, scissors and glue

Simplification	Extension
Wherever possible have 3D solids available for students to look at. This will also help with identifying the key features.	Students could be asked to draw the nets of simple 3D shapes and make them out of card.

Literacy	Links
The words pyramid and prism are important categories of 3D shapes, but students may well have particular shape perceptions associated with each and therefore this needs to be fully exposed and explored. That cubes and cuboids are also prisms may not be appreciated by many students. However, students may well bring knowledge of other 3D shape terms with them, such as octahedron, and so on. Celebrate and share their knowledge.	There is a collection of nets for paper models of more complex solids at http://www.korthalsaltes.com/index.html

Alternative approach

If there is a set of 3D shapes in your department, use these with groups of students. Label them and circulate them for student groups to examine carefully, decide whether the shape is a prism, pyramid or other, name it if possible and record the number of faces, edges and vertices. This activity can be carried out with a collection of cardboard cartons of a variety of shapes. Share and discuss the students' results fully.

Checkpoint

1	How many faces does a cube have?	(6)
2	How many edges does a square-based pyramid have?	(8)
3	How many vertices does a cuboid have?	(8)

Starter – Describe the shape

Describe features of a 2D shape to the students and see who can identify it first. For example: My shape has four sides… it has four right-angles… It has four equal sides (square). Penalise those jumping in too quickly before they can name it beyond doubt.

Teaching notes

This lesson requires a lot of visualisation and logical reasoning. Activities such as the suggested starter can be used to get students' 'mind's eye' working and actual objects can be used to help here as well. It is important that the students use the correct mathematical words rather than 'oblong', for example.

When it comes to identifying shapes from their descriptions as in question **3**, ask students how they know beyond doubt that they are correct.

Plenary

Describe 3D shapes in a similar way to the 2D shapes in the starter. Again, penalise those students jumping in too quickly. An example could be: My shape has 5 faces… Four of the faces are triangles… One face is a square (square-based pyramid).

Exercise commentary

Question 1 – Students could be encouraged to sketch each of the shapes, using a ruler to try and draw the relevant parallel lines.

Questions 2 and **3** – These questions can be done in pairs and, again, take time to sketch 3D shapes.

Answers

1. **a** sphere **b** cube **c** square-based pyramid
    d cylinder **e** cone **f** triangular based pyramid
    g triangular prism **h** cuboid
2. Drawing **c**
3. **a** **A** cylinder **B** cuboid
    C cube **D** triangular prism
    E sphere **F** square-based pyramid
    b, c Check students' sketches

Objectives	
• Use 2D representations to visualise 3D shapes and deduce some of their properties	(L6)

Key ideas	Resources
1 Isometric grids can be used to draw 3D shapes when orientated correctly 2 Shaded faces with the same orientation helps to visualise the shape	Isometric grid and isometric dots for whole-class use

Simplification	Extension
Ensure that students have the isometric paper the right way round. Use shading to help determine which *face* of the object is being drawn. Students can shade surfaces as soon as they are complete; for example, top faces can be shaded heavily; LHS faces shaded lightly; RHS faces shaded medium or not at all.	Discuss other 2D representations of 3D shapes, such as nets, plans and elevations. Students draw the plans and elevations of some of the shapes in the exercise. Students use the Internet to research the work of M.C. Escher.

Literacy	Links
The word *isometric* comes from Greek words meaning 'equal measure'. All three dimensions of an object, length, width and height, are 'measured equally' when drawn as the grid is formed from equilateral triangles. When drawing on isometric paper, shapes stand out more clearly on dotted paper, but the lines on the lined grid give more help when drawing.	The sugar cube was invented in 1841 by Jakub Kryštof Rad in Dacice, Bohemia (now in the Czech Republic). At this time, sugar was produced in a large, solid cone shape and had to be cut for the customer. Rad invented the sugar cube after his wife cut her finger slicing the sugar. Sugar cubes first appeared in shops in Vienna in 1843. A granite monument of a sugar cube stands in the town square in Dacice. There is a picture of the monument at http://www.radio.cz/pictures/czech/dacice_cukr.jpg

Alternative approach

Use the cubes of a construction kit to build solids that students then draw. It could well be worth practising drawing copies of shapes as in questions **2** and **3** of the students' book, but the real challenge comes when they draw in 2D what they make and handle in 3D.

If the scale of the drawings is such that each edge of the cubes is just the side of one triangle on the isometric paper, then the drawings will be small. They could be scaled up by counting two or three triangles for one unit of edge length.

Checkpoint

1 Using a piece of isometric paper, draw a cube of side length 4 (diagonal) squares.

   On the same piece of paper, draw a cuboid of dimensions (side lengths) of your own choice.

   Compare your drawings with your neighbour's drawings.

Starter – Quick fire

Recap basic number work and include questions on fractions, decimals and percentages and questions using mental and written computation. Ask rapid response questions. Students reply by writing on their mini whiteboards. Discuss questions when their answers indicate a need.

Teaching notes

Draw three cubes on dotted isometric paper – two of them $2 \times 2 \times 2$, the other $3 \times 3 \times 3$. Students explain why one of them is different. Give pairs of students enough interlocking cubes to make the $2 \times 2 \times 2$ cube. Point out that, on the drawings, three directions represent with the width, length and height of the cubes – with the height being vertical and the width and length following the diagonal directions.

Issue isometric paper and ask students to orientate it the same way as the drawings of the cubes. Point out that, when correct, there are vertical lines on the grid but no horizontal lines. Ask students to describe what the grid looks like when incorrect. Ensure all have it the correct way before drawing.

Demonstrate on the isometric grid how to draw a shape other than a cube. Students follow the steps on their own paper. Now show how shading can be used to distinguish between the 'top', 'left side' and 'right side' as in 'Simplification' above.

Plenary

Show a 3D shape drawn on isometric paper. Ask how many faces can be seen. Using the convention for shading as described in 'Simplification' above, ask what shading should be used on each face.

As another task, students use isometric paper to draw as many 3D shapes that use five unit cubes. They shade the faces.

Exercise commentary

Questions 1 and **2** – Contrast the free-hand drawings of question **1** with the isometric drawings of question **2**. Ask which method is quicker and which is the more accurate representation.

Question 3 – Students draw copies on isometric paper of shapes without a background grid.

Question 4 – Students need to visualise each shape's side elevation to decide which has the smallest area.

Answers

1 Check students' work against the drawings in Student Book
2 Check students' work
3 **a** 4
   b Check students' work
   c Discuss with students
4 Discuss with students

Objectives	
• Use 2D representations to visualise 3D shapes	(L6)

Key ideas	Resources
1 A net is a 2D plan of a 3D shape 2 A 3D shape can have several different nets	Nets of 3D shapes (1106) Various types of packaging to disassemble Various solid 3D shapes Square grid paper and pre-cut nets Scissors, rulers and sticky tape or glue Commercial construction kits

Simplification	Extension
Students can investigate 3D shapes by using: • nets already made for them • commercial construction kits that click together • transparent 3D shapes that allow students to see the back from the front • commercial cartons and packaging that they can disassemble.	Students cut out the nets created in question **2** and make the two 3D shapes. For all the 3D shapes they have made, students count the number of faces, F, vertices, V and edges, E and record them in a table with five columns labelled: Name of shape, F, V, E and F + V − E. The students discover an unusual result (that the last column is always 2).

Literacy	Links
The family of *prisms* has members all of which have cross-sections which are constant along their lengths. When the cross-section is rectangular, the prism is a *cuboid*. When it is circular, the prism is a cylinder. When it is triangular, the prism can be a *wedge*. The family of *pyramids* all have cross-sections that decrease to a point. When the base of the pyramid is circular, the pyramid is a *cone*. The pyramids in Egypt have square-based pyramids.	Nets of shapes have immense practical and commercial significance in packaging, which in turn has implications for waste management and care of the environment. There is a collection of nets for paper models of complex solids at http://www.korthalsaltes.com/index.html

Alternative approach
The disassembling of packaging and the assembling of pre-cut nets are important experiences in helping students visualise 3D shapes. In addition, there are various commercial construction kits of plastic 2D shapes that clip together easily to make 3D shapes. This website also provides various nets that can be printed ready for construction: http://www.senteacher.org/Worksheet/12/3D.html

Checkpoint
1 Using a piece of squared paper, draw the net for a cube of side length 5 squares. Now cut it out and fold it up to make the cube.   (Check students' nets.) 2 Using a piece of squared paper, draw the net for a cuboid of side lengths 5 squares by 6 squares by 4 squares. Now cut it out and fold to make the cuboid.   (Check students' cuboids.)

Starter – Quick fire

Recap basic number work and include questions on fractions, decimals and percentages and questions using mental and written computation. Ask rapid response questions. Students reply by writing on their mini whiteboards. Discuss questions when their answers indicate a need.

Teaching notes

Show students an empty cereal box and discuss how it is manufactured. Disassemble it and show that it is made from a flat piece of card folded to make the 3D shape. Explain that this flat shape will need to include all surfaces and discuss what shape and size these will be. There is also the need for overlapping tabs that are used to stick the box together.

Students disassemble boxes of various kinds. Introduce the name **net** for the flat 2D shape and explain that, strictly, the net does not include the tabs used to stick the edges together. Point out the equal faces and edges indicating clearly the edges that meet up when folded.

Show students another 3D shape and discuss what its net will look like. Explain the need to include each surface. Students name the shapes of the different faces and find how many of each shape will be equal.

Plenary

Show students four 'nets' and ask them to identify the one that will *not* create a cube. The students then draw a different net of a cube on their mini whiteboards. (There are 11 of these nets in all). Compare results.

Exercise commentary

Question 1 – Students will need to count squares on the faces of the 3D shapes to help them match the nets of the cuboids to 3D shapes.

Question 2 – This demands careful counting of squares to make accurate copies of the half-nets.

Question 3 – This may be done by imagining the triangular faces folding around the square bases. Otherwise, students may need to make the nets.

Answers

1 a 5   b 2   c 4
   d 6   e 3   f 1

2 Check students' drawings. Square-based pyramid and triangular prism

3 Net **B**

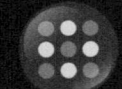

Objectives	
• Calculate the surface area of cubes and cuboids	(L6)

Key ideas	Resources	
1 The surface area of a cuboid is the total of the areas of its six faces 2 The surface area of a cuboid is the same as the area of its net	⊞ Nets, surface area Cuboids of various sizes Square grid paper; plain paper	(1107)

Simplification	Extension
Students record their working methodically. For example: Top = base × height = 3 cm × 4 cm = 12 cm² Bottom = 12 cm² Left side = base × height = 4 cm × 5 cm = 20 cm² Right side = 20 cm² etc. Or use labels A =…, B = …, etc., so that all surfaces can be accounted for.	Students measure the faces of various commercial boxes that have the shape of cuboids. They then calculate the surface area of each box.

Literacy	Links
3D shapes with curved surfaces also have surface area. Some ice-cream cones are made from cardboard. It would be interesting for students to see such a cone opened out so that the surface area is seen to come from a sector of a circle. A sphere also has a surface area. Students might have ideas about how to find it (such as sticking small squares on it). Mention that the Earth is a sphere and that also has a surface area – we live on it!	Human skin has a total surface area of about 1.8 m^2. It accounts for between 15% and 20% of the total weight of the human body and helps to protect the body from the environment. It helps keep body fluids in and water and germs out and it constantly renews itself. Over 90% of common house dust is made up of dead skin cells. There is more information about human skin at http://yucky.discovery.com/flash/body/pg000146.html

Alternative approach
a) Nets make only hollow cuboids. A solid cuboid cannot be made from a net. To find the surface area of a solid cuboid, stand each face of the cuboid on cm² paper, line up the edges with the grid, draw round the edges and then cut out each face. Discuss that equal faces can be paired. Calculate the area of each and hence the surface area. Plain paper can be used instead of cm² paper. The faces have then to be measured with a ruler. Essentially, it is the same method as with a net, but it is worth making the distinction between a hollow shape and a solid shape. b) Distinguish the three pairs of opposite faces of a cuboid by colouring the pairs in different colours. If a commercial construction kit is used, this can be easily achieved. Then ask for the areas of the six rectangular faces, but ask for them in pairs, colour by colour.

Checkpoint
1 What is the surface area of a cuboid that measures 4 cm by 5 cm by 2 cm? $(2 \times 4 \times 5 + 2 \times 4 \times 2 + 2 \times 5 \times 2 = 76 \text{ cm}^2)$

Starter – Quick fire

Recap basic number work and include questions on fractions, decimals and percentages and questions using mental and written computation. Ask rapid response questions. Students reply by writing on their mini whiteboards. Discuss questions when their answers indicate a need.

Teaching notes

Show a cuboid and discuss how much paper would be required to wrap it without any overlaps. State that the students are finding the **surface area** of the cuboid, which is the **total area of all the surfaces of a cuboid**.

Show the cuboid from the student book and discuss how to calculate the area of each surface. Use words such as 'top', 'front' and 'side'. Point out that, for each face, there is an identical face, so that each area of a face can be used twice.

Discuss the net of the cuboid and that each face of the cuboid becomes part of the net. Demonstrate how the area of the net is equal to the surface area of the cuboid. So, one way to find the surface area of a cuboid is to find the area of its net.

Plenary

Show various nets with straightforward dimensions. Students calculate the surface area of each cuboid that they form.

Show various cuboids with straightforward dimensions. Students calculate the surface area of each of them.

They write their working and answers on their mini whiteboards. Discuss their responses where necessary.

A cube (stress the word 'cube') has a surface area of 24 cm². Students calculate the dimensions of the cube. (2 cm × 2 cm × 2 cm)

Exercise commentary

Question 1 – Encourages students to visualise the hidden faces of a cuboid before calculating its surface area.

Question 2 – Students calculate the surface area of a cube or cuboid from its net.

Question 3 – Students have to imagine all the faces of each cuboid (or draw the net) to calculate the surface area from a drawing.

Question 4 – Requires students to find the dimensions of the cuboid before finding its surface area.

Question 5 – This can be done in pairs.

Answers

1 **a** D   **b** A   **c** E
  d 52 cm^2 **e** 52 cm^2
2 **a** 24 cm^2 **b** 10 cm^2 **c** 32 cm^2
  d 16 cm^2 **e** 28 cm^2
3 **a** 34 cm^2 **b** 38 cm^2 **c** 24 cm^2
4 56 cm^2
5 **a** $2 \times 2 \times 3, 1 \times 2 \times 6, 1 \times 1 \times 12, 1 \times 3 \times 4$
  b $2 \times 2 \times 3$

Objectives

- Calculate volumes of cuboids and shapes made from cuboids (L6)

Key ideas	Resources
1 The volume of an object is measured by how much space it occupies 2 Volume is measured in centimetres cubed (cm³) or metres cubed (m³)	Volume of cuboids (1137) At least 24 unit cubes for each student or pair of students

Simplification	Extension
If students cannot find the volume from a diagram of a shape, then they can build the shape from the unit cubes provided and count the cubes that they use.	Referring to the 'Teaching notes' below, students tabulate their results for cuboids of volume 24 cm³ using headings of length, width and height. Can they see a link between the dimensions of the various cuboids and their volumes?

Literacy	Links
This book generally uses the words '3D shapes' rather than '3D solids', as the shapes may be either solid or hollow. If they are hollow, they may well be used as containers for liquids. Students need to know the difference in meaning between *volume* and *capacity*, even though they are both measured using the same units. A solid has a volume, such as the volume of an iron bar or a brick. A container has a capacity, such as the capacity of a petrol tank or a bath.	The largest building in the world by volume is the Boeing aircraft factory at Everett, Washington in the USA. The volume of the building is 13 300 000 m³ and it has a floor area of 398 000 m² or 98 acres. There is more information about the factory at http://www.boeing.com/commercial/facilities/index.html

Alternative approach

The approach used in the Example and question **3** in the student book is worth spending time on, as it provides the foundation for the formula used to find the volume of a cuboid.

As a whole-class activity, have pairs of students build identical rectangular layers of interlocking cubes, preferably with each layer in one colour and different layers in different colours. Acknowledge that the volume of one layer is the number of cubes that make the layer. By placing layer upon layer, build up a multi-layered 3D solid. Discuss how to find its volume.

The capacity of various near-cuboid containers such as juice cartons can be found by (a) reading the label, (b) filling the container and pouring the water into a measuring jug (from the science department), and (c) from making a layer of 1 cm³ cubes to be the same size as the base of the juice carton and then putting layer upon layer to build up the height. How do these three methods of finding the capacity of the carton (or the volume of juice in a full carton) compare?

Checkpoint

1 The base of a cuboid is 4 cm by 5 cm and it is 6 cm high.

How many centimetre cubes can fit inside the box? (120)

Starter – Quick fire

Recap basic number work and include questions on fractions, decimals and percentages and questions using mental and written computation. Ask rapid response questions. Students reply by writing on their mini whiteboards. Discuss questions when their answers indicate a need.

Teaching notes

Provide students with at least 24 unit cubes per student or per pair of students. They build a cuboid from 24 cubes.

Collate the dimensions of their different cuboids under the headings: length, width, height.

State that the **volume** of each cuboid is the same and ask students to define the term 'volume'. Agree that volume is a measure of the space that a 3D object occupies. Introduce the cm³ and m³ as standard units of measurement.

Show a different cuboid. Students find its volume by counting how many unit cubes it contains. Point out that the number of cubes in the top layer can be seen but other layers have hidden cubes. Agree that each layer has the same number of cubes as the top layer. Demonstrate that multiplying the number of cubes in the top layer by the number of layers gives the total number of cubes in the whole cuboid – and that this is its volume.

Plenary

Show students several cuboids with straightforward dimensions. On their mini whiteboards for each cuboid, they write (a) the number of cubes in one layer, (b) the number of layers and (c) the volume of the cuboid. Discuss the results.

Extend students by building up to the formula for volume of a cuboid. Ask how they can find the number of cubes in one layer from the length and width of the cuboid. Agree that one layer = length × width.

Ask how they can find the number of layers from the length, width and height of the cuboid. Agree that the height gives the number of layers, so:

Volume of a cuboid = one layer × height

= length × width × height.

Show them several straightforward cuboids. Students write the volume on their mini whiteboards.

Exercise commentary

Questions 1 and **2** – Students count the cubes of these irregular single-layer 3D shapes.

Question 3 – Students find the volume of the given cuboids by counting the cubes in one layer and then multiplying this by the number of layers.

Question 4 – The volume of shape **D** is ambiguous because you cannot tell if there is a cube in the bottom far corner. However, whether there is or is not, the shape does not need ten cubes.

Question 5 – The diagram no longer shows the centimetre cubes and the student has to imagine the layers.

Answers

1 a 5 cm³   b 10 cm³   c 10 cm³
   d 12 cm³   e 14 cm³   f 10 cm³
2 a 11 cm³   b 12 cm³   c 20 cm³
3 a 4 cm³   b 8 cm³   c 12 cm³
   d 18 cm³   e 24 cm³   f 36 cm³
4 Shapes **B**, **C** and **D**
5 2400

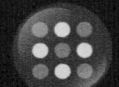

Key outcomes	Quick check
Recognise and name 3D shapes. L4	What is the mathematical name for the shape of a tin of baked beans? (Cylinder)
Use isometric drawings to visualise 3D shapes. L5	Using isometric paper, draw a cuboid. How many edges does it have? (8)
Use nets of 3D shapes. L5	Draw the net of a cuboid 4 cm by 5 cm by 2 cm.
Find the surface area of cubes and cuboids. L5	What is the surface area of the cuboid you have just drawn the net for? $(2 \times 4 \times 5 + 2 \times 4 \times 2 + 2 \times 5 \times 2 = 76 \text{ cm}^2)$
Find the volume of a 3D shape by counting cubes. L5	How many centimetre cubes can fit inside this cuboid ? $(2 \times 4 \times 5 = 40 \text{ cm}^3)$

⊞ MyMaths extra support

Lesson/online homework	Description
Plans elevations 1098 L6	Drawing plan, side and front views of 3D objects

My Review

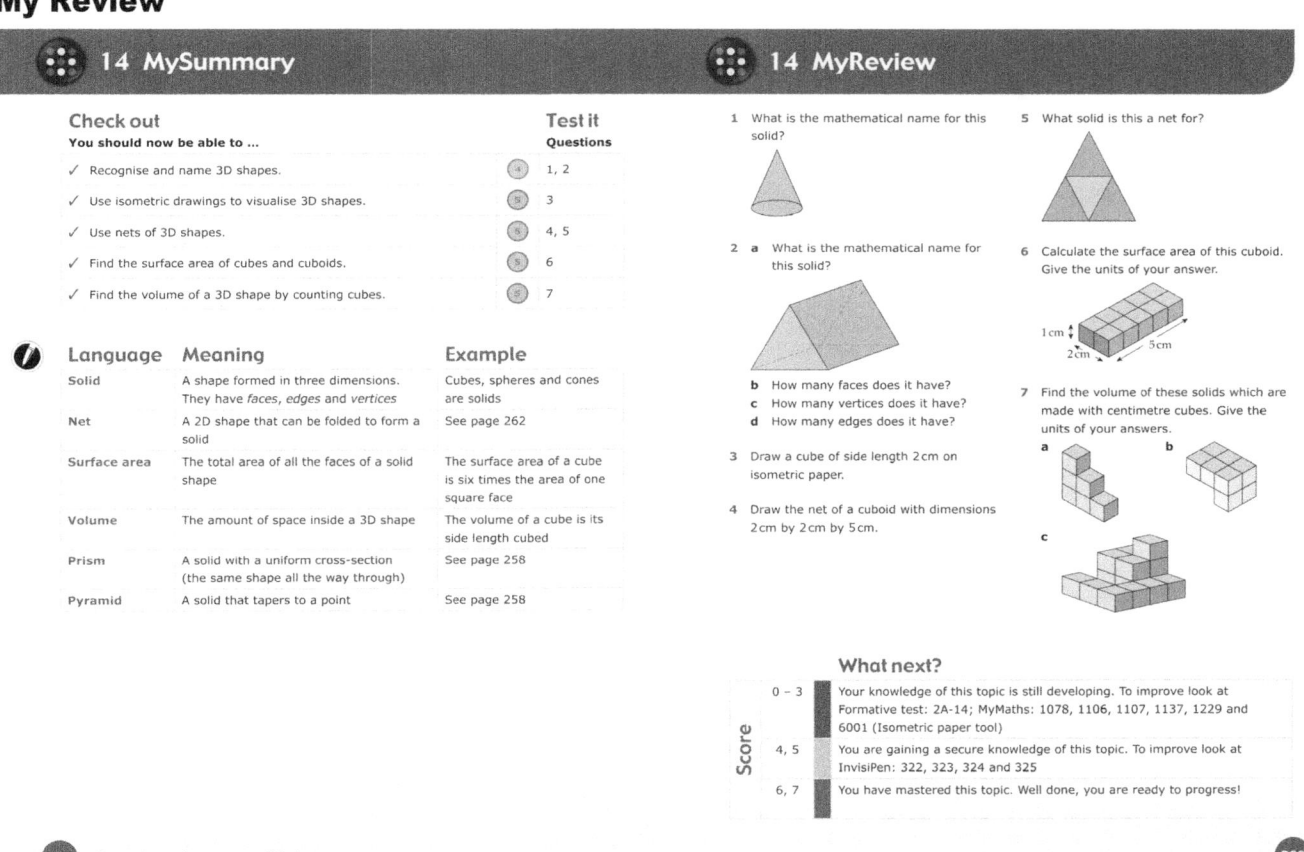

Check out
You should now be able to ...

	Test it Questions
✓ Recognise and name 3D shapes.	1, 2
✓ Use isometric drawings to visualise 3D shapes.	3
✓ Use nets of 3D shapes.	4, 5
✓ Find the surface area of cubes and cuboids.	6
✓ Find the volume of a 3D shape by counting cubes.	7

Language	Meaning	Example
Solid	A shape formed in three dimensions. They have *faces*, *edges* and *vertices*	Cubes, spheres and cones are solids
Net	A 2D shape that can be folded to form a solid	See page 262
Surface area	The total area of all the faces of a solid shape	The surface area of a cube is six times the area of one square face
Volume	The amount of space inside a 3D shape	The volume of a cube is its side length cubed
Prism	A solid with a uniform cross-section (the same shape all the way through)	See page 258
Pyramid	A solid that tapers to a point	See page 258

1 What is the mathematical name for this solid?

2 a What is the mathematical name for this solid?

   b How many faces does it have?
   c How many vertices does it have?
   d How many edges does it have?

3 Draw a cube of side length 2 cm on isometric paper.

4 Draw the net of a cuboid with dimensions 2 cm by 2 cm by 5 cm.

5 What solid is this a net for?

6 Calculate the surface area of this cuboid. Give the units of your answer.

7 Find the volume of these solids which are made with centimetre cubes. Give the units of your answers.
   a   b
   c

What next?

Score	
0 – 3	Your knowledge of this topic is still developing. To improve look at Formative test: 2A-14; MyMaths: 1078, 1106, 1107, 1137, 1229 and 6001 (Isometric paper tool)
4, 5	You are gaining a secure knowledge of this topic. To improve look at InvisiPen: 322, 323, 324 and 325
6, 7	You have mastered this topic. Well done, you are ready to progress!

Question commentary

Questions 1 and **2** – Students may need reminding of terminology.

Question 3 – Students may find it easier to draw a cube of 2 units long rather than 2 cm.

Question 4 – Students can compare answers and check by cutting out the net and folding it up.

Question 5 – Students can check by drawing out the net and folding it to create the 3D shape.

Question 6 – Students may find it helpful to draw out the net first.

Question 7 – Students may need help visualising the cubes that are hidden in the diagram.

Answers

1 a cone/circular-based pyramid
2 a triangular prism
  b 5   c 6
  d 9

3 Check accuracy of students' diagram
4 Check 2 lots of 2×2, 4 lots of 5×2 and 2 lots of 5×5, squares/rectangles and that it will fold into a cuboid
5 Triangular-based pyramid/tetrahedron
6 34 cm^2
7 a 6 cm^3 b 8 cm^3 c 15 cm^3

14 MyPractice

1 Copy and complete the following table, giving information about these 3D shapes.

Name	3D shape	Faces	Vertices	Edges
Cube	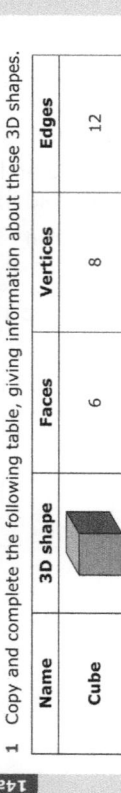	6	8	12
Cuboid				
Cylinder				
Triangular Prism				

2 Sketch these 3D shapes on isometric paper.

a b c

3 On square grid paper, draw the net of these solid shapes.

a b c

4 These cuboids are made from centimetre cubes.
Find the **surface area** of each cuboid.

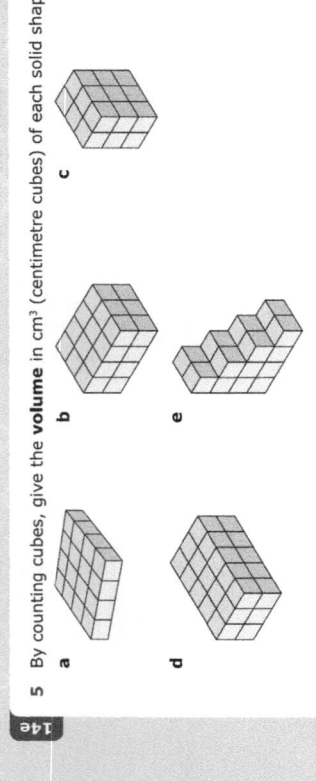

a b c

5 By counting cubes, give the **volume** in cm³ (centimetre cubes) of each solid shape.

a b c

d e

Question commentary

Question 1 – The cylinder can give rise to discussion. Can a face be curved? Can an edge be curved?

Questions 2 and **3** – Encourage students to compare answers.

Question 4 – Students can draw nets to help.

Question 5 – In part **e** students may need to break the shape down into layers.

Answers

1. 6, 8, 12
   6, 8, 12
   3, 0, 2
   5, 6, 9
2. Check accuracy
3. Check accuracy
4. **a** 76 cm^3 **b** 52 cm^3 **c** 90 cm^3
5. **a** 16 cm^3 **b** 24 cm^3 **c** 18 cm^3
   d 30 cm^3 **e** 20 cm^3

Related lessons		Resources	
3D shapes	14a	3D shapes	(1078)
		2D and 3D shapes	(1229)
		Cubes and cuboids	
		Old newspapers or magazines	

Simplification	Extension
Prepared templates could be used for task **2**. Encourage students to complete one very good drawing rather than trying to complete too many of the tasks in the time available.	Students could look in old magazines or newspapers for examples of pictures that show single or two point perspective. They could draw guidelines on the pictures to find their vanishing points and eye-lines. Whilst searching for these, ask them to look out for pictures that seem to have more than two vanishing points. They might come across some such as looking upwards at an edge on a skyscraper that show tapering of the vertical edges as well as the horizontal ones. Students could also research the use of reverse perspective, where the exact opposite of perspective happens and the vanishing point would be behind or on the person viewing the picture rather than its more natural position in the distance away from the viewer.

Links

Design and technology uses perspective drawing when creating designs for objects to be manufactured. Links can be made to other types of technical drawing and the rationale behind them. Consider the need for such drawing techniques. http://en.wikipedia.org/wiki/Technical_drawing

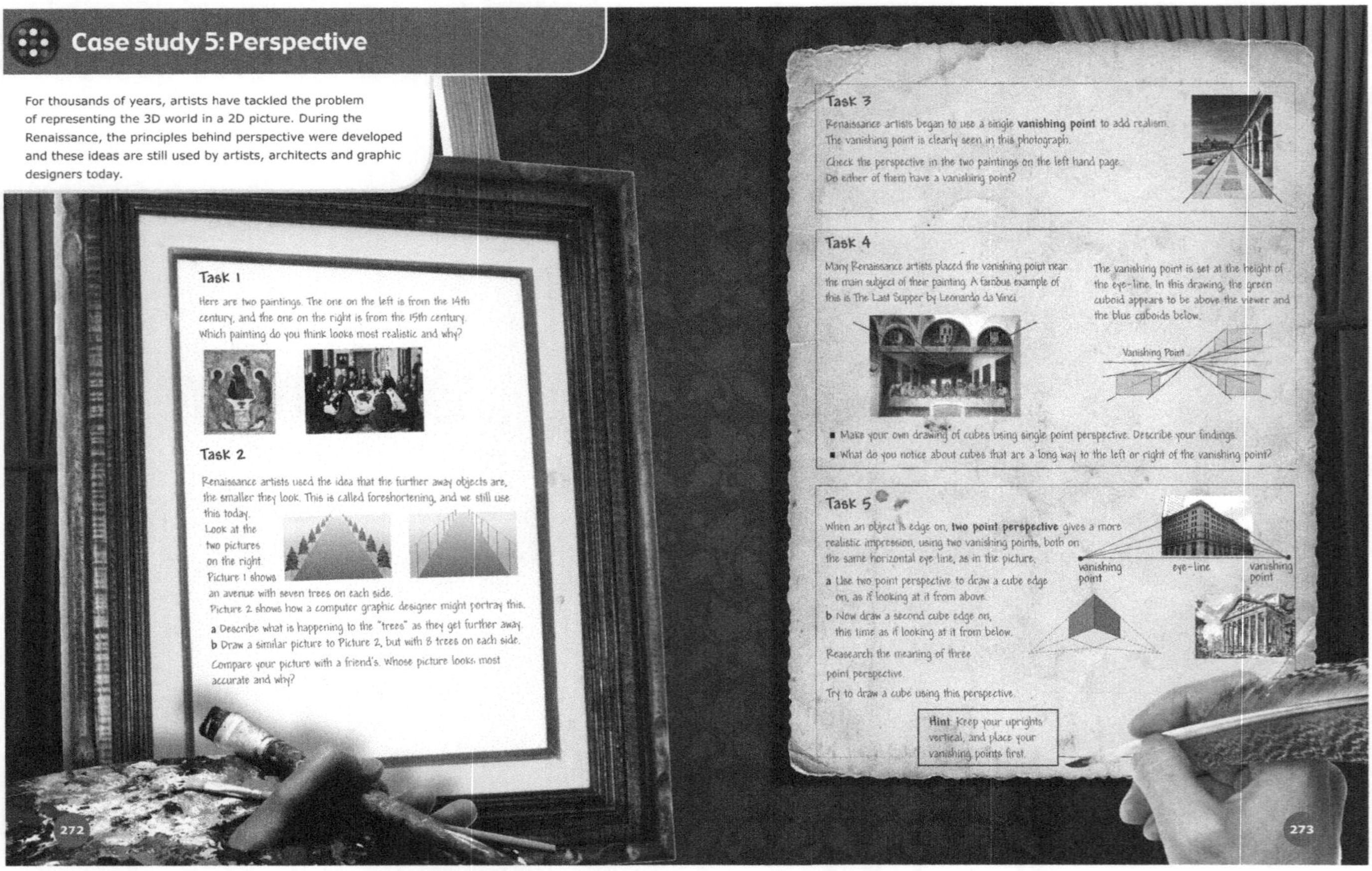

Case study 5: Perspective

For thousands of years, artists have tackled the problem of representing the 3D world in a 2D picture. During the Renaissance, the principles behind perspective were developed and these ideas are still used by artists, architects and graphic designers today.

Task 1

Here are two paintings. The one on the left is from the 14th century, and the one on the right is from the 15th century. Which painting do you think looks most realistic and why?

Task 2

Renaissance artists used the idea that the further away objects are, the smaller they look. This is called foreshortening, and we still use this today.

Look at the two pictures on the right.

Picture 1 shows an avenue with seven trees on each side.

Picture 2 shows how a computer graphic designer might portray this.

a Describe what is happening to the "trees" as they get further away.

b Draw a similar picture to Picture 2, but with 8 trees on each side.

Compare your picture with a friend's. Whose picture looks most accurate and why?

Task 3

Renaissance artists began to use a single **vanishing point** to add realism. The vanishing point is clearly seen in this photograph.

Check the perspective in the two paintings on the left hand page. Do either of them have a vanishing point?

Task 4

Many Renaissance artists placed the vanishing point near the main subject of their painting. A famous example of this is The Last Supper by Leonardo da Vinci.

The vanishing point is set at the height of the eye-line. In this drawing, the green cuboid appears to be above the viewer and the blue cuboids below.

Vanishing Point

■ Make your own drawing of cubes using single point perspective. Describe your findings.

■ What do you notice about cubes that are a long way to the left or right of the vanishing point?

Task 5

When an object is edge on, **two point perspective** gives a more realistic impression, using two vanishing points, both on the same horizontal eye line, as in the picture.

vanishing point — eye-line — vanishing point

a Use two point perspective to draw a cube edge on, as if looking at it from above.

b Now draw a second cube edge on, this time as if looking at it from below.

Research the meaning of three point perspective.

Try to draw a cube using this perspective.

Hint Keep your uprights vertical, and place your vanishing points first.

Teaching notes

During the Renaissance period (from the 14th century to the 17th century), artists strived to produce paintings that gave a more realistic representation of the world than had been the case in many paintings prior to the Renaissance period. In the Renaissance, artists became interested in using perspective to represent 3D objects in a 2D picture in a way that showed them as they were seen in the real world.

Talk about the Renaissance period and look together at the two paintings shown on the left hand page. Remind students that both pictures are painted on a flat 2D surface and are trying to show a 3D world. Ask them which one they think is more realistic and how this realism is created.

Task 1

Discuss angles in the pictures. In the right hand picture, lines that lie along the sight line and would be parallel in the real world are shown converging to a common point. In the left hand picture, the angle of the seat and the platforms under the feet are tapering in an unnatural looking manner, as are some parts of the building in the background. Discuss how sizes are used to create depth in the right hand picture. People in the foreground are shown slightly larger than those further away, windows that are closer are taller than those that are further away, etc. In comparison, the left hand picture looks almost flat, even though there are things in the background.

Task 2

Students will need to create the 'framework' onto which to put their trees. They should ensure that they consider the vanishing point along the sight lines.

Task 3

Talk about the vanishing point and look again at the original two paintings to see if either of those have a vanishing point (you should find that the right hand painting does). Discuss how the vanishing point is on the eye-line and how the angles converge from above for things that are above the eye-line and from below for things below the eye-line.

Task 4

Look at the diagram of cuboids and discuss with the students how to draw diagrams with single point perspective. Establish that, to draw a cube, you would set an eye-line and vanishing point and then draw the front face as a square. Then you would draw guidelines from the corners of this face to the vanishing point and use these to help construct the diagram. Give students time to draw their own diagram of cubes, positioning at least one above the eye-line

and using different amounts of horizontal offset either side of the vanishing point.

Task 5

Discuss how, when the building is viewed edge on, the two walls either side of the edge appear to taper away in different directions to form two vanishing points that lie on the same eye-line. Discuss how you would use two point perspective to draw a cube edge on and give the students some time to make their own drawings as described.

Answers

1   The 15th century painting looks more realistic. The people in the foreground look larger than the people in the background.

2   **a**   The trees get smaller

    b   Students' own answers

3   Yes, the right hand one

4   Students' own answers

5   Students' own answers

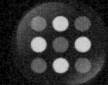

Learning outcomes

R3	Express one quantity as a fraction of another, where the fraction is less than 1 and greater than 1	(L5)
R4	Use ratio notation, including reduction to simplest form	(L5)
R5	Divide a given quantity in two parts in a given part : part or part : whole ratio; express the division of a quantity into two parts as a ratio	(L5)
R7	Understand that a multiplicative relationship between two quantities can be expressed as a ratio or a fraction	(L5)
R8	Solve problems involving percentage change, including: percentage increase, decrease and original value problems and simple interest in financial mathematics	(L5)

Introduction

This chapter starts with simplify ratios and dividing into ratios. An introduction to proportion is followed by sections on solving proportion problems and problems that mix ratio and proportion. The chapter moves on to looking at comparing proportions as fractions or percentages before finishing with a section on calculations involving money.

The idea of creating things which are in proportion is vital to art and architecture. However there is one number, called the 'Golden Proportion', which is supposed to be the most pleasing to the eye.

The Golden Proportion relates to a rectangle whose ratio of length to width is 1.6180339887 : 1. There is evidence that the ancient Greeks and Egyptians used this proportion in the design of many of their buildings, and Renaissance artists used it commonly in their paintings.

Prior knowledge

Students should already know how to…

* Identify factors and multiples
* Convert between fractions, decimals and percentages
* Calculate simple percentages of an amount

Starter problem

Students should be encouraged to collect their own data on height and head circumference as well as the sizes of other body parts (which could link to work in statistics). This data can then be used to quantify various ratios and proportions. Opportunities can be taken to emphasize the need to use common units and how to draw scale drawings. Posing the question 'In an accurate 10 cm tall model of an adult, how big should the head be?' allows a discussion of dividing in a given ratio. Similar modelling questions can be used to introduce direct proportion.

Students could investigate the age dependence of measurements. What are the percentage changes in the size of body parts as people grow? How should you compare relative proportions? At birth a baby is about four heads tall but only $7\frac{1}{2}$ heads tall as an adult.

The theory of art contains several examples of the ideal proportions for bodies and faces. How do you quantify these proportions and how realistic are they? One famous example is da Vinci's version of Vitruvian man. Manga comics illustrate the effect of modifying ratios.

Resources

🌐 MyMaths

Fractions of amounts	1018	Percentages of amounts 2	1031	Proportion unitary method	1036
Proportion	1037	Ratio dividing 1	1038	Ratio dividing 2	1039
Ratio introduction	1052	Best buys and value for money			1243

Online assessment

Chapter test	2A–15
Formative test	2A–15
Summative test	2A–15

InvisiPen solutions

Calculator methods	129	Simplify and use ratio	191
Simple ratio and proportion	192	Comparing proportions	194

Topic scheme

Teaching time = 7 lessons/3 weeks

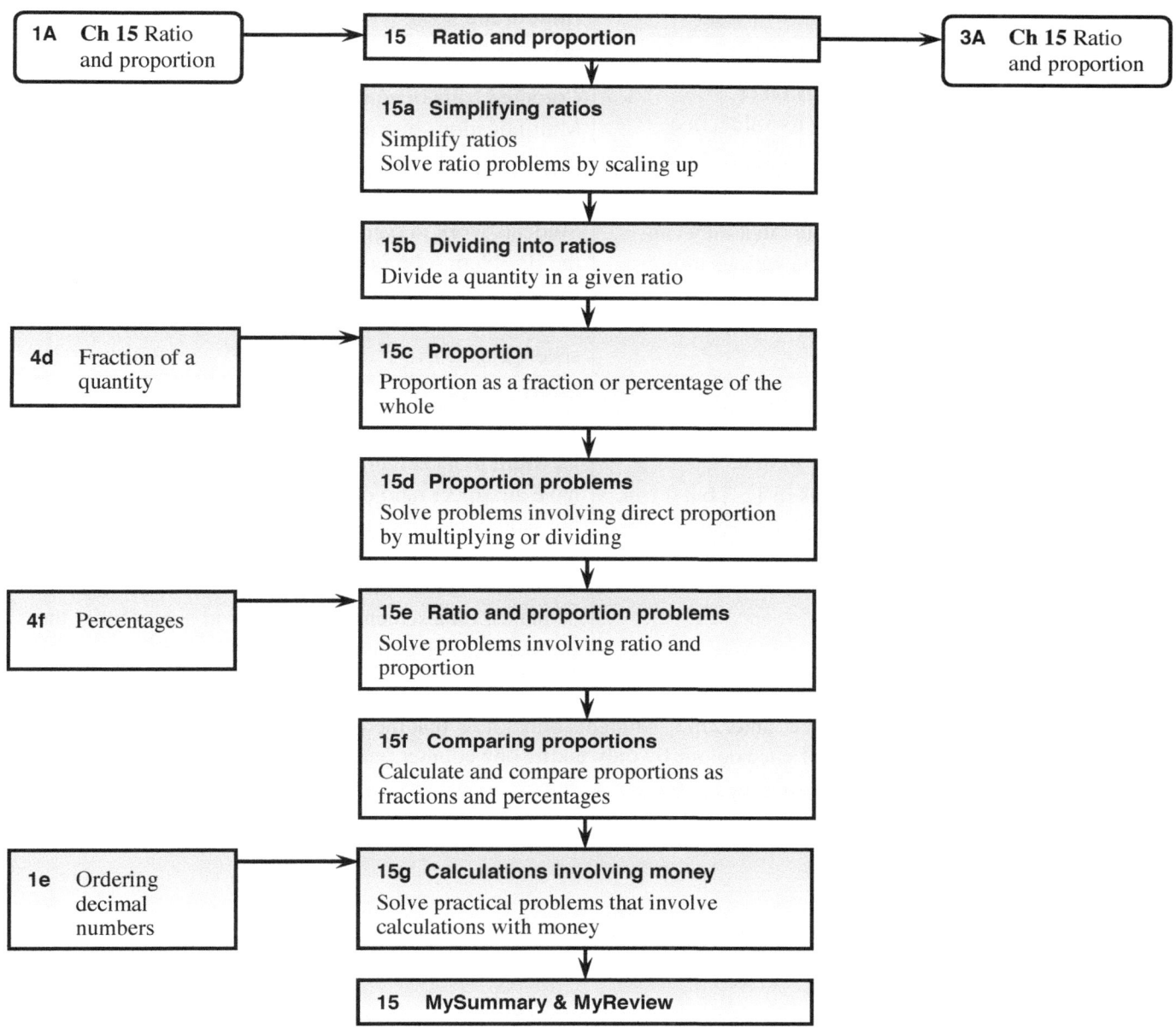

| 1A | Ch 15 Ratio and proportion |

| 15 | Ratio and proportion |

| 3A | Ch 15 Ratio and proportion |

15a Simplifying ratios

Simplify ratios
Solve ratio problems by scaling up

15b Dividing into ratios

Divide a quantity in a given ratio

| 4d | Fraction of a quantity |

15c Proportion

Proportion as a fraction or percentage of the whole

15d Proportion problems

Solve problems involving direct proportion by multiplying or dividing

| 4f | Percentages |

15e Ratio and proportion problems

Solve problems involving ratio and proportion

15f Comparing proportions

Calculate and compare proportions as fractions and percentages

| 1e | Ordering decimal numbers |

15g Calculations involving money

Solve practical problems that involve calculations with money

15 MySummary & MyReview

Differentiation

Student book 2A   274 – 293

Simplifying ratios
Dividing into ratios
Proportion
Proportion problems
Ratio and proportion problems
Comparing proportions
Calculations involving money

Student book 2B   266 – 283

Ratio
Division in a given ratio
Direct proportion
Ratio and proportion
Percentage increase and decrease
Comparing proportions

Student book 2C   268 – 285

Ratio
Division in a given ratio
Direct proportion
Ratio and proportion
Comparing proportions
Algebra and proportion

Objectives

- Use ratio notation and simplify ratios   (L5)

Key ideas	Resources
1 A ratio is often written using a colon, such as 1 : 2 2 A ratio can be simplified by division or multiplication without changing its value, in a similar way to fractions	⊞ Ratio introduction (1052) Coloured balls or equivalent Multiplication square

Simplification	Extension
Students have counters in two colours that they can physically divide up according to the various ratios being described. Provide more visual examples like those in question **1** before moving to the more abstract concepts in question **2**.	Students work in pairs to invent similar questions to the 'Problem solving' question **5**. They consider problems such as 'Divide £30 in the ratio 2 : 1 (for every pound that Bob gets, his older sister gets £2)'.

Literacy	Links
The word *ratio* was first used with its mathematical meaning in England over 350 years ago. A ratio is written using the colon, as in 1 : 2 but it can be written as '1 to 2'.	The aspect ratio of a screen or an image is the ratio of its width to its height. HD televisions and monitors have an aspect ratio of 16 : 9 (also known as 1.78 : 1) but older style screens have an aspect ratio of 4 : 3 (1.33 : 1). Common cinema film ratios are 1.85 : 1 and 2.35 : 1. When an image filmed in one aspect ratio is displayed on a screen with a different aspect ratio, the image has to be either cropped or distorted.

Alternative approach

Have a bag with 25 red and 75 blue counters in it. Students only know that there are 100 counters in two colours. The problem is to find how many of each colour by only taking one counter out at any time.

Select a counter, record its colour and return it to the bag. Repeat a total of 5 times. Enter the results in a table. For example, if 2 red and 3 blue are selected in the first 5 turns, the table reads:

	Red : Blue	1 : n
After 5 turns	2 : 3	1 : 1.5
After 10 turns		1 :
After 20 turns		1 :

Continue and record results after 10, 20, 50, 100, … turns. Each time, find the ratio in the form 1 : n by division. See if the 1 : n ratio settles down and ask students how many reds and blues they think there are in the bag. Check by emptying the bag.

Checkpoint

1 The colour mid purple is made by mixing 3 litres of red paint to 1 litre of blue paint.
   a Does mixing 12 litres of red to 4 litres of blue make mid purple?   (Yes)
   b Does mixing 21 litres of red to 5 litres of blue make mid purple?   (No)

Starter – Amazing digits

Students think of any 2-digit number where the two digits are different; for example, 35.

They reverse the two digits; 53.

They subtract the smaller number from the larger number; 53 – 35 = 18.

They add the answer's two digits together; 1 + 8 = 9.

Repeat with another 2-digit number. What do they notice? (The answer is always 9.)

Extend the task to see if it works with any 3-digit number. If the last step gives a 2-digit answer, then adds those two digits together as an extra step. (It does work!)

Teaching notes

Show students a simple recipe, such as:

2 litres of lemonade
Juice of 6 lemons
1500 ml fizzy water
300 grams sugar.

Discuss how much of each ingredient there needs to be if only 1 litre of lemonade is used. Then if 3 litres of lemonade is used; and if 6 litres is used.

Explore how the recipe can be re-written by increasing (or decreasing) each ingredient at the same rate. In each case, the lemonade will taste exactly the same.

Make the link to *ratio*. Refer to the example in the students book of mixing paint. Point out that:
1) the notation of ratio uses a colon, and
2) the order of the ingredients is critical.
Red : blue is different from *blue : red*.

Demonstrate how to **simplify** a ratio by decreasing both parts of the ratio at the same rate by dividing by the same number. Simplifying in this way will keep the same taste of lemonade and keep the same shade of the colour purple.

Practise finding equivalent ratios by multiplying (or dividing) both parts by the same number.

Students find the solution to problems such as 'If I have two litres of blue and I want to make light purple, how much red will I need? How many litres of light purple will this mixture give me?'

Plenary

Give ratios such as 2 : 3 = 4 : *n*. Students write the value of *n* on their mini whiteboards.

Give ratios such as 4 : 12. Students write the ratio in its simplest terms by using division and show their answers on their mini whiteboards.

Exercise commentary

Questions 1 and **2** – In question **1**, students count the red and blue tins, write the ratio and then simplify it. In question **2**, the ratio is already written for them.

Question 3 – Students take the ratio 2 : 1 for dark purple and find the required equivalent ratio by multiplication.

Question 4 – This is a significantly harder question as it involves increasing parts by a fractional value.

Question 5 – The required strategy is more demanding but the arithmetic is easier than question **4**.

Answers

1. a. mid purple   b. dark purple
   c. dark purple
2. a. dark purple   b. mid purple
   c. dark purple   d. light purple
   e. mid purple   f. dark purple
   g. dark purple   h. light purple
3. a. 6 tins   b. 10 tins   c. 14 tins
4. a. 3 : 2
   b. 8 tins of white and 3 tins of red. For the mixture in **a**, you would need $4\frac{1}{2}$ tins of white to mix with 3 tins of red, so the mixture given will be *lighter*
5. a. 2
   b. 8 yellow beads and 7 blue beads

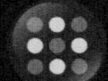

Objectives

- Divide a quantity into two parts in a given ratio (L5)
- Solve simple problems involving ratio and proportion using informal strategies (L5)

Key ideas	Resources
1 A ratio shows the relative sizes of two or more values 2 Find the total number of parts and the value of just one part	Ratio dividing 1 (1038) Ratio dividing 2 (1039) Counters of different colours for support

Simplification	Extension
Students use the method shown in the student book where they systematically increase the ratios and find the total value of all the parts. For example, £3 : £1 gives £4 in total Now × 2 on both sides £6 : £2 gives £8 in total Now × 3 on both sides £9 : £3 gives £12 in total.	Students work with ratios of three individual parts and involve decimal values. For example, repeat question **3** after introducing an extra person, Emma. Alex, Charlie and Emma share the amounts in the ratio 2 : 1 : 3.

Literacy	Links
The word *scale* has many meanings, from a scale pan on a balance, a fish scale, a social scale and the scaling of a mounting. It is also the name of a line with graduated markings on a map. This meaning has the numbering on the line in the correct ratio for measuring distance on the map.	The Golden Ratio occurs in mathematics, art and nature and is calculated as 1 : 1.618 (to 3 dp). It can be used to divide an object into two parts so that the ratio of the smaller part to the larger part is the same as the ratio of the larger part to the whole object. The ratio is used in architecture to produce buildings of aesthetically pleasing proportions. There are pictures of buildings built on the Golden Ratio at http://goldennumber.net/architecture.htm

Alternative approach

Quantities can be divided into more than 2 parts in a given ratio. For example, when the Hooper family go on holiday, their three children get pocket money in proportion to how much help they give by doing jobs at home. Sam, Toni and Una get a total of £84 divided amongst them in the ratio 2 : 1 : 3. How much pocket money did each one get?

The total of the parts is 2 + 1 + 3 = 6.

Divide using short division. Each part is worth £84 ÷ 6 = £14 each

$$\frac{1\ 4}{6\,)\,8^2 4}$$

Multiply for each child. Sam gets 2 × £14 = £28

Toni gets 1 × £14 = £14

For Una, use one of two methods: (a) 3 × £14 = £42; (b) 3 is half of 6, so Una gets half of £84 = £42.

Checkpoint

1 Max and George divide £20 in the ratio 1 : 3.
   a How much money does Max receive? (£5)
   b How much money does George receive? (£15)

Write these percentage calculations.

50% of 28	75% of 30	15% of 70	25% of 90
75% of 20	10% of 350	25% of 56	40% of 30
25% of 60	100% of 35	10% of 120	25% of 42

Students find the answers and match up pairs of answers in the shortest possible time.

Teaching notes

Draw three red squares and one white square. Students give the ratio of red to white. Explain that the ratio compares the two parts, red and white.

Introduce Alex and Charlie from the student book. Work through the first method shown there using the ratio $2 : 1$. Emphasise the methodical recording of **each part** and the **total**.

Introduce the second method (which uses proportion from the next lesson) for the same ratio $2 : 1$. The total number of parts is $2 + 1 = 3$. Alex delivers $\frac{2}{3}$ of the papers and so earns $\frac{2}{3}$ of the money. One third of £9 = £9 ÷ 3 = £3, so two-thirds is $2 \times £3 = £6$. Charlie gets $\frac{1}{3}$ of £9 = £3. (See Chapter 4 for finding a fraction of a quantity.)

Practise this method in different contexts. For example, pink paint is made by mixing red paint and white paint in the ratio of red : white = 1 : 5. How much of each colour is required to make 42 litres of pink?

Students first consider the proportion that each colour is of the total. The total number of parts is $1 + 5 = 6$. So, red is $\frac{1}{6}$ of the total and $\frac{1}{6}$ of 42 is…, whereas white is $\frac{5}{6}$ of the total and $\frac{5}{6}$ of 42 is …, etc.

Plenary

Students share £42 in a number of different ways; for example, in ratios 3 : 4 and 2 : 5 and 1 : 2 : 4. They use the proportion method on their mini whiteboards. Discuss the method and the answers.

Exercise commentary

Questions 1 and **2** – Students divide a number (in question **1**) and an amount (in question **2**) into a given ratio with diagrammatic support. One way is to copy the diagrams and circle what Alex and Charlie have.

Question 3 – No diagrams are given, so the method of finding proportions can be used, where $2 + 1 = 3$ gives a need for thirds.

Questions 4–6 – Extend the problems into different real-life contexts.

Answers

1 Alex 6, Charlie 2
2 Alex £12, Charlie £3
3
a	A £8, C £4		b	A £12, C £6
c	A £16, C £8		d	A £20, C £10
e	A £10, C £5		f	A £200, C £100
g	A £14, C £7		h	A £22, C £11
i	A £42, C £21		j	A £60, C £30
k	A £24, C £12		l	A £50, C £25

4 a 6   b 18
5 3 kg of cement and 15 kg of aggregate
6 a 8 litres   b 12 litres

Objectives

- Understand the relationship between ratio and proportion (L5)
- Recognise the equivalence of percentages, fractions and decimals (L4)

Key ideas

1 Ratio is a comparison between two or more parts of a whole. It is written using a colon
2 Proportion is a comparison between one of the parts with the whole itself. It is written as a fraction (or decimal or percentage).

Resources

⊞ Proportion (1037)

Counters of various colours

Simplification

Students give all proportions only as fractions. Recall that proportion is a comparison of a part with the **whole**. (When the whole is split into 5 parts in the ratio 2 : 3, some students may write a proportion incorrectly as $\frac{2}{3}$ rather than $\frac{2}{5}$.)

Extension

Students give all proportions as fractions, decimals and percentages. Students can also write ratios of the given parts for each question where possible (in question **2**, these are recurring decimal values).

Literacy

Ratio and *proportion* are different. Ratios compare different quantities within a batch, such as red : blue is 2 : 3 within a pile of red and blue beads. Whereas a proportion gives the fraction of one thing as part of the whole. So, $\frac{2}{5}$ of all the beads are red, which is to say that the proportion of the red beads is $\frac{2}{5}$.

Links

For every 100 girls born in the UK, there are around 105 boys. What ratio is this of male to female? What percentage of all babies born in the UK are boys? In 2011 the population of the UK was 31 million males and 32.2 million females. What percentage of the population is male? Why is this different to the percentage at birth? (Life expectancy for females is longer than for males.)

Alternative approach

Have a bag with 25 red and 75 blue counters in it. Students only know that there are 100 counters in two colours. The problem is to find the *proportion* of the bag that is red by only taking one counter out at any time.

Select a counter, record its colour and return it to the bag. Repeat a total of 5 times. Enter the results in a table. For example, if 2 red and 3 blue are selected in the first 5 turns, the table reads:

| | Red | Blue | Total | Proportion that is red | | |
				fraction	decimal	percentage
After 5 turns	2	3	5	$\frac{2}{5}$	0.4	40%
After 10 turns						
After 50 turns						

Continue and record results after 10, 20, 50, 100, ... turns. Each time, find the proportion that is red and write it in three different ways. See if the proportion settles down with increasing turns and ask students how many reds and blues they think there are in the bag. Check by emptying the bag.

Checkpoint

1 There are 20 students in a class. Eight cycle to school.
   a What proportion of the class cycle to school? (8/20 = 2/5 or 0.4 or 40 %)
   b What proportion of the class do not cycle to school? (12/ 20 = 3/5 or 0.6 or 60 %)

Starter – Countdown

Ask students for six numbers: five chosen from 1 to 9, and then either 50 or 100. Write the six numbers for all the class to see.

Throw a dice three times to generate a 3-digit target number.

Students try to reach this target number (or get as close as possible to it) using their six numbers with any of the four basic operations $+$, $-$, $\times$ and $\div$.

Teaching notes

Recall the previous lesson. Show students a number of counters, say three red and seven white. Students give the ratio of red : white and also white : red (that is, 3 : 7 and 7 : 3).

Recall that ratio is used to compare one part with other parts. Introduce the word **proportion** and explain this word is used to compare one part with the **whole**. Students now find the proportion that is red; that is, they compare the number of red counters with the total number of counters and give their answers as a fraction, decimal or percentage. ($\frac{3}{10}$, 0.3, 30%) They repeat for the white counters. ($\frac{7}{10}$, 0.7, 70%)

Describe other contexts, such as class of 25 students having 12 boys and 13 girls (where the total number provides easy calculation of percentages). Each time, students find ratios and proportions. Take time to emphasise the distinction between these two concepts.

When necessary, remind students how to convert fractions to percentages by finding the equivalent fraction with 100 as the denominator.

Plenary

Show a bar chart of eye-colour of a group of friends. Students give the ratio of blue : green : brown.

They also find the proportion of blue eyes as a fraction, decimal and percentage. They repeat for green eyes and for brown eyes.

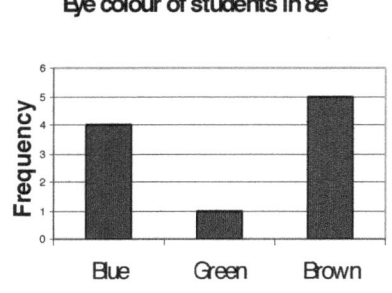

Eye colour of students in 8e

Exercise commentary

Questions 1–4 – These questions give different contexts in which students find proportions of parts of a whole. Throughout the exercise, more confident students should be encouraged to give their answers in fractional, decimal and percentage form.

Question 5 – This gives the proportion (as a percentage) and students calculate the size of parts of the whole.

Answers

1 a $\frac{1}{10}$ b orange   c $\frac{4}{10}$

2 a $\frac{1}{3}$ b $\frac{2}{3}$

3 a $\frac{3}{5}$ b Less than half, as $2\frac{1}{2}$ slices is one half

4 a $\frac{13}{20}$ b $\frac{7}{20}$

5 a 1000   b $\frac{9}{10}$ or 90%   c 10

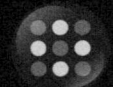
Objectives	
• Use direct proportion in simple contexts	(L5)
• Solve simple problems involving ratio and proportion using informal strategies	(L5)

Key ideas	Resources
1 Direct proportion occurs when two variables increase at the same rate	Proportion unitary method (1036) Proportion (1037) Square grid paper A multiplication square for support

Simplification	Extension
Students firstly consider which two quantities are being compared before setting the information in a diagram and lining up corresponding quantities. They label clearly the multiplier and directional arrows as in the examples in the student book.	Students consider a problem involving inverse proportion; for example, 'It takes 6 people 12 days to build a wall. How long will it take 3 people?' They should use their common sense to judge the reasonableness of their answer.

Literacy	Links
The two most common types of proportion are *direct proportion* and *inverse proportion*. Direct proportion is involved when one variable increases as a linked variable increases at the same rate. Whereas, inverse proportion occurs when one variable decreases as the other increases at the same rate. Offer students pairs of variables and they decide if they are linked by direct or inverse proportion. For example, distance travelled by car and the petrol used; speed on a motorway and the time taken.	As part of the design process for a product, manufacturers draw up a list of all the components incorporated in the assembled product. This is called a parts list. The manufacturer decides how many of the product he is going to build, and then orders the number of parts required. The number he needs is in direct proportion to the number on the parts list. There is are examples of parts lists at http://www.turbocharged.com/catalog/parts_list.html and at http://www.wellsdental.com/Techbull/U801/u801.htm

Alternative approach

a) The rate of increase of the two linked variables is more clearly seen graphically. Consider the cost of various numbers of items. The graph of *direct proportion* is a straight-line graph. For example, the number and cost of certain chocolate bars vary as in this table:

Number	1	2	3	4
Cost, p	80	160	240	320

and, when graphed, this gives a straight line.

b) Question **3** in Exercise **15d** mentions the method of finding the final answer by first finding an intermediate answer for 1 person. This is an example of the *unitary method*. It is useful in problems where a direct one-stage multiplication (or scaling) is awkward.
For example, find the weight of 6 biscuits if 7 biscuits weigh 224 grams.

$$1 \text{ biscuit weighs } 224 \div 7 = 32 \text{ grams (scale down by 7)}$$
$$6 \text{ biscuits weight } 6 \times 32 = 192 \text{ grams (scale up by 6)}$$

A one-stage multiplier from 7 to 6 is not as easy as a two-stage process via '1 biscuit'. Setting out the working as here is equivalent to the arrowed diagrams in the student book.

Checkpoint

1 What is the weight of 4 biscuits if 5 of them weigh 140 grams? (112 grams)

Starter – Grandad Bob

Bob wanted to share £240 between his two grand-children. He decided to give the money in the ratio of their ages. Simon was 12 and Jo was 8.

Find how much money each grandchild would receive. (Simon £144, Jo £96)

However, he decided that he would also include his great-niece, Megan, who is 4 years old. How much does each child receive now? (£120, £80, £40)

Teaching notes

Practise direct proportion by asking oral questions. For example, if a bag of chips cost 90p, how much do 2 bags, 3 bags, 12 bags cost? (£1.80, £2.70, £10.80) Students explain their methods. Point out that the two variables (bags and cost) are in *direct proportion* because they increase at the same rate using the same **multiplier**.

Introduce other examples; for example, 'Two carpenters build 7 wardrobes in a day. How many wardrobes can 6 carpenters build in a day?' (21)

Students specify the variables and set out their work using a diagram with arrows as in the student book. Discuss how to find the multiplier to use with the variables in each case. Remind students to include units in their answers when necessary.

This topic links with the use of scale factors when studying enlargements and scale drawings.

Introduce a problem with a fractional multiplier; for example, if three magazines cost £3.60, how much will five magazines cost?
Point out that there are two methods:

- Find a multiplier (perhaps using a calculator) that multiplies 3 to give 5. The multiplier m has to be such that $3 \times m = 5$. Division will be needed.

- Use the unitary method and find the cost of one magazine as a stepping-stone to five magazines.

Plenary

Present students with several straightforward problems in context that use direct proportion. They work them out mentally and write their answers on mini whiteboards. Discuss as necessary.
Repeat with problems that require simple short division.

Exercise commentary

Questions 1 and **2** – In question **1**, students use a simple multiplier based on a first line of '1 necklace needs 6 beads'. In question **2a**, the reverse is the case, with students using '7 beads make 1 necklace' as a first line.

Question 3 – Part **a** uses simple multipliers (or dividers). Part **b** uses the unitary method.

Question 4 – Parts **a–e** use simple multipliers. Part **f** requires the unitary method.

Question 5 – It may be helpful to use a calculator for parts **a-c**.

Question 6 - Straightforward

Answers

1 a 12   **b** 18   **c** 30
2 a i 2   **ii** 4   **iii** 6
   b i 8   **ii** 4
3 a

Miles	5	10	15	25	50
Kilometres	8	16	24	40	80

b

Tickets	1	2	3	4	5	6
Cost	7.5	15	22.5	30	37.5	45

4 a £24   **b** £6   **c** £25
   d £3.50   **e** £4   **f** 1200 g
5 a 96p   **b** $7.40   **c** £31.20   **d** 96p
6 6 potatoes, 3 chilli, 22 g of peas, 75 g plain flour

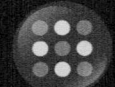

Objectives	
• Solve simple problems involving ratio and proportion using informal strategies	(L5)

Key ideas	Resources
1 A ratio deals with the relative sizes of different categories of items 2 Equivalent ratios can be found by multiplication (or division)	Proportion unitary method (1036) Proportion (1037) Ratio dividing 2 (1039) Red and white counters or squares A calculator A stop watch for question **4**

Simplification	Extension
When simplifying ratios (as in question **2a**), students may intuitively choose to divide by a scale factor (of 2 in question **2a**). Otherwise, suggest that a ratio is first written in its simplest form.	Students find and simplify various ratios from their own school timetable. Examples can be the **ratio** of English time to science time, and the ratio of science to mathematics. Can they identify any equivalent ratios? For example, French : history = 1 : 3 is equivalent to geography : mathematics = 2 : 6.

Literacy	Links
Ratio and *proportion* are different. Ratios compare different quantities within a batch, such as red : blue = 2 : 3 within a pile of red and blue beads. Whereas a proportion gives the fraction of one thing as part of the whole. The red beads are $\frac{2}{5}$ of all the beads, so the proportion of the red beads is $\frac{2}{5}$.	Beads have been found dating back 100 000 years. They are the oldest form of jewellery ever found. There are pictures of ancient shell beads at http://www.nhm.ac.uk/about-us/news/2007/june/news_11808.html How long is a necklace made from 12 shells (each 1 cm long), 6 shells (each 1.5 cm long) and 2 shells (each 2 cm long)? What proportion of the shells are 2 cm long?

Alternative approach	

In problems where scenarios are described in words, it can be useful to write the working using words rather than the arrowed diagrams of the student book.

For example, necklaces are made from patterns of 18 beads which repeat every 12 cm. Find the number of beads needed for a necklace 60 cm long.

Write a sentence so that what is required (in this case, the number of beads), is on the right-hand end of the sentence.	12 cm of necklace need 18 beads.
Then write what you want underneath.	60 cm of necklace need… beads.
Find a multiplier; in this case, × 5, because 12 × 5 = 60.	60 cm of necklace need 18 × 5 = 90 beads.

If there is no easy multiplier, use the *unitary method*. For example, find the beads for a 50 cm necklace.

Write the sentence.	12 cm of necklace need 18 beads.
Find 1 cm of necklace by ÷ 12.	1 cm of necklace need 18 ÷ 12 = 1.5 beads
Find 50 cm of necklace by × 50.	50 cm of necklace need 1.5 × 50 = 75 beads.

Checkpoint	

1 Damian mixes pink paint by mixing white and red paint in the ratio 2 : 3.
   a He has 10 tubes of white paint. How many tubes of red paint does he need?   (15)
   b On another occasion, he has 18 tubes of red paint. How many tubes of white paint does he need? (12)

Starter – Emergency!

Students arrange the digits 1 to 9 to make three 3-digit numbers that will add up to a total of 999.

Students find different ways to get this total.

(One possible way is 498 + 375 + 126 = 999)

Teaching notes

Recall from previous lessons on ratio and proportion that:
- ratio compares different parts with one another;
- proportion compares one part with the whole.

Show a selection of coloured squares to the class; for example, six red and four white squares. Students give the ratio of red : white and the ratio white : red.

Discuss whether these two ratios can be simplified. Demonstrate the equivalences visually by dividing the squares into two equal groups to give three red and two white in each group and hence the equivalent ratio 3 : 2. Point out that finding an equivalent ratio by division is similar to find equivalent fractions by division.

Using the simplified ratio, students find how many reds are needed for 10 whites, 20 whites and 18 whites. Invite students to give the *proportion* of red in each case, noting that, by using equivalent fractions, the proportion of red is always $\frac{3}{5}$ of the total number of squares.

This topic is linked to finding and using scale factors with enlargements and scale drawings.

Plenary

Describe various scenarios, such as a box of 28 chocolates with plain chocolate to milk chocolates in the ratio 3 : 4. Students find the number of each type of chocolate in the box, using mini whiteboards to show their answers.

Pose the question 'Can you split a class of 25 students in the ratio of 3 : 4?'. Discuss in pairs and then as a whole class.

Exercise commentary

Throughout this exercise, students may benefit from working in pairs to discuss and agree on the method to use and on the way that their working will be set out. In some questions, they may find that more than just one method is possible.

Questions 1 and 2 – These questions involve finding equivalent ratios in context.

Question 3 – Students will need to know how to divide a quantity into a given ratio.

Question 4 – This question entails an experiment with students working in pairs. Each pair will need a stopwatch or a watch with a second hand. Students will need to take care with units of time in this question.

Answers

1   12
2   **a**   **i**   Dark   **ii**   Light   **iii**   Mid
    b   6 litres of white and 9 litres of black
3   **a**   5   **b**   15 green; 10 red   **c**   2
    d   **i**   no   **ii**   yes
4   Check students' working

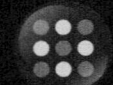
Objectives

- Find proportions by calculating percentages and fractions of quantities (L5)
- Compare two proportions using percentages and fractions (L5)

Key ideas	Resources
1 Different proportions of quantities can be compared by finding percentages or fractions of the quantities	Fractions of amounts (1018) Percentages of amounts 2 (1031) Multiplication tables (for support)

Simplification	Extension
The combining of fractions and percentages may prove too confusing for some students and it may be beneficial to concentrate on *either* percentages *or* fractions, but not both at the same time. Subsequent lessons can tackle fractions and percentages at the same time.	Students calculate and compare percentages of amounts, where the percentages are not multiples of 10%. For example, 32% of 400 and 46% of 600.

Literacy	Links
The word *proportion* comes from the Latin words *pro portione* which roughly means 'division into parts'. To compare proportions, fractions (or percentages) of two quantities have to be found and then compared.	Proportional representation is a system of election where the number of seats given to a particular political party is proportional to the number of votes that it receives. In an election in the UK, only the winning candidate in each constituency becomes a Member of Parliament. Smaller parties might win a sizeable proportion of the vote without winning any seats.

Alternative approach

Exercise **15f** is based on finding multiples of 10% of various amounts. There is a common misunderstanding if finding percentages of quantities are always based on 10%. The faulty logic says:

> 10% of 650 is 650 ÷ 10.
> So, 20% of 650 is 650 ÷ 20
> and 30% of 650 is 650 ÷ 30, etc.

The pattern is seductive but wrong. This misunderstanding can be avoided (a) by continually emphasising that, for example, 20% is 2 × 10%, or (b) by working with 1% which returns to first principles based on 'percent' meaning 'hundredth'.

For example, for 30% of £120,

> 1% of £120 = £1.20   by dividing by 100
> so 10% of £120 = £12   by multiplying by 10
> so 30% of £120 = 3 × £12 = £36   by multiplying by 3.

Checkpoint

1 Calculate
   a 10% of 60   (6)
   b 40% of 60   (24)
   c 1/5 of 60   (12)
   d 3/5 of 60   (36)

Starter – Paper round

Sam earns £20 each week doing a paper round. As a bonus, Sam is offered a choice of three options:

- an extra lump sum of £8 for just 1 week
- an extra £2 each week for the next 4 weeks
- a pay rise of 50% for 1 week followed by a pay cut of 50% the following week.

Students advise Sam on his choices and give their reasons.

Teaching notes

Students match equivalent expressions and identify the odd one out (2.5×200):

0.4×200	$200 \div 100 \times 40$	40% of 200
2.5×200	$200 \div 5 \times 2$	2% of 4000
$\frac{2}{5}$ of 200	$\frac{40}{100}$ of 200	0.4 of 200

Use the activity to recall:

- equivalence of fractions, decimals and percentages
- finding a fraction of an amount
- finding equivalent fractions with denominator of 100 in order to convert a fraction to a percentage
- dividing a percentage by 100 to find the decimal equivalent
- 'of' meaning 'multiply'.

Introduce the problem: 'Which is bigger, 40% of £60 or $\frac{2}{10}$ of £120?' Discuss students' initial responses. The comparison can only be done after making each calculation. Students discuss the two methods.

The exercise centres on the students' ability to calculate percentages and fractions of various quantities using a variety of methods.

Plenary

Write the four computations:

A $\frac{1}{4}$ of 24   B 5% of 200

C 0.3 of 30   D $\frac{2}{5}$ of 20.

Students calculate and compare the answers. They write the letters A, B, C and D in the ascending order of their answers (that is, smallest first) on their mini whiteboards. Discuss their results and methods.

Repeat with four other computations.

Exercise commentary

Question 1 – Students calculate 10%, multiples of 10% and, in part **i**, half of 10% of various numbers.

Questions 2 and **3** – Students calculate and then compare unit fractions of amounts (in question **2**) and multiples of 10% of amounts (in question **3**).

Question 4 – Students calculate and compare non-unitary fractions of amounts.

Question 5 – Students calculate the reductions using percentages and then subtract the reductions to find the actual sale prices.

Question 6 – The clearest comparison is made by converting fractions to percentages *either* by finding equivalent fractions with denominators of 100 *or* by using a calculator to change to decimals first.

Question 7 – Students will likely see that changing all results to percentages is the best way to compare them.

Answers

1	a	8	b	3	c	9	d	16
	e	16	f	6	g	27	h	64
	i	3	j	140				

2 a 8 cm < 9 cm   b 12 m < 15 m
   c £9 > £8   d 4 kg < 5 kg
   e €5.6 > €3   f 9p > 8p

3 a 10% of £90 < 30% of £40; 9 < 12
   b 30% of 110 km > 20% of 160 km; 33 > 32
   c 30% of 200 g < 80% of 80 g; 60 < 64
   d 90% of €90 > 50% of €100; 81 > 50
   e 60% of 50 mm > 40% of 70 mm; 30 > 28
   f 20% of £60 < 50% of £26; 12 < 13

4 a both equal; 30
   b $\frac{4}{5}$ of 45; 35 < 36
   c $\frac{2}{3}$ of £75; 50 > 45

5 The first item

6 Julie has 65%, Sophie has 68%. So, Sophie.

7 70% in art, 72% in English, 69% in history, 71% i maths, 60% in science. So English was best.

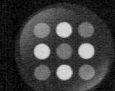
Objectives	
• Calculate accurately, selecting mental methods or calculating devices as appropriate	(L5)
• Record methods, solutions and conclusions	(L4)

Key ideas	Resources
1 Multi-stage problems require an overall strategy 2 Students need to judge whether a mental method, a written method or a calculator is the best choice for a given calculation	Best buys and value for money (1243) A calculator

Simplification	Extension
Undue reliance on calculators can be a real problem for some students. Ensure that students make a mental estimate of an answer initially for any question where a calculator is used.	Students share their reports for question **3** with one another. Do they understand their partner's reasoning and do they agree with it? They combine reports, improve upon the wording and arguments used in the joint report and, if possible, make a PowerPoint presentation which can be presented to the class.

Literacy	Links
The problems in this exercise require a good degree of numerical fluency. All three forms of computational skill – mental, written and calculator – are required, as well as skills of estimation. In addition, the ability to understand a problem and have an overall strategy, even before making any calculation, is needed.	Before electronic calculators became widely available in the mid-1970s, slide rules were widely used to perform calculations. A slide rule is a device shaped like a ruler with two or more scales that can slide against each other. It converts multiplication and division into addition and subtraction. There is more information about slide rules at http://en.wikipedia.org/wiki/Slide_rule and at http://www.sliderulemuseum.com/

Alternative approach
These longer problems can lead to fruitful discussions when students work in pairs. Students can decide a joint strategy, agree an estimate before any calculation is made, decide when to use a mental, written or calculator method, and can check their computations.

Checkpoint
1 A particular brand of shampoo is available in two sizes. 200 ml for £2.40 and 500 ml for £5.40. Which is the best value? Hint: work out what 100 ml costs in each case. <div align="right">(2.4 ÷ 2 = 1.2 , 5.4 ÷ 5 = 1.08 , so the 500 ml bottle is better value)</div>

Starter – Quick fire

Recap basic number work. Include questions on fractions, decimals and percentages and questions using mental and written computation. Ask rapid response questions. Students reply by writing on their mini whiteboards. Discuss questions when their answers indicate a need.

Teaching notes

Split the class into three groups, A, B and C. Each group finds the answers to these calculations, which are given one at a time:

$1 + 2 + 3 + 1 + 2 + 2 + 1$

3×4

7×24

$182 \div 7$

$340 \div 10$, etc.

Group A must only use mental methods.
Group B can use mental or written methods.
Group C must use only a calculator.

Point out that:

– mental methods can be as quick, if not quicker, than a calculator

– mental methods are not appropriate for harder calculations

– written methods can evaluate most calculations accurately but they are sometimes not as fast as a calculator

– reliance on a calculator can be a false security, as wrong answers are possible.

Refer to the example about cereal bars in the student book. Discuss which method is most appropriate for each calculation.

Discuss how to check each calculation, including:

– estimating answers and assessing the reasonableness of answer;

– using inverses, such a checking a division by a multiplication

– breaking a complex calculation into parts with jottings when using a calculator.

Plenary

Work through the questions of the exercise as a class, inviting students to make suggestions and share views on appropriate methods.

Exercise commentary

Students working in pairs could be beneficial for all this exercise.

Question 1 – This is similar to the worked example in the student book. Students use all three methods – mental, written and calculator – to divide a 3-digit number by a 1- or 2-digit number.

Questions 2 and **3** – revisit similar multi-step questions from previous lessons. The emphasis should be on deciding on strategy. Students can work in pairs. To avoid overreliance on a calculator, ensure that estimates and approximate calculations are **shown** for any questions where a calculator is used.

Question 4 – This question is a substantial piece of work. Students use many sources of information to compare two types of transport. They use their literacy skills to write a report. Some students are likely to need specific support by being asked appropriate questions, such as:

- which is the shorter journey – by car or train?
- how many days does Stephen work?
- how much in total is it for this many train tickets?
- what is total annual cost of the car, including petrol?

Answers

1 **a** A : 17p B : 16p C : 16.5p
   b Packet B as this is the cheapest per biscuit

2 £36

3 **a** 182 miles   **b** £17 290

4 *By Car* Fixed costs

per year	= £1180
Petrol costs (48 weeks for 5 days)	= £1.40 × 6 × 5 × 48
	= £2016
Total cost	= £3196 per year
Travelling time	= 90 min per day
By train Total cost	= £1760 per year
	OR
	= 44 × 48
	= £2112 per year
Cheaper to buy season ticket (1 year)	
Travelling time	= 1 hour per day

It is more cost effective and faster to use the train, although having the car means it can be used for other things such as holidays and shopping.

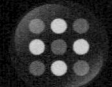
Key outcomes		Quick check
Simplify ratios.	L5	There are three pairs of equivalent ratios in this list. Find the three pairs. 2 : 3 1 : 2 3 : 1 4 : 8 9 : 3 10 : 15 (2 : 3 and 10 : 15; 1 : 2 and 4 : 8; 3 : 1 and 9 : 3)
Divide amounts into ratios.	L5	Divide £30 in the ratio 1 : 4 (£6 : £24)
Express one amount as a proportion of a whole.	L5	Kate has £50 and spends £10. What proprtion of her money does she spend? (1/5 or 0.2 or 20%)
Recognise and use direct proportion.	L5	5 oranges cost £2. How much would eight oranges cost? (1 orange costs 40p, so 8 cost £3.20)
Compare proportions of amounts using fractions and percentages.	L5	Which is larger 2/5 of £200 or 30% of £300? (30% of £300 = £90)
Solve problems involving money using mental methods, written methods or using a calculator.	L5	Which is the better deal on some shampoo: a pack of two half litre bottles at £2.20, or a 1.2 litre bottle at £2.40? (220 ÷ 100 = 2.2p or 240 ÷ 120 = 2p The second deal is cheaper)

MyMaths extra support

Lesson/online homework		Description
Frac dec perc 1	1029 L4	Converting well known fractions, decimals and percentages

MyReview

Check out
You should now be able to ...

		Test it ➡ Questions
✓	Simplify ratios.	⑤ 1
✓	Divide amounts into ratios.	⑤ 2, 3
✓	Express one amount as a proportion of a whole.	⑤ 4, 5
✓	Recognise and use direct proportion.	⑤ 7, 8
✓	Compare proportions of amounts using fractions and percentages.	⑤ 9
✓	Solve problems involving money using mental methods, written methods or using a calculator.	⑤ 10

Language	Meaning	Example
Proportion	Compares a part to the whole	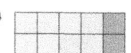
Ratio	Compares two or more parts and is usually written using a colon	Proportion of red is $\frac{8}{20} = \frac{2}{5}$ Ratio of red to blue is $8:12$ $= 2:3$
Simplify a ratio	Divide both sides of a ratio by their highest common factor	$16:24 = 2:3$
Scaling	Multiplying or dividing a pair of quantities to help solve a problem	See page 282

1 Write each of these ratios in its simplest form.
  a $3:12$
  b $15:20$
  c $12:18$
  d $24:20$
  e $40:80$
  f $18:90$

2 Share each amount in the given ratio.
  a £30 in the ratio $2:1$
  b £24 in the ratio $1:3$
  c £35 in the ratio $2:3$
  d £27 in the ratio $4:5$

3 There are 12 people working for a charity. The ratio of men to women is $1:5$. How many men and how many women are there?

4

What proportion of the rectangle is shaded
  a yellow
  b pink
  c blue?

5 In a box of tiles, 2 are broken and 6 are intact. What proportion of the tiles are broken?

6 A recipe for 4 people requires 320g of potatoes. How much will be needed for 6 people?

7 100g of cake contains 300 calories. A slice of cake is about 130g. Approximately how many calories does it contain?

8 Blackcurrant squash is made by mixing 1 part cordial with 7 parts water.
  a How much cordial is needed to make 24 litres of squash?
  b How much cordial will need to be mixed with 70ml of water?
  c How much water will need to be mixed with 5 litres of cordial?

9 Which is larger?
  a $\frac{1}{4}$ of 32 or $\frac{1}{3}$ of 27
  b 70% of 60 or 60% of 80

10 Which deal on fruit juice is the best value for money?
  Deal A: two 1.35 litre bottles for £4.50
  Deal B: a 1 litre bottle for £1.75
  Deal C: three 900ml bottles for £5

What next?

Score		
0 – 5	▮	Your knowledge of this topic is still developing. To improve look at Formative test: 2A-15; MyMaths: 1018, 1031, 1036, 1037, 1038, 1039, 1052, 1243 and 1245
6 – 8	▮	You are gaining a secure knowledge of this topic. To improve look at InvisiPen: 129, 191, 192 and 194
9, 10	▮	You have mastered this topic. Well done, you are ready to progress!

⚫ **MyMaths**.co.uk

Question commentary

Question 1 – This may need some explanation as students have not formally been asked to simplify ratios before.

Questions 2 and **3** – Straightforward

Questions 4 and **5** – Proportion can been answered in the forms of ratio, percentage or fractions.

Questions 6 and **7**– Encourage the use of the unitary method.

Question 8 – Students may need help interpreting what each part is asking.

Question 9 – Straightforward

Question 10 – Students may be guided to find the cost of 100 ml in each case.

Answers

1	a	$1:4$		b	$3:4$
	c	$2:3$		d	$6:5$
	e	$1:2$		f	$1:5$
2	a	£20, £10		b	£6, £18
	c	£14, £21		d	£12, £15

3 2 men, 10 women

4 a $\frac{1}{2}$ / 0.5 / 50%   b $\frac{3}{10}$ / 0.3 / 30%

    c $\frac{1}{5}$ / 0.2 / 20%

5 $\frac{1}{4}$ / 0.25 / 25%

6 480 g

7 390 calories

8 a 3 litres   b 10 ml
    c 35 litres

9 a $\frac{1}{3}$ of 27   b 60% of 80

10 *Deal A*

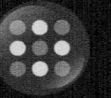

15 MyPractice

15a

1 Jane mixes green paint in three shades, using yellow and blue.

Light green 4:1   Leaf green 5:2   Lincoln green 2:1

Use Jane's mixes of green to decide upon the shade of each of these mixes.

a   b

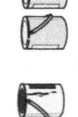

c   d

15b

2 Using the same mixture ratios as in question **1**, what is the shade of each of these mixtures?

	y:b		y:b		y:b		y:b
a	12:3	b	15:6	c	16:8	d	16:4
e	20:8	f	18:9	g	24:12	h	60:15

3 a Demelza and Alex share some money in the ratio 2:5. After they have shared the money, Alex has £30. How much did Demelza receive?

b At a swimming club, the ratio of boys to girls is 3:4. There are nine boys at the club. How many girls are there?

15c

4 Write your answers to these questions as **i** fractions **ii** percentages.

1/10	1/10	1/10	1/10	1/10	1/10	1/10	1/10	1/10	1/10

What proportion of the rectangle is

a blue **b** yellow **c** pink?

d Another row has been added and the colours have been jumbled.
Have any of the colours kept the same proportions of the whole rectangle? If so, which?

e As fractions, write the proportions of all three coloured areas.

15d

5 Use direct proportion to solve each of these problems.

a Four pizzas cost £8. What is the cost of 12 pizzas?

b Three bars of chocolate cost £1.20. What is the cost of nine bars of chocolate?

c 3.5kg of cheese costs £11. What is the cost of 14kg of cheese?

d 20 text messages cost 90p. What is the cost of 100 text messages?

e A recipe for six people uses 720g of rice. How much rice is needed for nine people? How much rice is needed for three people?

15e

6 Anna shares out some sweets between herself and her friend Susie.
Anna gets 21 sweets and Susie gets 14 sweets.

a Write down the ratio of Anna's sweets to Susie's sweets.

b Write down the proportion of the sweets that were given to Susie.

7 All the following questions are to do with ratio and proportion.

a There are 5 soft centre chocolates in every 8 chocolates in a box.
There are 52 chocolates in the box.
How many of them are soft centre chocolates?

b At a drama workshop there are 2 boys for every 7 girls.
35 girls go to the drama workshop.
How many boys attend the drama workshop?

c $\frac{3}{8}$ of the pupils at Dana's school are girls.
What is the ratio of boys to girls at Dana's school?

15f

8 Compare these percentage proportions of amounts.
Use these signs (>, < or =) to say whether they are larger, smaller or equal.

a 10% of £70 and 50% of £16   **b** 25% of £15 and 20% of £25

c 10% of 250g and 30% of 90g **d** 60% of 60m and 70% of 50m

e 40% of 50mm and 20% of 100mm **f** 70% of €60 and 80% of €60

9 Which would cost less?
'Niki' were £90, now increased by 20%.
'Base' were £100, increased by 10%.

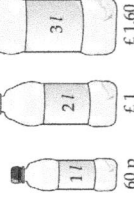

10 Which bottle of water is the best value?

3l £1.60   2l £1   1l 60p

MyMaths.co.uk

Question commentary

Questions 1 and **2** – Remind students that the order of a ratio is important. All the ratios in these questions are yellow : blue.

Question 3 – Encourage students to write down the corresponding ratios, e.g. 2 : 5 = ? : 30.

Questions 4 –6 – Straightforward

Question 7 – This question is quite difficult. Students could work in pairs to understand what each part of the question is asking.

Questions 8 and **9** – Encourage clear working.

Question 10 – Students could work in pairs to find a strategy.

Answers

1   a   Lincoln green   b   Leaf green
    c   Light green   d   Lincoln green

2   a   Light green   b   Leaf green
    c   Lincoln green   d   Light green
    e   Leaf green   f   Lincoln green
    g   Lincoln green   h   Light green

3   a   £12   b   12

4   a   i $\frac{2}{5}$ ii   40%

    b   i $\frac{1}{10}$ ii   10%

    c   i $\frac{1}{2}$ ii   50%
    d   Yes, yellow
    e   Blue $\frac{7}{20}$ Yellow $\frac{1}{10}$ Pink $\frac{11}{20}$

5   a   £24   b   £3.60   c   £44
    d   £4.50   e   1080 g; 360 g

6   a   3 : 2   b $\frac{2}{5}$

7   a   32.5   b   10   c   5 : 3

8   a   10% of £70 < 50 % of £16
    b   25 % of £15 < 20% of £25
    c   10% of 250 g < 30% of 90 g
    d   60% of 60 m > 70% of 50 m
    e   40% of 50 mm = 20% of 100 mm
    f   70% of €60 < 80% of €60

9   Niki

10   21

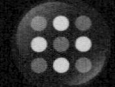

Learning outcomes

P1 Record, describe and analyse the frequency of outcomes of simple probability experiments involving randomness, fairness, equally and unequally likely outcomes, using appropriate language and the 0-1 probability scale (L5/6)

P2 Understand that the probabilities of all possible outcomes sum to 1 (L5)

P3 Enumerate sets and unions/intersections of sets systematically, using tables, grids and Venn diagrams (L5)

P4 Generate theoretical sample spaces for single and combined events with equally likely, mutually exclusive outcomes and use these to calculate theoretical probabilities (L5)

Introduction

The chapter starts by looking at the language of probability and the probability scale is then covered before covering equally likely outcomes. Experimental probability is covered before the final section that looks at sets and Venn diagrams.

The introduction discusses the use of probability in clinical trials for things like new drugs. The idea of giving a 'control group' a placebo in order to measure the effect of the real drug on the other patients relies heavily on the idea of probability. What is the probability, for example, of the drug failing to work on a patient who has the disease being looked at? What is the probability of the patient who takes the placebo actually recovering from the illness being tested on despite not getting the real drug?

Mathematicians can help the scientists and doctors solve these kinds of problems by working out the chances of 'false positives' and errors in the trial. This kind of statistical analysis goes way beyond Key Stage 3 mathematics, but the fundamentals are important to understand at this level by analysing the probabilities of single events and looking at the effect of combining probabilities into two or more sequential or related events.

Prior knowledge

Students should already know how to...

- Work with simple fractions and/or decimals
- Understand simple probability
- Order fractions and decimals

Starter problem

The starter problem looks at the probability of getting one of the numbers from one to twelve when you roll a pair of dice. This is an example of a sample space where the outcomes are recorded in a table:

	1	2	3	4	5	6
1	2	3	4	5	6	7
2	3	4	5	6	7	8
3	4	5	6	7	8	9
4	5	6	7	8	9	10
5	6	7	8	9	10	11
6	7	8	9	10	11	12

As you can see from the table, the chances of getting a one are zero – hence the residents at number 1 are *very* low risk!

Student should be able to see that number 7 is the most at risk while as the numbers go to the extreme ends of the street, the risk gets less so that numbers 2 and 12 are the least risky (with *some* risk still attached).

Resources

MyMaths

Probability intro	1209	Simple probability	1210

Online assessment

Chapter test	2A–16
Formative test	2A–16
Summative test	2A–16

InvisiPen solutions

Probability scale and vocab	451	Finding probabilities	452
Experimental and theoretical probability			461
Finding probabilities	471

Topic scheme

Teaching time = 5 lessons/2 weeks

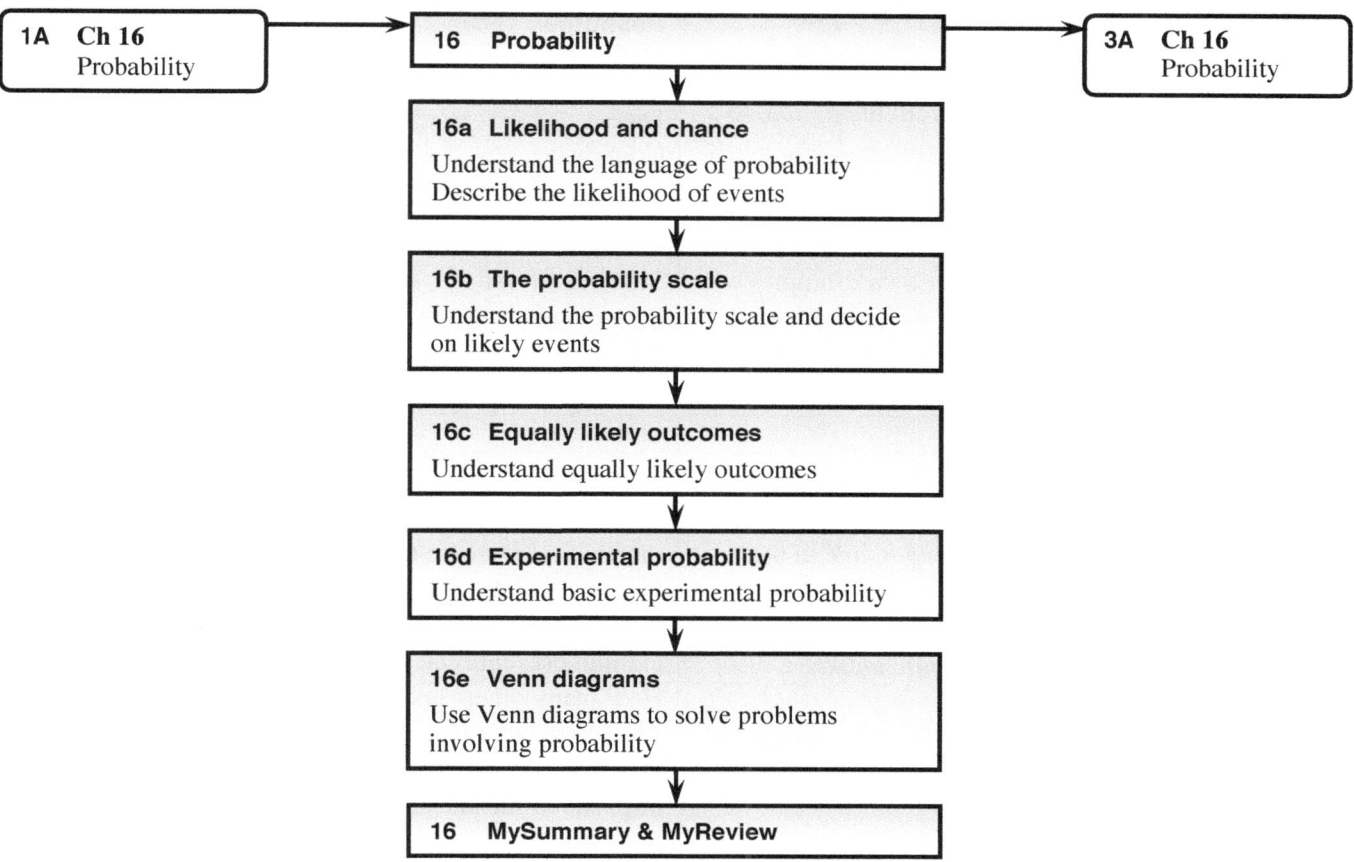

1A   Ch 16
Probability

16   Probability

3A   Ch 16
Probability

16a   Likelihood and chance
Understand the language of probability
Describe the likelihood of events

16b   The probability scale
Understand the probability scale and decide on likely events

16c   Equally likely outcomes
Understand equally likely outcomes

16d   Experimental probability
Understand basic experimental probability

16e   Venn diagrams
Use Venn diagrams to solve problems involving probability

16   MySummary & MyReview

Differentiation

Student book 2A   294 – 309

Likelihood and chance
The probability scale
Equally likely outcomes
Experimental probability
Venn diagrams

Student book 2B   284 – 299

Listing outcomes
Probability
Experimental probability
Theoretical and experimental
    probability
Sets

Student book 2C   286 – 305

Two or more events
Tree diagrams
Mutually exclusive outcomes
Experimental probability
Comparing experimental and
    theoretical probability
Simulating experimental data
Venn diagrams and probability

Objectives

- Use the vocabulary and ideas of probability   (L4)

Key ideas	Resources
1 A range of words can be used to describe the different likelihoods of events from *impossible* to *certain*	 Probability intro (1209) Dice Coins Drawing pins

Simplification	Extension
Encourage students to think of their own examples of likely and unlikely events. Linking events to 'winning' may help. Then they think of their own examples of certain and impossible events.	Students investigate which is more likely when a drawing pin is dropped, that it lands point up or point down.

Literacy	Links
Extend students' range of vocabulary to describe probabilities. Students place these words on the probability scale from *Certain* to *Impossible* in the most appropriate order. *Quite likely, Almost impossible, Evens chance, Very unlikely, Almost certain, Quite unlikely, Very likely, Fifty-fifty* (Note that *evens chance* and *fifty-fifty* are equivalent.)	Many superstitions are based on the belief that a particular action can bring good or bad luck and so increase or decrease the chance of an event happening. For example, breaking a mirror brings seven years bad luck and catching a falling leaf on the first day of autumn prevents catching a cold during the winter. How many other superstitions does the class know? The origins of some common superstitions are explained at http://www.allsands.com/history/originscommons_ssd _gn.htm

Alternative approach

Students place these words on the probability scale from *Certain* to *Impossible* in the most appropriate order.

Quite likely, Almost impossible, Evens chance, Very unlikely, Almost certain, Quite unlikely, Very likely, Fifty-fifty

(Note that *evens chance* and *fifty-fifty* are equivalent.)

Students are given a list of events on a set of cards. They allocate each event to a description on the scale and discuss their results. The events could be:

Dogs will bark.	*It will snow on Mount Everest today.*
I will arrive at school on time.	*The postman will deliver a letter to my home today.*
A dice will roll to give an even score.	*A dice will roll to give a 6.*
The local shop will run out of chocolate today.	*Someone will swim across Niagara Falls today.*
The sun will rise tomorrow.	

Checkpoint

1 Joe puts tickets numbered 1 to 20 in a box.
   Using words from this list – impossible, unlikely, an evens chance, likely, certain – describe how likely the following events are:
   a Joe picks the number 20   (unlikely)
   b Joe picks an odd number   (an evens chance)
   c Joe picks the number 40   (impossible)

Starter – Ice cream

Students find how many different combinations of ice cream they could make, choosing two different flavours from the following six flavours: vanilla, strawberry, toffee, mint choc, pistachio and banana. (15)

Teaching notes

Pairs of students describe events that are certain to happen and events that are impossible to happen. They need to be clear what it means for an event to be certain or impossible. They share their ideas with the class.

Repeat with examples and definitions of likely and unlikely events and events with an evens chance of happening. They can refer to the definitions in the student book.

Use the example of a dice to highlight these ideas of probability. Students explain, for example, why an event is certain, such as getting a score of less than 7, or why an event is unlikely, such as getting a score less than 2.

Show students a normal coin. Ask them which is more likely – tails or heads – and discuss why.

Show students a drawing pin and discuss which side it is most likely to land on – point up or point down. Discuss how this could be investigated.

Draw a line and label its ends with *Certain* and *Impossible*. Discuss that the probability of an event happening falls somewhere on this line. Write some of the students' own examples from the introductory discussion at appropriate places on the line and also include the dice 'events'. The discussion about where 'rolling a number less than 2' should be placed can extend to an informal introduction of allocating a fraction to a probability.

Plenary

Offer various events. Students choose the most appropriate description of the probability of each event happening. They write their choice of word on their mini whiteboards. Discuss their responses.

Exercise commentary

In this exercise, students will benefit greatly from working in pairs when discussing probability.

Questions 1–3 – Students acquire an informal understanding of the likelihood of events. They can begin to think of attaching numerical values to the probability of the events.

Question 4 – Extends to an informal consideration of combined events and of the erratic nature of chance. The nature of bias in a coin can be discussed. Students could use a coin of their own to investigate.

Answers

1 a   even chance   b   unlikely   c   likely
   d   certain   e   impossible
2 Various answers possible – discuss with students
3 a   Even chance
   b   Both blue and yellow have less than an even chance, with blue slightly more likely than yellow
4 If the coin is fair, there is an even chance of getting a head next time. However, the coin could be biased (weighted) towards heads.

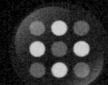

16b The probability scale

Objectives

- Understand and use the probability scale from 0 to 1   (L5)

Key ideas	Resources
1 Probabilities can be allocated numerical values 2 The numerical values for probability range from 0 to 1	Probability intro (1209) Simple probability (1210) Number line from 0 to 1 with 10 intervals

Simplification	Extension
Give students more use of the words such as 'impossible', 'highly likely', and 'not very likely' before moving to working with fractions. They can allocate events such as in question **4** to the probability scale before considering numerical fractions.	Students, in pairs, consider each other's placing of various events on the probability scale. They are given a bag containing 10 counters of different colours. They allocate the probability of selecting each colour to the number line in question **3**.

Literacy	Links
The words used on the probability scale in the previous lesson are now given numerical values on the scale from 0 to 1. The value 0 is given to impossible events and the value 1 is given to events which are certain to happen.	Many people ponder over the probability of snow on Christmas day! Snow can still fall even when the air temperature is above freezing. As snowflakes fall, they gain heat from the surrounding air by conduction but they also lose heat by evaporation. If the flakes lose more heat than they gain, the flakes will remain frozen and the snow will reach the ground. Climatologists decide whether it is likely to snow by considering both the temperature of the surrounding air and the relative humidity. There is a snow probability calculator at http://www.sciencebits.com/SnowProbCalc&calc=yes

Alternative approach

Students are given a set of nine cards with the events below written on them. They are also given a set of eleven cards labelled 0, 0.1, 0.2 up to 1. They match the nine events with nine of the eleven numerical cards.

They then think of two events of their own to match the two remaining numerical values. They discuss their outcomes with a partner.

The events could be:

Dogs will bark.	*It will snow on Mount Everest today.*
I will arrive at school on time.	*The postman will deliver a letter to my home today.*
A dice will roll to give an even score.	*A dice will roll to give a 6.*
The local shop will run out of chocolate today.	*Someone will swim across Niagara Falls today.*
The sun will rise tomorrow.	

Checkpoint

1 You have a bag of ten sweets. 2 are red and 8 are yellow.
   a Describe the probability of picking a red sweet. Can you give this probability a numerical value?
   (Unlikely, 0.2)
   b Describe the probability of picking a yellow sweet. Can you give this probability a numerical value?
   (Likely, 0.8)

Starter – Quick fire and Higher or lower

Recap basic number work. Ask rapid response questions. Students reply by writing on their mini whiteboards. Discuss questions when their answers indicate a need.

Then, using either a set of playing cards or a set of numbered cards, show students the first card and ask whether they think the next card will be higher or lower. Repeat several times. Discuss when 'higher' or 'lower' is the better answer.

Teaching notes

Draw a line for the probability scale ranging from impossible to certain. Explain that the probability of all events can be placed somewhere on this scale, because nothing can be more definite than certainty or impossibility. Students suggest where to label the scale with *likely*, *unlikely* and *evens*.

Explain that probabilities can be given numerical values with 1 being certain and 0 being impossible. Discuss what numbers could be used to represent probabilities between these two extremes. Agree that fractions, decimals or percentages could be used.

Show a number line from 0 to 1 with 10 intervals. Students suggest the labelling of the various intervals with the appropriate fraction, decimal or percentage. Discuss the equivalences between fractions, decimals and percentages. Also discuss that some of the tenths can have equivalent fractions, such as four-tenths and two-fifths.

Students suggest some events and discuss what would be a reasonable numerical value for the probability of the event happening. The event is added as a label to the probability scale. Repeat with other events.

Plenary

Students work in pairs to find events which they think are impossible, certain, unlikely, likely and have an evens chance of happening. They allocate numerical values to indicate where they consider the best places to be for the events on the scale from 0 to 1.

Pairs of students give feedback to the whole class to confirm or modify their decisions.

Exercise commentary

In this exercise, students will benefit greatly from working in pairs to discuss probabilities of events.

Question 1 – Students allocate descriptions to the numerical probability scale.

Questions 2 and 3 – Students allocate numerical values to the probability scale.

Question 4 – It is not essential find numerical values for the probabilities to answer this question. Students match the worded descriptions to the pictures of the bags.

Question 5 – Students need to interpret the likelihoods in terms of the number of cards of that value.

Answers

1 Working from left to right
   first box – very unlikely
   second box – quite likely
   third box – very likely

2 Missing labels are
   $20\%, 30\%, 40\%, 60\%, 70\%, 80\%, 90\%$

3 Missing labels are
   $\frac{3}{10}$ $\frac{2}{5}$ $\frac{3}{5}$ $\frac{7}{10}$ $\frac{4}{5}$ $\frac{9}{10}$

4 **a** 2   **b** 4   **c** 5   **d** 2
   e 3

5 Three 2s, Two 1s, One 3

Objectives	
• Find and justify probabilities based on equally likely outcomes	(L5)

Key ideas	Resources
1 Theoretical probabilities are based on events being equally likely 2 Theoretical probabilities can be found using a simple formula	Simple probability (1210) Dice Coins Copies of hundred squares (for support)

Simplification	Extension
In question **4,** students will find it useful to have a hundred square on hand. They can then count the desirable outcomes of the events of the question.	The activity described in 'Teaching notes' using the word STATISTICS can be extended by using the words PERCENTAGES FRACTIONS which contain 20 letters. Students calculate various probabilities of, for example, choosing a vowel, and express each probability using fractions, percentages and decimals in each case.

Literacy	Links
New vocabulary includes the words *equally likely*, *biased* and *random*. Because certain objects have the same shape and size (such as beads in a bag) or because an object has a certain symmetry (such as a dice), it is reasonable to suppose that certain outcomes of an action (selecting a bead or rolling a dice) are *equally likely* to happen. This notion of 'equal likeliness' allows us to assume the turn of events without having to do any experiment to see if the events truly are equally likely to happen.	Dice that are deliberately biased are often called crooked or loaded dice. Dice can be loaded by adding a small amount of metal to one side or by manufacturing the dice with a hollow gap inside, so that one side is lighter than the others. One way of testing for a loaded die is to drop it several times into a glass of water. If it is hollow it will float with the hollow side uppermost; if it is weighted, it will sink with the same number always facing down.

Alternative approach

Is a coin fair? Students can test the fairness of a coin by comparing results based on theoretical probability with the results of a practical experiment. For example, if a coin is fair (that is, heads H and tails T are equally likely), then the probability of a head $= \frac{1}{2}$ and, in 50 spins of the coin, a head is likely, in theory, to occur 25 times – and a tail to occur 25 times also.

Working in pairs, each pair spins their coin 50 times and records their results in a table:

Outcome	H	T	
Tally			Totals
Observed frequency			
Expected frequency	25	25	50

Is it reasonable to expect *exactly* 25 heads? Are your results near enough to 25 to be satisfied that the coin is fair and that H and T are equally likely? What might make a coin unfair (or biased)?

Checkpoint

1 Lilia rolls an ordinary dice.
   a What is the probability that she rolls a four?   (1/6)
   b What is the probability that she rolls more than four?   (2/6 = 1/3)
   c What is the probability that she rolls an odd number?   (3/6 = ½)

Starter – Quick fire

Recap basic number work. Include questions on fractions, decimals and percentages and questions using mental and written computation. Ask rapid response questions. Students reply by writing on their mini whiteboards. Discuss questions when their answers indicate a need.

Teaching notes

Use a line from 0 to 1 with ten intervals and label the ends 0 for impossible and 1 for certain. Recall the use of fractions, decimals and percentages to label the various points along the line. Discuss the simplification of some of the fractions and the equivalence of fractions to decimals and percentages.

Write the word STATISTICS. Imagine the letters on separate cards placed in a bag. Discuss the likelihood of picking a vowel from the bag. Students find the number of vowels (3) and the total number of cards with letters (10). Make two statements:

1) There is a 3 in 10 chance of picking a vowel out of the bag

2) The probability of picking a vowel is $\frac{3}{10}$.

Repeat with different events, such as picking a letter S, picking a consonant, etc. Refer to the student book and introduce the formula.

Students place these events from STATISTICS on the probability scale, derive the decimal and percentage equivalences and match them with the appropriate vocabulary using words such as *quite likely, unlikely,* etc.

Plenary

Refer to question **5** in Exercise **16c**. When rolling a dice six times, would the students expect each number to come up just once? Ask them to justify their answers.

How many times would they expect the number 4 to come up if the dice was rolled 60 times? Does reality work so predictably?

Roll a dice 60 times. Record the result and discuss them. Were they as expected?

Exercise commentary

Questions 1–4 – All these questions require students to use the probability formula to calculate probabilities of simple events. In question **4c**, note that 'less than 4' does not include 4 itself. Students should simplify fractions where possible.

Question 5 – Makes students consider a calculated probability in the context of the unpredictability of real life.

Answers

1   $\frac{1}{2}$

2   $\frac{1}{3}$

3   **a** $\frac{1}{5}$ **b** 0   **c** $\frac{3}{5}$ **d** $\frac{2}{5}$

4   **a** $\frac{1}{10}$ **b** $\frac{39}{100}$ **c** $\frac{11}{100}$ **d** $\frac{1}{2}$

5   Not necessarily. Over a large number of rolls, e.g. 1000, would expect an even number to turn up roughly half the time.

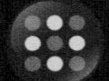

Objectives	
• Estimate probabilities by collecting data from a simple experiment	(L5)

Key ideas	Resources
1 When events are not equally likely, probabilities are estimated from experimental data	Simple probability (1210) Drawing pins Dice Packs of playing cards

Simplification	Extension
For a practical approach, keep the number of possibilities small (use coins, three-sector spinners or dice). Although dice have more possibilities than coins or spinners, they are easier to handle in class than coins and spinners.	Referring to the drawing pin data in 'Teaching notes', students draw a graph showing how the experimental probability changes as the number of trials increases. Label the horizontal axis 'Number of trials' and the vertical axis 'Experimental probability'.

Literacy	Links
Experimental probability is found by experiment involving many *trials*, where a trial is one repetition of the same event. The more trials there are, the more accurate the experimental probability will be. When events are not 'equally likely', then the results are biased. *Bias* is a systematic (rather than a random) deviation for the true value. For example, when the weight of a dice is not uniformly distributed, it is a biased dice. The probability of a biased result can only be found experimentally.	Question **1** refers to data on the speed of cars. It is estimated that around a third of all road accidents are caused by motorists speeding. Speed cameras measure the speed of passing cars and identify vehicles travelling over the legal speed limit. There are around 5000 speed camera sites in the UK. Maps showing their positions are at http://www.speedcamerasuk.com/speed-camera-database.htm and at http://www.abd.org.uk/cameras/map.htm

Alternative approach

This investigation compares experiment and theory.

A traditional pack of 52 cards has a *success* when it is cut at a diamond. Cut the pack ten times, record the number of successes and write the experimental probability of cutting a diamond as a decimal. Repeat a further 10 times making a total of 20 cuts. Repeat for 50 cuts, 100 cuts and even 200 cuts by combining the results of students across the class. Enter all results into a table with these headings. The first results suppose that 3 of the first 10 cuts were at a diamond.

Number of cuts	10	20	50	100	
Number of diamonds	3				
Experimental probability of a diamond	$\frac{3}{10} = 0.3$				

Analyse the results. Do the values of the experimental probability seem to be settling down as the number of cuts increases? Estimate this value 'in the long run' far beyond 100 or 200 cuts.

What value would a theoretical approach give if all four suits of the pack are assumed to be equally likely to be cut? What is the theoretical probability of cutting a diamond? Do theory and experiment agree?

How would you introduce bias into this experiment? (Do not have equal numbers of each suit.)

Checkpoint

1 Matt is interested to see how popular silver grey is as the colour for a car.

   He notes the colours of 200 parked cars. There are 125 silver grey cars.

   Estimate the probability that the next parked car is NOT silver grey.   (75/200 = 3/8)

Starter – What colour?

Put coloured cubes in a bag; for example, six red, three blue and one yellow. Tell students that there are 10 cubes inside.

Take a cube from the bag without looking, note the colour and return it. Repeat and record the results. Continue to repeat until students think they know the colours in the bag and the number of different colours.

Teaching notes

Briefly recap how to calculate probabilities using the notion of 'equally likely'. Introduce the idea of conducting a statistical experiment. Introduce the word *trial* as a single enactment of a repeated event. Students need to appreciate that a statistical experiment involves a lot of repetition.

Define experimental probability. Say that they will conduct an experiment to determine the probability of a drawing pin landing 'point up'. Explain that this will involve working in pairs, with one student dropping the drawing pin and the other student recording the outcomes. (Don't be too prescriptive in how they record – let them work out a system for themselves.)

Encourage students to repeat the experiment many times (say, at least 40, but no more than 100). The important notion to understand is that the greater the number of trials, the greater the accuracy of the experimental probability.

Students initially to do the experiment in pairs and then they combine their results with another pair. The results for all the class could be combined to get an outcome for a much larger number of trials. Discuss the results and how reliable the experimental probability of the drawing pin landing 'point up' is likely to be.

Plenary

Give students a result such as 'Three of the first ten cars passing the school were red'. They write the experimental probability of a red car as a fraction and as a decimal. They find how many of the first 50 cars might be expected to be red. They write the probability and the expected number on their mini whiteboards and discuss their results.

Repeat for similar scenarios.

Exercise commentary

All questions require students to calculate experimental (not theoretical) probabilities from the probability formula.

Questions 1–5 – These all involve rather long wordy scenarios for which some students might need further explanation.

Question 5 – Students make a biased dice; the question calls it a 'trick dice'. When making the net, the edge length of the final cube needs to be not less than 2 cm for the construction to be manageable.

Answers

1. $\frac{1}{5} = 0.2$

2. $\frac{13}{50} = 0.26$

3. $\frac{8}{60} = \frac{4}{30} = \frac{2}{15} = 0.13$

4. a

Colour	Tally	Frequency
Red	5	16.66%
Purple	5	16.66%
Green	10	33.33%
Blue	5	16.66%
Yellow	5	16.66%

  b 16.66%   c Green

5. Discuss with students.

Objectives

- Enumerate sets and unions/intersections of sets systematically, using tables, grids and Venn diagrams   (L5)

Key ideas	Resources
1 Interpret and draw Venn diagrams 2 Work out probabilities using Venn diagrams	⊞ Simple probability (1210)

Simplification	Extension
Question **4** can be omitted as a general simplification. Further examples such as question **1** with no 'outside' number can also be used to get students used to using the circle parts of the Venn diagram.	Ask students to come up with their own problem similar to Ella's puzzle in question **4**. Can they give *just enough* information so that a partner can solve the Venn diagram?

Literacy	Links
The language of sets and Venn diagrams contains many words that may be unfamiliar to students such as 'union' and 'intersection'. Encourage students to write a glossary of terms as each new word or phrase is introduced.	Students may be familiar with these classic 2-circle Venn diagrams but can they come up with a way of representing three 'events'? What about four, or even five events? A quick search on the Internet will provide students with some pretty amazing Venn diagrams for these situations. The Wikipedia page for Venn diagrams with several of these on is at http://en.wikipedia.org/wiki/Venn_diagram

Alternative approach

A two-way table provides a good way to link work on sample spaces, etc. with this work on Venn diagrams. For example consider a two-way table showing two types of chocolate split into 'like' and 'dislike':

	Like B	Dislike B
Like A	18	6
Dislike A	12	15

How can this information be translated into a Venn diagram? Students should be able to see that the four numbers in the table match the four regions in the Venn diagram and they can use this to complete the diagram. Follow-up questions can then be used such as 'what is the probability that…?'

Checkpoint

1 Draw a Venn diagram with two overlapping circles.
   The diagram represents a group of 20 students who study History and/or Geography.
   a There are no students who study neither. Write 0 (zero) in the relevant region.
   (Write 0 in the area outside the circles)
   b 7 students study both History and Geography. Write 7 in the relevant area.
   (Write 7 in the intersection of the two circles)
   c 12 students study History. How many of these only study History?   (5)
   d Complete the Venn diagram. How many students study only Geography?   (8)

Starter – How many people?

In a recent survey, 18 people said they liked rugby, 13 people said they liked hockey and 5 people said they liked both. 4 people said they liked neither. How many people were asked? (30)

Similar logic problems can be given like this and the level of challenge varied accordingly. For example, you might have no-one who liked both, or no-one who liked neither.

Teaching notes

Students need to be able to comprehend the general structure of the Venn diagram and explain, in words, what each region represents. Encourage them to do this first rather than diving straight into the questions. They can produce a glossary of terms since much of the language will be unfamiliar.

Walk the students through the second example where it is the probability that is required rather than the number.

In question **3a**, encourage students to link all their work together and provide a full written explanation of what they are doing.

Plenary

Return to the starter problem. Can the students now draw a Venn diagram to illustrate the results of the survey? Questions can also be asked such as 'what is the probability that a person chosen at random likes hockey?' (13/30)

Exercise commentary

Questions 1 and **2** – Students may need help interpreting the language used.

Question 3 – This could be done in pairs.

Question 4 – Students will need to know 'intersection' and 'union', which is explained on the previous page.

Answers

1	a	40	b	22	c	16	d	34
2	a	55.17%	b	34.48%				
3	a	£393						
	b	Check students' work						
4	a	Check students' work						

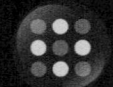

Key outcomes	Quick check
Understand and use the probability scale from 0 to 1. L5	Draw a probability scale from 0 to 1, dividing it into tenths. A bag contains 3 white and 7 red counters. Mark on the probability scale the probablity of : Selecting a white counter (3/10 or 0.3) Seleceting a blue counter (0)
Use vocabulary to describe the likelihood of events. L5	Place the following words in order of likeliness: certain unlikely likely impossible evens (impossible, unlikely, evens, likely, certain *or the other way round*)
Find probabilities based on equally likely outcomes. L5	Ben puts number cards marked 1 to 10 in a box. He chooses a card from the box at random. Find the probability that the number on the card is greater than 6. (4/10)
Use experiments to estimate probabilities. L6	Sarah travels to work by train each day. In 50 working days, the train was late 8 times. Estimate the probability that the train will be on time the next day. (42/50)
Use Venn diagrams to find probabilities. L5	20 people are asked whether they listened to the radio and if they watched TV. 12 people did both. 1 person did neither. 2 people listened to the radio only. Draw a Venn diagram and fill in the four sections. What is the probabilty of selecting a person who watches TV only? (5/20)

⊞ MyMaths extra support

Introducing data 1235 L3	Sorting data into groups using Venn diagrams and tally charts; bar charts and histograms

MyReview

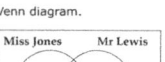
Check out

You should now be able to ...

Test it ➡
Questions

✓	Understand and use the probability scale from 0 to 1.	⑤ 1
✓	Use vocabulary to describe the likelihood of events.	⑤ 2
✓	Find probabilities based on equally likely outcomes.	⑤ 3 – 5
✓	Use experiments to estimate probabilities.	⑥ 6, 7
✓	Use Venn diagrams to find probabilities.	⑤ 8

Language	Meaning	Example
Probability	A measure of the chance that an event happens	The probability of a flipped coin showing tails is $\frac{1}{2}$ or 0.5 or 50%. This is an evens chance
Evens chance	A 50% chance of happening	
Equally likely	Events with the same chance of happening	For a fair dice 1, 2, 3, 4, 5, and 6 are all equally likely. The probability of each outcome is $\frac{1}{6}$
Trial	A statistical experiment	Throwing a dice to see which number is on top
Outcome	A possible result of a trial	For a dice the possible outcomes are 1, 2, 3, 4, 5 and 6
Event	A collection of outcomes	The event 'an even number' consists of the outcomes 2, 4 and 6
Experiment	A series of trials which can be used to estimate a probability	Rolling a dice 600 times and recording the outcomes is an experiment
Venn diagram	Uses circles to sort things into sets. The circles can overlap	See page 304

1 An ordinary dice is rolled. Draw a probability scale and add labels to show the probabilities of rolling
  a an odd number
  b a 7
  c a 1.

2 Use one of the following words to describe the events in question **1**.
  impossible   unlikely   evens
  likely   impossible

3 A bag contains 2 white and 6 red counters. What is the probability that a randomly chosen counter will be
  a white   b red   c blue?

4 A number from 1–12 is selected at random. Find the probability it is
  a a prime number
  b a square number.

5 In a playgroup there are 6 boys and 9 girls. A child is selected at random. What is the probability it is a boy?

6 Ashley travels to work by train. In 35 days the train was late 7 times. Estimate the probability that the train will be late the next day.

7 The test results of 10 students are as follows:

8	8	3	7	4
9	4	2	2	6

A mark of more than 7 was needed to pass.
Estimate the probability that a student chosen at random would have passed the test.

8 Adam asked 20 students in his class whether their science teacher is Miss Jones and their history teacher is Mr Lewis.
His results are shown on the Venn diagram.

Adam picked one student at random. Find the probability that they
  a are taught by Miss Jones.
  b are taught by Miss Jones and Mr Lewis.

What next?

Score		
	0 – 4	Your knowledge of this topic is still developing. To improve look at Formative test: 2A-16; MyMaths: 1209 and 1210
	5, 6	You are gaining a secure knowledge of this topic. To improve look at InvisiPen: 451, 452, 461 and 471
	7, 8	You have mastered this topic. Well done, you are ready to progress!

MyMaths.co.uk

Question commentary

Question 1 – The scale could be divided into sixths.

Question 2 – This could lead to a discussion about the numerical value that likely and unlikely might be given.

Question 3 – Straightforward

Question 4 – Students may need reminding about prime and square numbers.

Question 5 – Straightforward

Questions 6 and **7** – These questions cover experimental probability.

Question 8 – The answers are fractions out of 20.

Answers

1 a   marked in middle   b   marked at 0
  c   marked about $\frac{5}{6}$ along line

2 a   even chance   b   impossible   c   likely

3 a $\frac{1}{4}$ b $\frac{3}{4}$ c   0

4 a $\frac{5}{12}$ b $\frac{1}{4}$

5   $\frac{2}{5}$

6   0.2

7   0.3

8 a $\frac{13}{20}$ b $\frac{9}{20}$

16 MyPractice

1 Betty puts tickets numbered 1–100 into a bag, and picks a ticket at random.
Give an example of an outcome that is:

a Certain   b Very likely

c Very unlikely   d Impossible

2 Here are some events that could happen when you roll an ordinary dice.

a The score on the dice is 3.   b The score is a multiple of 3.

c The score is 7.   d The score is less than 10.

e The score is 4 or more.

Write this list out in order, from the least likely event to the most likely.
Explain your answers.

3 Josie spins a coin five times. Explain how likely you
think the following results are.

a Five heads

b Two heads and three tails

c Three heads and three tails

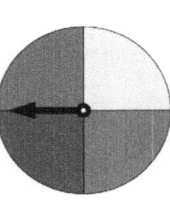

4 Explain in words the likelihood of events with these probabilities.

a 2%   b 50%

c 99%   d 75%

5 How likely are events with these probabilities?

a 0.4   b 0.01

c 0.95   d 0.5

6 Jessica rolls an ordinary six-sided dice.
Use the formula for probability to calculate the probability that
the score on Jessica's dice is:

a exactly 6

b more than 4

c an odd number.

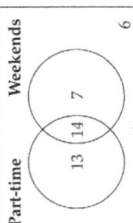

7 If you pick a day of the week at random, what is the probability that the name of
the day contains the letter T? Show all your working.

8 If you choose a month at random, what is the probability that the name of the
month contains the letter R? Show your working.

9 A spinner has sections coloured red, blue, green and yellow.
The table shows the results of an experiment to test the spinner.

Colour	Frequency
Red	71
Blue	74
Yellow	33
Green	22

Use the results in the table to estimate the experimental
probability of each result.
Give your answers as percentages and decimals.

10 Sam and Dave both take penalties for the football teams they
play for. In one season, Sam takes eight penalties, and scores
with seven of them. Dave takes twelve penalties, and scores ten times.

a Work out the probability of each player scoring with
a penalty. Give your answers as decimals.   You can use a calculator.

b Which player is the best penalty-taker? Explain your answer.

11 Julie is the manager of a supermarket. She asked 40 employees whether
they work part-time and if they work on weekends.
Her results are shown on the Venn diagram.

Part-time   Weekends

13   14   7

6

Julie picked one employee at random.
Find the probability that they

a don't work on weekends

b work part-time and work on weekends.

Question commentary

Questions 1 and **2** – These could be done in pairs.

Question 3 – This is quite tricky but could lead to investigational work on combinations.

Questions 4 and **5** – Students may want to qualify likely and very likely, for example.

Question 6 – Straightforward

Question 7 – Students need to remember Saturday.

Question 8 – Students may benefit from writing out the names of the twelve months of the year.

Question 9 – Each of the four colours can be given, initially, as a fraction out of 200. Students may need reminding how to convert to decimals and percentages.

Question 10 – Students need to compare 7/8 with 10/12.

Question 11 – Students can work in pairs and check they understand what the question is asking.

Answers

1 Various answers possible, for example
   a picking a ticket numbered less than 101
   b picking a ticket numbered less than 100
   c picking a ticket numbered 1
   d picking a ticket numbered 0

2 Order is **c, a, b, e, d**

3 a very unlikely $\left(\frac{1}{32}\right)$
   b unlikely $\left(\frac{10}{32}\right)$
   c impossible (0)

4 a very unlikely   b even chance
   c very likely   d likely

5 a little less than evens   b very unlikely
   c very likely   d even chance

6 a $\frac{1}{6}$ b $\frac{1}{3}$ c $\frac{1}{2}$

7 $\frac{3}{7}$

8 $\frac{2}{3}$

9 a

Red	35.5%	0.36
Blue	37%	0.37
Yellow	16.5%	0.17
Green	11%	0.11

10 a Sam 0.875
       Dave 0.83
   b Sam. Higher probability of scoring

11 a 0.325   b 0.35

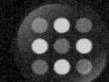

Case study 6: Free-range

Related lessons		Resources	
Written multiplication	11b	Divide decimals by whole numbers	(1008)
Written division	11c	Multiply decimals by whole numbers	(1010)
Scale drawing	12d	Scale drawing	(1117)
Proportion	15c	Proportion	(1037)
		Examples of food packaging with 'free range', 'fair trade' or 'organic' labels	

Simplification	Extension
Concentrate on just the outside area in task **1**. In task **2**, encourage students to work together to find possible areas before proceeding to plan the layout. Tasks **3** and **4** involve proportion and could be simplified by reducing the number of parts or changing some of the values.	Allowing students to assume that caged and free-range hens lay the same amount of eggs per day and that farmers would be able to sell all the eggs they produced regardless of type, students could explore each of the free-range farms and calculate the number of caged hens the farmer could keep to make more profit than they do selling their eggs as free-range.

Links

Students could look at the various rules for other produce labelled as 'free-range', 'fair trade' or 'organic'. Lots of information on this and other ethical foodstuffs can be found on the internet. An example can be found at http://www.co-operativefood.co.uk/food-ethics/ and a quick search in Google will throw up lots of other examples. Students could also keep a diary of their eating to record when they eat products that are labelled as ethical.

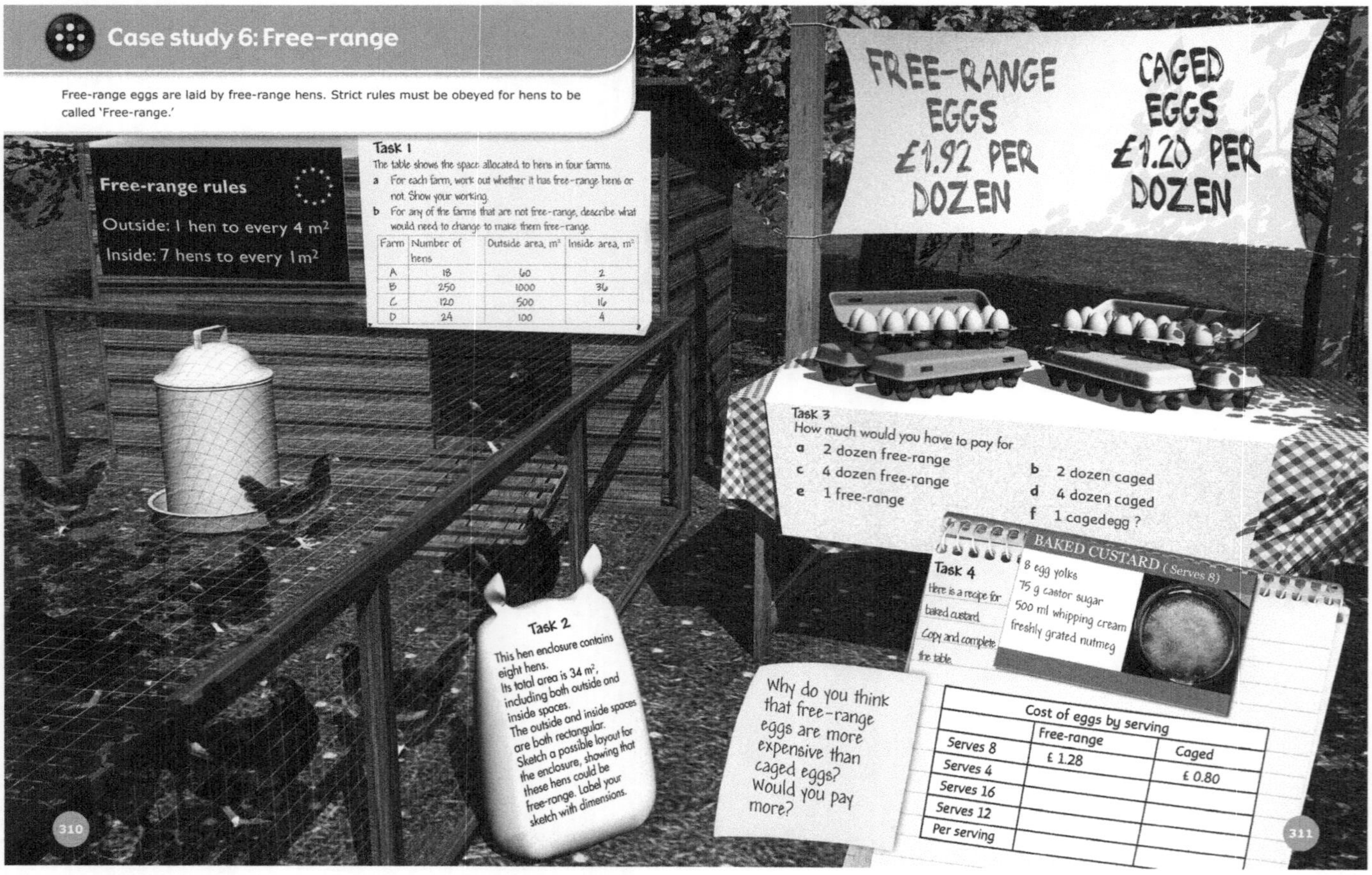

Case study 6: Free-range

Free-range eggs are laid by free-range hens. Strict rules must be obeyed for hens to be called 'Free-range.'

Free-range rules

Outside: 1 hen to every 4 m²

Inside: 7 hens to every 1 m²

Task 1

The table shows the space allocated to hens in four farms.

a For each farm, work out whether it has free-range hens or not. Show your working.

b For any of the farms that are not free-range, describe what would need to change to make them free-range.

Farm	Number of hens	Outside area, m²	Inside area, m²
A	18	60	2
B	250	1000	36
C	120	500	16
D	24	100	4

Task 2

This hen enclosure contains eight hens.

Its total area is 34 m², including both outside and inside spaces.

The outside and inside spaces are both rectangular.

Sketch a possible layout for the enclosure, showing that these hens could be free-range. Label your sketch with dimensions.

FREE-RANGE EGGS £1.92 PER DOZEN

CAGED EGGS £1.20 PER DOZEN

Task 3

How much would you have to pay for

a 2 dozen free-range

b 2 dozen caged

c 4 dozen free-range

d 4 dozen caged

e 1 free-range

f 1 caged egg ?

Task 4

Here is a recipe for baked custard.

Copy and complete the table.

BAKED CUSTARD (Serves 8)

8 egg yolks

75 g castor sugar

500 ml whipping cream

freshly grated nutmeg

Why do you think that free-range eggs are more expensive than caged eggs? Would you pay more?

	Cost of eggs by serving	
	Free-range	Caged
Serves 8	£ 1.28	£ 0.80
Serves 4		
Serves 16		
Serves 12		
Per serving		

Teaching notes

Many students are interested in animal welfare and how animals farmed for produce are kept. Mathematics can be used to explore some of these issues by considering the extra cost of free-range eggs versus eggs from caged hens. Not only can students explore the legislation that enables a farmer to label their eggs as free-range, they can compare costs and discuss the reasons why people may choose to pay more for free-range eggs.

Ask students whether they have heard of free-range eggs and what their understanding of the term is. Explain that there are rules in place to determine whether a farmer can sell their eggs as free-range.

Task 1

Ask students how big they think 4 m^2 is. Consider the size of the classroom to get a feel for relative size. Look at farms A to D. Discuss with the students how to decide whether they are free-range. Make sure they take account of both the outside and inside dimensions.

Task 2

Look at the farm in the picture and the dimensions given on the feed bag. Ask students to plan with a partner a possible layout of the farm pen so they can consider the hens to be free-range.

Task 3

Now look at the costs of the different types of eggs. Ask students to find the answers to questions **a** to **f**. Discuss the different strategies used.

Task 4

Ask students to spend a few minutes looking at the baked custard recipe with a partner. How would you calculate the cost of the eggs for the different amounts of the pudding? Share ideas then ask students to complete the recipe card.

Answers

1 a A: No; B: Yes; C: No; D: Yes

   b A: Outside area to 72 m^2, inside to 2.57 m^2

   C: Inside area to 17.14 m^2

2 Check students' drawings

3 a £3.84

   b £7.68

   c 16 pence

   d £2.40

   e £4.80

   f 10 pence

4 64 pence/40 pence

   £2.56/£1.60

   £1.92/£1.20

   16 pence/12 pence

MyAssessment 4

These questions will test you on your knowledge of the topics in chapters 13 to 16.
They give you practice in the types of questions that you may eventually be given in your GCSE exams. There are 75 marks in total.

1 Write the term-to-term rule for each of these sequences.
a 3, 14, 25, 36, ... (1 mark) b 39, 35, 31, 27, ... (1 mark)
c 7, 14, 28, 56, ... (1 mark) d $\frac{1}{8}, \frac{1}{4}, \frac{1}{2}, 1, ...$ (1 mark)

2 For these sequences
a write the term-to-term rule b give the position-to-term rule.
i 4, 7, 10, 13, ... ii 17, 14, 11, 8, ... iii 1, 10, 19, 28, ... (6 marks)

3 Adding two consecutive triangular numbers gives a square number.
What square number is obtained by adding the
a 5th and 6th triangular numbers (2 marks)
b 11th and 12th triangular numbers? (3 marks)

4 On isometric paper draw these shapes.
a A cuboid 2cm × 3cm × 6cm. (2 marks)
b A square-based pyramid with base length 4cm and height 6cm. (3 marks)

5 Look at these nets of common 3D objects.
Name the solid made by each of these nets. (3 marks)
a b c

6 These cuboids are made from centimetre cubes.
a Draw the net of each cuboid. i ii (2 marks)
b What is the surface area of each cuboid? (2 marks)
c Work out the volume of each cuboid. (2 marks)

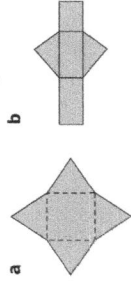

7 For the following cuboids
a copy the shapes onto isometric paper (4 marks)
b work out the volume of each cuboid. (2 marks)
i ii

8 Change the ratio of these quantities to give them in their simplest form.
a 5:10 b 6:30 c 28:49 d 3.2:1.6 (4 marks)

9 Concrete is made by mixing cement and sand in different amounts.
a Lean concrete is made by mixing cement and sand in the ratio 1:5.
How much cement and sand is used to make 30kg of concrete? (2 marks)
b Hard concrete uses a ratio of cement to sand of 1:2.
How much cement and sand is used to make 27kg of concrete? (2 marks)
c Write the proportion of cement in lean concrete as a fraction. (2 marks)
d Write the proportion of sand in lean concrete as a percentage. (2 marks)

10 Use direct proportion to solve these problems.
a 40 litres of petrol will allow a car to travel 500km.
How far will the car travel on 8 litres of petrol? (2 marks)
b A worker earns £87 for a 12 hour shift.
How much does she earn in 3 shifts? (2 marks)

11 Health bars are sold in different multipacks.
A : 6 bars for £1.20, B : 10 bars for £1.98 and C : 15 bars for £2.96.
Which multipack is the better value for money?
Choose the most appropriate method and show all your working. (4 marks)

12 a Draw a probability scale, using arrows, mark on the scale:
events that are impossible, an evens chance and certain. (4 marks)
b Now write in words three events that match your probabilities
of impossible, evens chance and certain. (3 marks)

13 In a bag there are 11 red marbles and 5 blue marbles.
What is the probability of randomly picking
a a blue marble (1 mark) b a red marble (1 mark)
c a green marble (1 mark) d a red or blue marble? (1 mark)

14 A bag of balloons are being inflated for a party. Before being released
there are 35 red balloons and 15 white balloons inflated. What is
the probability that the first balloon to be burst is a white balloon? (2 marks)

15 An octahedral (8-sided) dice is rolled 100 times and the scores are
recorded in the table.

Score	1	2	3	4	5	6	7	8
Frequency	16	12	9	15	10	14	13	11

a Calculate the experimental probability of throwing a 7. (2 marks)
b Compare this with the theoretical probability of obtaining a 7. (2 marks)
c How could the experimental probability be improved? (1 mark)
d How many times would you expect to throw a 2 if the dice is
rolled 500 times? (2 marks)

 MyMaths.co.uk

Mark scheme

Questions 1 – 4 marks
a 1 start from 3 and +11 each time
b 1 start from 39 and − 4 each time
c 1 start from 7 and × 2 each time
d 1 start from $\frac{1}{8}$ and × 2 each time

Questions 2 – 6 marks
a i 1 start from 4 and + 3 each time
  ii 1 start from 17 and − 3 each time
  iii 1 start from 1 and + 9 each time
b i 1 position number $= \times 3$ then $+1$
  ii 1 position number $= \times(-3)$ then $+20$
  iii 1 position number $= \times 9$ then $- 8$

Questions 3 – 5 marks
a 2 6^2; 15 + 21 seen
b 3 12^2; 66 + 78 seen

Questions 4 – 5 marks
a 2 Ensure drawing correct size; ruler used; any orientation acceptable
b 3 Correct base size and height; -1 each error

Questions 5 – 3 marks
a 1 square-based pyramid
b 1 wedge
c 1 cube

Questions 6 – 6 marks
a i 1 Correct net drawn
  ii 1 Correct net drawn
b i 1 $42\ cm^2$
  ii 1 $56\ cm^2$
c i 1 $18\ cm^3$
  ii 1 $24\ cm^3$

Questions 7 – 6 marks
a i 2 Check correct copy drawn; -1 mark each error
  ii 2 correct copy drawn; -1 mark each error
b i 1 $7\ cm^3$
  ii 1 $25\ cm^3$

Questions 8 – 4 marks
a 1 1 : 2
b 1 1 : 5
c 1 4 : 7
d 1 2 : 1

Questions 9 – 8 marks
a 2 5 kg cement, 25 kg sand
b 2 9 kg cement, 18 kg sand
c 2 $\frac{1}{6}$ or any equivalent fraction; may see 6 parts in total; 1 part out of 6
d 2 83.3%; accept 83%; 1 mark for 5/6 or equivalent fraction

Questions 10 – 4 marks
a 2 100 km; 1 mark for 40/8 = 5
b 2 £261; 1 mark for attempt at 87×3

Questions 11 – 4 marks
 1 £1.20/6 = £0.20; Multipack **A**
 1 £1.98/10 = £0.19(8); Multipack **B**
 1 £2.96/15 = £0.19(7); Multipack **C**
 1 Multipack **C** is the best value for money

Questions 12 – 7 marks
a 4 Ensure correct scale between 0 and 1; arrows drawn at 0 (impossible), 0.5 or ½ for even chance ; 1 for certain
b 3 Any three sensible events

Questions 13 – 4 marks
a 1 $\frac{5}{16}$ or 31.3%
b 1 $\frac{11}{16}$ or 68.8%
c 1 0
d 1 1

Questions 14 – 2 marks
 2 $\frac{15}{50}$ or $\frac{3}{10}$ or 0.3

Questions 15 – 7 marks
a 2 $\frac{13}{100}$ or 13%
b 2 $\frac{1}{8}$ or 12.5%
c 1 By throwing the dice more times
d 2 $\frac{500}{8} = 62–63$

Learning outcomes

DF2 Select and use appropriate calculation strategies to solve increasingly complex problems (L5)

DF3 Use algebra to generalise the structure of arithmetic, including to formulate mathematical relationships (L5)

DF5 Move freely between different numerical, algebraic, graphical and diagrammatic representations (for example, equivalent fractions, fractions and decimals, and equations and graphs) (L5)

DF7 Use language and properties precisely to analyse numbers, algebraic expressions, 2D and 3D shapes, probability and statistics (L5)

RM2 Extend and formalise their knowledge of ratio and proportion in working with measures and geometry, and in formulating proportional relations algebraically (L5)

RM6 Interpret when the structure of a numerical problem requires additive, multiplicative or proportional reasoning (L5)

RM7 Explore what can and cannot be inferred in statistical and probabilistic settings, and begin to express their arguments formally (L5)

SP1 Develop their mathematical knowledge, in part through solving problems and evaluating the outcomes, including multi-step problems (L5)

SP2 Develop their use of formal mathematical knowledge to interpret and solve problems, including in financial mathematics (L5)

SP4 Select appropriate concepts, methods and techniques to apply to unfamiliar and non-routine problems (L5)

Introduction	Prior knowledge
The chapter consists of a sequence of five spreads based on the theme of a school trip to France. This allows questions to cover a wide range of topics taken from algebra, statistics, geometry and number. The questions are word-based and often do not directly indicate what type of mathematics is involved. Therefore students will need to work to identify the relevant mathematics and in several instances which of a variety of methods to apply before commencing. This approach is rather different from the previous topic based spreads and students may require additional support in this aspect of functional maths.	The chapter covers many topics; lessons which contain directly related material include • 1f • 2b, d, e • 3f • 4f • 5a • 6a • 7b • 8c, d, e, g • 11a, d, e, f • 12a, d • 15g

Using mathematics

The student book start of chapter suggests three areas of everyday life where aspects of the ability to apply mathematical ideas prove highly valuable.

Fluency: If you run a small business you need to be able to do your accounts. Are you making a profit? Is the money you make from sales bigger than all your overheads – wages, rent, materials…? People often use spreadsheet type programs to help them to so their accounts. However, should you trust what they say? It helps if you have a 'feel' for what the right answer should be and if you can quickly do simpler versions of the calculations yourself as checks.

Mathematical reasoning: Sometimes finding the answer to a mathematical problem is the easy part. The hardest part can be convincing other people that your solution is the right one. One way to help persuade other people is by choosing the best graph to show your results. You also need to be able to back up your results with carefully reasoned explanations.

Problem solving: Controlling a robot is surprisingly complex. It requires breaking down into smaller tasks in order to be manageable. Each of these smaller tasks might need skills from several different areas of mathematics. To control a robot's movements you will need to use geometry, coordinates and algebra to represent instructions.

Topic scheme

Teaching time = 5 lessons/2 weeks

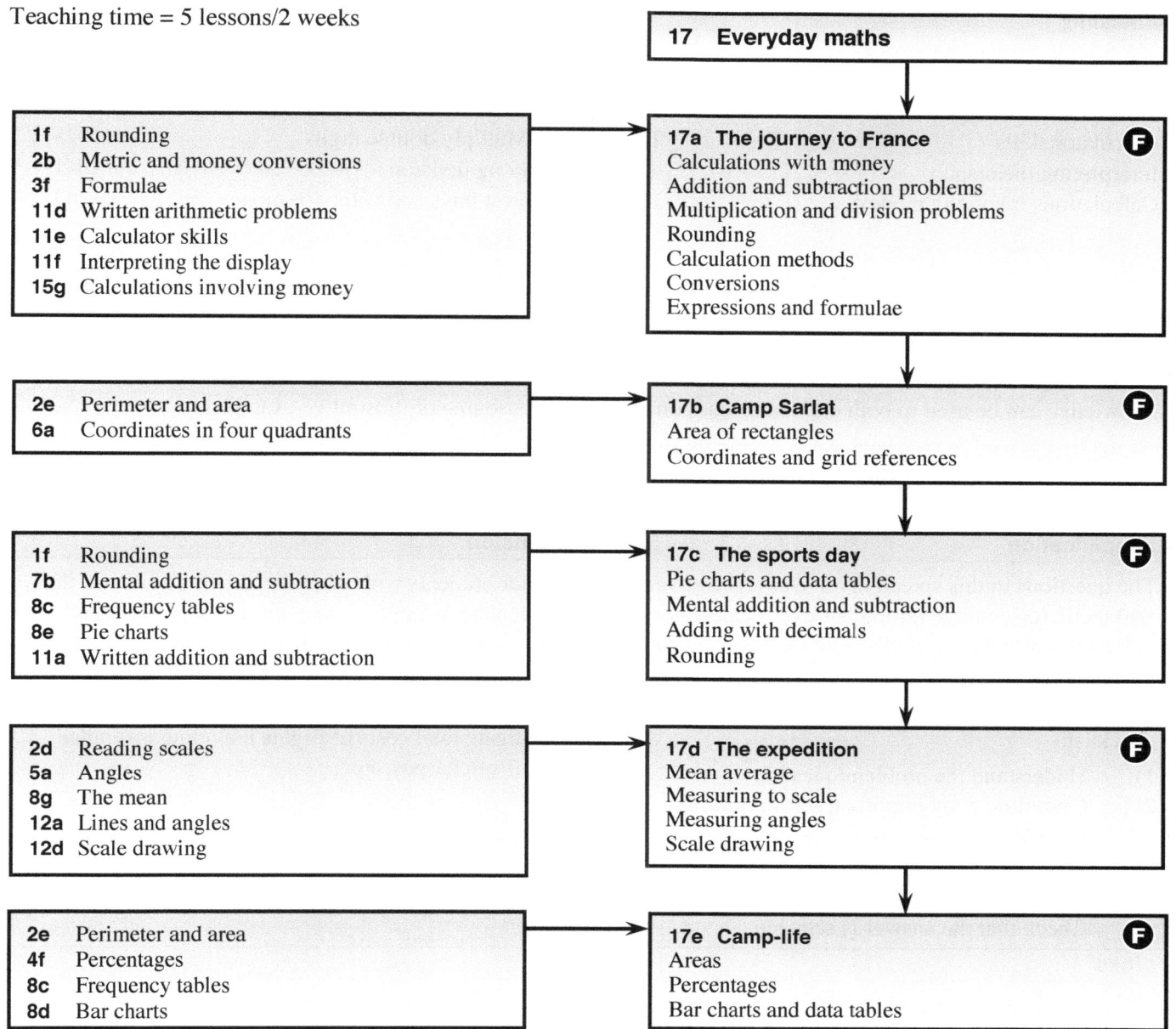

17   Everyday maths

1f	Rounding
2b	Metric and money conversions
3f	Formulae
11d	Written arithmetic problems
11e	Calculator skills
11f	Interpreting the display
15g	Calculations involving money

17a The journey to France **F**
Calculations with money
Addition and subtraction problems
Multiplication and division problems
Rounding
Calculation methods
Conversions
Expressions and formulae

2e	Perimeter and area
6a	Coordinates in four quadrants

17b Camp Sarlat **F**
Area of rectangles
Coordinates and grid references

1f	Rounding
7b	Mental addition and subtraction
8c	Frequency tables
8e	Pie charts
11a	Written addition and subtraction

17c The sports day **F**
Pie charts and data tables
Mental addition and subtraction
Adding with decimals
Rounding

2d	Reading scales
5a	Angles
8g	The mean
12a	Lines and angles
12d	Scale drawing

17d The expedition **F**
Mean average
Measuring to scale
Measuring angles
Scale drawing

2e	Perimeter and area
4f	Percentages
8c	Frequency tables
8d	Bar charts

17e Camp-life **F**
Areas
Percentages
Bar charts and data tables

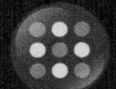
Related lessons		Resources	
Rounding	1f	Rounding decimals	(1004)
Metric and money conversions	2b	Metric conversion	(1061)
Formulae	3f	Converting measures	(1091)
Written arithmetic problems	11d	Rules and formulae	(1158)
Calculator skills	11e	Multiply double digits	(1025)
Interpreting the display	11f	Long division	(1041)
Calculations involving money	15g	Best buys and value for money	(1243)
		Calculators	
		Travel brochures	

Background

This spread focuses on the logistics and finances of the trip and largely exercises number skills. Issues surrounding costs, deposits and exchange rates may be familiar to some students from family holidays and this knowledge can be used to both enliven discussion and provide a source of illustrative examples.

As the first spread in the chapter it is important to establish how the students should approach the work, whether as individuals, as pairs or small groups, etc., should they work at their own pace, will they be expected to start straightaway or will an introduction be given, etc.

Simplification

The questions in this spread involve straightforward arithmetic (discourage falling back on a calculator), the difficulties are likely to arise from the language and understanding what is required. Pair weaker students and encourage breaking down a problem using a checklist:

1) Understand the problem/question
2) Underline/copy important information
3) Decide which operation is necessary
4) Make an approximation
5) Work out the answer
6) Check that the answer is sensible

Extension

Provide students with a holiday brochure and ask them to calculate an approximate cost for two adults and two children to go on holiday. Ask them to include approximate costs for food, activities, etc. If access to the internet is available, encourage students to investigate total costs of flights including insurance and all surcharges, etc.

Links

Planning a trip of any kind takes a lot of organisation and links can be drawn to both school trips and family holidays. It is also a good opportunity to discuss with students the idea of planning any kind of expenditure such as saving to buy a new games console, shopping on the high street and working out if you have enough money to buy your food and drink in the local café.

Teaching notes

Invite pairs of students to imagine that they are a teacher planning a school trip and ask them to suggest what they need to consider. Focus on the costs involved: how should they calculate deposits, deal with exchange rates, etc. The student book can be used as a prompt. The subsequent discussion should concentrate on generic approaches, what is required and a suitable method, rather than specific details.

Supply students with some example calculations and ask them to explain how they would complete them. Total cost £3782, 20 students: cost per student, 15% deposit, £435 to be paid in Euros at £1= €1.28. Ask how they decide whether to use mental, written or calculator methods: can they give two pros and two cons for each method? Also ask how they would go about checking their answers (against an approximation, using an inverse operation, is it reasonable, is it to an appropriate degree of accuracy?)

Ask students if they can supply some handy hints for doing calculations, especial using mental methods. These can be collected on the board as a reminder for students as they work through the spread.

Exercise commentary

Question 1 – Encourage students to work without a calculator in the first instance. Encourage them to look for simple ways of calculating, for example, 20% (÷ 5). In part **f**, a slightly simpler way of working out the conversions is to divide first by 10 and then multiply by 12. Can students justify this method as being equivalent to the formula given? Discourage the use of a calculator for part **g**, emphasising that it is only necessary to know which currency is cheaper, not by how much.

Question 2 – Students may begin by using a trial and improvement approach but encourage them to develop a systematic method of checking the distances. Parts **b** to **e** build on the initial calculation in part **a** so this should be checked first of all. Again, discourage the use of a calculator.

Answers

1. a £9476
   b yes, £10 000 ÷ 50 = £200
   c £189.52, £190
   d £15
   e £692
   f (1050 + 1770 + 1740 + 2040) = €6600
   g i £1.10 < €2   ii £2.20 < €2.40
      iii £26 > €30   iv £80 > €90
2. a Cherbourg–St. Lô–Alencon–Le Mans–Tours–Poitiers–Angoulême–Sarlat (713 km) 710 km
   b 10 hours 10 min   c 8:10 p.m.
   d Tours (after 352 km)   e 450 miles
   f $\frac{1}{4}$

Related lessons		Resources	
Perimeter and area	2e	Area of rectangles	(1084)
Area of a rectangle	2f	Coordinates 2	(1093)
Coordinates in four quadrants	6a	Local area map	
		Small name cards	

Background

This spread takes up the theme of the school trip and arriving at the camp where they have to organise the accommodation and familiarise themselves with the campsite. The mathematics involves areas of rectangles, arithmetic with decimals, the use of coordinates (with direct cross-curricular links to geography) and logical reasoning.

Simplification	Extension
In question **1**, the decimals may cause difficulty. Suggest, for example, that students think about the area of a 2×2 tent and a 22×15 tent. Encourage students to think this through rather than simply use a calculator. For question **2**, provide cards with the five names on to allow students to experiment with their order.	Supply students with a scale for the map, the large squares are $10 \text{ m} \times 10 \text{ m}$, and ask them to determine the sizes of various features. How long is the football pitch? What is its area? If the swimming pool is 1.5 m deep, what is its volume?

Links

Working out areas from plans forms a link to design subjects and to architecture and town planning in the real world. Work on maps, coordinates and grid references link directly to geography and navigation in the wider sense.

Teaching notes

The first question involves the multiplication of decimals. It will be useful revision to ask students to explain how to do this and how to check their answer. Test their understanding by asking them to calculate the area of a rectangular tent. Ask how they think this is related to how many people the tent will comfortably sleep. Is the ground area the only thing that needs to be considered? What about the tent's shape?

Question 2 is likely to be new to the students in the context of mathematics. It may help to provide a similar example and ask students to provide a 'method' for solving the puzzle and for verifying any solution.

Questions 3 to 5 involve interpreting a map and finding locations. Using a local area map, ask students to specify the positions of local landmarks. Can they do this is such a way that they don't refer to other locations on the map? This may be familiar from geography and the method used in the questions is easily tied in with the use of coordinates in mathematics. The map is also a scale drawing and students could be asked to think about how they could calculate real-life distances based on either the local area or campsite maps. One way to approach this is by asking students to say how they would go about creating an accurate map of the school.

Exercise commentary

Question 1 – Calculators are not necessary. It will be important to check the size of the answers using approximate integer calculations. Check that units are given. What is the area per person for the three tents?

Question 2 – This is a new type of question; students will need to be systematic in their reasoning and be careful to use each piece of information given.

Question 3 – Check that students can read the grid squares and take account of the 'zero' squares. The postcard on the previous page may help with interpreting the map.

Question 4 – Students now have to identify the grid squares from the information given. Encourage them to extend this by giving a partner further examples such as 'In which grid square is tent L?'

Question 5 – Students could be given cut out versions so that they can orient them to match the map of the camp.

Answers

1   a $3\,\text{m}^2$ b $5\,\text{m}^2$ c $8.75\,\text{m}^2$

2   A: John, B: Mark, C: Karl, D: Lilly, E: Cherry

3   a   i   Football pitch (centre circle)
        ii   Pool
        iii   Sports hall entrance
        iv   Shower block
    b   H, I, J
    c   A

4   a $(3, 0)$
    b $(4, 0)$
    c $(0, 2), (1, 2), (2, 2), (0, 3), (1, 3), (2, 3)$
    d   Café-shop
    e $(2, 0)$
    f $(2, 2)\ (3, 2)$

5   a $(2, 1)$ b $(0, 1)$ c $(3, 2)$

Related lessons		Resources	
Ordering decimal numbers	1e	Rounding decimals	(1004)
Rounding	1f	Ordering decimals	(1072)
Fractions and decimals	4b	Decimal place value	(1076)
Mental addition and subtraction	7b	Reading pie charts	(1206)
Addition and subtraction problems	7d	Large copies of question 2 table	
Collecting data	8b		
Pie charts	8e		
Written addition and subtraction	11a		
Interpreting the display	11f		

Background

The sports day theme can be made even more real for the students if data from sports competitions in which they are involved can be used as illustrations or to replace numeric values in the questions.

A large range of mathematics is encountered in this spread broadly on the theme of statistics, including: interpreting pie charts, collating data and finding summary statistics, solving 'algebraic' problems, rounding and making and justifying decisions.

Simplification

The wide variety of topics in this spread may prove discouraging to a student. At the same time it presents an opportunity to find questions with which they feel more comfortable, allowing them to build confidence. It will also help to organise students into small groups to share ideas and work together; this will be most helpful for questions 2 and 3. For question 2, provide students with a large version of the table and, working one team at a time, enter tallies of games' results and goals scored. In a second stage these can be added up and entered into the final table.

Extension

A number of checks are available for question 2c. Ask students to investigate the following questions. Does the total number of won games have to equal the total number of lost games? Can the total number of drawn games be odd? How does the total number of won, drawn and lost games relate to the total number played? What is the difference between the total number of goals for and total number of goals against? How does this relate to the answer in part a?

Links

Sports and the results from sports may be of interest to a large number of students who regularly follow a local football team or athletics events. A league table from the newspaper could be used to provide a contrast to that given in question 2, while results from events at the Olympics could be analysed in discussion with other questions.

Check out http://espn.go.com/olympics/summer/2012/results for a full list of all results from London 2012.

Teaching notes

Given the breadth of knowledge being tested here it will be most useful to focus attention on those areas which are likely to cause the students most difficulty, rather than try to address all potential issues.

A majority of the class is likely to be familiar with scoring in football. Using results from the school or an international competition will allow several of the issues associated with question **2** to be discussed. In particular, cover how to systematically collate the raw results into the summary table.

Put students into groups and pose a question similar to **3**. Ask students for their ideas on how to go about solving it; did they get it right? How do they know? Several approaches are possible and it will be instructive to get students to compare their relative merits.

Exercise commentary

Question 1 – One student = 7.2° so angles are only needed to this accuracy; can they be estimated? Ask students to measure the angles and calculate the numbers to check their answers.

Question 2 – In part **a**, encourage students to write down an ordered list of the number of goals scored per match. In part **c** students need to be very careful, what checks can be made?

Question 3 – Different mental methods can be used and students could be asked to 'compete' against each other to work out their given total the quickest.

Question 4 – In part **b**, check times go from smallest (fastest) to largest (slowest).

Question 5 – Discourage the use of a calculator here.

Question 6 – Refer back to question **2** of **17b** if necessary to highlight the nature of the logic problem and suggest a systematic approach.

Answers

1 a i Football   ii Tennis
   b i Archery   ii Tennis
   c 25

2 a All stars v Cheetahs, 7 goals
   b 4
   c Check students' work
   d Superstars/Champions (joint first), High 5, Cheetahs, All Stars
   e Students' answers: goal difference Superstars (4) > Champions (3)

3 a 24   b 27   c 25   d 22
   e 27   f 30

4 a i 16.4 s ii 14.4 s   iii 17.3 s
     iv 15.1 s v 14.6 s
   b 14.4, 14.6, 15.1, 16.4, 17.3

5 Carl (14.4), Darren (13.9), Hussain (13.7), Reece (13.6) Hamed (13.5)

6 Jenny (first), Marta, Lilly, Gulsum, Sarah, Carley (last)

Related lessons		Resources	
Fraction of a quantity	4d	Angle sums	(1082)
Angles	5a	Position and turning	(1231)
Mental addition and subtraction	7b	Mean and mode	(1200)
Addition and subtraction problems	7d	Map scales	(1103)
Mode, median and range	8f	Scale drawing	(1117)
The mean	8g	Bearings	(1086)
Written addition and subtraction	11a	Proportion	(1037)
Scale drawing	12d	Protractor	
Proportion	15c	Ruler	
		Enlargement of map and cliff face	
		OS maps	

Background

Students who are involved in the Duke of Edinburgh award scheme, Boy Scouts, Girl Guides, Woodcraft Folk, Combined Cadet Force, etc. may have direct experience of going on expeditions. Sailors and orienteerers may also have knowledge of navigation. These students' experiences of how mathematics can be applied should be used to enliven and inform classroom discussion.

The mathematics in this spread is broadly on the theme of geometry and includes giving compass bearings, measuring angles and measuring distances on scale drawings, as well as averages, time scales and finding proportions. There are direct links to the geography syllabus.

Simplification

Measuring some of the angles may prove awkward. Provide students with an enlarged copy of the map/cliff face or advise laying a ruler over the top of the protractor to make reading the scale easier. (Enlarged diagrams should not be used for measuring distances.)

Extension

Supply students with an OS map and ask them to plan a walk between given points. To begin they should specify the route as a list of directions/bearings and distances read off the map. They should then give timings for the journey assuming a typical walking pace of 15 min/km on even, level ground. This could be refined to take account of the type of terrain, any altitude changes (allow 10min/100 m climbed) and any rest stops.

Links

Route finding and planning can link into many different aspects of real life from walking to the shops to driving to a destination far away. Curriculum links to geography are very clear to see and other scenarios can be envisaged where map reading and calculating with angles is necessary in real life.

http://www.ordnancesurvey.co.uk/ is a good place to start exploring maps and the principles of mapping.

A link to history is provided by question **3**.

Teaching notes

In question **1c**, the mean can be thought of as a 'balance point' for the distribution of students' weights. This provides a means of checking the answer: the sum of the differences between individual students' weights and the mean should be zero. This provides a more formal definition of 'it should be in the middle'.

Question **2** has obvious links to geography with directions being specified by compass points, whilst in question **4**, angles are measured in degrees. The approaches can be combined to give directions as three-figure bearings.

A further option is to show how locations can be 'triangulated': what place is on a bearing 045° as seen from point A and 030° as seen from point B? (Cave/grotto) Can students provide their own examples, perhaps using a different base-line that requires larger angles to be measured? This could even be used as a challenge: can students produce an accurate scale drawing given the line AB and pairs of bearings for other locations? Distance can then be measured with a ruler and converted into a real-life distance using a scale; this skill is required for question **5**.

The first part of question **3** is likely to cause trouble due to the lack of a year zero – which some students might not appreciate. This is most easily clarified using small values and a number line.

Exercise commentary

Question 1 – A calculator is not necessary (1/4 = ÷ 4). In part **c** how does the mean compare to the median? Which is more representative?

Question 2 – Aim for ±1 mm accuracies in measurements. Students could be asked to give three-figure bearings as well as compass directions.

Question 3 – In part **a**, link BC dates to negative numbers. Explain the numbering 2 BC, 1 BC, 1 AD, 2 AD (no year zero). Encourage students to test their calculation with smaller numbers that can be shown on a 'number/time line'. In part **b**, what is a sensible accuracy for the answer?

Question 4 – Aim for ±1° accuracy. Encourage students to make estimates of the angles first (at least to the level acute, obtuse) to help to choose the correct scale to read.

Question 5 – If 1 cm represents 1 m and you want answers accurate to 0.5 m, how accurately do you have to measure the lines with your ruler?

Answers

1 **a** Tom   15 kg
         Lau It   12 kg
         Debbie   18 kg
         Rick   11 kg
         Darren   20 kg
         Marta   12.5 kg
   b 64 kg
   c Tom (mean 59 kg)

2 **a** **i**   500 m, North-East
         ii 250 m, South-East
         iii 50 0m, North
         iv 100 m, South
   b anticlockwise
   c 90°, clockwise

3 **a** 85 years
   b 2010 + current year.
         (E.g. if now 2014, then 2010 + 2014 = 4024)

4 **a** 120° obtuse   **b** 45° acute
   c 51° acute   **d** 97° obtuse
   e 112° obtuse   **f** 125° obtuse
   g 157° obtuse   **h** 90° right angle

5 **a** **i** 5 m   **ii** 3 m   **iii** 6 m   **iv** 5 m
   b 10 m
   c 13 m

Related lessons		Resources	
Rounding	1f	Rounding decimals	(1004)
Perimeter and area	2e	Area of rectangles	(1084)
Area of a rectangle	2f	Frequency tables and bar charts	(1193)
Real-life graphs	6e	Simple equations	(1154)
Bar charts	8d	Solving equations	(1182)
One-step equations	10a		
Two-step equations	10c		
Making equations	10d		

Background

The spread has a loose focus on incidents that occur in the life of Miss Perry and the students. It allows a breadth of mathematics to be covered including: finding areas, applying algebra, using systematic approaches to problem solving, reading and constructing bar charts.

An aspect of camp life is giving awards for various types of achievement. This could be mirrored in this final spread with, for example, bronze, silver and gold awards being given to students in recognition of their 'effort', 'achievement' and 'support to others'. This ties in with a suggestion for an **extension** activity.

Simplification	Extension
Each question in this spread focuses on a different aspect of mathematics. In the first instance, direct students to questions on topics that they feel more comfortable with and are most likely to succeed. Allow students to work in small groups and do the questions collectively; as well as providing mutual support it is important that they discuss and share their approaches.	If it was decided to run an awards scheme students could be charged with collating class members' marks in the various categories, ranking them and deciding appropriate boundaries for gold, silver and bronze awards.
	This can be developed further with students producing pie charts and other graphs showing, for example, the differences between boys' and girls' achievements.

Links

There are lots of problem-solving type questions and puzzles similar to the ones here that can be provided to students as 'end-of-term' activities, enrichment puzzles and maths club activities.

Some examples of number puzzles can be found at http://www.mathsisfun.com/puzzles/number-puzzles-index.html and a quick google search will certainly turn up more puzzles from other strands of mathematics.

Teaching notes

Question **1** involves finding areas. It may be instructive to ask students to explain where the formula for the area of a rectangle comes from.

Question **2** could be tackled using algebra but most students will be able to reason through the 'clues'. Also ask how they could check that their answers are correct.

Question **3** is a comprehension question where the students read from the given graphs before constructing their own graphs in question **4**.

Summary graphs could also be made and conclusions drawn as to which group of students performed best overall.

Exercise commentary

Question 1 – Students should not require a calculator. For part **c** ask them to work out the percentage as a fraction first and compare to 'recall' facts.

Question 2 – Students should be able to logically reason their way through this question. Again, insist on no calculators.

Question 3 – A comprehension question. Check students are reading from the frequency scale correctly on both graphs.

Question 4 – Use the graphs in question **3** as a model and get the students to draw their own axes carefully. Overall combined awards can also be used to create a fourth example and draw conclusions.

Answers

1 **a** $12 \, \text{m}^2$ **b** $24 \, \text{m}^2$ **c** 67%

2 **a** A holds 15 litres
   B holds 6 litres
   C holds 2 litres
 b 21 litres

3 **a** 12   **b** 12   **c** Expedition
 d Expedition   **e** 14   **f** 47

4 Check students' bar charts